THE ARMIES OF EUROPE

TODAY

THE
ARMIES
OF
EUROPE
TO-DAY

OTTO VON PIVKA

This book was designed and produced by
Alban Book Services Limited,
147 London Road, St. Albans, Herts, England

OSPREY PUBLISHING LIMITED
Member of the George Philip Group
137 Southampton Street,
Reading, Berkshire RG1 2QZ

First published 1974
© *Otto von Pivka, 1974*

Filmset in 9/10 pt. Times New Roman 327
Printed in Great Britain on 118 gsm paper by
W. S. COWELL LIMITED
at the Butter Market, Ipswich, England

ISBN 0 540 07121 8

CONTENTS

FOREWORD

It is the purpose of this book to capture, for one moment of time, impressions of the armies which currently are maintained by the European powers. Armies are dynamic, living things, and their uniforms, weapons, equipment and organisation are constantly changing. It is thus inevitable that by the time this book is published it will already be out of date in certain points of detail. The only way to keep truly abreast of current military developments is to devote considerable amounts of time and money to the acquisition and digestion of the numerous military magazines which are nowadays available on the international market. The point should perhaps be made that all the information collated in this book is freely available to the layman, if he knows where to look.

Changes which are known to be impending at the time of going to press include new uniforms for the Swedish, Swiss, Bulgarian, Austrian and Italian armies; major reorganisation of the Austrian, Greek, German and Turkish armies; expansion of all armies of the Warsaw Pact states; and re-equipment with new generation armoured vehicles in the United Kingdom, France, Belgium, Austria, and the Warsaw Pact states. In the longer term, the events of the 1973 Arab–Israeli War will no doubt have a far-reaching effect. The world's powers watch such conflicts with no less interest than an earlier generation displayed towards the Spanish Civil War, whatever their ostensible political positions. The dominant place as queen of the battlefield so long enjoyed by the tank may now require some re-assessment, menaced as it is by the light, long-ranging and easily-concealed guided missile. A particular lesson has been the loss of reputation suffered by the much-vaunted T62 when it confronted the much older Centurion of the Israeli armoured brigades.

The nature and abilities of any army can change quite rapidly, with the acquisition of new equipments – or doctrines – ready-made and "off the shelf" from the great powers. The smaller European states are generally dependent upon such equipments, as the cost of developing major modern weapons is far too high to be borne by any but the major powers. The pages which follow will demonstrate that the armies of Europe fall quite naturally into three categories, the categories into which they are grouped in this book. The North Atlantic Treaty Organisation forces range from the United Kingdom and Germany, with large and capable indigenous armament industries, to the small states such as Belgium and Norway which are dependent on American equipment. (France belongs alongside Britain and Germany in all but name – her removal from NATO was a purely political gesture which does not affect the realities of the armed balance.) The Warsaw Pact nations provide the awesome spectacle of a vast alliance directed and equipped along standardised lines from a single nerve-centre. The sturdy example set by Yugoslavia only throws into more sombre relief the apparent success of the "Breschnew Doctrine" throughout the rest of Eastern Europe. The standardisation of equipment, organisation and doctrine within the Soviet bloc is so complete that I have stepped out of the alphabetical sequence generally adopted, to place the USSR at the beginning of WARPAC section – any other arrangement would have forced the reader into constant forward referral. The third group are the neutral and ostensibly "non-aligned" nations, who provide an interesting study. They are generally equipped with a mixture of indigenous weapons – some of them of high quality, *vide* Sweden – and foreign hardware acquired from sources on both sides of the Iron Curtain.

At the beginning of each national section I have included a necessarily brief summary of the other forces maintained by the nation concerned, and of the political structure to which those forces are answerable. Brief technical details of weapons and vehicles will be found throughout the book: in some cases it seemed logical to describe them under their country of origin, in some cases in relation to some foreign user, and in yet other cases in the appendices.

I should like to express my thanks to the many people who have been of assistance to me in the production of this book – particularly to Herr Spiering, Dr Wiener, and Rosie.

Hamburg, October 1973   O. vP.

The following abbreviations will be found in many places throughout the text of this book:

AA   = Anti-aircraft
AAGW = Anti-aircraft guided weapon
APC   = Armoured personnel carrier
AT   = Anti-tank
ATGW = Anti-tank guided weapon
LMG   = Light machine gun
SAM   = Surface to air missile
SMG   = Sub-machine gun
SP   = Self-propelled
SSM   = Surface to surface missile

THE NORTH ATLANTIC TREATY ORGANISATION (NATO)

The North Atlantic Treaty, foundation document of the Western alliance, was signed in Washington on 4 April 1949 by Belgium, Canada, Denmark, France, Iceland, Italy, Luxemburg, the Netherlands, Norway, Portugal, the United Kingdom and the USA. Greece and Turkey formally joined on 18 February 1952, and the Federal Republic of Germany on 9 May 1955. The text of the treaty is reproduced below:

"The Parties to this Treaty reaffirm their faith in the purposes and principles of the Charter of the United Nations and their desire to live in peace with all peoples and all Governments.

They are determined to safeguard the freedom, common heritage and civilization of their peoples, founded on the principles of democracy, individual liberty and the rule of law.

They seek to promote stability and well-being in the North Atlantic area.

They are resolved to unite their efforts for collective defence and for the preservation of peace and security.

They therefore agree to this North Atlantic Treaty:

Article 1
The Parties undertake, as set forth in the Charter of the United Nations, to settle any international dispute in which they may be involved by peaceful means in such a manner that international peace and security and justice are not endangered, and to refrain in their international relations from the threat or use of force in any manner inconsistent with the purposes of the United Nations.

Article 2
The Parties will contribute toward the further development of peaceful and friendly international relations by strengthening their free institutions, by bringing about a better understanding of the principles upon which these institutions are founded, and by promoting conditions of stability and well-being. They will seek to eliminate conflict in their international economic policies and will encourage economic collaboration between any or all of them.

Article 3
In order more effectively to achieve the objectives of this Treaty, the Parties, separately and jointly, by means of continuous and effective self-help and mutual aid, will maintain and develop their individual and collective capacity to resist armed attack.

Article 4
The Parties will consult together whenever, in the opinion of any of them, the territorial integrity, political independence or security of any of the Parties is threatened.

Article 5
The Parties agree that an armed attack against one or more of them in Europe or North America shall be considered an attack against them all, and consequently they agree that, if such an armed attack occurs, each of them, in exercise of the right of individual or collective self-defence recognized by Article 51 of the Charter of the United Nations, will assist the Party or Parties so attacked by taking forthwith, individually and in concert with the other Parties, such action as it deems necessary, including the use of armed force, to restore and maintain the security of the North Atlantic area.

Any such armed attack and all measures taken as a result thereof shall immediately be reported to the Security Council. Such measures shall be terminated

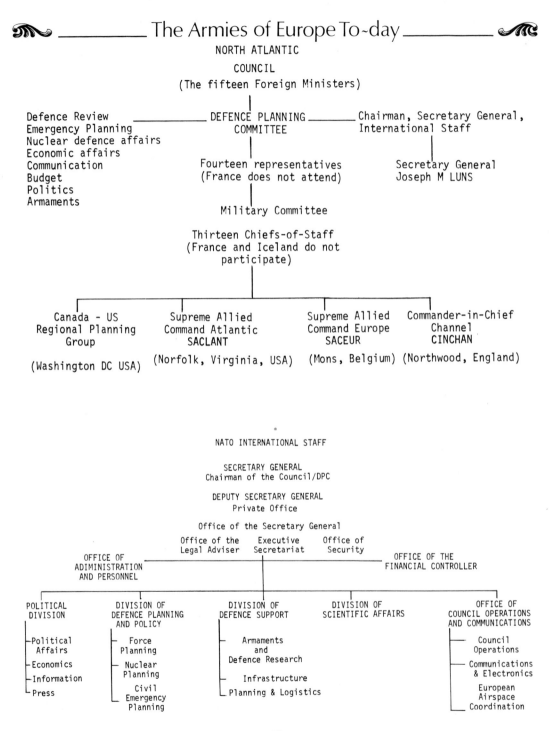

NORTH ATLANTIC
COUNCIL
(The fifteen Foreign Ministers)

Defence Review ——————— DEFENCE PLANNING ——————— Chairman, Secretary General,
Emergency Planning   COMMITTEE   International Staff
Nuclear defence affairs
Economic affairs
Communication   Fourteen representatives   Secretary General
Budget   (France does not attend)   Joseph M LUNS
Politics
Armaments

Military Committee

Thirteen Chiefs-of-Staff
(France and Iceland do not
participate)

Canada - US	Supreme Allied	Supreme Allied	Commander-in-Chief
Regional Planning	Command Atlantic	Command Europe	Channel
Group	SACLANT	SACEUR	CINCHAN
(Washington DC USA)	(Norfolk, Virginia, USA)	(Mons, Belgium)	(Northwood, England)

NATO INTERNATIONAL STAFF

SECRETARY GENERAL
Chairman of the Council/DPC

DEPUTY SECRETARY GENERAL
Private Office

Office of the Secretary General

Office of the   Executive   Office of
Legal Adviser   Secretariat   Security

OFFICE OF   OFFICE OF THE
ADIMINISTRATION   FINANCIAL CONTROLLER
AND PERSONNEL

POLITICAL DIVISION	DIVISION OF DEFENCE PLANNING AND POLICY	DIVISION OF DEFENCE SUPPORT	DIVISION OF SCIENTIFIC AFFAIRS	OFFICE OF COUNCIL OPERATIONS AND COMMUNICATIONS
├─Political Affairs	├─ Force Planning	├─ Armaments and Defence Research		├─ Council Operations
├─Economics	├─ Nuclear Planning			├─ Communications & Electronics
├─Information	└─ Civil Emergency Planning	├─ Infrastructure		└─ European Airspace Coordination
└─Press		└─ Planning & Logistics		

NATO MILITARY STRUCTURE

MILITARY COMMITTEE
MC

INTERNATIONAL MILITARY STAFF
IMS

(Brussels)

Supreme Allied Commander Europe SACEUR (Shape, Belgium) 1	Supreme Allied Commander Atlantic SACLANT 2	Allied Commander-in-Chief Channel CINCHAN (Northwood, England) 3	Canada US Regional Planning Group CUSRPG (Washington DC USA)

Shape Technical Centre STC (The Hague)	SACLANT Anti-Submarine Warfare Research CENTRE Centre SACLANTCEN (Le Spezia, Italy)	NATO Defence College NDC (Rome)	Military Agency for Standardization MAS (Brussels)	Advisory Group for Aerospace Research & Development AGARD (Paris)	ACSA ALLA ARFA ANCA 4

when the Security Council has taken the measures necessary to restore and maintain international peace and security.

Article 6*

For the purpose of Article 5, an armed attack on one or more of the Parties is deemed to include an armed attack

– on the territory of any of the Parties in Europe or North America, on the Algerian Departments of France**, on the territory of Turkey or on the islands under the jurisdiction of any of the Parties in the North Atlantic area north of the Tropic of Cancer;

– on the forces, vessels, or aircraft of any of the Parties, when in or over these territories or any other area in Europe in which occupation forces of any of the Parties were stationed on the date when the Treaty entered into force or the Mediterranean Sea or the North Atlantic area north of the Tropic of Cancer.

* *As amended by Article 2 of the Protocol to the North Atlantic Treaty on the accession of Greece and Turkey.*
** *On 16th January, 1963, The French Representative made a statement to the North Atlantic Council on the effects of the independence of Algeria on certain aspects of the North Atlantic Treaty. The Council noted that insofar as the former Algerian Departments of France were concerned the relevant clauses of this Treaty had become inapplicable as from 3rd July, 1962.*

Article 7

This Treaty does not affect, and shall not be interpreted as affecting, in any way the rights and obligations under the Charter of the Parties which are members of the United Nations, or the primary responsibility of the Security Council for the maintenance of international peace and security.

Article 8

Each Party declares that none of the international engagements now in force between it and any other of the Parties or any third State is in conflict with the provisions of this Treaty, and undertakes not to enter into any international engagement in conflict with this Treaty.

Article 9

The Parties hereby establish a Council, on which each of them shall be represented to consider matters concerning the implementation of this Treaty. The Council shall be so organised so as to be able to meet promptly at any time. The Council shall set up such subsidiary bodies as may be necessary; in particular it shall establish immediately a defence committee which shall recommend measures for the implementation of Articles 3 and 5.

Article 10

The Parties may, by unanimous agreement, invite any other European State in a position to further the principles of this Treaty and to contribute to the security of the North Atlantic area to accede to this Treaty. Any State so invited may become a party to the Treaty by depositing its instrument of accession with the Government of the United States of America. The Government of the United States of America will inform each of the Parties of the deposit of each such instrument of accession.

Article 11

This Treaty shall be ratified and its provisions carried out by the Parties in accordance with their respective constitutional processes. The instruments of ratification shall be deposited as soon as possible with the Government of the United States of America, which will notify all the other signatories of each deposit. The Treaty shall enter into force between the States which have ratified it as soon as the ratifications of the majority of the signatories, including the ratifications of Belgium, Canada, France, Luxemburg, the Netherlands, the United Kingdom and the United States, have been deposited and shall come into effect with respect to other States on the date of the deposit of their ratifications.

Article 12

After the Treaty has been in force for ten years, or at any time thereafter, the Parties shall, if any of them so requests, consult together for the purpose of reviewing the Treaty, having regard for the factors then affecting peace and security in the North Atlantic area including the development of universal as well as regional arrangements under the Charter of the United Nations for the maintenance of international peace and security.

Article 13

After the Treaty has been in force for twenty years, any Party may cease to be a Party one year after its notice of denunciation has been given to the Government of the United States of America, which will inform the Governments of the other Parties of the deposit of each notice of denunciation.

Article 14

This Treaty, of which the English and French texts are equally authentic, shall be deposited in the archives of the Government of the United States of America. Duly certified copies will be transmitted by that Government to the Governments of the other signatories."

In 1952 the existing command structure was adopted and is shown on the relevant charts.

NATO is primarily a defensive political alliance of independent states and only comparable to the

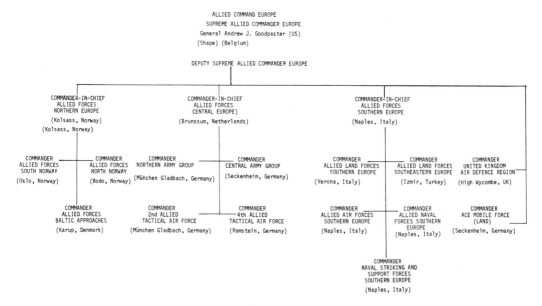

AMF - Allied Command Europe Mobile Force (Land)

HQ at SCHENKEN Near MANNHEIM

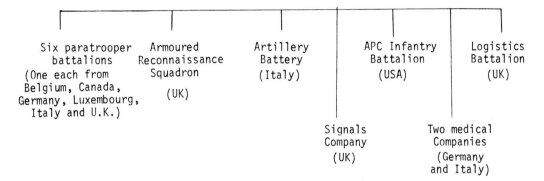

Warsaw Pact (and the secondary network of treaties which render this showpiece almost superfluous) in a limited way. The problems of achieving concensus between the varying political and military organisations of NATO's member states have to some extent been overcome by the adoption of official NATO languages (English and French) and agreed procedures for various military tasks, ranging from drafting orders for operations to procedures for ordering a single screw for a radio set. These standardised procedures are called STANAGs (Standard NATO agreements).

A considerable blow to NATO's effectiveness came on 10 March 1966 when President de Gaulle of France announced his country's intention of withdrawing from the military side of the NATO organisation and requiring that NATO remove its military headquarters, Supreme Headquarters Allied Powers in Europe (SHAPE), from outside Paris. SHAPE was invited by Belgium to rehouse itself in Casteau where it is now situated.

Over the last three or four years a deceptive aura of mildness has come over the Soviet bloc and this has been expressed in various international meetings ostensibly aimed at reducing tension and armament levels in Europe and the world. Some of these discussions are SALT (Strategic Arms Limitation Talks), and MBFR (Mutual Balanced Force Reduction talks). The Soviet delegation insisted that the word "balanced" be removed from the meeting place, and cynics now interpret these initials to mean "More Battalions For the Russians."

It is doubtful if the Soviets have any intention of disarming (indeed, in recent years they have considerably increased their nuclear and conventional potential) but they have every hope of achieving the dissolution of NATO merely by appearing at these various conference tables and reciting political cant for years on end while the Western nations are gradually lulled into a sense of false security and disarm unilaterally. Recent events in Denmark, Belgium, Federal Germany and Norway indicate how this creeping ailment is spreading.

NATO military co-operation is quite highly developed, and this applies even to the intelligence services since the Czech crisis of 1968. Officer training at the national staff and defence colleges is fully integrated and officers of most NATO nations regularly attend courses in other nations of the alliance. Joint exercises are regularly carried out and all rough edges of the multinational mobilisation and command system have now been smoothed out. France takes no part in these exercises.

THE KINGDOM OF BELGIUM

Population – 9,800,000.   **Capital** – Brussels.

Armed Forces:

    Army – 66,000 men; 600 tanks; Honest John nuclear rockets.

    Navy – 4,200 men; 30 minesweepers.

    Air Force – 20,500 men, 190 combat aircraft: 100 F-104Gs, 27 Dassault Mirage 5BAs, 63 Mirage 5 BRs. Transports – app. 45 C-119G Packets, C-47 and C-54, and C-130H Hercules. Air defence – 8 squadrons Nike-Hercules missiles.

Para-military forces – Gendarmerie of 13,500 (soon to be increased by 1,000 men).

Reserves – Army – 2 brigades.

    Navy – 7,000 men.

Defence Spending – 31,700 million francs ($1 = 43·8 francs) in 1972 (2·3% GNP).

Belgium, as a kingdom, was set up after the Napoleonic wars and today still harbours the potential seeds of national disunity in that there exist deep tensions between the northern, Flemish-speaking and currently richer half of the country and the southern, French-speaking and recently increasingly depressed half. This schism is so definite that even in the armed forces candidates for promotion to higher levels must fit into a fifty-fifty allocation scheme which ensures a linguistic balance, and thus strives to avoid charges of discrimination against one or other community.

King Baudouin comes from the line of Sachsen-Coburg-Gotha, the same house which gave Queen Victoria of England her consort, Albert. Belgium has a constitutional monarchical system; the prime minister at time of writing is Edmond Leburton, a Socialist. Defence minister (also member of the Co-ordinating Committee for Commerce and Social Services) is Paul Van den Boeynants, a Christian Socialist. The king is supreme commander of the armed forces, and the chain of command then passes to the defence minister who is advised by a Defence Council formed of politicians and the chiefs of staff of the three armed services.

The army falls into three main parts:

1. The field army (1st Belgian Corps).
2. The territorial army (which is composed of 10% regular cadre and 90% reservists).
3. The logistic base, which is a NATO base more than a national undertaking.

The field army has a strength of about 30,000 men and has its headquarters in Köln in West Germany. Its organisation is shown on the relevant chart.

    Commander 1st Belgian Corps is Lieutenant-General L. M. Teysen

    Commander 1st Division is Major General R. Raucq

    Commander 16th Division is Major General G. Henon

About 60% of the men are professional soldiers, the other 40% are conscripts serving for twelve months at a time. Both these divisions are fully mechanised, and the tank battalions use the German Leopard tank, which has replaced the British Centurion. The Belgian army is proud of its traditions, which it has maintained since the formation of the kingdom. The cavalry, for instance, embraces four regiments of Chasseurs á Cheval (of which the 1st, 2nd and 3rd regiments are currently active and undertake reconnaissance duties); three regiments of Guides (of which the 1st and 2nd Regiments are currently active and equipped with Leopards); ten Lanciers regiments (1st, 2nd, 3rd and 4th currently active and equipped with Leopards); four Escadrons de Reconnaissance (non-active); and two Bataillons de Tanks Lourds (the 1st and 4th) both non-active.

The reserve army also includes nine "Bataillons Legers de Province" each named after the province in which it is located and each maintaining the tradition of an old cavalry regiment. The infantry is similar in this respect.

14

Corps troops include two Honest John SSM battalions; two heavy air defence battalions equipped with Hawk SAM; four air corps squadrons with 80 Alouette II helicopters and 12 Dornier DO-27 fixed wing aircraft. Corps artillery is equipped with American weapons (M-55, 203 mm SP howitzers and towed 203 mm howitzers); brigade artillery batteries use the American M-108, 105 mm and M44 and M109, 155 mm SP howitzers.

Tank strength is currently 330 Leopards with 55 more due for delivery by 1976; 175 M-47 American light tanks and 135 American M-41 light tanks. It is planned to replace these light tanks with the new British "Striker" tracked reconnaissance vehicle.

Mechanised infantry battalions are mounted in the French-built AMX-VTT APC.

In order to reduce defence expenditure, Belgium has decided that two brigades of its 4-brigade 1st Belgian (BE) Corps must be withdrawn from Germany back into Belgium. Complete with corps troops, the 1st (BE) Corps has a strength of 32,000 men. One brigade is armoured and the others are mechanised. The chain of command and organisation is as the accompanying chart.

The Belgian Gendarmerie

As in Italy and France, the Belgian Gendarmerie is subordinate in time of war to the Ministry of Defence. Under normal conditions it answers to the ministries of the Interior and Justice. It is organised into five territorial commands (which number 3,000 men) and two Mobile Legions each of one horsed squadron, one squadron of motorised infantry, one reconnaissance squadron and one logistics squadron. The Gendarmerie provide the guard for the royal palaces, the courts and the ministries.

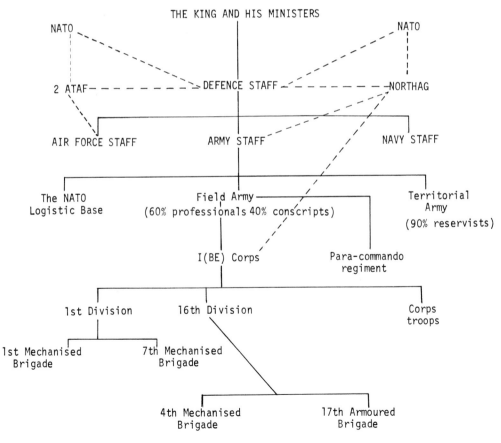

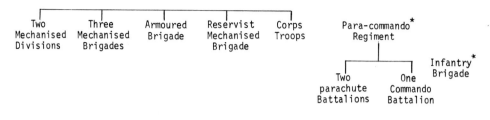

1st BELGIAN CORPS

HQ

- Two Mechanised Divisions
- Three Mechanised Brigades
- Armoured Brigade
- Reservist Mechanised Brigade
- Corps Troops
- Para-commando* Regiment
  - Two parachute Battalions
  - One Commando Battalion
  - Infantry* Brigade

* = One battalion of the Para-Commando regiment is part of ACE AMF; the rest of these formations are held in Belgium and will only be assigned to NATO if needed.

Total established strength is 12,500 all ranks. They wear a striking, dark blue uniform with kepi and red collar tabs.

Belgian Army Equipment
Small Arms *9 mm Browning pistol, 9 mm Vigneron M-2 machine* pistol with collapsible butt; loaded weight – 3·96 kg; length – 61 cm/89 cm; blow-back action; 32 round straight magazine below the breech, rate of fire – 600 rpm; effective range – 100 m.
7·62 mm FN SLR; 7·62 mm FN "Typ D" LMG; weight – 9·21 kg; length – 1·145 m; 20 round magazine below the breech; gas assisted action; rate of fire – 350 to 600 rpm variable; effective range – 600 m.
7·62 mm FN "Typ MAG" General Purpose Machine Gun (GPMG); weight with bipod – 10·91 kg; weight of tripod – 10·5 kg; gas assisted action; length – 1·26 m; belt fed, rate of fire – 600 to 1,000 rpm; effective range – 600 m.
81 mm and 120 mm mortars; 100 mm Blendicide AT rocket launcher; length of barrel – 1·8 m; weight – 12 kg; weight of hollow charge rocket – 2·75 kg; VO – 195 m/sec; effective range – 220 m.
Canon anti-tank d'Infanterie (CATI) Light Tank Destroyer
Based on the British Lloyd Bren carrier of World War II; weight – 4·5 tons; length – 4·41 m; width – 2·06 m; height – 1·57 m; engine – 85 hp, water-cooled, petrol; max road speed – 48 km/hr; road range – 190 km; armour – 8 mm; armament – 90 mm reduced recoil cannon; crew – 3.

Vehicles
FN AS24 3 × 2 light paratrooper's jeep. A collapsible jeep which can be dropped by parachute.

Empty weight – 220 kg; can carry – 4 men or 330 kg; length – 1·89 m; width – 1·64 m; height – 0·89 m; engine – 15 hp, 2-cylinder, air-cooled, petrol; max road speed – 57 km/hr; road range – 200 km.
FN4RM Ardennes, 1½ ton, 4 × 4 forward control Truck and FN 4RM 652/3, 4 ton, 4 × 4 forward control truck.

Belgian Army Uniforms
There is great similarity between the uniforms of the Belgian army and their comrades in the British army. Conscripts wear khaki battle dress of British pattern, British 1937 pattern canvas webbing equipment, black boots, and berets in various colours as follows: armoured troops – black; 1st and 3rd Battalions of the Para-Commando Regiment – maroon, 2nd Battalion – dark green; infantry – khaki.

Senior NCOs and officers have, apart from the battle dress, a light khaki service dress with regiment and rank shown on the buttons, the collar patches and the breast pocket badge. This is topped off by a khaki peaked cap with the Belgian cockade over the badge of arm. Officers have fudge-coloured, double-breasted "British Warm" coats with leather buttons for uniform wear off parades, and they also wear British pattern brown leather "Sam Browne" belts. Brown gloves and brown shoes complete their costume.

Apart from badges, ranks are indicated in the *colour* of the cap badges, officers' being gold, NCOs' silver and privates' brass.

Branch of service badges are worn on the peaked cap, the collar (cavalry regiments) or the shoulder-strap (infantry); and cavalry and infantry regiments wear their own regimental badges on their berets and their breast pockets (different badges in each case). Officers wear regimental badges on the gold buttons of their service dress jackets, beret and button badges being the same. Behind the beret badge is a shield-shaped plastic backing in the regimental facing colour.

Generals have crimson hatbands and wear winged thunderbolts on their collars; their cap badge is a golden winged thunderbolt flanked on each side by two vertical golden stripes, and the chin strap and cap bottom band are also gold. Officers on the general staff retain their regimental facing colour but wear the gold thunderbolt on collar and peaked cap (and on the epaulette in shirt sleeve order). Officers of field rank (major – colonel) wear badge of branch on their peaked caps flanked by a single vertical bar of gold on each side and with gold chin strap and bottom band; subaltern officers have branch cap badges and gold chin straps; warrant officers (adjudant-chef and adjudant) silver branch badges and chin straps; senior NCOs (Opperwachtmeester, 1ste Wachtmeester and Wachtmeester) silver badges and brown leather chin straps. Corporals and below do not wear peaked caps.

Belgian shirt sleeve order is as follows: very light khaki shirt and tie (sleeves worn buttoned at the cuff), khaki trousers and narrow web belt with oblong silver buckle plate; black boots and gaiters for men, brown shoes for officers.

Badges of rank for sergeants and below are worn on the sleeve; for officers and warrant officers (Adjudant 1er Classe and Adjudant) are worn on the shoulder-straps on plastic slides in the regimental facing colour.

Belgian army combat uniform consists of the American style "NATO" helmet, and camouflaged jacket and trousers. Badges of rank are worn on cloth slides on the shoulder-straps.

Belgian Army Flags

The cavalry units of the Belgian army carry "Etendards", dismounted units carry "Flaggen".

Representative Belgian collar patches: left, Lieutenant-General; right, Adjutant 1ere Classe of Ardense Jägers. Officers' rank patches are in sequence one, two and three stars (Sous-Lieutenant to Capitaine); three under a bar (Capitaine-Commandant); and one, two and three stars over a thick bar (Major to Colonel). Top centre, cap badge of line infantry (5, 6, 7, and 12 Bns.); below, Carabiniers cap badge.

Both are of the same design but Etendards are about half the size of Flaggen. Unlike the British Artillery, the Belgian artillery carries an "Etendard". The design of both colours is the national flag; three vertical stripes, black (next to the pike) yellow and red, fringed with gold and having regimental battle honours, "citations" and title embroidered on it in gold. The pike staff is black and has a very unusual tip which consists of a golden rampant lion standing on a tablet over a golden wreath. Older regiments have cravats attached to the pike: these cravats are in the regimental facing colour and bear the regimental title and badge in gold.

Belgian beret badges, left to right: 3rd Bn. Para-Commando Regt., Tank Destroyers, Artillery, Engineers, Signals.

Table of Belgian Facing Colours and Badges

Arm or regiment	Collar patch colour	Shoulder* or Collar** badge	Hat badge	Hatband colour	Beret colour***
General Officers	Black with crimson edge	A gold winged thunderbolt**	A gold winged thunderbolt	Crimson	
Cavalry Chasseurs à Cheval	Orange	Hunting horn and crossed sabres*	Hunting horn and crossed sabres	Khaki	Black
Guides	Crimson with green edge	A crown over crossed sabres*	A crown over crossed sabres	Khaki	
Lanciers	White with a black edge (2nd Regt White only)	Crossed lances*	Crossed lances	Khaki	
Artillery (Artillerie)	Dark blue with red edge	As for the hat badge**	Crossed cannon barrels behind a vertical rocket	Khaki	Light chocolate brown
Horse Artillery	Dark blue with red edge	A horseshoe over crossed cannon barrels**			
Engineers (Genie)	Black with red edge	Roman helmet**	Roman helmet	Khaki	Khaki
Signals (Troupes de Transmissions)	Black with white edge	As for the hat badge*	Flaming torch amid lightning flashes	Khaki	Khaki
Infantry of the Line (Linie)	Red with black edge	Crown*	Crown	Khaki	Light chocolate brown
Carabiniers	Dark green with yellow edge	Hunting horn** and *	Hunting horn	Khaki	Light chocolate brown
Ardennes Rifles (Chasseurs Ardennais)	Dark green with red edge	Boar's head** Crown*	Boar's head	Khaki	Light chocolate brown
Grenadiers	Red	Grenade* and **	Grenade	Khaki	Light chocolate brown
1st and 3rd Battalions of the Para-Commando Regt	Crimson	A winged sword, point down, and a scroll with: "Who dares wins"*	Not worn	Not worn	Crimson with winged parachute badge
2nd Battalion, Para-Commando Regiment	Black with white edge	A dagger*	Not worn	Not worn	Dark green with an upright two-handed sword badge, without a black patch behind it
Army Air Corps			A crowned bee and the motto "Semper labora"	Khaki	Light blue
Medical Corps	Red	A snake coiled round a staff*	As for the beret	Khaki	Khaki with red patch bearing a yellow crowned shield having an æsculab in the centre
Dental Corps	Purple with red edge				
Veterinary Corps	Dark Blue with black edge				
Apothecaries	Dark green with light green edge				

Arm or regiment	Collar patch colour	Shoulder* or Collar** badge	Hat badge	Hatband colour	Beret colour***
Logistics Corps (supply, transport and repair) (Quartier-maitre, transport et Ordonnance)	Light blue	A crowned cog wheel bearing and wing and two lightning flashes Beneath it the motto: "Pugnantes adjuvo"*	As for the shoulder badge	Khaki	Khaki with badge as for the hat but flanked by two lions
Recruits in basic training	Red	—	Not worn	Not worn	Khaki with a golden lion badge
Officers on the general staff	Regimental facings	A gold thunderbolt with wings; slightly smaller than that of a general and of a different design**	Khaki		Regimental colour and badge

*** Those units which at the end of World War II belonged to the Belgian armoured division now still wear black berets although this division has long since been disbanded. Units which at that time belonged to the infantry divisions still wear light chocolate brown berets and corps which belonged to other formations wore, and still wear, khaki berets. With the beret a regimental badge is worn on a shield shaped plastic backing which is in the main colour of the collar patches.

THE KINGDOM OF DENMARK

Population – 4,951,000 in Denmark.   **Capital** – Kopenhagen.
       –   46,500 in Greenland.
           38,700 in the Faroe Islands.
Armed Forces:
       Army – 27,000 men; 250 tanks.
       Navy – 6,600 men; 6 submarines, 2 destroyers, 4 frigates, 4 escorts, 22 MTBs, 7 minelayers, 12 minesweepers; 8 Alouette helicopters.
       Air Force – 9,800 men, 112 combat aircraft: 16 SAAB F-35 Draken, 16 RF-35 Draken, 32 Super Sabre F-100D/7, 32 F-104G, 16 Hawker Hunter, plus small transport and helicopter elements.
Para-military forces – 55,100 men in the *Heimwehr* (Home Guard).
Reserves   – Army 65,000.
                   Navy 3,000.
                   Air Force 11,500.
Defence Spending – $438,500,000 in 1972 (2·4% of GNP).

Denmark is a constitutional monarchy, head of state since 15 January 1972 being Queen Margerethe II. Her consort is Prince Henrik de Monpezat. The government is elected by secret ballot every four years; it consists of the single-chamber *Volketing* of 179 elected members – including two each from Greenland and the Faroes. The current government is Social-democratic; the prime minister is Anker Jørgensen and the defence minister is K. Olesen.

Denmark has never permitted NATO to station nuclear weapons on her soil, and there are plentiful signs that she is tending increasingly towards a neutralist policy. Allied NATO troops are also excluded from the country in peacetime, as in Norway. Occupying the vital exit from the Baltic Sea as she does, Denmark is essential to NATO because, with her co-operation, the Soviet Baltic fleet can be bottled up and rendered almost ineffective. It is against this background that one should see the apparent dwindling of military will on the part of the Danish government. Conscription for all males between 18 and 50 years of age, for a period of 16 months' national service, was recently reduced to 12 months. A further cut to 6 months' service has now been announced. At the end of this short training period the conscripts would be transferred to reserve units. Speaking of the future shape of the Danish army, Olesen stated that the current figure of 13,000 professional soldiers may well be cut to 7,000 with some 1,500 civilian technicians in a back-up group to help maintain complex equipment. The country's defence budget has recently been cut by 5% in accordance with these plans.

Together with Norway and Schleswig-Holstein (where the 6th Panzer-Grenadier Division of the West German *Bundeswehr* is stationed), Denmark forms part of NATO's northern region. The supreme command of the Danish defence forces

moved to its new home in Vedbaek, north of Kopenhagen, on 1 April 1973. HQ Combaltap remains at Karup, which in time of war is also the seat of the Danish defence HQ incorporating the Eastern and Western Army Regional Commands, the navy and air force commands.

The Danish army has quite modern equipment but is weak in numbers. Each regiment retains the

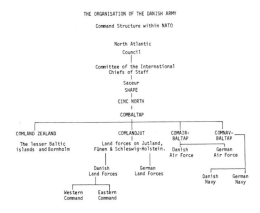

THE ORGANISATION OF THE DANISH ARMY

Command Structure within NATO

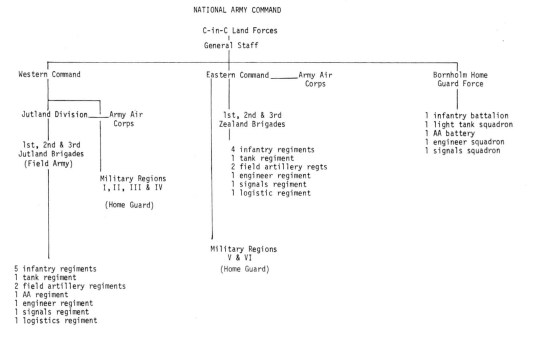

Danish troops during a combat exercise on the island of Bornholm, 1973. (Keystone)

traditions which it has inherited from units raised as early as the 17th century. Each regiment has three or four battalions of which the first is active and the remainder are reserve units. The army consists of six armoured infantry brigades, of which two are reserve formations; the four active formations are maintained at about 75% war strength. Each brigade consists of three "Battle Groups" of battalion size; one of these groups is strong in armour, the other two are strong in infantry.

The infantry groups are of two types, APC-mounted and motorised. Each battalion of APC infantry consists of HQ company, two APC (M-113) infantry companies and a squadron (company) of tanks. The motorised battalion has HQ Company and three motorised companies. Special volunteer units have also been raised, and these men are given "Ranger" training and are proficient in parachuting, commando and frogman-type duties.

Armoured battalions consist of HQ squadron, two tank squadrons and an APC infantry company.

Artillery battalions have an HQ battery, two SP medium batteries and a towed medium battery. There are also light batteries (105 mm) and, at divisional level, heavy batteries and rocket artillery.

Danish Army Equipment
Small Arms. 9 mm Sig pistols of Swiss manufacture, 9 mm sub-machine guns, 7·62 mm American carbines, 7·62 mm remodelled "M-42" German machine gun of World War II design, and 12·7 mm MGs on APCs.
Danish-produced small arms:
9 mm Hovea M/49 SMG with collapsible tubular steel

butt Weight – 4·04 kg; length (extended) – 0·81 m; blow-back action; rate of fire – 600 rpm; 35 round magazine; effective range – 100 m.
7·62 mm Madsen M1948 LMG Weight – 10·2 kg with bipods; length – 1·16 m; blow-back action; rate of fire – 600 rpm; effective range – 600 m; 30 round magazine.

For the heavy role there is a 14 kg tripod mount which increases the effective range to 1,200 m. Ammunition supply is then by belt.
Mortars 60 mm, 81 mm and 120 mm.
Anti-tank weapons M72 100 mm anti-tank GW; American 106 mm recoilless anti-tank rifles mounted on jeeps.
APCs M-113.
Tanks M-41 Walker Bulldog light tanks, Centurions with 76 or 84 mm cannon (some 105 mm now also in use).
Field Artillery Towed 105 mm American M-50 howitzers; towed 155 mm American M-52 and SP 109G (M-64) howitzers; towed 203 mm American howitzer and Honest John 762 mm SSM (these last two have nuclear capacity but no nuclear warheads are stationed on Danish soil).
AA Artillery Bofors 40 mm, radar controlled M-63 MG.
Engineers The British Medium Girder Bridge known to the Danes as the "Feltbro M-71".
Signals Largely German "Telefunken" equipment.
Vehicles are a mixture of American (Jeeps and GMC) and British (Bedford 3-tonners).

Danish Army Uniforms

From the end of World War II until 1969 the Danish Army had worn British style khaki battle dress, or, in the case of officers, service dress. After this date, all ranks received a new uniform for parade, walking out and everyday wear. The jacket is dark bottle green and of service dress cut with five front buttons, the trousers dark grey with a dark green side piping. Buttons are yellow and bear the regimental badge, and the yellow collar badges also show the regiment. For infantry units these are on a coloured cloth backing which indicates the battalion of the regiment in which the wearer serves. The colour code is as follows: Regimental HQ – crimson; 1st Battalion – red; 2nd Battalion – white; 3rd Battalion – yellow; 4th Battalion – blue.

With the peaked cap there are three different styles of cap badge: one for generals, one for officers and one for other ranks. Other headgear is the "Schiffschen" or side hat, which is dark green and worn with a red and white cockade in the front centre and the army badge on the left side; and the beret, also dark green, with the army badge (a crowned shield in a laurel wreath bearing three lions) is worn over the left eye.

Badges of rank are worn by officers on the epaulettes and by other ranks on the upper arms. These badges are shown in the list below. Shoes and gloves are black; shirt white for walking out, light green for duty wear; and tie black. For everyday wear in barracks, a khaki battle dress (BD) of British pattern is worn with either a beret or a side hat. Combat dress consists of the "M58", lime green jacket and trousers with '58 pattern British webbing and American style steel helmet. Badges of rank in combat dress are of cloth and are worn on the upper arms. In summer a very light khaki service dress may be worn, open necked, four button front, four patch pockets with buttoned flaps, plain cuffs. With this are worn light khaki shirt, tie and trousers. Shirt sleeve order consists of the light khaki shirt and tie with sleeves buttoned at the cuff, light khaki trousers and narrow web belt with yellow buckle plate or the same garments but with open neck and sleeves rolled up. For winter wear a dark green greatcoat and a raincoat are provided. The gold buttons on the SD jacket bear the arm of service (infantry, cavalry, artillery) device.

Badges of Rank

Privates

Konstabel	– one horizontal braid bar
Overkonstabel 2nd Grade	– two horizontal braid bars
Overkonstabel 1st Grade	– three horizontal braid bars
Korporal (conscript)	– two buff chevrons, point up
Korporal (professional)	– two buff chevrons, point up the lower apex of the chevrons closed by the arc
Sergent (conscript)	– three chevrons
Sergent (professional)	– three chevrons and an arc beneath
Oversergent	– four chevrons and an arc beneath
Senior sergent 2nd Grade	– four chevrons and two arcs beneath
Senior sergent 1st Grade	– four chevrons and three arcs beneath
Sekondløjtnant	– one small five-pointed gold star
Løjtnant	– one star under a gold "triangle"
Premierløjtnant	– two stars
Kaptajn	– three stars
Major	– one large, six-pointed gold star
Oberstløjtnant	– two such stars
Oberst	– three such stars
Generalmajor	– one very large, six-pointed gold star
Generalløjtnant	– two such stars
General	– three such stars

THE FEDERAL REPUBLIC OF GERMANY

Population – 61,489,000 (including West Berliners). **Capital** – Bonn.

Armed Forces:

Army – 328,200 men.

Navy – 32,500 men; 12 destroyers (3 with missiles), 8 frigates, 12 submarines, 76 minesweepers, 40 MTBs.

Air Force – 101,000 men, *c.* 850 combat aircraft: *c.* 490 F-104G ("Starfighter"), *c.* 300 Fiat G-91 fighters; RF-4-E Phantom Mk IIs will replace the Starfighters, and some 88 are already in service.

Para-military forces – 20,000 Grenzschütz (Frontier Guards) equipped with light and heavy armoured cars (including the British Saladin with 76 mm gun).

Reserves – 1·7 million men.

Defence Spending – 24,219 million marks in 1972.

After World War II, West Germany was reconstructed by the Allies as a federal republic, the individual states conforming fairly closely to the old kingdoms and principalities which Bismark bound together with his policy of blood and steel in the 1860s and 70s. These states are as follows: Schleswig-Holstein, Hamburg, Bremen, Nordrhein-Westfalen, Niedersachsen, Hessen, Rheinland-Pfalz, Saarland, Baden-Württemberg and Bayern.

West Berlin used to be considered automatically as an integral part of West Germany but the position of this oddity thrown up by the chances of Mr Churchill's red pencil has become increasingly unclear in recent years.

Head of state is the Bundespräsident, currently Walter Scheel, who was elected to office by the federal assembly in May 1974 and serves for five years, maximum ten. The political system is carefully designed to ensure that extremists cannot again come to power easily; there are two "houses of parliament" – the Bundestag, or lower house, and the Bundesrat or upper house. The Bundestag consists of 496 elected members from the federal states in the main body of the republic and 22 elected members from West Berlin, who, however, have no valid votes in the debates. From the members of the governments of the individual states 45 men are chosen to form the Bundesrat or upper house.

The leader of the majority party in the Bundestag is the Chancellor (currently the Social-democrat Helmut Schmidt) and real political power rests with him. West Germany has just become a member of UNO, as has the GDR.

The modern German Army bears no relation whatever to the Wehrmacht of the Second World War. Due to a prolonged and intensive re-education programme to which the Western allies (France, Britain and America) subjected the West Germans after 1945, modern German youth has not the slightest urge to don a uniform or to carry a weapon, and left-wing activities have reached an alarming scale in the German universities. This, in turn, has led to a massive number of "Kriegsdienstverweigerer" or conscientious objectors – in 1972 they totalled over 32,000. There is no para-military training of school children in Germany, neither are uniforms worn by school-children.

Order of Battle of the Bundeswehr

I Corps (HQ – Münster in Westfalen; deployed in Schleswig-Holstein, Niedersachsen and Nordrhein-Westfalen)

1st Panzer-Grenadier-Division (Hannover)
1st Panzer-Grenadier-Brigade
2nd Panzer-Grenadier-Brigade
3rd Panzer-Brigade
3rd Panzer-Division (Buxtehude)
7th Panzer-Grenadier-Brigade
8th Panzer-Brigade
9th Panzer-Lehr-Brigade

WEST GERMAN CORPS TROOPS

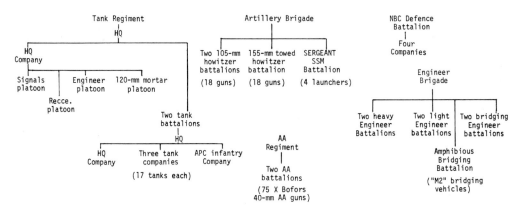

Other units include medical, transport, repair, logistics and air transport battalions.

*6th Panzer-Grenadier-Division** (Schleswig-Holstein)
16th Panzer-Grenadier-Brigade
17th Panzer-Grenadier-Brigade
18th Panzer-Brigade
7th Panzer-Grenadier-Division (Unna)
19th Panzer-Grenadier-Brigade
20th Panzer-Grenadier-Brigade
21st Panzer-Brigade
11th Panzer-Grenadier-Division (Oldenburg)
31st Panzer-Grenadier-Brigade
32nd Panzer-Grenadier-Brigade
33rd Panzer-Brigade
Panzer-Regiment 100
II Corps (Bavaria and Baden-Württemberg)
4th Jäger-Division
10th Jäger-Brigade
11th Jäger-Brigade
12th Panzer-Brigade
10th Panzer-Grenadier-Division
28th Panzer-Grenadier-Brigade
29th Panzer-Grenadier-Brigade
30th Panzer-Brigade
1st Gebirgsdivision (Bad Reichenhall-Garmisch-Partenkirchen area)
22nd Gebirgs-Jäger-Brigade
23rd Gebirgs-Jäger-Brigade
24th Panzer-Brigade
Panzer-Regiment 200

III Corps (HQ Koblenz; deployed in Hesse, Rheinland-Pfalz and Saarland)
2nd Jäger-Division
4th Jäger-Brigade
5th Panzer-Grenadier-Brigade
6th Panzer-Brigade
5th Panzer-Division (Koblenz)
13th Panzer-Grenadier-Brigade
14th Panzer-Brigade
15th Panzer-Brigade
12th Panzer-Division (Würzburg)
34th Panzer-Grenadier-Brigade
35th Panzer-Grenadier-Brigade
36th Panzer-Brigade
Panzer-Regiment 300
1st Airborne Division (Luftlande-Division)
25th Fallschirm-Jäger-Brigade
26th Fallschirm-Jäger-Brigade
27th Fallschirm-Jäger-Brigade
Ceremonial troops consist of the "Wachbataillon" (Guards Battalion) which has three companies, one each from the army, navy and air force. They wear a cuffband in black with silver Gothic lettering "WACHBATAILLON" and are armed with the World War II German infantry carbine.

West German Weapons and Equipment
Small Arms
Pistole P1
This 9 mm weapon is produced by the Walther firm of James Bond fame in Ulm and its civil designation is the "P38". The weight of the pistol with full

* This Division is under COMBALTAP, in NATO's northern sector with the Danish army.

Above, the West German army's *Marder* infantry armoured combat vehicle, one of the family of armoured vehicles. Below, the new Swiss-German anti-aircraft tank *Fla-Panzer 1*.

THE WEST GERMAN DIVISION

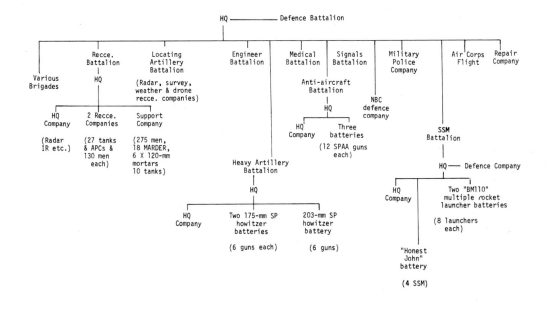

THE WEST GERMAN PANZER GRENADIER BRIGADE

(Armoured Infantry)

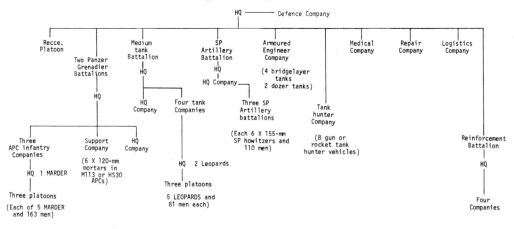

magazine is 0·89 kg; VO – 330 m/sec; combat range – 50 m; magazine content – 8 rounds.

Maschinenpistole MP2

9 mm calibre, wooden butt and a 25 or 32 round bar magazine are the trademarks of this automatic pistol-cum-sub machine carbine (SMC). It is a blow-back principle of operation; 4·3 kg in weight (full magazine of 32 rounds). Only 0·64 m long, the bulk of the weapon is further reduced by having the magazine inserted up through the pistol grip. VO – 395 m/sec; combat range 200 m.

Maschinenpistole MP2A1

Details as for the MP2 except that this weapon has a collapsible metal butt making its length (butt extended) 0·65 m and (butt closed) 0·47 m. Weight with 32 rounds in the magazine – 4·1 kg.

Gewehr G3 (CETME Carbine)

Although employing NATO calibre 7·62 mm ammunition, this semi-automatic carbine differs in construction from the Belgian FN NATO pattern weapon. Weight (with full 20 round magazine) – 4·7 kg; length – 1·02 m; principle of operation – gas pressure; rate of fire – 600 rpm; VO – 780 m/sec; combat range – 400 m. As well as the G3 with wooden butt, there is the "G3 Kurz" with collapsible metal butt and the "G3ZF" with telescopic sights and wooden butt.

Maschinengewehr (MG) 1 or MG3 with bipod

This weapon is a copy of the World War II "MG 42" and is highly complex in construction, with a very high rate of fire (1,200 rpm) which guzzles ammunition. It is also used by the armies of Austria, Italy and Switzerland. Weight (empty) – 11·6 kg; length – 1·23 m; calibre – 7·62 mm; combat range – 600 m; VO – 733 m/sec; principle of operation – blow-back action; ammunition feed – self disintegrating belt; crew – 2. When the MG1 is mounted on a vehicle its effective range increases to 1,000 m.

20 mm Bordkanone HS820

Many APCs in the Bundeswehr are equipped with this weapon; weight – 57 kg; length – 2·57 m; rate of fire – 1,000 m/sec; combat range – 1,200 m; VO – 1,050 m/sec.

Mortars

81 mm Tampella Mortar (Finnish design)

Weight – 45·4 kg; calibre – 81 mm; length of barrel – 1·6 m; rate of fire – 15 rpm; range – from 500–4,500 m; crew – 1 + 3. This weapon can be broken down into three man-packable loads.

120 mm Brandt Mortar

Weight (with base plate) – 260 kg; with 2 wheel chassis – 224 kg; calibre – 120 mm; length of barrel – 1·75 m; rate of fire – 15 rpm; range – from 750–6,500 m; VO – 285 m/sec; crew 1 + 5. Normally either towed by the Unimog 1·5 ton 4 × 4 lorry or mounted in the HS30 APC, this weapon can also be broken down into seven loads for man or animal transport.

120 mm Tampella Mortar (Finnish design)

Normally transported and fired from APCs, this 120 kg weapon can be broken down into three loads for pack transport purposes.

Multiple Rocket Launchers

During World War II the German Wehrmacht used multiple rocket launchers both in the towed version (the 6-barrelled "Nebelwerfer") and in a vehicle-borne 8-barrelled model mounted on an armoured half-track. This tradition has recently been taken up again with the introduction into service in 1970 of the "36-barrelled 110 mm Mehrfachraketenwerfer", mounted on a 7 ton 6 × 6 lorry. The crew consists of 3 men. Each rocket weighs 55 kg and is 2 m long with a single stage, solid fuel motor. The weapon is ballistic with a maximum range of 15 km. Ammunition types include HE, smoke and anti-tank mines. It takes 18 seconds for the 36 barrels to fire their rockets. The prime mover has a multi-fuel motor, max road speed – 73 km/hr, road range – 500 km; length – 7·6 m; width – 2·5 m; height – 2·6 m.

Nuclear Rockets

Although forbidden to manufacture nuclear weapons, Germany has received not only the old "Sergeant" rocket but also the "Pershing" strategic rocket (the latter weapon belongs to the Luftwaffe as the German Army could not provide the manpower to crew this complex system). Nuclear warheads are held in Germany by American Custodian Units and would be handed over to the Germans for use if the need arose.

Sergeant Surface-to-Surface Guided Missile

This ageing equipment has an inertial guidance system and is transported on a vehicle which is not its starting ramp. Immediately prior to firing, the warhead must be married up with the rocket, a single stage, solid fuel motor; speed – 3·5 Mach; range 40 km–140 km. Weight of rocket – 4,536 kg; weight of "XM-15" warhead – 650 kg; length of assembled rocket – 10·5 m. Non-nuclear warheads

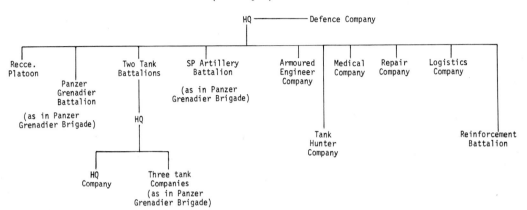

WEST GERMAN PANZER BRIGADE

(Tank Brigade)

(HE) can also be used. The firing ramp vehicle is the Magirus-Deutz, 7 ton, 6 × 6 "Jupiter" tractor; max road speed – 60 km/hr. A complete firing group includes a crane vehicle and a rocket transport vehicle.

Anti-aircraft weapons

Rheinmetal Rh 202 HS699 20 mm AAMG

This weapon is towed on a 2-wheeled chassis, has a crew of 1 + 3 and weighs 0·57 tons. It is optically controlled, max combat range (AA) – 1,200 mm; combat ammunition – 250 rounds; rate of fire – 1,000 rpm.

Bofors 40 mm L70 AA Cannon

Once again a towed equipment, this weapon is also used in many other NATO states. Normally deployed in batteries or half batteries, it is radar controlled. Crew – 6; weight of trailer mounted weapon – 4·7 tons; length – 7·28 m; width – 2·2 m; height – 2·35 m. Max combat range AA (optical) – 1,500 m, AA (radar controlled) – 3,000 m; rate of fire – 240 rpm. The twin 40 mm L60 Bofors AA cannon mounted on the "M42" light tank chassis have the same ranges as above but their rate of fire is 2 × 120 rpm. The "M42" is a very obsolete weapon and is currently being replaced by the "Fla-Panzer 1".

Anti-Aircraft tank "Fla-Panzer 1"

Produced by the firm Oerlikon-Contraves, this new weapon system can fire either HE or AP projectiles and is thus effective against hard ground targets. The AP ammunition is held in two small

magazines and the change over from the normal mode of fire against air targets, to the secondary, anti-armour, role is achieved simple by throwing a lever which changes the ammunition feed to the guns. For AA purposes, the Fla-Panzer 1 has target acquisition and target tracking radar (whose aerials are stowed away in the ground combat mode) and a computer which controls the alignment of the guns. The chassis for the weapon is the Leopard Tank.

Redeye

This American-developed, one man crew, use-and-throw-away AAGM is being (1973) introduced into service in the German Army. Employing an infra-red target acquisition principle, *Redeye* homes in on the heat source of any passing plane. It requires no maintenance in storage and the storage container is also the missile launcher.

The German Territorial Army

The *Territorialheer* is composed of over 80% reservists and is thus an organisation which requires time to become effective in its wartime role: security of CENTAGs rear areas; protection of vital points and the defence of certain areas; damage control; military traffic control and NBC warning and reporting. The TA is divided into six Wehrbereiche (defence regions) as follows:

Wehrbereiche		Territorialkommandos
Schleswig Holstein	I	Territorialkommando Schleswig-Holstein
Niedersachsen	II	Territorialkommando
Nordrhein Westfalen	III	Nord

Rheinland-Pfalz and		
Hessen	IV	Territorialkommando
Baden-Württemberg	V	Süd
Bayern	VI	

The six regions are grouped into three Territorial-kommandos (Territorial Commands): Schleswig-Holstein, Nord and Süd as shown. Each Wehrbereich is subdivided into Verteidigungsbezirke (defence areas) which in turn fall into Verteidigungskreise (defence districts). Static defence units are the Wehrbereich-level Sicherungskompanien (security companies) and the Jäger bataillone (light infantry battalions) at Verteidigungsbezirk level which are used for the defence of vital points and of areas. These units are lightly equipped and not very mobile. Mobile TA forces are represented by the Heimatschutzkommando (Home Guard Command) which equates to a brigade size formation. It has mobility in the shape of lorries and has an emphasis on anti-tank defence.

German Army Uniforms
Officers
Mess Kit No 1 (Gesellschaftsanzug)

Civilian style dinner jacket with badges of rank on the shoulders, sash (cummerbund) in the regimental facing colour.

Mess Kit No 2 (Zweitaschenrock)

Light grey, double-breasted jacket with four buttons, two slit pockets in the skirts, regimental collar patches (Kragenspiegel), badges of rank on the shoulder-straps, black trousers with side piping in the regimental facing colour, peaked grey cap with black headband, silver (gold for generals) army badge (crossed swords over an oak wreath) black-within red-within yellow cockade, silver (gold) peak embroidery according to rank, silver (gold) piping to top and bottom of black headband and the top of the cap. White shirt, black tie and shoes, grey gloves.

Walking Out Dress (Ausgehanzug)

Hat as for Mess Kit No 2 (tank troops wear a black beret, paratroopers a maroon beret and Jägers a dark green beret), white shirt, black tie, trousers, gloves and shoes as for Mess Kit No 2, light grey, single-breasted, open-necked jacket with single rear vent, regimental collar patches, regimental piping to shoulder-straps; silver edging to collar and shoulder-straps, silver matt buttons (all silver gold for generals), four pockets. A formation badge is worn on the upper left arm.

Service Dress (Kleine Dienstanzug)

As for walking out dress but with light blue shirt.

Parade Dress (Grosse Dienstanzug)

As for Service Dress but with mid calf length

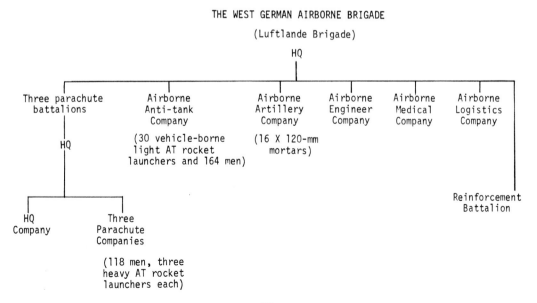

THE WEST GERMAN AIRBORNE BRIGADE

(Luftlande Brigade)

29

WEST GERMAN JÄGER BRIGADE

(Light Infantry Brigade)

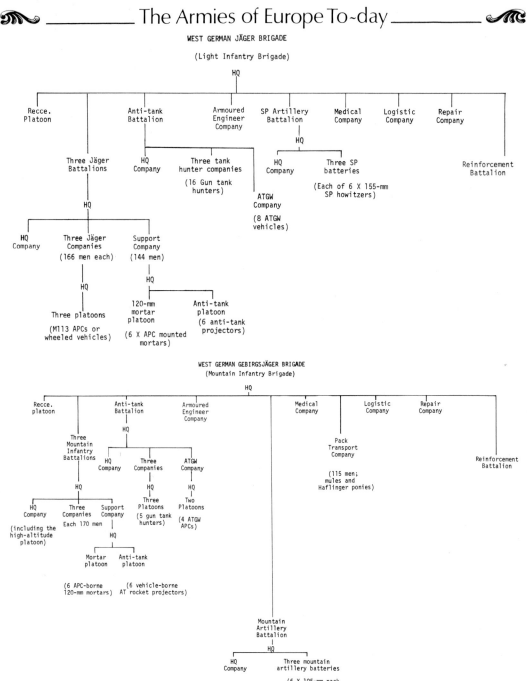

HQ

Recce.
Platoon

Anti-tank
Battalion

Armoured
Engineer
Company

SP Artillery
Battalion

Medical
Company

Logistic
Company

Repair
Company

HQ

Three Jäger
Battalions

HQ
Company

Three tank
hunter companies

(16 Gun tank
hunters)

HQ
Company

Three SP
batteries

(Each of 6 X 155-mm
SP howitzers)

Reinforcement
Battalion

ATGW
Company

(8 ATGW
vehicles)

HQ

HQ
Company

Three Jäger
Companies
(166 men each)

Support
Company
(144 men)

HQ

Three platoons

(M113 APCs or
wheeled vehicles)

120-mm
mortar
platoon

(6 X APC mounted
mortars)

Anti-tank
platoon
(6 anti-tank
projectors)

WEST GERMAN GEBIRGSJÄGER BRIGADE
(Mountain Infantry Brigade)

HQ

Recce.
platoon

Anti-tank
Battalion

Armoured
Engineer
Company

Medical
Company

Logistic
Company

Repair
Company

HQ

Three
Mountain
Infantry
Battalions

Pack
Transport
Company

(115 men;
mules and
Haflinger ponies)

Reinforcement
Battalion

HQ
Company

Three
Companies

ATGW
Company

HQ

HQ

HQ

Three
Platoons

(5 gun tank
hunters)

Two
Platoons

(4 ATGW
APCs)

HQ
Company

(including the
high-altitude
platoon)

Three
Companies
Each 170 men

Support
Company

HQ

Mortar
platoon

Anti-tank
platoon

(6 APC-borne
120-mm mortars)

(6 vehicle-borne
AT rocket projectors)

Mountain
Artillery
Battalion

HQ

HQ
Company

Three mountain
artillery batteries

(6 X 105-mm pack
howitzers each)

black boots (into which the trousers are gathered) and a black leather waist belt with square silver (gold) buckle plate bearing an eagle and the inscription "RECHT UND EINIGKEIT UND FREIHEIT".

Shirt sleeve order (Hemdenaermel)

Either light blue shirt and black tie with sleeves worn buttoned at the cuff or open-necked light blue shirt with short sleeves, regimental epaulettes (as for service dress).

Combat Dress (Kampfanzug)

US-style NATO helmet, "moss-grey" jacket and trousers with national flag at the tops of the sleeves, jack boots, fawn webbing equipment which is practically a copy of the World War II black leather equipment of the Wehrmacht.

Miscellaneous

Medals are worn optionally and many from the last war can still be seen. Younger soldiers wear the following medals (or their ribbons) on the left breast: sport medal (in bronze, silver or gold); life saving qualification medal (in 3 classes); the Hamburg flood catastrophe (1962) medal. Paratroopers wear their "wings" on the upper right breast as do army pilots; Einzelkämpfer (Rangers) wear their green and silver badge on the right breast pocket, and the military sports badge (in bronze, silver or gold) is worn on the left breast pocket. Medical, dental and veterinary officers wear their specialist badges on their epaulettes above the badges of rank. Officers of the military geographical service wear their globe badge on the right cuff.

Dress for other ranks

Basically the same as for officers, the differences only are listed here:

1. Peaked cap – the regimental facing colour is worn as a piping to both edges of the black hatband and to the edge of the top of the cap by corporals and below. Senior NCOs wear bronze piping.

2. Collars – the collar patches have white cotton lace embroidery instead of silver; collars are not piped along the edge for corporals and below, senior NCOs have bronze piping.

3. All rank badges are worn on the epaulettes since June 1973. Prior to this date the various grades of private soldier had worn these badges on the upper sleeve.

4. Buttons are bronze, matt metal.

Miscellaneous

Crews of armoured vehicles which are not tanks (SP howitzers, APCs) wear brown berets with the

West German field officer's peaked cap.

German cockade over crossed sabres as a badge over the left eye.

Mountain troops (Gebirgsjäger) wear grey peaked caps of special design with an edelweiss badge on the left hand side and a front badge consisting of the German cockade over crossed sabres. They also wear short, close fitting, double-breasted, hip length grey jackets and either black ski trousers and ski boots (winter) or knee breeches and grey woollen socks and mountaineering boots.

NBC protective clothing consists of grey rubber smock with hood, grey rubber gloves, trousers and boots.

In the grey-green combat clothing, a narrow strip in the regimental facing colour is worn around the base of the shoulder-strap.

Facing colours in the German Army (worn on collar badges, trouser seams, shoulder-straps and hats):
Generals – red with gold collar decoration
General staff officers – light crimson with special silver collar lace
Armoured troops (Tanks) (Panzer) – pink
Armoured Recce troops (Aufklärer) – deep yellow
Field Artillery (Feld-Artillerie) – brick red
Anti-aircraft Artillery (Flug-Abwehr-Artillerie) – coral red
Engineers (Pioniere) – black
Signals (Fernmelde) – lemon yellow
Infantry (Panzer-grenadiere) (Fallschirmjäger) (Jäger & Gebirgsjäger) – grass green
Technical Troops (Technische Truppe) (Logistics, transport, repair & medical) – dark blue
Army Air Corps (Heeresflieger) – light grey

NBC Defence Corps (NBC Schütztruppe) – dark crimson
Military Police (Feldjäger) – orange
Military bands (Militar Musik) – white

German Army Flags

In the Bundeswehr all units of battalion size carry a flag (Truppenfahne). The size and design is the same for all units whether infantry, cavalry or navy and consists of the national flag (three horizontal stripes – black over red over gold with a gold shield bearing the black German eagle in the centre). The flag is 1 meter square and edged in black, red and gold cord and gold fringes. No unit decoration appears on the flag itself, this is carried engraved on a brass ring around the pike staff. The pike staff is black and has a spear-point tip bearing an oval of oak leaves enclosing the black and silver iron cross (1813 pattern). Distinctions appear in the form of cravats attached to the pike staff. These cravats are in the facing colour of the unit concerned, are about 10 cm wide by 1 meter long and bear the national emblem at the top (eagle on gold shield on black-over red over gold ground) and bear the unit designation or a dedication in gold. The lower end is gold fringed.

The colour bearer is an NCO and wears white gauntlets when on parade with the flag. The flag bandolier is a simple black leather belt with small bucket and silver buckle and is worn over the left shoulder to the right hip.

When old flags are no longer required, the flag itself is returned to the army depot at Itterbeck, the cravats (up to three may be carried at any one time on each flag) and the ring from the pike are sent to the Militärgeschichtlichen Museum in Rastatt in Baden-Württemberg.

| | | | | Overall | |
Wheeled Vehicles	Weight (kg)	Length (m)	Width (m)	Height (m)	Engine
¼ Ton Auto-Union, 4 × 4 Jeep	1,245	3·4	1·7	1·7	Three cylinder, two stroke, water-cooled, 44 hp petrol engine; max road speed – 95 km/hr; wades – 0·5 m
¾ Ton Borgward, 4 × 4 cargo vehicle	2,450	5·3	1·9	2·2	Six cylinder, four stroke, water-cooled, 82 hp petrol engine; max road speed – 95 km/hr; wades – 0·75 m
¾ Ton Borgward, 4 × 4 staff vehicle	2,470	5·3	1·9	2·15	As above
1½ Ton Unimog, 4 × 4, "S" type cargo vehicle	2,900	4·92	2·14	2·53	Six cylinder, four stroke, water-cooled, 80 hp petrol engine; max road speed – 95 km/hr; wades – 0·8 m
1½ Ton Unimog, 4 × 4 box-bodied signals vehicle	?	4·92	2·14	2·49	As above
1½ Ton Unimog, 4 × 4 box-bodied vehicle	3,224	4·92	2·14	2·59	As above
1½ Ton Unimog, 4 × 4 ambulance	3,224	4·9	2·14	2·59	As above
3 Ton Ford, 4 × 4 cargo vehicle	4,300	7·25	2·44	2·94	Eight cylinder, V, water-cooled, 92 hp petrol engine; max road speed – 85 km/hr; wades – 1 m
3 Ton Ford, 4 × 4 box-bodied vehicle	4,770	7·0	2·45	2·97	As above
5 Ton Daimler-Benz, 4 × 4 cargo vehicle	7,500	8·1	2·5	3·05	Six cylinder, four stroke, water-cooled, 145 hp multi-fuel motor; max road speed – 70 km/hr; wades – 0·85 m

Federal German Military Equipment

5 Ton MAN 630L2A, 4 × 4 cargo vehicle	7,400	7·9	2·5	2·85	Six cylinder, four stroke, water-cooled, 130 hp multi-fuel engine; max road speed – 67·5 km/hr; wades – 0·85 m
5 Ton MAN 630L2A, 4 × 4 box-bodied vehicle	8,050	7·7	2·5	2·97	As above
5 ton Henschel HS-115, 4 × 4 cargo vehicle	6,050	4·5	2·35	?	Six cylinder, four stroke, 125 hp diesel engine
7 ton KHD Jupiter, 6 × 6 cargo vehicle	7,850	8·0	2·5	2·8	Eight cylinder, four stroke, 178 hp multi-fuel, air-cooled engine; max road speed – 73 km/hr; wades – 0·85 m
10 ton Faun 8/15, 4 × 4 limber	13,500	6·6	2·8	2·8	Eight cylinder, V form, four stroke, multi-fuel, air-cooled, 178 hp engine; max road speed – 67·5 km/hr; wades – 0·97 m. This vehicle *carries* the 105 mm howitzer of the brigade artillery
10 ton Faun 912/21, 6 × 6 ammunition carrier	16,800	8·4	2·5	3·5	Twelve cylinder, V form, four stroke, air-cooled, 265 hp, multi-fuel motor. This vehicle is fitted with a crane to speed the loading and unloading of ammunition

Trails of 105 mm mountain howitzer packed on German artillery mule.

Wheeled Vehicles	Weight (kg)	Length (m)	Width (m)	Overall Height (m)	Engine
10 ton Faun Z912/21-203, 6 × 6 ammunition carrier	17,150	8·3	2·5	2·85	As above; this vehicle is designed to operate with the 155 mm and 203 mm medium howitzers
12 ton Faun Z912/21 Skysweeper, 6 × 6 auxiliary artillery vehicle	16,500	9·0	2·5	2·88	Engine as above; with its dozer blade, this vehicle lends valuable support to the 155 mm M2 and 203 mm M2 medium howitzers
12 ton Faun L912/45a, 6 × 6 artillery tractor	11,500	7·6	2·5	2·77	Engine as above; the 155 mm M2 and the 203 mm M2 are pulled by this vehicle
7 ton Jupiter TW-931, 6 × 6 mobile crane	14,560	9·4	2·5	3·1	Eight cylinder, V form, 178 hp, air-cooled, multi-fuel engine. This is a general recovery vehicle
12 ton Faun LK 12/21-400, 6 × 6 mobile crane	17,700	8·8	2·5	3·15	Twelve cylinder, V form, four stroke, air-cooled, 265 hp, multi-fuel engine; max road speed – 60 km/hr

Federal German Tracked Vehicles

Weapon	Date into B/W service	Weight in firing position (kg)	Range (km)	Rate of fire (rpm)	Muzzle velocity (m/sec)	Combat ammunition load (rounds)	Crew	Length Width Height (meters)	Remarks
Hotchkiss-Brandt light artillery observers APC		8,200	—	—	—	—	4	4·48 2·34 1·60	Built under licence in Germany by Klockner-Humboldt-Deutz. Six cylinder, water-cooled, 164 hp Hotchkiss engine; road range – 290 km; max speed – 58 km/hr, consumption – 85 litres/ 100 km; tank capacity – 245 litres; wades – 0·7 m
Hotchkiss-Brandt armoured ambulance		8,200	—	—	—	—	1 + 4 sitting or 1 + 2 lying	4·66 2·34 1·90	Engine details as above
Hispano-Suiza-30 APC		14,600	—	—	—	—		5·56 2·55 1·85	Eight cylinder, Rolls-Royce, water-cooled, 230 hp engine; max road speed – 51 km/hr; consumption – 145 litres/ 100 km; tank capacity – 245 litres; road range – 170 km. A multi-purpose vehicle, the uses include – APC (8 men), command, signals, mortar carrier, fire control and rocket tank hunter

THE REPUBLIC OF GREECE

Population – 9,030,000.   **Capital** – Athens.

Armed Forces:

    Army – 118,000 men; 450 medium tanks.

    Navy – 18,000 men; 3 submarines (3 more to be delivered in 1974), 8 destroyers, 4 destroyer escorts, 3 patrol vessels, 2 minelayers, 20 minesweepers, 13 MTBs, 4 patrol boats with Exocet SSM, 15 landing ships (8 tank, 6 medium and 1 dock), 8 landing craft; 12 HU-16 maritime patrol craft.

    Air Force – 21,000 men, 190 combat planes: 6 fighter-bomber squadrons (3 with F-84Fs, 2 with F-104Gs, 1 with F-5As); 3 interceptor squadrons (2 with F-5As, 1 with F-102As); 2 reconnaissance squadrons (1 with RF-5s and 1 with RF-84Fs). Transport – 3 squadrons with 15 C-47s and 45 Noratlas. Helicopters – 2 squadrons (1 with 12 H-19s and 6 AB-205s, 1 with 10 Bell 47Gs). Air defence – 1 battalion with Nike-Hercules SAM.

Para-military forces – 22,500 Gendarmerie; 65,000 National Guard.

Defence Spending   – $495,134,000 in 1972 (3·3% of GNP).

Head of State until late 1973 was former intelligence colonel Georgios Papadopoulos. (He was then deposed by other elements within the military regime, and the current picture is not clear.) His former military duties included the study of psychological warfare. He was the brain behind the bloodless coup of 21 April 1967, and until December 1967 he was a minister in the government of Mr Kollis. When ex-King Konstantin II mounted his abortive counter-coup on 13 December 1967 (and subsequently fled to Italy), Papadopoulos became President and vice-regent. Greece remained nominally a kingdom until June 1973 when the king (still in voluntary exile in Italy) was dethroned, a plebiscite was held and Papadopoulos was confirmed as head of state.

Parliament was suspended on 24 April 1967 and since then a Consultative Council of 56 (since September 1971 raised to 75) replaced them. Of the 75 members fifteen are chosen by the head of government (then Papadopoulos), the others are elected by 15,000 "electors" (mayors, leading professional people and others). Since April 1967 all political parties have been forbidden in Greece.

Greece had been a kingdom since her liberation from Turkish rule in 1830, when many Germans helped the Greeks in their revolt to achieve independence. The first king of Greece was of the royal house of Bavaria, Otto I.

Greece is divided into seven provinces – Attika (Athens, Central and West Macedonia, Peloponnese (Patras), Thessalien (Larissa), Crete, Epirus and East Macedonia and Thrace. The monks' republic of Athos is also part of the state.

Greece is an active member of NATO and receives much military aid from the USA and West Germany. There is universal military service liability (two years, or two and a half years in specialist units) for all males from 21 to 50 years of age. After this active service, the men revert to the 1st Reserve for nineteen years and thence to the 2nd Reserve for a further ten years. They are annually mobilised for four-week exercises in the next four years following their national service. About 50,000 men per year are called up, in four quarterly batches. General mobilisation involves all able-bodied persons regardless of age and sex. The civil defence organisation normally draws the line at 40 for men and 35 for women.

The pre-June 1973 constitution made it clear that the armed forces were responsible not only for defence of Greece against external and internal enemies but also were dedicated to maintain the existing political order.

After the Second World War Greece fought a bitter civil war against the Communists and there is a small but active left wing group in the country. The Soviets exploit civil unrest in the state so that

NATO will be weakened and the access to the Mediterranean for her Black Sea Fleet will be eased.

In August 1950 the three ministries of the Greek armed forces were fused into one and in 1952 the British Army's Training Mission was replaced by an American team. The Greek army is mainly American equipped and organised, and her officers receive training in the staff colleges of other NATO countries. Characteristics of Greek equipment may be seen in the NATO equipment Tables. Assessment of the morale and reliability of the Greek army is difficult as most reports publicised in the West have a strong leftist slant. The Greek army performed well in Korea in 1956; their discipline is strict and haircuts short! Drawing their recruits from a largely peasant economy, it is likely that the men are tough, good in fieldcraft, resourceful and undemanding logistically. The place of the Greek army officer in society is currently firmly established. Agitation against them comes from the left but indications are that this is a minority view.

Organisation

The Greek army consists of one armoured division, one armoured brigade, eleven infantry divisions and a para-commando division. There are also twelve independent light infantry battalions which are the mobile part of the Territorial Defence Force. One of the infantry divisions is deployed in Crete and is retained at national disposal; the headquarters of the three Corps, the armoured division and eleven infantry divisions are assigned to NATO in the form of COMLANDSOUTHEAST at Izmir in Turkey. Apart from the twelve light infantry battalions, the Territorial Defence Force has one hundred battalions of reservists which are used as a basis for prolonged guerrilla warfare in their home areas should the country be overrun by an enemy and the field army be forced to leave the country.

THE GREEK ARMY 1973

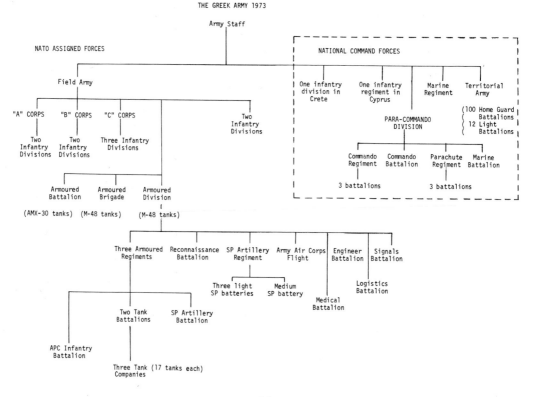

Greek Army Equipment

Small Arms (All of American origin) 9 mm Pistols; 9 mm SMGs; 7·62 mm Rifles and MGs; 81 mm mortars, 120 mm mortars.

APCs American M-113, M-2, M-3 and M-59.

Armoured Cars American M-8, 6 × 6 and M-20.

Tanks 200 American M-47s, 220 M-48s and 30 French AMX-30 medium tanks.

Artillery (American equipments) 105 mm howitzers, 155 mm and 203 mm towed guns, 105 mm, 155 mm, M-109G and 175 mm SP howitzers.

AA Artillery 40 mm, 75 mm and 90 mm guns.

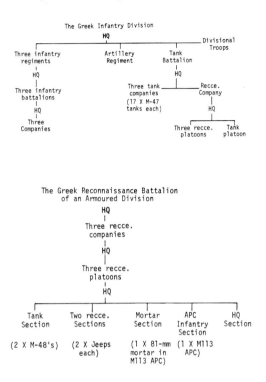

Greek Army Uniforms

During the last year the appointments on Greek uniforms have undergone several swift changes. Firstly, in 1970 the artillery collar badge changed from a flaming gold grenade to a crossed rocket and cannon barrel also in gold. At about the same time, general staff officers (who previously had been distinguished by a gold edging to their collar patches) received a new badge in the shape of a light blue oblong shield bearing a gold owl superimposed on a sabre which is worn on the upper right breast. With the deposition of King Konstantin in June 1973, all crowns were removed from Greek uniforms and there was then a pause until August 1973 when new badges (a phoenix in gold rising from red flames) was designed, made and delivered. The uniforms of strongly British flavour which had been worn from 1945 until 1968 have since been replaced by American olive green garments.

The following forms of dress are worn:

Officers

Ceremonial – midnight blue.

Winter Service Dress (SD)

Olive green, single-breasted, four button front tunic with open collar, two pleated patch pockets on the chest, two slit pockets in the skirts, single vent rear, two buttons at the rear of the cuff. The jacket has an olive green waist belt with yellow open buckle. Regimental collar badges are worn and badges of rank consist of stars and phoenixes on the shoulder-straps. General officers wear red gorget patches: general, lieutenant-general and major-general with gold button and central oak leaf embroidery; brigadier and colonel with gold button and crimson centre cord. The gold buttons bear the phoenix over a shield bearing a crested Greek helmet superimposed on the Greek cross. The olive green, peaked cap has a gold chin strap and black peak; the cap badge is a large version of the button badge in gold, blue and white enamel and surrounded with golden oak leaves. Olive green trousers, black shoes and gloves, black tie and fawn shirt complete the suit.

Summer SD

Very light khaki in colour, open-necked single-breasted, four patch pockets (the top two pleated), buttoned cuffs and a triple-pleated back with two vents. Buttons, collar badges and rank badges as before. This jacket can be worn with tie and shirt as in winter SD or open necked and without shirt or tie in which case the sleeves are rolled up and a detachable collar liner is worn inside the collar. Very light khaki trousers, black shoes. Hat as before or a beret in the following colours: Army Air Corps – red, paratroops – green, tank troops – black, other units – khaki.

Battle Dress (BD)

Olive green in colour and of the same cut as British, post-war BD. Collar badges, rank badges, tie, shirt as before, concealed buttons, olive green trousers, black boots and gaiters or shoes. Peaked cap or beret, black gloves.

Combat Dress

As for BD but in rougher material and with cloth rank badges; collar badges not worn; British-style 1950's pattern steel helmet and '37 pattern khaki webbing, increasingly replaced by U.S.-style issue.

Dress – Other ranks

Conscripts wear only BD and berets; professional senior NCOs have SD as described above but the cap badge is the phoenix over the shield, in brass, without the flanking oak leaves.

Badges of Rank

Other ranks (worn on the upper arms):

Lance corporal	– one yellow chevron, point down
Corporal	– two chevrons

Greek Army march-past on Independence Day 1973; note American-style kit and American weapons. Until recently British-style personal equipment was widely used. (Keystone)

Sergeant (conscript)	– three chevrons
Sergeant (professional)	– three chevrons over a short, horizontal gold bar
Company Sergeant Major	– three chevrons surmounted by a phoenix
Battalion Sergeant Major	– three chevrons surmounted by a phoenix over a short, horizontal gold bar
Officer cadet	– a gold cord along the shoulder strap.

Officers (worn on the shoulder-strap):

Second Lieutenant	– a six-pointed silver star
Lieutenant	– two silver stars
Captain	– three silver stars
Major	– a six-pointed gold star under a phoenix
Lieutenant Colonel	– two gold stars and a phoenix
Colonel	– three stars (in line) under a phoenix
Brigadier	– a large six-pointed silver star under crossed gold baton and sabre under a phoenix
Major General	– as above but two stars one alongside the other

Lieutenant General – as above but three stars in pyramid formation

General – a gold phoenix over crossed gold batons.

Miscellaneous

Army Air Corps pilots wear a golden eagle on the upper left breast.

Greek Army Collar Badges

Arm of Service	Facing Colour
Cavalry (tanks)	– Dark green
Artillery	– Black
Engineers	– Light crimson
Signals	– Dark blue
Infantry	– Red
Medical Corps	– Crimson
Pharmacists	– Medium green
Veterinary Corps	– Pale purple
Postal service	– Equal halves, dark brown and dark green
Supplies & Transport	– Mid-green with light yellow edging
Quartermaster Corps	– Orange with dark blue edging
Technical Troops	– Dark blue with orange edging
Legal Services	– Very dark purple with light yellow edging
Recruiting or Mobilisation Corps	– Dark blue with mid-green edging
Topographical Service	– Equal halves, dark brown and grey
Military Geographical Corps	– Crimson with dark brown edging
Finance Corps	– Pink with crimson edging

Greek paratrooper on summer exercise; this unit wears camouflaged combat clothing.

Finance Control Corps	– Light red with pink edging
Supervisory Clerical Corps	– Equal halves, dark brown and pink
Military Bands	– Mid-blue

Greek Army Flags

Square cloth, light blue, bearing an upright white cross; the cloth is edged in gold fringes. In the centre are embroidered pictures of various saints, eg St George slaying the dragon – a different saint for each service. The pike staff is spirally striped light blue and white; the rhombic, gilt tip bears the upright cross. Gold cords and tassels are tied around the base of the flagstaff tip and extend to below the level of the bottom of the flag.

THE REPUBLIC OF ITALY

Population – 54,490,000.   **Capital** – Rome.

Armed Forces:

> **Army** – 393,000 men including 86,300 Carabinieri and 1,000 "Lagunari" (marines); 1,100 tanks.
>
> **Navy** – 44,000 men (including the naval air arm); 9 submarines, 3 cruisers with Terrier SAMs (one with ASROC anti-submarine missiles as well) and anti-submarine helicopters, 6 destroyers (2 with Tartar SAMs, 4 equipped for anti submarine operations), 10 destroyer escorts, 12 coastal escorts, 61 minesweepers of various sizes, 5 fast patrol boats with Otomat SSMs, 7 MTBs, 4 landing ships.
> Naval air arm: 3 maritime patrol squadrons with 30 Grumman S-2 Trackers and 18 Breguet Atlantics; helicopters: HU-16As, 24 SH-3Ds, 9 SH-34s, 30 AB-204Bs and 12 Bell-47s.
>
> **Air Force** – 76,500 men and 320 combat aircraft: 5 fighter-bomber squadrons (3 with F-104G, 1 with F-104S and 1 with Fiat G-91Y), 4 light attack squadrons with Fiat G-91-R; 6 all weather fighter squadrons (4 with F-104S, 1 with F104G and 1 with F-86K); 3 reconnaissance squadrons with 27 RF-84F and 20 RF-104G. Transport – 3 squadrons with some C-119s and 14C-130E Hercules. Air defence – 12 SAM battalions with Nike-Hercules SAM.

Reserves   – 660,000.

Defence Spending   – $3,244 million in 1972 (2·6% of GNP).

Command Structure of the Italian Armed Forces:

The President of the Republic

The Supreme Defence Council: Chairman, the President. Members: Prime Minister, Minister of Home Affairs, Minister of Defence, Foreign Minister, Finance Minister, Minister of Trade and Industry, Chief of Defence Staff.

Defence Staff: Committee of Chiefs of Staff – Chairman, Chief of the Defence Staff (at the time of writing Admiral Eugenio Henke). Members: Army Chief of Staff, Navy Chief of Staff, Air Force Chief of Staff, General Secretary for Defence (at the time of writing General Andrea Cucino).

Army, Navy and Air Force Staffs

Italian Army Formations

The Field Army (*Three Corps*)
Two tank divisions
Five armoured infantry divisions
Five mountain brigades
One reconnaissance brigade

One marine regiment
One fortress regiment
One rocket artillery brigade
Three/five heavy artillery regiments
Two amphibious and one railway engineer regiments
Four anti-aircraft rocket regiments
Three air transport battalions
The Territorial Army (*Six Corps*)
Four armoured infantry brigades
One parachute brigade
One Carabinieri armoured infantry brigade
Two infantry battalions plus two infantry companies (on mobilisation).

Military Doctrine

Italy's present military doctrine is very closely tailored to fit the standard NATO model. All formations of the field army are NATO-assigned, one Alpine brigade being part of the ACE Mobile Force.

Although the peace treaty of 1945 forbade Italy to manufacture her own nuclear weapons, nuclear ammunition for those cannon with atomic capability and warheads for the Honest John rockets are

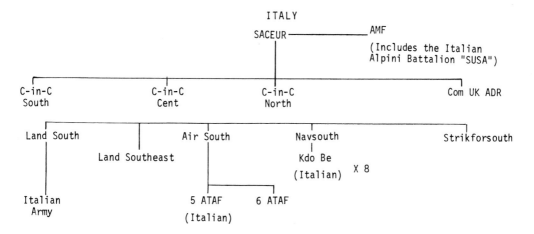

ITALY

SACEUR ——————————— AMF

(Includes the Italian
Alpini Battalion "SUSA")

| C-in-C South | C-in-C Cent | C-in-C North | Com UK ADR |

Land South — Air South — Navsouth — Strikforsouth

Land Southeast — Kdo Be (Italian) X 8

Italian Army — 5 ATAF — 6 ATAF (Italian)

held in Italy by American custodian units and, until Breschnew's visit to Nixon in late June 1973, would have been released for use if NATO had deemed it necessary.

The effects of the "death" of the Cold War have yet to be analysed but up to now the Italian Army has followed the strategic concept of the flexible response with its increased emphasis on conventional forces.

The present-day regiments of the Italian army are descended from those units which fought on the allied side after 1943 and those units which have since been newly raised. In spite of the civil war, which raged in Italy in late 1943 and caused much tension and damage within the army, these regiments have managed to retain their traditional links up to the present day. This is particularly true of the cavalry.

The peace treaty of 1947 limited Italy's armed forces but the Communist menace of 1949 caused Italy to demand military assistance and guarantees of security from America. This led to Italy joining NATO on 4 April 1949, but still with force levels limited by the 1947 treaty. In 1951 Italy demanded that these limits be lifted and this was done in spite of the protests of the USSR, Czechoslovakia and Poland. From this point on Italy has developed her armed forces to the modern and capable standard which they display today.

Until 1960 the Italian army was almost entirely equipped with American or British weapons, but since then a change has been made to equipment produced in Italy, where necessary under licence from the originating country. In 1962 a comprehensive series of reforms was initiated which has modernised the command, supply and equipment of the army.

Italy occupies a sensitive position in NATO's geography; isolated from Federal Germany in the north by the neutrals Austria and Switzerland, her Eastern neighbour is Yugoslavia. This state, currently out of the Warsaw Pact and pursuing a pro-western line, may well fall back into Moscow's sphere of influence when Tito dies; this would increase Italy's exposure and perhaps make seaborne communication with her eastern NATO partner, Greece, more problematic. Based on these factors, and on the geography of the country, Italy has been divided for defence purposes into the following Territorial Commands: North-west, North-east, Emilia-Toscana, Central (including Sardinia), and Sicily.

The field army is divided into four corps disposed as follows: *III Corps* (HQ Milan) one tank division, two infantry divisions and one mountain brigade; *IV Corps* (HQ Bolzano) is charged with the protection of the Brenner Pass and consists of three mountain brigades; *V Corps* (HQ Vittorio Veneto), with the task of protecting the north-east borders to Austria and Yugoslavia and the coast around Venice, consists of one tank division, two infantry divisions and a mountain brigade; *VI Corps* (HQ Bologna) consists of an infantry brigade and various support units. Apart from these four corps there are also

THE ITALIAN ARMOURED DIVISION

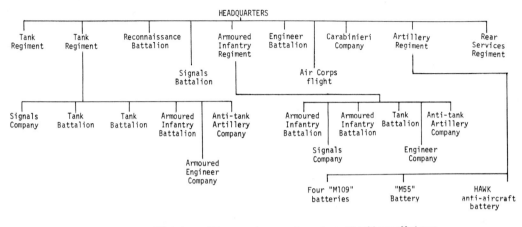

HEADQUARTERS

Tank Regiment | Tank Regiment | Reconnaissance Battalion | Armoured Infantry Regiment | Engineer Battalion | Carabinieri Company | Artillery Regiment | Rear Services Regiment

Signals Battalion

Air Corps flight

Signals Company | Tank Battalion | Tank Battalion | Armoured Infantry Battalion | Anti-tank Artillery Company | Armoured Infantry Battalion | Armoured Infantry Battalion | Tank Battalion | Anti-tank Artillery Company

Armoured Engineer Company

Signals Company

Engineer Company

Four "M109" batteries | "M55" Battery | HAWK anti-aircraft battery

330 tanks   560 armoured personnel carriers   80 self-propelled guns

THE ITALIAN INFANTRY DIVISION

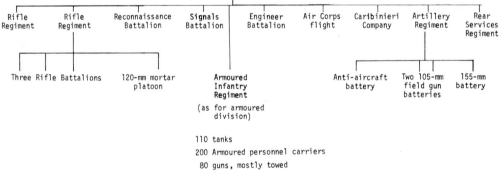

Headquarters

Rifle Regiment | Rifle Regiment | Reconnaissance Battalion | **Signals Battalion** | Engineer Battalion | Air Corps flight | Caribinieri Company | Artillery Regiment | Rear Services Regiment

Three Rifle Battalions | 120-mm mortar platoon

Armoured Infantry Regiment

(as for armoured division)

Anti-aircraft battery | Two 105-mm field gun batteries | 155-mm battery

110 tanks

200 Armoured personnel carriers

80 guns, mostly towed

THE ITALIAN ALPINI BRIGADE

Headquarters

Mountain Infantry Regiment | Fortress Battalion | Mountain Signals Company | Mountain Engineer Company | Air Corps flight | Caribinieri platoon | Mountain Artillery Regiment | Rear Services Regiment

Three or four battalions

Three or four Mountain batteries

42

the following independent formations: a parachute brigade in Livorno, an armoured cavalry (reconnaissance) brigade in Gorizia, an anti-aircraft Hawk missile brigade in Portogruaro, and the "Lagunari" or marine regiment of two battalions which is in and around Venice and is specially equipped to fight in the swamps and lagoons along the northern Adriatic coast. These latter three formations could be easily called upon to support V Corps in the Yugoslavian border area.

Up to now the defence of the southern part of the Italian peninsular has been given over to the navy, air force and territorial army; the centre of gravity as far as the field army was concerned was the northern part of the country, with attention focused in particular against the north-east. The massive increase in the strength of the Soviet fleet in recent years has not gone unnoticed, however, particularly that fleet's marine infantry component with its PT76 amphibious tanks. It is thus likely that a redisposition of the Italian field army to counter invasion threats in the south of the country may come about.

During peacetime four brigades of the territorial army are maintained in being, based on Messina, Bologna, Florence and Bari. In case of mobilisation, these brigades would be reinforced by further territorial brigades and engineer units made up of reservists, and by Carabinieri units including an armoured regiment. Although functioning in time of peace largely as civil police and coming under control of the Minister of Home Affairs, the Carabinieri are completely trained along army lines and have their own armoured infantry brigade, parachute battalion and armoured regiment. Their commander is a lieutenant-general of the army who is not a Carabinieri himself but must come from one of the other arms of the army. The Carabinieri is thus more than a para-military force.

The conscription system embraces all Italian males 21 years old, although service can be deferred for a time if the conscript has a genuine case to present. Conscientious objection is now recognised and allowed for, but to date this has caused no problems to the Italian government and is certainly not on the same scale that has been reached in Federal Germany, where the younger generation's attitude to military service would have brought even Bismark to the verge of tears. Conscription is for fifteen months in the Italian army (two years for the navy, fifteen months for the air force) and conscripts may reach the rank of lieutenant in this time if suitably qualified. (Most of the non-commissioned officers are conscripts and there is a dearth of the traditional, hard-bitten professional NCO who formed – and still forms – the absolute backbone of many Western armies. Thus in the Italian army it is, perforce, often the senior officers who are perhaps more frequently seen roaring at the men than would be the case in, say, the British Household Brigade.) After completing their conscript service the men revert to the reserve where they remain until the age of 45. Here they are periodically recalled for refresher training and also take part in exercises.

Italy's armed forces have not been involved in combat since the Second World War where their performance, certainly in the latter years, suffered due to a lack of conviction and motivation. It is thus very difficult to pronounce a "combat value" verdict over this army although it can be pointed out that modern warfare devolves more and more heavily on the junior leaders in an army, that is to say the section and platoon commander level. In view of the Italian army's apparent lack of a strong corps of seasoned NCOs at all levels, this may be a disadvantage, particularly in the employment of armoured formations. The likely disruptive effects of Italy's ten million Communist voters should not be too highly valued.

The Training System

Conscripts are given their initial training in Training Regiments which form part of the Territorial Army. Following this they go to their units in the field army formations or to the training schools of the various technical arms according to specialisation. NCO candidates are filtered off at time of entry into service and are given a three-month course in the school of their future arm after which they are appointed lance-corporal. After further training or employment in a unit they are promoted to Sergente. Professional NCO candidates are trained in the Junior Leaders Academy in Viterbo and then in the school of their own arm. Conscripts with matriculation qualification are considered for appointment as officers, receive six months training in the school of their arm and are then promoted to lieutenant. Professional officers are selected from volunteers either with matriculation qualifications or from those who do not yet have matriculation but who have the potential to obtain this qualification in the army officer training school in Naples.

THE ITALIAN PARACHUTE REGIMENT

Headquarters

Parachute Battalion	Parachute Battalion	Carabinieri Parachute Battalion	Sabotage Battalion	Parachute Artillery Battalion

(105-mm guns)

Qualified officer cadets then serve two years at the Military Academy in Modena, after which they are lieutenants. There follow a further two years in the "Scuole d'applicazione d'arma" in Turin, where training is according to the officers' arm of service. This four years' training is mainly academic with a 60% devotion to science, and is followed by a "down to earth" three months at the officers' school of arm.

Staff training, previously available only to the elite who had proved themselves worthy of it, will in future be given to all officers in the rank of captain and will last one year. Selected officers from this course will then receive a further two years intensive staff training to fit them for later positions of command. It is also intended to train certain qualified staff officers at the Joint Services Staff College ("Instituto Stati Maggiori Interforze") in Rome with their air force and naval colleagues. Those officers (and civil servants) who are destined for the very top positions receive further training at the "Centro Alti Studi Militari". Under the NATO exchange system, Italian officers also attend the staff colleges of other NATO countries and fill positions in the Allied headquarters.

Italian Army Equipment

Armoured Vehicles

A small number (*c.* 200) of M60-A1 American tanks are still in service as are some 600 M47s, which are steadily being replaced by the West German Leopard tank of which there will eventually be 800. The ubiquitous M113 American APC in all its variations is present to the tune of 3,300, but the Italian army is studying the development of the "Infantry Combat Vehicle" (eg the Russian BMP 76 and the West German "Marder") with considerable interest. Financial considerations and the MBFR talks may well render replacement plans stillborn; meanwhile, a number of the new French AMX-VTT amphibious APCs are already in use in the Italian armoured formations.

Amphibians

The Lagunari regiment has been using the American LVT-4 for its tactical operations since 1950 but, following successful troop trials along the Adriatic coast of the British SRN6 Mark II hovercraft, it seems likely that these will replace the LVT-4s in the near future.

Anti-tank weapons

In the guided-missile field the French SS11 and the "Mosquito" and "Cobra" systems have been in use for some years and are being replaced by "Tow" until an Italian missile system is developed. In anti-tank guns, the M36 "Jackson" has rendered excellent service but is now unquestionably obsolescent. The recoilless projectors 75 and 106 mm are also used.

Artillery

105 mm mountain howitzer
105 mm towed field gun (not proved to be too robust!)
155 mm medium howitzer and 155 mm medium field gun
203 mm heavy howitzer
105 mm M7 self propelled howitzer
155 mm M109 self propelled howitzer
175 mm M107 self propelled gun
203 mm M55 self propelled howitzer
"Honest John" Surface to Surface missile (to be replaced by "Lance")

Anti-aircraft weapons

20 mm Hispano Suiza cannon on various vehicles
40 mm Bofors L70 towed cannon
90 mm M2A2 gun
M-42 self propelled 40 mm cannon for armoured unit protection
Hawk MIM-23A guided missile
Soft skinned vehicles are almost entirely native Italian production.

Small arms and mortars 120 mm mortars, 81 mm mortars, West German "MG 42" 7·62 mm heavy machine gun, FAL 7·62 mm rifle, Beretta 9 mm sub machine-carbine (Carabinieri only) and pistols.

Aircraft: Fixed Wing: 100 Cessna 0-1E Bird Dog, 50 Piper L-18 or L-21. On order are one hundred S1A1 Marchetti SM109B and a smaller number of Aeritalia AM-3C. *Helicopters:* Agusta-Bell AB-47G and AB-47J and AB-204B multi-purpose helicopters. On order are 84 AB-206A and A-1 "Jet Rangers" for reconnaissance tasks and 26 Meridionale-Boeing CH-47C Chinook transport helicopters. Troop trials with various helicopter-borne weapon systems including anti-tank guided weapons are already being conducted.

Italian-manufactured Equipment
Small Arms
9 mm M1951 Beretta pistol

Weight – 0·71 kg, 8 round magazine; effective range – 50 m.

9 mm M38/49 Beretta SMG

Weight – 3·3 kg; blow-back action, wooden butt, 20 or 40 round straight magazine below the breech; rate of fire – 550 rpm; length – 80 cm; effective range – 100 m.

7·62 mm Self-Loading carbine BM59/Mk Ital (Fucile automatico leggero)

Weight – 4·22 kg; gas assisted action, 20 round magazine; rate of fire – 750 rpm; length – 1·09 m; effective range – 300 m. This is an Italian development of the American Garand M-1 carbine; another version, the BM59/Mk Ital-A has a pistol grip and collapsible metal butt.

Artillery
100 mm Light Multiple Rocket Launcher (Razziera a 24 colpi mod 1A 100/R). 24 barrels in three rows; normally mounted on the Fiat AR-59 4 × 4 jeep. Performance unknown.

Wheeled Vehicles
OM CL/52 1 ton 4 × 4 truck

Empty weight – 2,490 kg; length – 4·41 m; width – 2 m; height – 2·21 m; engine – 56 hp, water-cooled, petrol; max road speed – 85 km/hr.

Fiat CM/52 4 ton 4 × 4 forward control truck

Empty weight – 5,360 kg; length – 6·19 m; width – 2·37 m; height – 2·95 m; engine – 92 hp, water-cooled, diesel; max road speed – 58 km/hr; road range – 600 km.

OM 5 ton 4 × 4 forward control truck

Empty weight – 3,030 kg; length – 6·44 m; width – 2·07 m; height – 2·24 m; engine – 85 hp, water-cooled, diesel; max road speed – 85 km/hr. This vehicle is used as an artillery tractor.

Lancia TL/51 1½ ton 4 × 4 tractor

Empty weight – 2,900 kg; length – 4·48 m; width – 1·97 m; height (to canopy top) – 2·67 m; engine – 58 hp, water-cooled, petrol; max road speed – 60 km/hr. This vehicle is used as tractor for the 155 mm howitzer and also carries the crew.

Alfa-Romeo AR-51 ¼ ton 4 × 4 jeep. Produced in 1951, now obsolete, it has a 4 cylinder, 65 hp petrol engine, seats 6; max road speed – 103 km/hr; road range – 330 km; wades – 70 cm.

Fiat AR-51 ¼ ton 4 × 2 jeep. 4 cylinder, 53 hp petrol engine, seats 6; max road speed – 100 km/hr; road range – 480 km; wades – 60 cm. Produced in 1951, now largely replaced by newer versions.

Fiat AR-55 ¼ ton 4 × 4 jeep. A development of the Fiat AR-51; differences – engine 59 hp; top road speed – 116 km/hr.

Fiat AR-59 ¼ ton 4 × 4 jeep. The latest in the Fiat AR line; 56 hp engine, otherwise as for the AR-55.

New Vehicles
Fiat, M.A.N., Saviem (FMS)

Class A tactical, 4 × 4, amphibious ¼ ton jeep. This is a new Franco-Italo-German product. Load ½ ton or 6 men; 4 cylinder, 73 hp rear mounted petrol engine; max road speed – 125 km/hr; max water speed – 10 km/hr (propulsion by hydrojet); road range – 720 miles; empty weight – 1·95 tons.

Piaggio 4 × 2 paratroopers' jeep. Basically a motorised platform 2·2 m × 1·6 m × 1 m high. Air droppable, it has a 10 hp petrol engine, rear wheel drive and can carry 2 men and ½ ton of cargo. Max road speed – 38 km/hr.

Fiat X-11/1 ¼ ton 4 × 4 jeep. 79 hp petrol engine; max road speed – 125 km/hr; carries 6 men.

Fiat 4 × 4 light tactical supply vehicle. Very low profile with a centrally mounted, 4 cylinder, 40 hp petrol engine; max road speed 75 km/hr; can carry 2 men and 0·7 tons cargo.

Fiat TM/69 6 × 6 artillery tractor, 6 cylinder, 220 hp, petrol engine; max road speed – 82 km/hr; weight – 12 tons. This truck carries the entire gun crew of 12 men plus first line ammunition. There is also a crane equipped version being produced.

Fiat CM/62 4 × 4. A scaled-down version of the TM/69.

45

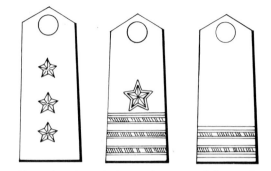

Fiat 4 × 4 2 ton amphibious truck.

Very similar in appearance to the famous American DUKW of World War II and designed to go into service with the Lagunari marines, the vehicle has a light aluminium alloy body. 120 hp 6 cylinder, diesel engine; max road speed – 90 km/hr, max water speed – 10 km/hr (propulsion by hydrojet); road range – 500 km. Empty weight – 4·5 tons; can carry 2 tons of cargo or 1 + 12 men. It is 7·5 m long, 3·6 m wide and 3·8 m high.

Fiat 4 × 4 amphibious armoured car

Boat shaped hull; 6 cylinder, 145 hp diesel engine mounted in the rear; max road speed – 100 km/hr, max water speed – 5 km/hr; road range – 710 km; crew – 3; armament 1 × 20 mm Rheinmetall MK-20, Rh-202 cannon; 1 × 7·62 mm Rheinmetall MG-3 machine gun and an 81 mm mortar/ grenade launcher.

Italian Army Uniforms

There has been little change in Italian uniforms since the end of the First World War and some of the costumes such as those of the Alpini and the Bersaglieri are known the world over. The following forms of dress are to be seen in the Italian Army today:

Gala Uniform (Uniforme da Cerimonia)

Very dark blue, service dress type jacket but without epaulettes, gold buttons (bearing a trophy of arms device) and rank badges.

Service Dress (Uniforme Ordinaria)

Light khaki gaberdine jacket and trousers with four patch pockets and gaberdine belt. Gold buttons (design as above); regimental facing colour worn on the collars with a silver star in the front corner. Very light tan shirt and tie, black gloves, brown shoes. The hat varies according to regiment (Alpini wear their famous mountaineers' hat with

Examples of new Italian rank insignia, left to right: Generale di Divisione, Colonello Commandante di Corpo (gold stars edged red), Tenente Colonello (gold stars), Capitano (gold stars), Aiutante di Battaglia (gold star, bars, edged red), Maresciallo Capo (gold, edged black).

its eagle feather; the Bersaglieri either a normal, light khaki peaked cap or their well known, wide-brimmed hat with its bush of cocks' feathers; Carristi (armoured troops) a black beret; Paracadutisti (paratroopers) a crimson beret; Granatieri (Grenadiers) a khaki beret, and so on. The hat bears the regimental badge. For parades officers wear a light blue silk sash from right shoulder to left hip passing under the waist-belt and a sabre (or sword according to regiment) is carried. Badges of rank are worn on the upper arm for NCOs and on the shoulder-straps for officers. Formation badges are worn on the upper left arm.

Battle Dress (Uniforme di Servizio)

Tailored in a heavy, woollen material, khaki in colour, this uniform is very reminiscent of the British battle dress of the Second World War except that it is slightly longer in the waist. This uniform can be worn with shoes or with boots and gaiters. A British 1937 pattern web waist-belt is worn with the battle dress and for parades officers may wear sashes and sabres as with service dress. Hats as for service dress. Badges of rank, regiment and formation as for service dress.

Working Dress

The ubiquitous drab denim suit worn with beret or forage cap and boots and gaiters.

Combat Dress (Uniforme da Combattimento)

The helmet is of the familiar pre-war Italian design and appears with regimental distinction even when camouflaged (Alpini, an eagle's feather and a pompon on the left side; Bersaglieri, the cock's feather bush on the right side); camouflaged jacket and trousers, web equipment in olive drab shade, boots and gaiters.

Summer Dress

Very light khaki, service dress style jacket and trousers in lightweight cloth, collar badges in enamelled metal, rank badges as for service dress, formation badge worn on a hanging brassard from the left shoulder-strap.

Shirt Sleeve order

Very light tan shirt with black tie and sleeves worn buttoned at the wrist, collar badges in enamelled metal or plastic, rank badges for officers on slides over the shoulder-straps, formation badge as for Summer Dress. Off parade a thin khaki web belt with dull silver buckle plate bearing a trophy of arms is worn; on parades the wide web belt, sashes for officers as with service dress, gloves and boots and gaiters if ordered. The hat would be either the peaked cap, beret, "regimental special" or the forage cap.

Specialist Qualification Badges

Parachutist — white metal parachute and wings worn on the right breast above the pocket flap.

Pilot — gold eagle with lowered head and spread wings surmounted by a flaming torch worn on the left breast above the pocket flap.

Officer of the — a golden eagle, upright with spread
General Staff   wings and a red shield bearing
(employed on   "RI" on its chest worn on the left
regimental   breast above the pocket flap.
duties)

Italian Army Flags

The national flag, a tricolour in green (next to the pike), white and red, on a wooden pipe with gold spearpoint tip. Attached to the pike tip is a light blue silk cravat with the unit designation in gold and gold fringed ends. Units with long traditions may have other cravats as well.

Italian Army Collar Patch Colours (all bear the silver star of Savoy).

Armour (*cavalry*) The collar patch has three peaks to the rear.

Regiment Nizza (1°)	– dark red
Regiment Piemonte Reale (2°)	– light red with black edge
Regiment Savoia (3°)	– black with red edge
Regiment Genova (4°)	– bright yellow
Regiment Novara (5°)	– white
Regiment Aosta (6°)	– light red
Regiment Firenza (9°)	– orange
Regiment Saluzzo (12°)	– black
Regiment Monferrato (13°)	– dark red with black edge
Regiment Alessandria (14°)	– orange with black edge
Regiment Guide (19°)	– white with light blue edge
Cavalry depot	– orange
Kürassiers	– silver lace, oblong in shape
Armoured Car (Carri Armati)	– red with two rear peaks

Artillery

Artiglieria da Campagne	black patch, with one peak to the rear, edged in yellow
Artiglieria Pesante Campale	
Artiglieria Pesante	
Artiglieria Corazzata	as above but on a light blue oblong
Artiglieria a Cavallo	

Engineers (*Genio*) – black, single point, crimson edge

Signals (*Trasmissioni*) – black, single point, light blue edge

Infantry

Line Infantry (Fanteria de Linea	– oblong patch with various colours and stripes according to regiment
Specialist Infantry:	
Grenadiers (Granatieri)	– oblong silver lace as for Kürassiers
Mountain troops (Alpini)	– medium green; two peaks to rear
Light Infantry (Bersaglieri)	– crimson; two rear peaks
Paratroops (Paracadutisti)	– light blue, oblong, with silver, winged sword badge
Marines (Lagunari)	– red, oblong with gold anchor badge
Armoured Infantry (Carristi)	– red, two rear points on a light blue oblong
Infantry training depot	– red, two rear points

Transport (*Automobilist*)	– light blue, two rear points on a black oblong
Logistics (*Commissariat*)	– crimson with one rear point
Medical (*Sanita*)	– pink with one rear point

NBC defence corps – black, oblong with silver badge

Officers serving with the general staff wear regimental collar patches but with small, oblong silver lace decoration under the star.

THE NETHERLANDS ARMY

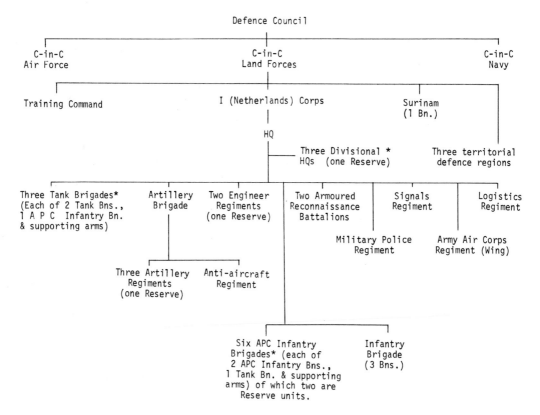

* = According to operational situation, these brigades will be formed into three divisions under command of existing divisional HQs.

THE KINGDOM OF THE NETHERLANDS

Population – 13,325,000.

Capital – den Haag.

Armed Forces:

    Army – 80,000 men (of whom 26,000 are regulars); 885 tanks.

    Navy – 15,200 sailors, 2,800 marines and 2,000 naval air force; 6 submarines, 2 cruisers (one with Terrier SAM), 6 frigates with Seacat SAM, 12 destroyers, 6 corvettes, 6 logistic support ships, 5 MTBs, 42 minesweepers, 1 high speed combat support ship. Naval air force – 44 combat planes: 2 squadrons Bréguet BR-1150 Atlantic anti-submarine planes and P-2 Neptunes; 18 Wasp and Agusta-Bell 204B anti-submarine helicopters, 23 SH-3D search and rescue helicopters.

    Air Force – 22,200 men, 144 combat aircraft: 36 F-104G fighter-bombers, 54 NF-5A fighter-bombers, 36 F-104G interceptors, 18 RF-104G reconnaissance planes. Twelve F-27 transport planes. Eight squadrons Nike-Hercules SAM; eleven Hawk SAM squadrons.

    Reserves – 42,000 men.

Para-military forces – 3,200 Reichspolizei.

Defence Spending – $1,562 million in 1972 (2·9% of GNP).

Head of state is Queen Juliana, Princess of Orange-Nassau, Duchess of Mecklenburg, born 30 April 1909. Her consort is Prince Bernhard; the heir to the throne is Princess Beatrix (born 1938). Holland is a constitutional monarchy, and the parliament (Die Generalstaaten) is a two-chamber house. The upper chamber (Senat) has 75 seats with two-thirds of these seats split between the Catholic Peoples Party and the Labour Party. Members are elected to the Senat by the provincial governments and serve a six-year term. The second chamber has 150 directly elected members who serve for four years. There are fifteen political parties.

Holland employs universal conscription, terms of service being: army – 16–18 months; navy – 12–24 months; air force – 18–21 months. After completion of active service, refresher training is carried out until the age of 35 (40 for reservist NCOs, 45 for reservist officers).

The Netherlands contribution to NATO is the 1st Netherlands Corps of two armoured brigades and four armoured infantry brigades organised into two divisions. Corps HQ is at Apeldoorn in Holland and the Corps commander is Lt. Gen. F. E. Meynderts. Divisional headquarters are at Arnhem (1 Div.) and Harderwijk (4 Div.). In peacetime the brigades are at 85% of war establishment; the Corps troops units are at 40% of war strength. National defence forces consist of the training depots and schools; in case of mobilisation territorial brigades with support and logistics units are formed and Holland is divided into three Army Territories. Certain Dutch army units are earmarked for UNO peace keeping operations. There is also an organised Civil Defence Force.

The Dutch army of today finds itself in an increasingly precarious situation as regards the maintenance of discipline over its conscripted soldiers. The hitherto conventional conduct and appearance of the men began its now somewhat alarming trend in 1971 when the Dutch defence ministry permitted the men to wear their hair long; on 1 August 1972 the now hirsute conscripts held a day of protest against the military custom of saluting commissioned officers (which they regarded as degrading) and exactly a year later the Secretary of State for Defence, J. Mommersteg, declared that saluting in the Dutch Army would no longer be obligatory. He added however, that he "hoped" that Dutch soldiers stationed abroad would continue to regard saluting as being the thing to do when in contact with other armies. The average Dutch soldier of today (even

Top, Dutch YP 408 8 × 6 armoured personnel carrier. Centre, DAF 6 × 6 3-ton truck. Bottom, DAF YA 126 4 × 4 Wapendrager. Opposite, Dutch officer in service dress, with rank badges on shoulder-straps, branch patches on collar, and national emblem on upper arm. (Courtesy Netherlands Army)

up to the rank of Sergeant) presents a most disquieting appearance with his mass of unkempt and often greasy hair flowing from under his helmet. If this "democratisation" of the Dutch military continues, the combat value of their forces must be adversely affected. The length of a soldier's hair is in itself, of course, quite irrelevant to his fighting efficiency: but in the current climate of social opinion it is one of several symptoms of a basically un-military attitude which could have disastrous consequences in time of emergency.

Dutch Army Equipment
Small Arms

9 mm Browning FN pistol. 11·34 mm M3-A1 American SMG: Weight – 3·63 kg; length – 58 cm (76 cm with extended steel wire butt); blow-back action; 30 round straight magazine below the breech; rate of fire – 450 rpm; effective range – 90 m. *7·62 mm CETME SLR; 7·62 mm FN "Typ MAG" GPMG; 7·62 British Bren-L4A2 LMG*: Weight – 10·5 kg (with bipod); gas assisted action; 30 round, curved magazine above the breech; rate of fire – 550 rpm; effective range – 600 m. Can also be mounted on a 13·6 kg tripod which increases the range to 1,000 m.

81 mm and 120 mm mortars, 106 mm recoilless AT rifle.

Vehicles

French AMX "105A" 105 mm SP howitzer; AMX 13 Turenne light tank; Leopard MBT. *DAF YP104 4 × 4 scout car*: Weight – 5·4 tons; crew – 2; length – 4·33 m; width – 2·08 m; height – 2·03 m (to top of MG); engine – 131 hp, petrol; max road speed – 98 km/hr; road range – 500 km; armament – 1 × 7·62 mm MG.
French AMX-VTT tracked APC.
DAF YP 408 8 × 6 APC: Weight – 11 tons; length – 6·1 m; width – 2·4 m; height – 1·8 m; engine – 165 hp diesel; max road speed – 90 km/hr; road range – 600 km; crew – 2 + 10 men; armament – 1 × 0·5 inch Browning MG; wades – 1·2 m without preparation, has infra-red driving and fighting equipment. Access either through two rear doors or through roof hatches.
Variants:
PW1-5 Platoon commander's vehicle, crew 2 + 7; armament MG plus one 84 mm Carl Gustav AT weapon.
PWCO – Company and battalion command vehicle; crew 2 + 4.
PW-GWT – Ambulance; crew – 2 + 2 lying and 4 sitting wounded.
PW-V Cargo carrier; crew – 2, capacity – 1,500 kg.
PW-MT Mortar tractor; crew – 2 + 5; tows the 120 mm Brandt-Raye mortar and carries 50 rounds.

Wheeled Vehicles

DAF YA 126 Wapendrager, 1 ton, 4 × 4 truck. Empty weight – 3,400 kg; length – 4·55 m; width – 2·1 m; height – 2·18 m; engine – 102 hp, 6 cylinder, water-cooled, petrol; max road speed – 90 km/hr;

road range – 440 km; crew – 2 + 8. Variants –
ambulance and signals trucks.

DAF YA314 3 ton, 4 × 4 truck. Empty weight –
4,700 kg; length – 6·09 m; width – 2·4 m; height –
2·79 m; engine – as for YA126; max road speed –
80 km/hr; road range – 700 km; crew – 2 + 16.
Variants – tipper, signals and workshop vehicles.

DAF YA616 (ZKW) 10 ton, 6 × 6 truck. Empty
weight – 10,130 kg; length – 7·16 m; width – 2·45 m;
height – 2·95 m; engine – 232 hp, 6 cylinder, water-
cooled, petrol; max road speed – 70 km/hr; road
range – 500 km. Variants – tanker, tipper, crane
vehicle and artillery tractor.

DAF YA328 6 × 6 Artillery Tractor. Empty weight –
6,200 kg; length – 6·18 m; width – 2·4 m; height –
2·69 m; engine – 131 hp, 6 cylinder, water-cooled,
petrol; max road speed – 80 km/hr; road range –
500 km; crew – 2 + 12. This vehicle is the basis for
the YP408 8 × 6 APC.

DAF YT1500L, 4 × 2 tractor Can pull 10 tons, has
131 hp, 6 cylinder, water-cooled, petrol engine.

Dutch Army Uniforms

Officers
Ceremonial wear consists of midnight blue jacket
and trousers with high closed collar and facings,
badges and buttons according to regiment.

Service Dress
  Dark chocolate brown peaked cap with brown
leather chin strap and having the Netherlands lion
in a round plate enclosed by gold laurel leaves as a
badge. Dark chocolate brown jacket, open neck,
single-breasted, single rear vent, four button front,
gold buttons bearing the lion, four pockets, regimental collar patches. Rank badges are worn on the
shoulder-straps. Light khaki shirt and tie, brown
leather Sam Browne belt and gloves, light fawn
trousers, brown shoes. On the upper left arm is the
Netherlands lion in orange silk.

Battle Dress
  Beret according to regiment (armoured units –
black, other units khaki) with regimental badge on
coloured, rectangular patch; dark chocolate brown
jacket with two pleated pockets and bloused front
four dark chocolate brown front buttons in plastic
and bearing the lion; regimental collar patches, rank
badges on the shoulder-strap. Trousers, gloves,
shirt, tie and shoes and Netherlands lion sleeve
badge as above.

Shirt Sleeve Order
  Shirt and tie as above with dark chocolate brown

Left, Spanish infantry *cabo* (corporal) in the new service uniform, and Spanish paratrooper in camouflaged combat dress. Above, a Czech colonel (left) and lieutenant-colonel (right) of infantry in walking-out dress. Below, a group of Polish army colonels and a *Komandor* of the Polish navy gathering round an engineer lieutenant-colonel of the East German NVA.

slides over the shoulder-straps bearing the rank badges; sleeves worn buttoned at the wrist or, with open necked shirt, rolled to elbow level. Narrow fawn web belt with silver buckle plate, trousers and shoes or brown calf length boots as before. Beret as before.

Combat Dress

Olive green jacket and trousers with mid-calf length brown boots and British '37 pattern webbing; beret as before or US style NATO helmet. Badges of ranks on slides on the shoulder-straps.

Other Ranks

As for Officers but badges of rank are worn on the upper arms or, in shirt sleeve order and in combat dress, on dark chocolate brown cloth slides on the shoulder-straps. The peaked cap has a badge slightly different from that of officers in that it has fewer laurel leaves around it.

Dutch Army Flags

The flags and standards of the Netherlands army today are almost unchanged from those which they carried at Waterloo in 1815. Cavalry units carry standards which are smaller than the infantry flags but of the same design. The artillery carry no flags but have the crowned royal cypher "J" raised on their guns. The colours are orange, bear the crowned royal cypher "J" and are edged in gold fringes. The pike tip is similar to that of the Belgian army and consists of a gold lion "couchant" on a tablet over a golden wreath. Officers take the oath of alliegance on the flag of their unit; artillery officers swear on a "shabraque" laid over a gun.

THE KINGDOM OF NORWAY

Population – 3,935,000.   **Capital** – Oslo.
Armed Forces:
    Army – 18,000 men.
    Navy – 8,500 (800 coastal artillery gunners included); 15 submarines, 5 frigates, 2 escorts, 10 minesweepers, 5 minelayers, 20 high speed patrol boats with Penguin SSM, 26 MTBs, 2 logistic support ships, 4 landing ships.
    Air Force – 9,400 men, 117 combat aircraft: 80 Northrop F-5A fighters, 16 F-104G fighters, 16 RF-5A photo-reconnaissance planes, 5 P-3B maritime patrol planes. A transport squadron operates 4 C-47s and 6 C-130s; two squadrons of UH-1B helicopters and four squadrons of "Nike-Hercules" SAM.
    Reserves – 179,600 + 75,000 Home Guard in 14 regiments, subdivided into 84 district and 525 area commands.
Defence Spending – $490·78 million in 1972 (3·1% of GNP).

Head of State is King Olav V (born 2 July 1903), heir to the throne is Kronprinz Harald (born 21 February 1937). Norway is a constitutional monarchy, executive power lying with the king to be exercised through the State Council (Statsrad). The Statsrad consists of a Minister of State who nominates at least seven further members to the king, who approves them. The Minister of State is the leader of the strongest political party in parliament, the Storting of 150 elected members serving for a four-year term. Minister of State at time of writing and since 16 October 1972 was Lars Korvald of the Christian Peoples Party, and Defence Minister was Johna Kleppe of the Peoples' Party. The king is head of the armed forces.

Norway (in theory) permits no foreign troops to be stationed on her soil except in case of dire national emergency, neither will she allow nuclear weapons to the stationed within her borders. National service liability exists for all males between

20 and 44 years of age; terms of service for conscripts are: army – 12 months; navy and air force – 15 months. Periodic reserve training is also carried out, and Norwegian males up to 65 years of age are liable for Home Guard Service.

Norwegian Army Organisation

One brigade in north Norway, the remainder of the army split up into independent, battalion-sized battle groups. On mobilisation, eleven regimental combat teams, each 5,000 strong, would be formed as would logistic and territorial defence forces totalling 157,000 men.

Norwegian Army Equipment

Small Arms 9 mm pistols and sub-machine guns, 7·62 mm NATO FN rifles and 7·62 mm reworked "MG-42" of German, World War II design.
APCs American M113 and BV-202
Tanks Some German Leopards; M-48 American medium tanks and M-24 light tanks; M-8 American 6 × 6 armoured cars (on GMC chassis).

Other vehicles include the *Volvo L3314 ¾ ton 4 × 4 truck*: Empty weight – 1,510 kg; length – 3·99 m; width – 1·66 m; height – 2·05 m; engine – 68 hp, 4 cylinder, water-cooled, petrol; max road speed – 97 km/hr. Two thousand of these vehicles were bought from Sweden as were some Volvo BV 202 Bolinder Munktetell articulated, tracked over-snow vehicle. Apart from this the Norwegian army uses almost entirely American vehicles.
Artillery 105 mm towed guns, M109-G SP, 155 mm howitzers.
Air Corps L-18 and L-19 light fixed wing aircraft.

Norwegian Army Uniforms

Ceremonial Dress (Gallautstyr)

Very dark blue jacket (dark green and very short-skirted for dragoons – tanks) and trousers with regimental coloured piping to collar, cuffs, jacket edges and in three stripes (one narrow between two wide) on the trouser leg. Generals and dragoons have double-breasted jackets, other units single-breasted. Buttons bear the designs shown below and are gold for generals, artillery, transport, logistics and medical troops, and silver for infantry, dragoons, engineers and signals.

Regimental piping colours:	*Button design*
Generals – red	} The national lion
Infantry – red	} holding an axe

Cavalry	– red	– A hunting horn
Artillery	– red	– A flaming grenade
Engineers	– light blue	– A kürass
Signals	– light blue	– Crossed flags
Transport	– orange	– A wheel
Losistics (QM)	– light crimson	– A multi-rayed star
Medical	– light crimson	– The snake and staff
Repair	– light crimson	– A cog wheel

Headwear with ceremonial dress is a very dark blue peaked cap with dark blue within white within red cockade, gold loop and silver and red button bearing the national lion, gold chin strap; white gloves and black shoes, silver or gold waist-belt, gold hilted sword and sword knot and silver scabbard complete the outfit.

The gala uniform of the Kongensgarde (household troops):

Black round hat with broad brim and black drooping plume to right-hand side, black hatband edged white, blue within white within red cockade bearing the crowned royal cypher in gold. Single-breasted black jacket with nine silver buttons, collar, front and tops of Polish cuffs edged red; crimson silk waist sash with tassel; to left side for officers, black leather waist-belt with small, twin black ammunition pouches and silver buckle for the men. Silver lace loops to collar and cuffs, five silver buttons on each cuff, four buttons on rear skirts enclosed by red piped, vertical pocket flaps. Silver epaulettes on red backing for officers, green fringed epaulettes for other ranks. Black trousers with white side stripes, black shoes white gloves. All ranks wear a silver whistle and chain looped from the left shoulder to between the top and second buttons on the chest. Officers carry swords with gold hilts and knots, other ranks carry rifles with white slings.

Service Dress (Tjenesteantrekk)

Medium khaki green, single breasted, four button front, four patch pockets with buttoned flaps, Polish cuffs, no shoulder-straps, single rear vent; medium khaki green trousers, brown shoes and gloves, light khaki shirt and tie, medium khaki green peaked cap with brown chin strap and silver cap badge consisting of the silver national lion and axe on a crimson ground, surrounded by silver oak leaves. Buttons are gold or silver, as shown on the chart for ceremonial dress.

Working Dress

Medium khaki green battle dress of English style (with shoulder-straps); the front and breast pocket buttons are concealed, only those on the cuffs and shoulder-straps are in the regimental colour. Brown shoes or black boots and khaki webbing gaiters, khaki beret with silver badge in the form of the crowned royal cypher, capital V within an O. On the upper left sleeve is worn the regimental badge in the form of a short horizontal stripe in the following colours:

Cavalry (dragoons)	– green and yellow (vertical, equal divisions)
Artillery	– red and blue
Engineers	– blue and red
Signals	– blue and white
Infantry	– red
Transport	– blue and yellow
Repair	– red, blue, red
Logistics (QM)	– yellow
Medical	– crimson.

Norwegian collar rank badges – left, Generalmajor; right, Major. Top, royal cypher beret badge; below, national crest.

Shirt sleeve order

Very light khaki shirt and trousers, khaki tie and web belt with silver buckle plate, sleeves rolled up or buttoned down, brown shoes or black boots and web gaiters. Officers' rank badges are worn on very light khaki slides on the shirt shoulder-straps. The beret is worn.

Summer Service Dress (Officers)

Very light khaki jacket, shirt and trousers, khaki tie, brown shoes, peaked cap or beret. The jacket is of the same cut as the winter jacket and on the upper right arm is the Norwegian badge on a shield surmounted by the word **NORWAY**.

Combat Dress

Olive green jacket and trousers (officers rank badges on slides on the shoulder-straps), German World War II "coal-scuttle" pattern helmet or American-style NATO helmet; British '58 pattern khaki webbing; black boots and gaiters. Ski troops wear white camouflage suits and ski boots.

Greatcoats

Medium khaki green, double breasted, with half belt in rear; officers rank badges on the shoulder-straps.

Beret colours

Infantry – khaki; cavalry – black; long range recce groups (cavalry units) – maroon. The "Brigade North", based in the Arctic Circle against the

---

Badges of Rank

Other Ranks (worn on the upper arms)

Lance Corporal (Vize Korporal)	– one white chevron, point down.
Corporal (Korporal)	– two such chevrons.
Sergeant (Sersjant)	– three such chevrons.
Staff Sergeant (Oversersjant)	– three such chevrons with a horizontal white bar joining the tops of the chevrons.
Sergeant Major (Stabssersjant)	– as for Oversersjant with a white crown over the bar.

Officers (worn on the collar or shoulder-straps)

Second Lieutenant (Fenrik)	– one five-pointed silver star.
Lieutenant (Loytnant)	– two such stars.
Captain (Kaptein)	– three such stars.
Major (Major)	– one star and a silver lace edging.
Lieutenant-Colonel (Oberstløytnant)	– two stars and edging.
Colonel (Oberst)	– three stars and edging
Major-General (Generalmajor)	– one larger silver star on gold lace.
Lieutenant-General (Generalløytnant)	– two stars on gold lace.
General (General)	– three stars on gold lace.

Soviet border wear dark blue (cavalry retain black); the Finnmark troops wear "Umbra" green berets. All other units – khaki. A light khaki peaked cap with small crown and cockade is also worn.

Miscellaneous

Those members of the Norwegian forces who served with the British army during the Second World War still wear certain British badges from that period. These include: parachutist wings on top left sleeve (white parachute between light blue wings); the red legend "COMMANDO" on black backing on the top left sleeve (No. 45 Commando had a large Norwegian contingent). A Norwegian wartime sabotage unit has also been perpetuated by a badge: the words "KOMPANI LINGE" in silver on black.

Army pilots wear the national silver lion and axe

in a red circle with silver wings to both sides above the right breast pocket. Air crew observers have a winged, bursting grenade in gold on the right breast.

Parachutists have a gold or silver winged parachute on the right breast.

Norwegian Army Flags

Infantry and cavalry units still carry flags which are of the following design: cloth of varying colour according to unit; central design the Norwegian lion with an axe in silver; flag staff tip the crowned royal cypher (see above) in silver. Embroidered on the flag are the unit's battle honours. The Kongensgarde (household troops) have a white "Leibfahne"; the infantry brigade stationed in north Norway has a black flag – this colour always being awarded to the unit in the most exposed position.

THE REPUBLIC OF PORTUGAL

Population – 9,780,000*.   **Capital** – Lisbon.

Armed Forces:

> **Army** – 179,000 men.
> **Navy** – 18,000 including 3,300 marines; 4 submarines, 11 frigates, 6 corvettes, 16 patrol vessels, 16 minesweepers, 37 fast patrol launches.
> **Air Force** – 21,000 men, 150 combat aircraft: 2 squadrons B-26 Invader and PV-2 light bombers, 1 squadron F-84G fighter bombers, 2 squadrons Fiat G-91 fighters, 1 squadron F-86F interceptors, 6 counter insurgency flights with T-6s, 1 squadron maritime patrol P-2V5s. Transport planes – 22 Noratlas, 16 C-47s, 11 DC-6s, 15 C-45s. Light aircraft – 11 Dornier DO-27s; 85 Alouette II or III and SA-330 Puma helicopters. Reckoned as part of the air force is a three-battalion parachute regiment of 4,000 men.

Para-military forces – 9,700 National Republican Guard.

Reserves   – 500,000 men.

Defence Spending   – $459·5 million in 1972 (6·3% of GNP).

A s this book went to press Portugal experienced a military coup with considerable popular backing. The Thomaz/Caetano regime was overthrown and General Antonio de Spinola was sworn in as president. Wide-ranging constitutional reforms are

promised, and it would serve no purpose to describe the political structure before the coup.

Portugal has universal male military service liability, all men between 20 and 45 years of age being affected. Terms of service are as follows:

* This includes Madeira and the Azores; Portuguese Guinea has 550,000 – capital Bissau; Soa Tome and Principe (in the Gulf of Guinea) have 71,000; Angola has 5·5 million, capital Luanda; Mozambique has 7·5 million, capital Laurenco Marques; Macao 265,000 and Portuguese Timor 560,000, capital Dili.

Army	– 18–24 months (may be partly served in the Territorial Army or the Reserve).
Navy	– 4 years
Air Force	– 18 months to 4 years.

Pre-national service military training is given in the Mocidade Portuguesa (Portuguese Youth Movement) from seven to 21 years of age.

The President is commander-in-chief of the armed forces. Portugal is divided into four military districts; the Azores form another. The Portuguese Air Force has a base at Horta while the Americans also have base facilities in the islands. Madeira forms its own military district.

Portuguese Army Command Structure

Answerable to the government for army matters is the Army Minister, assisted by the Under-Secretary of State for the Army, the Chief of Army General Staff and the Inspector General of the Army.

The "family tree" of the army is as the diagram.

The Portuguese Army is racially a well-integrated force in which over 50% of the total strength deployed in Africa is made up of natives. If in possession of the necessary education, black Portuguese citizens can become officers and are often put in command of white subordinates.

A recent innovation has been the raising of native defence units to help bear the brunt of the fighting against the Communist-supported terrorist organisations which are trying to force Portugal to give up her African territories. These terrorist groups include: "Party for the Independence of Guinea and the Cape Verde Islands" (PAIGC) with about 10,000 men; the "People's Freedom Front for Angola" (MPLA) with 7,000 members, and the "National Front for the Liberation of Angola" (FNLA) with 5,000; and the "Frente de Libertacao de Mocambique" (FRELIMO) with 9,000 men mainly concentrated in the Mozambique provinces of Cabo Delgado, Niassa and Tete.

To combat these terrorists, Portugal's black militia have provided volunteers for two new formations in Mozambique, the "GE" (Grupos Especial) and the "GEP" (Grupos Especials Paraquedistas – Special Parachute Group). They wear black uniforms with bright yellow berets. These units were conceived by Mozambique's C-in-C General Kaulza de Arriaga, who has commanded the successful defence of the Cabora Bassa dam project and who is known to his men as "The Pink Panther". The "GE" and "GEP" contain many members of the fierce Maconde tribe who, until recently, provided the majority of the recruits for FRELIMO. In mid-1973 the 60,000 strong Portu-

guese forces in Mozambique were 65% black. (In 1961 the Portuguese had 16,000 men in this province; 9,600 in Angola, as against 55,000 now; and 5,000 in Guinea, as against 27,000.)

The anti-Portuguese guerrillas receive lavish financial support from Russia, China, the Organisation for African Unity (OAU), and even the Joseph Rowntree Social Service Trust of Britain. They are equipped with the most modern Soviet weapons including 122 mm rockets and are based and trained in Tanzania (where they receive instruction from militarily qualified members of the 30,000 Chinese in that country who are ostensibly engaged in railway construction), Malawi, Guinea and Zambia. They are even supposed to be getting Russian MiG fighters by 1974.

The recent coup was sparked partly by army discontent at the conduct of the African wars, and a cease-fire seems likely.

The Portuguese Army

The army consists of two tank regiments, eight cavalry regiments (the extent of the use of horses in these units is uncertain), 35 infantry regiments and seventeen coastal artillery regiments. These units are formed into divisions. Two divisions are stationed in Portugal, and are only partially up to strength, the missing men being reservists. The remainder of the army is split up throughout the African provinces and in Macao.

Portuguese Military Equipment

Portugal receives military aid from several European countries: Britain supplies warships (two in 1961), planes and Land Rover jeeps; France sends Alouette IIs and IIIs and Noratlas transport planes; West Germany supplies aircraft, Unimog vehicles and naval vessels; the Americans partially equip the Portuguese Air Force.

Infantry weapons are of the CETME 7·62 mm family as used in Spain and West Germany, and the ubiquitous "MG-42", the World War II German machine gun, is also issued. For details of performance of these weapons see the chapter on the Federal German Republic. Armoured vehicles include the M-47 and M-4 American medium tanks, the M-41 "Walker Bulldog" light tank, the British Humber Mk IV 4 × 4 armoured car, the French EBR-75 8 × 8 armoured car and the AML-60 4 × 4 scout car, the M-16 American half-track of World War II vintage, and the FV-1609. Artillery pieces are 105 mm and 140 mm howitzers.

Portuguese Army Uniforms

Certain items of Portuguese Army dress bear witness even today of the British influence which began with the Peninsular War (1808–1814) when the Anglo-Portuguese army under the Duke of Wellington fought against Napoleon's forces. In full dress officers wear crimson waist sashes – a very English custom.

Full Dress Uniform – General Officers

Very dark blue coat and light blue trousers; the coat single breasted, eight gold buttons on the front, no pockets, red standing collar and cuffs (with gold lace embroidery for generals), gold epaulettes with gold fringes, crimson silk (gold and crimson for generals) waist sash with knot and tassels to the left side, gold hilted sabre in steel sheath, gold and crimson sword knot, gold trouser stripe, white gloves, black shoes, cocked hat with gold edging and white feather trim.

General Officers, Walking Out, Winter

Grey peaked cap, gold badge, chin cords and peak decoration, dark blue pelisse with black astrakhan trim to collar, cuffs and edges; black frogging (five rows on chest) and black hungarian knots on the sleeves. Grey riding breeches, black boots and spurs, brown gloves.

Field Officers, Full Dress

Very dark blue cap with red piping to top edge and top of headband; gold cap badge over regimental

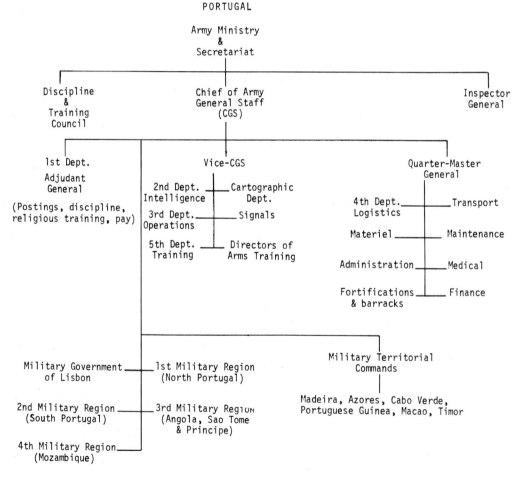

PORTUGAL

Army Ministry
&
Secretariat

Discipline & Training Council — Chief of Army General Staff (CGS) — Inspector General

1st Dept. Adjutant General (Postings, discipline, religious training, pay)

Vice-CGS

2nd Dept. Intelligence — Cartographic Dept.
3rd Dept. Operations — Signals
5th Dept. Training — Directors of Arms Training

Quarter-Master General

4th Dept. Logistics — Transport
Materiel — Maintenance
Administration — Medical
Fortifications & barracks — Finance

Military Government of Lisbon — 1st Military Region (North Portugal)

2nd Military Region (South Portugal) — 3rd Military Region (Angola, Sao Tome & Principe)

4th Military Region (Mozambique)

Military Territorial Commands

Madeira, Azores, Cabo Verde, Portuguese Guinea, Macao, Timor

badge; gold chin cords and peak decoration. Very dark blue jacket, single breasted, standing collar, six rows of black silk frogging across the chest; regimental collar patches, gold shoulder cords, gold chevrons above the cuffs; black silk edging to all parts of the jacket, black hungarian knots above the gold sleeve chevrons, white gloves. Light blue trousers with a red side stripe, black shoes, gold hilted sabre in steel sheath.

Summer Walking Out Dress – Officers

Grey peaked cap, gold cap badge over regimental badge, black chin strap, gold peak decoration. White shirt, black tie, grey, single-breasted jacket with four button front, two pleated pockets on the chest, two plain patch pockets on the skirts, two buttons at the cuffs; gold buttons and belt buckle, grey cloth belt, grey shoulder-straps, brown gloves, grey trousers, black shoes.

Winter Walking Out Dress – Officers

Hat as for summer walking out, grey single-breasted jacket, closed collar, six button front, regimental collar patches, two top pocket flaps with buttons, two skirt pocket flaps without buttons, two buttons at the cuffs, brown gloves, grey trousers, black shoes.

NCOs' Walking Out Dress, Winter

Hat as for officers walking out but no gold decoration to black peak; jacket as for officers winter walking out but with pleated patch pockets on the chest. Grey trousers, black shoes. Black leather waist-belt with yellow buckle.

Conscripts' Walking Out Dress (Portugal)

Dark blue side hat with regimental badge on the left side; dark blue, single-breasted jacket with closed collar and six button front; regimental collar patches, pleated patch pockets on the chest, gold buttons, black leather waist-belt with yellow buckle. Dark blue trousers, blue boots and gaiters.

Walking Out Dress (African Stations)

Dark red fez for native troops; light khaki jacket with closed collar and six button front, regimental collar patches, gold buttons, four pocket flaps

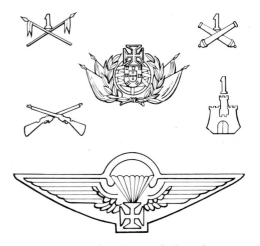

Centre, Portuguese upper cap badge, above para-troopers' badge. Left, regimental badges of 1st Cavalry and infantry; right, of 1st Artillery and 1st Engineers.

without buttons, badges of rank worn on black slides on the shoulder-straps; brown leather belt, yellow buckle; white gloves; light khaki shorts and puttees; black boots.

Combat Dress

Hat, jacket and trousers in brown, black and green camouflage pattern (rather similar to British DPM style); black calf-length boots; British style '37 pattern khaki webbing. A black beret with badge is often worn with this uniform. The steel helmet is a modernised version of the German "coal-scuttle", much smaller in size than the original.

Badges

Officers and senior NCOs wear two cap badges on their peaked caps; on the top part is the Portuguese crest within laurel wreaths and on four flags (the officers' pattern is slightly different from that of

---

Examples of regimental badges are:

1st and 2nd Cavalry Regiments	– crossed silver lances under the gold regimental number.
Other cavalry regiments	– crossed silver sabres under the gold regimental number.
Infantry regiments	– crossed gold rifles.
Field (SP) artillery	– crossed gold cannon barrels.
Foot artillery	– a bursting gold grenade.
Engineers	– a gold tower.

the Senior NCOs). Beneath this is worn the regimental cap badge which, for majors and above, incorporates a gold wreath. Regimental badges are also worn on the collars of ceremonial, walking out and service dress. Generals have crossed silver batons with a gold wreath.

Badges of Rank

Up to and including Staff Sergeant these are worn on the upper sleeves of walking out dress; in overseas stations, on black slides on the shoulder-straps – or on the right chest of the white, short sleeved singlet:

Private First Class	– one red chevron, edged in black, point down.
Lance Corporal	– one red chevron, edged in black, point up.
Corporal	– two red chevrons edged in black, point up.
Lance Sergeant	– three gold chevrons edged in black, point down.
Sergeant	– three gold chevrons edged in black, point up.
Staff Sergeant	– four gold chevrons edged in black, point up.
Sergeant Major	– gold edging to Polish cuff; above it the small Portuguese badge in gold.
Officer Cadet	– gold cuff edging and a diagonal gold stripe above it from low at the front of the sleeve, rising to the rear.

All officers' rank badges are worn on the cuffs of walking out and service dress and the cuff, of pointed or "Polish" style, is edged in gold:

Second Lieutenant	– one horizontal gold bar edged in black.
Lieutenant	– two horizontal gold bars edged in black.
Captain	– three horizontal gold bars edged in black.
Major	– one narrow over one wide such gold bar.
Lieutenant-Colonel	– two narrow over one wide such gold bar.
Colonel	– three narrow over one wide such gold bar.
Brigadier	– two five-pointed silver stars (horizontally disposed).
General	– three five-pointed silver stars in a pyramid.
Chief of the General Staff	– four five-pointed silver stars forming a truncated cone.
Marshal of the Army	– four five-pointed gold stars forming a truncated cone.

THE UNITED KINGDOM OF GREAT BRITAIN AND NORTHERN IRELAND (UK)

Population – 56,250,000.   **Capital** – London.

Armed Forces:

Army – 180,458 men, 1,000 tanks.

Royal Navy – 90,024 men (including 8,000 Royal Marines); 4 nuclear-powered submarines each with 16 Polaris A-3 SSMs, 30 attack submarines (6 nuclear powered, 24 diesel), 1 helicopter carrier, 2 commando carriers, 2 assault ships, 2 cruisers with Seacat SAM, 12 destroyers (9 with Seacat and Seaslug II SAM), 33 frigates, 21 ASW frigates, 4 AA frigates and 4 aircraft directing frigates, 38 coastal minesweepers, 6 inshore minesweepers, 10 patrol boats. (One fixed-wing aircraft carrier in service but soon to be withdrawn.)

The Fleet Air Arm has 96 combat aircraft: 2 strike squadrons with Buccaneer, 6 air defence squadrons – 2 with F-4K Phantom, 4 with Sea Vixen. 8 squadrons of Wessex helicopters, 3 squadrons Sea King ASW helicopters, 3 squadrons with Wasp and Whirlwind helicopters.

Royal Air Force – 109,849 men and 500 combat aircraft: 8 Vulcan medium bomber squadrons, 3 strike squadrons with Buccaneer; 7 strike/reconnaissance squadrons with F-4M Phantoms; 4 close support squadrons with Harrier; 9 air defence squadrons (8 with Lightnings, 1 with F-4M); 1 reconnaissance squadron with Victor SR-2s, 4 with Canberras; 1 airborne early warning radar squadron with Shackletons, 2 maritime patrol squadrons with Nimrods. 3 tanker squadrons with Victor K1/K1A. Transport capacity is 5 strategic lift squadrons with VC-10s, Belfasts and Britannias, 7 tactical lift squadrons with C-130 Hercules, 2 light communication squadrons with HS-125s.

Helicopters are organised in 7 squadrons with 60 Wessex or Whirlwinds and 30 SA-330 Pumas.

Ground and air defence of RAF airfields is carried out by the RAF Regiment which has 11 squadrons armed with L-40/70 Bofors AA guns and Bloodhound and Tigercat SAMs.

Reserves – Army – 361,600
Royal Navy – 34,300
Royal Air Force – 33,500.

Defence Spending – $6,900 million (£2,854 million in 1972) (4·7% GNP).

Deployment of the British Army

UK Base troops, training schools, depots, the Strategic Reserve (3rd Division) and one battalion of Gurkhas. Headquarters UK Land Forces (HQ UKLF) was formed as the result of a reorganisation on 1 April 1973. It contains ten Districts including Northern Ireland.

Northern Ireland

Normally one brigade is stationed permanently in this province but the present emergency, which began in 1969, has caused this force to be augmented by individual battalions drafted in for a 4-month unaccompanied tour. As in most European armies, manpower is short in the British army and these extra troops required in Northern Ireland have had to be withdrawn from their NATO roles in BAOR; this in itself would be enough to explain the willingness of the Soviet bloc to supply weapons to the IRA. Not only infantry battalions are employed for Internal Security (IS) duties; engineers, gunners and transport units are also trained and equipped for this role and recently even a complete cavalry regiment (Queen's Own Hussars) was re-equipped for dismounted duties and sent into the province.

British Army of the Rhine (BAOR)

This is the greatest concentration of tactical ground forces in the British Army today and is NATO assigned. It consists of HQ BAOR, Berlin Independent Brigade (BIB) and the 1st (British) Corps. HQ BAOR is in Rheindahlen up against the Dutch border of Germany; HQ 1 (BR) Corps is in Bielefeld and commands three divisions – 1st, 2nd and 4th Divisions – each of two brigades. The BIB consists of three infantry battalions, a squadron of tanks and engineer, signals and logistics units. There is no British artillery in Berlin.

The Mediterranean:

Cyprus (UNO contingent) One infantry battalion, one armoured car squadron and the "UK Sovereign Bases" which also give logistic support to the UNO peace-keeping force in that island.

Cyprus (Non-UNO) One infantry battalion, one armoured car squadron.

Gibraltar One infantry battalion and an engineer regiment.

The Caribbean:

British Honduras – an infantry battalion group.

The Far East:

Hong Kong Five infantry battalions (three of these Gurkhas), an armoured car squadron, a regiment of artillery, engineer and logistic units (including the British Army's last mule transport units).

Singapore One battalion group with logistic support.

Nepal Two recruiting depots (to replenish the five Gurkha battalions of the British Army).

Apart from these units, many individual officers and soldiers are seconded to Arab states in the Persian Gulf area or to the young Malaysian Army.

The tactical grouping of the British Army into the 1st, 2nd, 3rd and 4th Divisions has nothing to do with the Divisions into which the infantry is organised for recruiting purposes; this system is explained later.

Since the abolition of National Service 1961 the British Army has been a professional force and until recently recruiting has been no great problem. Parliament has, however, recently raised the school leaving age to 16 years and by this Act the Army has been robbed of a very valuable and important source of recruits.

Up to now, the technical arms of the British Army have trained the bulk of their Tradesmen in three "Apprentice Colleges" at Arborfield (Tradesmen for the REME and Engineers), Chepstow (REME, Engineers and RAOC) and Harrogate (Royal Signals). Apart from these units, there exist "Junior Leaders Regiments" for non-tradesmen of

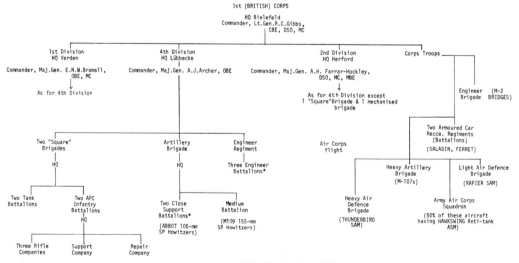

* = Normally deployed one battalion
in support of each Square Brigade.

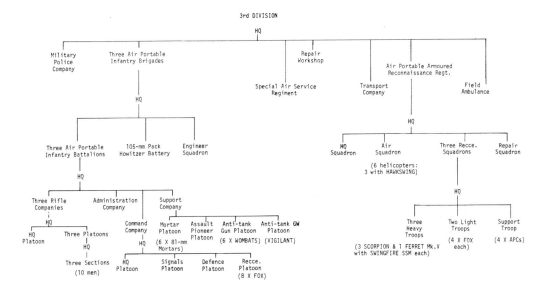

3rd DIVISION

the RAC, RA, Royal Signals and infantry, whose function it is to produce the future warrant officers of these arms. With the major source of their recruits now gone, the future of these units is in question, as is the continued flow of potential tradesmen and NCOs into the army.

The British soldier of today is well paid and enjoys general popularity among the civil population, largely due to his proven magnificent performance in Northern Ireland – where the soldiers' every move is subject to the relentless scrutiny of the television camera. It is questionable whether any other army in the world could have carried out a similar task with the limited bloodshed and the unbroken morale which the British soldier has achieved in that unhappy province. An interesting fact is that regiments recruited in Northern Ireland (eg Royal Irish Rangers) do not serve there during the emergency.

Recruiting of Officers

The mainstream of officer recruits pass through the Royal Military Academy (RMA) Sandhurst, although older potential officers (including many who have served in the ranks) can achieve commissions after a shorter course in Mons Officer Cadet School. This mainstream dwindled from 403 in 1971 to 337 in 1972, and this down-trend was followed by the University Cadet scheme (88 down

to 75) and short service entrants (67 down to 56). Only the Direct Graduate Entry Scheme increased its entrants, from 37 to 51, and the Army makes a great effort to attract graduates into its technical arms in order to be able to stay abreast of current weapon developments.

Army Reserve Forces

These fall into three categories:

1. The Regular Reserve (ex-servicemen with reserve service liability).

2. The Army General Reserve (certain key ex-National Servicemen).

3. The Territorial and Army Volunteer Reserve (TAVR); these are mostly civilians who volunteer to be trained as soldiers in their free time. On 1 January 1973 strength was 59,300 men. TAVR units which have mobilisation roles overseas train in their mobilisation locations once every three years, which means that about 23,000 men of the TAVR go to NATO countries, to Gibraltar and to Cyprus every year.

4. The eleven battalions of the Ulster Defence Regiment are similar in nature to TAVR units and replaced the disbanded "B Specials" of the Royal Ulster Constabulary. They now have a strength of 9,100 men, and at time of writing had lost 33 men killed by the IRA.

Military education starts at an early age in

Britain. Most schools maintain a "Cadet Force" in which boys of eleven years and older volunteer to receive military training once a week in uniform. Annual camps and visits to fostering units helps to make this training more effective, and the Cadet Forces are a valuable source of recruits for the army. In all there are the following Cadet Forces in Britain today: the Sea Cadet Corps, the Army Cadet Force, the Air Training Corps and the Combined Cadet Force. Strength of all these formations in January 1973 was 134,500.

Regiments and Divisions

For recruiting, administrative and traditional reasons the regiments of cavalry and infantry of the British army were reorganised into the following divisions in 1968. The dates in parentheses are those of the original raising of the unit, or the component units of an amalgamated regiment.

Cavalry:

The Household Cavalry
The Life Guards (1660)
The Blues and Royals (1661)
The Royal Armoured Corps
1st The Queen's Dragoon Guards (1685)
The Royal Scots Dragoon Guards (1681 and 1685)

4th/7th Royal Dragoon Guards (1685)
5th Royal Inniskilling Dragoon Guards (1685)
The Queen's Own Hussars (1685)
The Queen's Royal Irish Hussars (1693)
9th/12th Royal Lancers (Prince of Wales's) (1715)
The Royal Hussars (Prince of Wales's Own) (1715)
13th/18th Royal Hussars (Queen Mary's Own) (1715 and 1853)
14th/20th King's Hussars (1715 and 1858)
15th/19th The King's Royal Hussars (1759 and 1858)
16th/5th The Queen's Royal Lancers (1759 and 1680)
17th/21st Lancers (1759 and 1858)
1st Royal Tank Regiment ⎫
2nd Royal Tank Regiment ⎬ 1917
3rd Royal Tank Regiment ⎪
4th Royal Tank Regiment ⎭

Infantry: (Numbered line regiments from which traditions are traced are given in parenthesis).
The Guards Division
Grenadier Guards (two battalions) (1656)
Coldstream Guards (two battalions) (1650)
Scots Guards (two battalions) (1660)
Irish Guards (one battalion) (1900)
Welsh Guards (one battalion) (1915)

THE BRITISH TANK BATTALION

("Armoured Regiment")

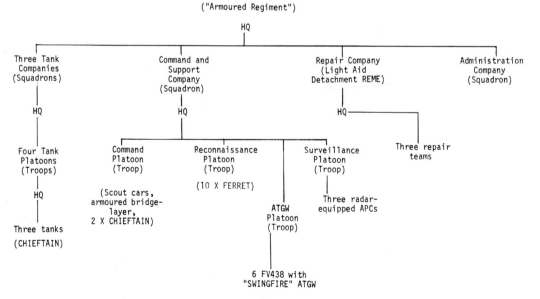

64

The Scottish Division (All regiments are represented by their 1st Battalions).
The Royal Scots (1st Foot) (1653)
The Royal Highland Fusiliers (21st/71st/74th Foot) (1678/1777/1787)
The King's Own Scottish Borderers (25th Foot) (1689)
The Black Watch (42nd/73rd Foot) (1739/1780)
The Queen's Own Highlanders (Seaforth & Camerons) (72nd/78th/79th Foot) (1777/1793)
The Gordon Highlanders (75th/92nd Foot) (1787/1794)
The Argyll & Sutherland Highlanders (Princess Louise's) (91st/93rd Foot) (1794/1800)
The Queen's Division
The Queen's Regiment (1st (2nd Foot), 2nd (3rd Foot), 3rd (35th/107th Foot) and 4th (57th/77th Foot) Battalions) (1661/1665/1701/1854/1755/1787)
The Royal Regiment of Fusiliers (1st (5th Foot), 2nd (6th Foot), and 3rd (7th Foot) Battalions) (1674/1673/1685)
The Royal Anglian Regiment (1st (9th Foot), 2nd (10th Foot), 3rd (16th Foot) and 4th (17th Foot) Battalions) (1685/1685/1688/1688)
The King's Division
The King's Own Royal Border Regiment (1st Battalion) (4th Foot) (1680)
The King's Regiment (1st Battalion) (8th Foot) (1685)
The Prince of Wales's Own Regiment of Yorkshire (1st Battalion) (14th/15th Foot) (1685/1685)

British Chieftain main battle tanks during an exercise. (RAC Tank Museum)

The Green Howards (1st Battalion) (19th Foot) (1688)
The Royal Irish Rangers (1st (27th/108th Foot) and 2nd (83rd/86th Foot) Battalions) (1689/1861/1973/1793)
The Queen's Lancashire Regiment (1st Battalion) (47th/81st Foot) (1741/1793)
The Duke of Wellington's Regiment (West Riding) (1st Battalion) (33rd/76th Foot) (1702/1787)
The Prince of Wales's Division (each regiment is represented by its 1st Battalion)
The Devon & Dorset Regiment (11th/39th/54th Foot) (1685/1702/1755)
The Cheshire Regiment (22nd Foot) (1689)
The Royal Welch Fusiliers (23rd Foot) (1689)
The Royal Regiment of Wales (24th/41st/69th Foot) (1689/1719/1758)
The Gloucestershire Regiment (28th/61st Foot) (1694/1758)
The Worcestershire & Sherwood Foresters Regiment (29th/6th/45th/95th Foot) (1694/1701/1741/1832)
The Royal Hampshire Regiment (37th/67th Foot) (1702/1758)
The Staffordshire Regiment (The Prince of Wales's) (38th/80th Foot) (1702/1793)
The Duke of Edinburgh's Royal Regiment (Berkshire & Wiltshire) (49th/66th and 62nd/99th Foot)

(1743/1758 and 1758/1824)

The Light Division

The Light Infantry (1st (13th/32nd/46th Foot), 2nd (51st/105th Foot) and 3rd (53rd/85th Foot) Battalions) (1685/1702/1741, 1755/1839 and 1755/1793)

The Royal Green Jackets (1st (43rd/52nd Foot), 2nd (60th Foot) and 3rd (53rd/85th Foot) Battalions) (1741/1755, 1755 and 1755/1793)

The Parachute Regiment

1st, 2nd and 3rd Battalions (1940)

Special Air Service Regiment

One battalion (22nd SAS)

The Brigade of Gurkhas

2nd Gurkha Rifles (two battalions) (1817 and 1866)

6th Gurkha Rifles (one battalion) (1817)

7th Gurkha Rifles (one battalion) (1902)

10th Princess Mary's Own Gurkha Rifles (one battalion) (1910)

The Ulster Defence Regiment

Eleven Battalions (1970)

Other regiments and corps, in order of seniority, include:

The Royal Horse Artillery

The Royal Regiment of Artillery

Royal Engineers

The Royal Corps of Signals

Army Air Corps

Royal Army Chaplains

Royal Corps of Transport

Royal Army Medical Corps

Royal Army Ordnance Corps

Corps of Royal Electrical and Mechanical Engineers

Corps of Royal Military Police

Royal Army Pay Corps

Royal Army Veterinary Corps

Small Arms School Corps

Military Provost Staff Corps

Royal Army Education Corps

Royal Army Dental Corps

Royal Pioneer Corps

Intelligence Corps

Army Physical Training Corps

Army Catering Corps

General Service Corps

Queen Alexandra's Royal Army Nursing Corps

Women's Royal Army Corps

British Army Equipment (detailed tables follow this brief summary).

Small Arms 9 mm Browning pistols, 9 mm Sterling sub-machine guns, Belgian FN 7·62 mm NATO

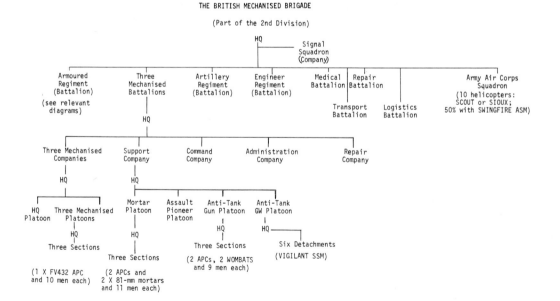

THE BRITISH MECHANISED BRIGADE

(Part of the 2nd Division)

pattern SLRs; 2-inch mortars and 81 mm mortars.
Anti-Tank Weapons Swedish Carl-Gustav 84 mm
anti-tank rocket projector; Swingfire, Beeswing,
Hawkswing, Malkara and Vigilant anti-tank GW;
Wombat recoilless anti-tank gun.
APCs 1 ton 4 × 4 Humber APC; Saracen 6 × 6
APC; AFV 432 tracked APC (derivatives serve as
GW carriers, command and recovery vehicles);
Scorpion, Striker, Spartan, Samaritan and Samson
versions of the new tracked light armoured vehicle
family.
Armoured Cars Saladin 6 × 6 with 76 mm cannon;
Ferret Mk. I, Mk. II and Mk V (with Swingfire
ATGW); Hornet 4 × 4 (with Malkara ATGW);
Fox 4 × 4 with 30 mm Rarden cannon; Vixen
4 × 4 with MGs.
Tanks About 1,000 Chieftain MBT with 120 mm
gun.
Artillery Italian pattern 'M-56' 105 mm pack
howitzers, British 105 mm armoured SP Abbot
howitzers, American M-109G 155 mm SP howitzers
and M-107 175 mm SP howitzers, M-110 203 mm
SP howitzers, "Honest John" tactical nuclear SSM.
Anti-aircraft artillery Blowpipe AAGW. Bofors
L-40/70, 40 mm radar-controlled AA guns now
being replaced by Rapier light AAGW (see below);
Thunderbird heavy AAGW.
Aircraft Beaver fixed wing light planes; 132 Scout
and 265 Sioux helicopters, now being replaced by
Lynx and Gazelle.
BAC Rapier ET-316

This light, air-portable low-level AA system is
already in service with the British Army and the
RAF and is selling in many other countries including Iran. The basic unit consists of two LWB
Landrovers with trailers. The one trailer is the
missile launcher with target acquisition radar and
generating set, the other is a missile magazine. The
equipment can be operated by one man; reloading
the launcher with four missiles requires two men.
The system can be lifted by Wessex helicopters in
two loads. Although basically an optical target
tracking system (and thus limited to fair weather)
an optional extra is an all-weather target tracking
radar, also trailer-mounted. Rapier can also be
mounted on wheeled or tracked and armoured
vehicles. Characteristics – combat range 600–6,000
km.

Thunderbird 2 Heavy Air Defence Missile System
Developed by British Aircraft Corporation, it

*The commander of an FV432 armoured personnel
carrier of the 2nd Royal Anglian Regiment, BAOR;
the DPM camouflage clothing is now worn as combat
dress by all infantry units, and the camouflaged cap is
being introduced. (COI)*

includes automatic IFF and is designed to combat
medium and high level air attacks. It has target
acquisition and target tracking radar and is computer
controlled. The system is mobile and the missile is
equipped with a semi-active homing device whereby
it homes in on a target "illuminated" by the ground-
based target tracking radar. Start motors are four,
single stage, solid fuel boosters which are discarded
after take-off. The missile itself has a single-stage,
solid-fuel rocket motor. The warhead is high
explosive detonated by a proximity fuse. The entire
system is air-portable. Thunderbird 2 has been in
service with the British Army since 1965.
Lance tactical SSM

Designed as a divisional level tactical nuclear GW
to replace Honest John and Sergeant. It is mounted
in a tracked carrier/launcher vehicle and is highly
mobile. Crew is six men, and range about 110 km.
The missile is air portable and air-droppable. The
guidance system is a simplified inertial type (cannot
be jammed) and the motor is a single-stage, liquid
fuelled rocket. The entire system comprises two
XM-667 tracked carriers (M113 derivatives) one of
which is the launcher, the other carrying two more
missiles and a loading crane. There is also a lightweight, wheeled, towed launcher for airborne operations. Lance completed testing in 1969 and is now
entering service.

British Army Infantry Weapons

Weapon	Calibre	Rate of fire (rpm)	Combat range	Magazine Capacity (rounds)	Loaded Weight	Remarks
Browning pistol	9 mm	72	25 m	13	2 lb 7 oz	Used by officers, senior NCOs and tank crews
FN Self Loading Rifle (SLR) L1A1	7·62 mm	20	300 m	20	11 lb 3 oz	The standard, Belgian-designed, NATO weapon
Sterling Sub Machine Gun (SMG) L2A3	9 mm		100 m	34	7 lb 10 oz	British produced, replaced the Sten gun in 1958
General Purpose Machine Gun (GPMG) in the light role	7·62 mm	100 (in bursts of 4–5)	800 m	Belt 50		The GPMG is converted from the light role (with bipod) to the SF role by addition of dial sight, tripod mount, two, heavy-duty barrels. Three such kits are held in each rifle company. It is also mounted on APCs.
GPMG sustained fire (SF) role	7·62	200	1,800 m	Belt 50		
Light mortar	2 inch	14	480 m	18 rounds carried		Platoon weapon, fires HE, Smoke and illuminating ammunition
Medium Mortar	81 mm	12	5,400 m	—	88 lbs	Support Company weapon, ammunition as for 2 inch mortar
Carl Gustav light anti-tank projector	84 mm		500 m	—		Swedish weapon, platoon anti-tank weapon
Wombat Battalion anti-tank gun	120 mm	4	1,000 m	—		British weapon, successor to BAT and Mobat guns. Six are in each support company
Light anti-tank rocket ("Heat")	66 mm	3	200 m	—	5 lbs	Section anti-tank weapon which replaced the No 94 "Energa" grenade fired from the rifle muzzle
Vigilant anti-tank GW	130 mm	3	1,400 m	—		
Royal Armament Research and Development Establishment (Rarden) Gun	30 mm	15	1,500 m	204 rounds in FV432 in clips of 3		Two mounted on APCs in the three companies of a mechanised battalion

British Army Wheeled Vehicles

Model	Weight (Pounds) Empty	Weight (Pounds) Loaded	Height (feet)	Length (feet)	Width (feet)	Max road speed (km/hr)	Road range (km)
Landrover ¼ ton Mk VIII (4 × 4)	3,365	4,460	6·4	12·5	5·5	75	570
Landrover ½ ton Mk 1 (4 × 4)	3,100	4,395	6·4	12·25	5·25	75	570
Landrover ¾ ton Mk XI (4 × 4)	3,685	5,766	6·75	15·25	5·5	75	448
Bedford "MK" (4 × 4)	10,755	20,835	11·2	21·5	8·0	75	586
Stalwart (6 × 6) (high mobility load carrier)	18,620	28,620	8·2	20·5	8·33	70	380

AEC "Militant" Mk I and Mk II (6 × 6)	21,950	41,950	11·75	28·0	8·0	50	480
Leyland 10 ton Artillery Tractor (6 × 6)	31,530	41,100	10·25	28·5	8·33	45	570
AEC "Militant" 10 ton Mk II recovery truck (6 × 6)	Not applicable	40,320	10·25	25·0	8·15	56	570
"Mighty Antar" tank transporter	85,000	220,000	14·5	62·0	13·1	45	320
Volvo BV 202 Arctic transport vehicle	6,400	9,300	6·66	20·25	5·75	45	320

British Army Helicopters

Type	Crew and passengers	Cruising Speed	Cruising Range	Flying Endurance	Remarks
Alouette Mk II	4	90 knots	270 nautical miles	3 hours	
Gazelle Mk I	4	120 knots	360 nautical miles	3 hours	Will replace Sioux by 1974
Lynx Mk I	9	158 knots	480 nautical miles	3½ hours	Will replace Scout and Alouette by 1975
Scout Mk I	5	100 knots	250 nautical miles	2½ hours	
Sioux Mk I	2	70 knots	190 nautical miles	2½ hours	

Gazelle can be armed with the 7·62 mm Minigun (6,000 rpm; 4,000 rounds carried, range 1,000 m) or with a 4 Hawkswing anti-tank GW with a range of up to 4,000 m.
Lynx can also take the Minigun or 6 Hawkswing.

The Alvis Stalwart high mobility load carrier.

British Armoured Fighting Vehicles

Model	Armament	Ammunition	Weight	Height	Length	Width	Fuel Capacity	Max road speed (km/hr)	Road range
Chieftain (MBT)	1 × 120 mm cannon 1 × 7·62 co-axial MG 1 × 5 inch ranging MG 1 × 7·62 commander's MG	53 rounds 120 mm 600 rounds 0·5 inch 4,500 rounds 7·62 mm	51 tons	2·81 m	7·46 m	3·5 m	200 gallons diesel	41·2	400 km
Saladin 6 × 6 armoured car	1 × 76 mm cannon 1 × 0·3 inch co-axial MG 1 × 0·3 inch commander's MG	42 rounds 76 mm 5,000 rounds 0·3 inch	13 tons	2·26 m	4·87 m	2·51 m	53 gallons	72	380 km
Saracen 6 × 6 wheeled APC	1 × 0·3 inch MG	3,000 rounds 0·3 inch	10 tons	2·5 m	5·0 m	2·51 m	44 gallons	70	352 km
FV 432 Mk I tracked APC	1 × 7·62 mm MG	3,000 rounds 7·62 mm	15 tons	2·18 m	5·1 m	2·97 m	80 gallons	54	482 km
FV 438 anti-tank GW vehicle	Swingfire SSM 1 × 7·62 mm MG	14 missiles 3,000 rounds 7·62 mm	16 tons	2·38 m	5·23 m	2·87 m	80 gallons	54	482 km
Ferret Mk I (Liaison) 4 × 4 scout car	1 × 0·3 inch MG	2,500 rounds	4 tons	1·4 m	3·83 m	1·9 m	21 gallons	91·3	320 km
Ferret Mk II (Recce) 4 × 4 scout car	1 × 0·3 inch MG (turret mounted)	2,500 rounds	4 tons	1·88 m	3·83 m	1·9 m	21 gallons	93·3	320 km
Ferret Mk V (GW Launcher)	Swingfire SSM 1 × 7·62 mm MG	6 missiles 2,500 rounds MG	6 tons	2·13 m	4·01 m	2·13 m	21 gallons	91	320 km

Both Centurion and Chieftain have main armaments stabilised in two planes and are very sophisticated weapon systems employing infra red night driving and firing aids. Three types of main armament ammunition are used: *High Explosive Squash Head* (HESH) – very destructive against armoured vehicles and fortifications and useful against other targets; *Armour Piercing Discarding Sabot* (APDS) – this World War II British developed ammunition type is a tungsten steel, sub-calibre round with a light metal "collar" which fits the gun and falls away from the round when it leaves the gun. The hard core thus has very high kinetic energy and can pierce any known tank armour; *Canister* – a modern version of the old grape shot and designed for use in the Korean War type of environment when human wave infantry attacks are expected.

British Army Vehicles

Machine type	Height Length Width (feet)	Weight (tons)	Max road speed (km/hr)	Road Range (km)	Armament	Ammunition (rounds)	Remarks
Centurion Mk XIII Main Battle Tank	9·8 28·75 11·27	51	34·6	190	1 × 105 mm cannon 1 × 0·5 inch ranging MG 2 × 0·3 inch MGs	64 600 4.500	

Vehicle	Dimensions						Armament		Remarks
Centurion Mk V bridgelayer	12·75	40·27 alone / 53·5 with bridge	14·75	49	34·6	185	1 × 7·62 GPMG		Can lay a 45 foot bridge (MLC 60) in two minutes. The bridge weighs 14 tons
Centurion Mk V Dozer tank	9·75	30·5	13·0	52·6	34·6	185	Either as for Centurion Mk XIII or, with engineer regiments, a 165 mm demolition gun		
Centurion ARK	12·75	34·3	12·5	52	34·6	100	As for bridgelayer		Forms a 75 foot MLC 80 bridge
Centurion Armoured Vehicle Royal Engineers (AVRE)	9·10/18·75*	28·6/29·75*	11·2/16·0*	51	33/12*	185	165 mm demolition 25 (HESH) gun, 2 × 0·3 inch MGs	3,500	*With fascine
Armoured Recovery Vehicle (ARV) II (Centurion)	9·5	29·4	11·2	49·5	34·6	140	None	None	Has 30-ton winch
Centurion Beach ARV	11·3	26·5	11·2	40·1	34·6	64	None	None	Used in amphibious operations. Can wade to 9·5 feet deep
Hornet	7·75	17·6	7·4	5·1	64	400	Malkara ATGW 1 × 7·62 GPWG	4 / 3,500	Air portable and air droppable; Malkara effective range – 700–4,000 m
Truck Humber 1 ton, armoured (known to the troops as "The Pig")	6·95	16·1	6·75	5·7	90	492	Non-mounted	—	Up-armoured in 1971–72 for use in Northern Ireland

Machine type	Height Length Width (feet)	Weight (tons)	Max road speed (km/hr)	Road Range (km)	Armament	Ammunition (rounds)	Remarks
FV 433; 105 mm SP howitzer (Abbot)	8·75 / 18·9 / 8·75	16·1	48	272	1 × 105 mm L13A1 cannon; 1 × 0·5 inch MG		Air portable, can swim with aid of screen

The New Range of British Light Armoured Vehicles

Name	Combat Wt/kg	Crew	Armament and Ammunition	Length	Width	Height	User Trials	Into Service	Possible Accessories
Scorpion; CVR(T) (tracked)	8,000	3	76 mm Gun 7·62 mm Coax GPMG 40 rounds 76 mm 3,000 rounds MG	4·3 m	2·2 m	2·1 m	1971	1972	Radiac Detector. CW Detector. Central Alarm System. Sperry Navigator. Turret and driver's passive viewers
Striker; CVT(T) GW (tracked)		3	5 ready Swingfire 5 stowed Swingfire 10 Total 7·62 mm MG	4·76 m	2·18 m	2·21 m	1972	1974	Radiac Detector. CW Detector, Radar No 14 (possibly). Sperry Navigator. Turret and driver's passive viewers. Central Alarm System
Spartan; CVR(T) APC (tracked)	8,165	2 + 5	7·62 mm GPMG 84 mm Karl Gustav 2,000 rounds 7·62 mm	4·6 m	2·2 m	2·2 m	1971	1973	Radar GS No 14. Turret and driver's passive viwers. Central Alarm System. CW detector. Radiac Detector
Sultan; CVR(T) Command (tracked)		2 + 3	7·62 mm GPMG (2,000 rounds)	4·99 m	2·1 m	2·2 m	1971	1973	Radiac detector. CW Detector. Central Alarm System. Driver's passive viewer. Sperry Navigator
Samaritan; CVR(T) Ambulance (tracked)	8,165	2 + 4 stretchers or 6 seated	None	4·6 m	2·1 m	2·2 m	197?	1973	Radiac detector. CW Detector. Central Alarm System. Driver's passive viewer
Samson; CVR(T) Rec (tracked)	8,332	3	7·62 mm GPMG	4·93 m	2·18 m	2·02 m	1971	1973	High speed winch Driver's passive viewer CW Detector Radiac Detector } Not yet finalised

72

Rear view of two Ferret Mk. II scout cars; this rather elderly design is currently being replaced by the new series of light armoured vehicles.

Scimitar; CVR(T) 30 (tracked)	7,713	3	30 mm Cannon, 7·62 mm Coax GPMG 200 rounds 30 mm; 3,000 rounds MG	4·3 m	2·2 m	2·1 m	1973	1972–3	30 mm in Scorpion Turret. Radiac detector. CW Detector. Radar GS No 14. Central Alarm System. Driver's and turret passive viewers
Fox; CVR(W) (wheeled 4 × 4)	5,670	3 (Can be fought by 2)	30 Cannon 7·62 Coax GPMG 96 rounds 30 mm 2,600 rounds MG	4·9 m	2·1 m	2·04 m	Mid 1968	1971	Radar GS No 14. Sperry Navigator. CW Detector. Radiac detector. Central Alarm System. Driver's and turret passive viewers
Vixen; CVR(W) L (wheeled 4 × 4)	?	2 + 2	1 × 7·62 mm GPMG	4 m	2:1	1·5 m to hull roof (excl. turret cupola and MG)	1969	1972	Radar GS No 14 (net yet finalised)

All these vehicles use the Jaguar 4·2 litre, 200 bhp, water-cooled petrol engine giving a power/weight ratio for the tracked vehicles of 25 bhp/ton and for the wheeled vehicles of 34 bhp/ton. Maximum road speed (all vehicles) is 80·5 km/hr and the road range – 480 km. Ground pressure (tracked vehicles) is 0·366 kg/cm² and (wheeled) 0·91 k1/cm².

British Army Uniforms

The following forms of dress are worn today in the British Army:

1. Full dress
2. No. 1 dress (only by officers and men in limited categories)
3. Service dress
4. Barrack dress
5. Combat dress including specialist clothing

Full dress

This is limited to the Household troops, including King's Troop Royal Horse Artillery (RHA). For the regiments of foot guards this consists of a bearskin bonnet with plume according to regiment, a red coat with blue facings, white piping and yellow buttons grouped according to regiment as follows:

Grenadier Guards – single
Coldstream Guards – in twos
Scots Guards – in threes
Irish Guards – in fours
Welsh Guards – in fives

Dark blue trousers with a red side piping are worn, with black boots, and white belts with yellow buckle plates.

The Life Guards wear a red coat, blue facings, yellow buttons, gold lace, white leather gauntlets and breeches, high jacked boots with spurs, silver helmets with white, falling horsehair plumes and heavy cavalry swords. The Blues and Royals wear a uniform of similar style but in blue with red facings and plume.

King's Troop RHA wears hussar-pattern dark blue uniform with red facings, yellow lace and spherical buttons, black busby with red bag and white plume, dark blue breeches with red side stripe, short boots and spurs.

No 1 Dress

Regimental pattern hat with regimental badge. This is generally a peaked cap in dark blue with headband and top piping in the particular facing colour of the regiment, but there are exceptions; for instance, the Parachute Regiment always wears its maroon beret, the Highland regiments wear their Glengarry, lancer regiments usually have red caps with yellow "quarter-welts" recalling the traditional lancer "Czapka" of square-topped design; the Royal Tank Regiment always wears its black berets with short bristle tufts behind the badge. Light infantry units have dark green caps, the Royal Military Police dark blue headbands and red tops, Irish regiments wear dark green large-topped berets

called Caubeens. Other examples are:

Royal Corps of Signals – all dark blue; Royal Corps of Transport – dark blue with white top piping; Royal Army Ordnance Corps – dark blue with red headband and top piping; Royal Electrical and Mechanical Engineers – as for RAOC; Royal Army Medical Corps – dark blue with crimson headband. This headdress is often also worn with Service Dress.

The No 1 Dress Jacket also varies in colour and cut with the regiment. the majority being dark blue; exceptions include Light Infantry – dark green, and Highland regiments – dark green and of cut-away Highland pattern. Cavalry regiments have chain mail shoulder pieces, other regiments and corps have shoulder-straps. The jacket has a high, closed collar with regimental collar badges, five button front and four pockets (buttons of regimental pattern). Trousers are generally dark blue with side stripe (or stripes) in the regimental facing colour. Exceptions are the Royal Hussars – crimson breeches; Highland regiments – either tartan trews or the kilt; Irish regiments – dark green trousers. Mounted regiments wear very close-fitting breeches and silver spurs, dismounted corps wear trousers of normal width.

A regimental pattern belt, either black or white with ornate belt buckle is often also worn; officers attending weddings and other festivities will wear golden shoulder cords, crimson silk waist sashes (dismounted arms) or regimental pattern pouch belt (mounted arms), swords of regimental pattern and white gloves. Dark brown gloves are worn on other occasions (light infantry – black). In tropical climates a white jacket replaces the usual No 1 dress jacket.

Service Dress (SD)

The No 1 Dress hat or the beret or a regimental pattern side hat (or forage cap) can be worn with SD. The jacket is khaki, single breasted, open necked, four button front, four pockets, single rear vent. Light khaki shirt and tie, regimental pattern collar badges, shoulder titles and buttons. Khaki trousers, boots or shoes (black for other ranks, brown for officers except Light Infantry officers and officers of highland regiments who wear black brogues). There are various minor differences between the style of the SD jackets of various regiments, particularly the cavalry and the artillery which have introduced their own patterns of jackets with buttons at the cuffs, no pleats on the top pockets, etc. Highland regiments have jackets with cut-away front skirts. Examples of some of the various regimental pattern berets, side caps and stable belts is included in a table in this chapter. In warm weather shirt sleeve order is worn, consisting of a khaki shirt with open neck and rolled up sleeves, khaki SD trousers, boots or shoes and regimental pattern canvas "stable belt" with either ornate clasp worn at the front centre or with black or brown leather buckles worn under the left arm. Regimental pattern shoulder titles and lanyards will also be worn and any of the three types of hat.

Barrack Dress

This form of dress crept into the British Army almost unnoticed from about 1962 onwards and in 1970, it was finally officially sanctioned. Praised by some as being comfortable, cursed by others as being unsoldierly, Barrack Dress is undoubtedly practical and cheap. It consisted originally of a khaki-green woollen pullover with round neck and shoulder straps, regimental stable belt and SD trousers or fatigue dress trousers, boots and gaiters or shoes. Nowadays, apart from the official khaki pullover, many other colours and patterns of pullover can be seen. These have been introduced by the individual regiments and corps. Examples are: Signals – dark blue with No 1 Dress epaulettes and buttons; Royal Hampshire Regiment – black; The Cheshire Regiment – red-brown; Intelligence Corps – dark green. Some units have also taken to wearing a neckerchief in the regimental colour in shirt sleeve order; examples are: Light Infantry – green; Royal Artillery and RAOC – dark blue.

Combat Dress

This exists in two patterns; the combat troops wear the new (1970) Disruptive Pattern Material (DPM) camouflaged suits in black, brown, yellow and olive green, while rear services wear the 1950s pattern suit, of similar cut to the new suit but in olive green. With this suit are worn the beret or steel helmet with camouflage net, boots and gaiters or puttees. Webbing equipment also comes in two patterns; combat troops wear the new 1958, olive green webbing; rear services the 1937, light khaki webbing. Specialist combat clothing includes the respirator and NBC protective clothing (made of impregnated paper compound and designed to be effective for up to one day), tropical and arctic clothing.

Regimental Badges

Unlike many other armies, a great variety of cap, collar, shoulder and button badges are worn by the

The band of the Queen's Own Hussars wearing a typical variation of No. 1 Dress, with cavalry and regimental features. There are considerable differences between one unit and another in matters of detail and in headgear. "Blues" are no longer issued to the rank and file as a whole.

various regiments of the British Army and since 1958 the infantry badges in particular have undergone many changes with all the amalgamations and reorganisations which have taken place. It would require a book of its own to explain and illustrate these badges fully; suffice to say that each cavalry regiment and each infantry battalion has its own cap, collar, shoulder and button badges.

Miscellaneous customs

All ranks are clean shaven except when they have permission to grow a moustache which must be kept neat and tidy. The Sergeant of Pioneers in each infantry battalion is required to wear a full beard.

Men of supporting arms and services attached to the Parachute Regiment and the Army Air Corps wear their own regimental badges on the berets of the units to which they are attached. Men of the REME serving in LADs with regiments will wear items of that unit's dress in addition to their own badges.

Officers of dismounted corps carry canes about 70 cm long and of regimental pattern in No 1 dress, SD and Barrack dress; this custom was adopted when officers ceased to wear swords on normal duty. Regimental Sergeant Majors (RSMs) and Company/Battery/Squadron Sergeant Majors often carry "pace-sticks" – highly polished wooden and brass dividers about 1·2 m long. These pace sticks can be set to the regulation "thirty inch pace" and thus used to plan parades meticulously.

Badges of Rank

For other ranks these are worn on the upper sleeves (lance corporal, corporal, sergeant and staff-sergeant (also called colour sergeant or company quartermaster sergeant (CQMS/BQMS/SQMS) according to appointment)) or lower sleeves (CSM, RSM, RQMS and drum/pipe major). They are:

Lance corporal   – 1 white chevron, point down
Corporal   – 2 white chevrons, point down
Sergeant   – 3 white chevrons, point down
   } specialist badges are worn above the chevrons.

Staff Sergeant   – 3 white chevrons surmounted by a crown (specialist badges are worn between the chevrons and the crown).
Warrant Officer 2nd Class (CSM)   – a crown.
Warrant Officer 2nd Class (RQMS)   – a crown within a laurel wreath.
Warrant Officer 1st Class (RSM)   – the full royal coat of arms.
Warrant Officer 1st Class with technical specialist training – the RSM's coat of arms surrounded by an edging in the regimental colour.
Warrant Officer 1st Class RAOC only (Conductor) – the RSM's coat of arms in a red circle.
Drum/Pipe Major   – four white chevrons, points up, surmounted by a brass drum or bagpipes, on the lower sleeve.

On parades, sergeants and above of infantry regiments wear a red sash from right shoulder to left hip.

Commissioned officers wear their rank on the shoulder-straps in the form of four-pointed stars and crowns which vary in colour, size and shape from regiment to regiment:

Second lieutenant – one star.
Lieutenant – two stars.
Captain – three stars.
Major – a crown.
Lieutenant-Colonel – a crown over one star.
Colonel – a crown over two stars
Brigadier – a crown over three stars in a pyramid formation
   } Red gorget patches with crimson central lace and gold button; hat badge a crowned lion standing on a crown.

Major-General – one star over crossed sabre and baton
Lieutenant-General – a crown over crossed sabre and baton
General – a crown over a star over crossed sabre and baton
Field Marshal – a crown over a wreath containing crossed batons
   } Red gorget patches with gold central lace and button. Cap badge as for the shoulder badge.

Examples of badges of rank and specialist badges are shown on the accompanying plates.

Flags and Standards of the British Army

This topic would justify a book on its own but it suffices here to give a brief guide to the subject.

Line infantry regiments in the British Army carry flags, rifle regiments do not. The 2nd Gurkha Rifles have a ceremonial truncheon instead of a flag; this has been brought into their British Army Service from the Indian Army (of British colonial days) when the 2nd Gurkha Rifles was part of that army.

Each regiment (battalion) has two flags called the Queen's Colour and the Regimental Colour. The Foot Guards have various patterns of colours but as a general rule for the line it may be said that the Queen's Colour is the Union Flag edged in gold

Above, the command version of the British army's FV432 armoured tracked personnel carrier series. Below, the American M109 self-propelled howitzer of 155 mm calibre, here in service with Britain's Royal Artillery.

fringes and bearing the regimental title in the centre. Around this title will be some of the most important battle honours which the regiment has earned in its history. The Regimental Colour will have the Union Flag in the top staff quarter and the rest of the flag will be in the regiment's facing colour and will bear more of the regiment's battle honours and various badges and devices. It is edged with gold fringes. British colours are embroidered and carried on polished brown wooden pikes with tips in the form of the crown surmounted by a golden crowned lion; golden cords and tassles reaching to the bottom of the flag complete the decoration. Certain regiments have cravats attached to the pikes (eg the "Glosters", for their action at the Imjin River in the Korean War in 1950–51, received the American presidential citation, which is worn on their pike and on the top of the men's sleeves in the form of a light blue silk oblong within a gold surround). Rifle regiments wear their battle honours on their cap badges, and the Royal Regiment of Artillery carries no colours as its guns are regarded as being the "rallying point". Thus batteries who have earned battle honours carry them painted on their guns. Examples are: "O" Battery RHA (Rocket Troop), who carry "Leipzig" (for the battle in 1813) and Minden Battery, who have a red rose and "Minden" (for the battle in 1759).

Only some cavalry regiments in the British army carry colours; Lancer and Hussar regiments do not. Regiments of Dragoons carry square, crimson "Standards" while regiments of Dragoon Guards carry swallow-tailed "Guidons". Both are gold fringed and the pikes are as for infantry colours although the size of cavalry colours is much smaller than that of their infantry counterparts. The design of cavalry colours has not really altered since Napoleonic days: in the centre is the regimental designation embroidered in gold; in the top staff and bottom fly corners the springing lower Saxon horse of the House of Hannover; and in the bottom staff and top fly corners, roundels containing either the regimental number or the slipped rose, thistle and shamrock. Battle honours fill up the vertical spaces flanking the central device.

When new colours are presented to a regiment, the old colours are usually laid up in the cathedral in the regiment's depot town and many of these old colours can be seen today, rotting dimly away far above the heads of interested sight-seers.

Examples of British beret colours and other regimental distinctions

Regiment	Beret	Side hat	Stable belt
Foot Guards	Khaki	Not worn	Dark blue with red centre stripe
Infantry of the Line	Dark blue	Various	Various
Light Infantry	Dark green	Dark green	Dark geeen; leather buckles
Parachute Regiment	Maroon	Not worn	Maroon with round silver belt plate bearing a pegasus
Army Air Corps	Light blue with a dark blue patch behind the badge	Not worn	Light blue with two royal blue stripes; leather buckles
SAS Regiment	Very light khaki	Not worn	Not known
RAMC	Dark blue with crimson patch behind the badge	—	Yellow over crimson with dark blue central stripe; leather buckles
RADC	As above but dark green patch	—	Dark green over dark blue with a narrow crimson centre stripe; side buckles
RA	Dark blue	Dark blue with red combe	Red with dark blue central band having a yellow central stripe; leather buckles

Regiment	Beret	Side hat	Stable belt
RHA (serves in the parachute brigade)	Maroon	Not worn	As for RA
Royal Hussars	Milk chocolate beret with crimson patch behind the badge	Not worn	Crimson centre band edged in yellow and with very dark blue on the outer edges; buckles to the side
Royal Tank Regiment	Black	Not worn	Red over green with a brown central stripe
1st Queen's Dragoon Guards	Dark blue	—	Royal blue; leather buckles
15th/18th Hussars	Dark blue	Red with yellow piping	Dark blue with a twin central stripe, yellow over red; leather buckles
Royal Engineers	Dark blue	Dark blue with red piping	Red with two dark blue stripes; silver, round buckle plate
Royal Corps of Transport	Dark blue	Dark blue with white piping	Dark blue, two white stripes in the centre, two red stripes nearer the edges; round silver buckle plate
Royal Army Ordnance Corps	Dark blue	Dark blue with red piping	Dark blue with three narrow red stripes; round silver buckle plate
Royal Military Police	Not worn (a khaki SD cap is worn instead)	Not worn	Red with leather buckles
Royal Electrical and Mechanical Engineers	Dark blue	Dark blue, red combe, yellow piping	Dark blue with two double stripes (yellow over red) and round silver buckle
Royal Army Education Corps	Dark blue	Dark blue with light blue combe	Dark blue with two, central light blue stripes and light blue edging; leather buckles
The Gloucestershire* Regiment	Dark blue	Dark blue with red piping	Dark blue with one central red stripe and two narrower yellow stripes towards the outer edges; leather buckles
The Royal Anglian Regiment	Dark blue	—	Dark blue with a central yellow stripe flanked by red bands; silver "web belt" buckle

* On all headgear the "Glosters" wear a small silver badge consisting of a sphinx within a wreath on the back of their hats to commemorate their participation in the battle of Alexandria in 1801.

THE TURKISH REPUBLIC

Population – 37,000,000.   **Capital** – Ankara.

Armed Forces:

Army – 435,000 men (including 75,000 Gendarmerie).

Navy – 39,000 men; 10 submarines, 10 destroyers, 6 escorts, 11 MTBs, 14 fast patrol boats, 20 minesweepers, 6 minelayers, some landing craft, 3 Agusta-Bell AB-204B anti-submarine helicopters.

Air Force – 50,000 men, 288 combat aircraft: 9 fighter-bomber squadrons (6 with F-100Ds, 2 with F-104Gs and 1 with F-5s), 2 (mothballed) F-86 interceptor squadrons, 2 all weather fighter squadrons with F-102A, 3 reconnaissance squadrons with RF-84F and RF-85. Transport – 3 squadrons with 30 C-47s, 8 C-130s and 16 Transalls. Air defence – 8 batteries "Nike-Hercules" SAM.

Reserves – 1·75 million.

Defence Spending – $573,324,000 in 1972 (3·3% of GNP).

Head of State at time of writing was President Fahri Korutürk, elected 6 April 1973 much against the wishes of the Turkish military, who had ruled the country since their coup on 12 June 1960. The Turkish Army Chief of Staff (Faruk Gürler) resigned his military office prior to these presidential elections with the heavily dropped hint that he would "accept" the office of president if elected. His ambitions were, unfortunately, not realised.

According to the revised constitution of September 1971, Turkey is to be a national democratic socialist lay state based on the rule of law. The freedom of the press and of religion is restored and police powers have been curbed. For some years the Turkish army has regarded itself as the guardian of the nation's conscience and only reluctantly has now handed over the reins of power to the "unreliable" politicians again. The parliament is the Great National Assembly (GNA), a single-chamber body of 450 elected members serving a four-year term. Over this chamber is the Senate with 182 members (150 of whom are elected, fifteen nominated by the president, the rest either ex-presidents or other ex-officer life-long members chosen from the ranks of the Revolutionary Committee of 1960). Term of office (for elected members) is six years;

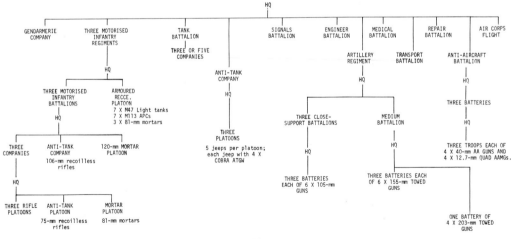

THE TURKISH INFANTRY DIVISION

THE TURKISH ARMOURED DIVISION

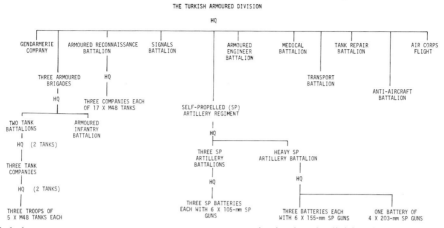

one-third change over every two years.

The president is elected by the GNA for a single, seven-year term. The prime minister is elected by the GNA and is at time of writing Naim Talu, an Independent; defence minister is Ilhami Sancar of the Confidential Party.

Turkey is still largely an agrarian state with a peasant economy. She receives development and arms assistance mainly from West Germany, USA and Italy. Social difficulties and the danger of a leftist takeover caused her right wing conservative army to seize power in 1960. Reforms are under way but much remains to be done. Turkish armed forces are almost exclusively American-organised and equipped (now becoming obsolete); discipline and training are hard, and pay low. Army officers are highly placed among the nation's élite and all Turkey's senior politicians are ex-army officers. The army enjoys great prestige among the mass of the people. Morale and combat value of the Turkish army is high, as demonstrated in Korea in 1956. Head of the armed forces is the president, who commands them through the National Security Council consisting of himself (chairman), the prime minister, defence, foreign affairs, home affairs, legal and finance ministers, the heads of the three services, and all army corps commanders and the chiefs of staff.

Universal conscription liability exists for all Turkish males from twenty to forty-six years of age, military service having just been reduced from twenty to eighteen months. About 175,000 conscripts are "called to the colours" each year.

Since 1945 the Turkish army has adopted the American system of corps, divisional and brigade organisation but the divisional structure is currently being revised so that their organisation and equipment will fit the terrain in which they are stationed. For instance, a division in the high mountains of east Anatolia will have far fewer armoured vehicles in the future than one stationed in the flatter lowland and desert areas. Horsed cavalry is still employed along inaccessible parts of the Turkish border, but this is a role which rotates between various units at about three-year intervals and most units who undertake this task are infantry battalions. The entire Turkish army is NATO-assigned and Turkey is one of NATO's most reliable members. Turkish officers attend the staff colleges of other NATO nations and operational doctrine is geared to agree with standard NATO procedures.

Turkish Army Organisation

One armoured division, one mechanised infantry division, eleven infantry divisions, six armoured brigades, one mechanised infantry brigade, three parachute battalions.

Turkish Army Equipment

Small Arms A wide range of American standard personal and automatic weapons, 81 mm and 120 mm mortars. The locally-made 9 mm Kirikkale pistol is also issued. Weight – 0·65 kg; 7 round magazine; effective range – 50 m. There is also a 7·65 mm version with an 8 round magazine.

Anti-tank weapons American 106 mm recoilless rifles, French SS-11 and Cobra anti-tank GW.

APCs American M-59 and M-113.

Armoured Cars American M-8 6 × 6.

Tanks American M-47 and M-48 medium tanks; M-24, M-26 and M-41 "Walker Bulldog" light tanks: M-36 tank destroyers.
Artillery American 105 mm, 155 mm and 203 mm towed howitzers; 105 mm and 155 mm SP howitzers; "Honest John" tactical nuclear SSM.
AA Artillery 40 mm, 75 mm and 90 mm radar controlled guns.
Helicopters 20 Agusta-Bell AB-204s.
Wheeled Vehicles American Jeeps, GMC and Dodge trucks.

Turkish Army Uniforms

Officers:
Ceremonial (Mess kit)
Midnight blue "monkey jacket" and trousers (the latter with a red side stripe), white shirt and gloves, black bow tie, black sash, gold buttons.
Service Dress
Dark olive brown peaked cap, gold chin strap and gold oak-leaf decoration to peak edge according to rank, gold cap badge consisting of crescent and star within an oak wreath all on a cloth backing of the regimental facing colour. Dark olive brown single-breasted, open-necked jacket, four (gold) button front, four pockets, regimental collar patches, badges of rank on the shoulder-straps, single rear vent. Button design is an oak wreath with a small crescent and star at the top opening. Majors, lieutenant-colonels and colonels wear on the shoulder the button design in gold on a cloth backing in the regimental facing colour; generals wear red backing and red collar patches. Fawn shirt, black tie, black gloves and shoes, dark olive brown trousers.
Battle Dress
Hat as above, or black beret (same badge), dark olive brown BD of British style but front buttons (brown plastic, plain) visible. The trousers have a large pocket on the side of the left thigh. American pattern webbing, black boots, US pattern helmet. The badges of rank on the shoulders are woven in yellow cloth.

Other Ranks:
As for officers except: hat badge is a star and crescent without oak leaves; no ceremonial or service dress is worn; brown leather chin strap to peaked cap; badges of rank in yellow cloth are worn on the upper arms.

Miscellaneous
Paratroopers and army pilots wear a winged crescent and star in gold metal on the left breast above the pocket. Officers having passed the general staff college course wear a crimson shield on the left breast pocket bearing a design in gold showing Kemel Attaturk's head in a sun burst, the winged crescent and star, crossed bayonets and an anchor.

Badges of rank
Yellow chevrons, point down, on the upper arms:
Lance corporal (Astsubay Adayi) – one chevron.
Corporal (Çavuş) – two chevrons.
Sergeant (Ustçavuş) – three chevrons.
Sergeant major (Başçavuş) – four chevrons.
Service stripes take the form of horizontal yellow bars on the left cuff and can be up to four in number.

Turkish Army Flags
Two flags are carried by infantry, cavalry and artillery units at regimental level. One, which could be equated to the British "Queen's Colour", is an adaptation of the national flag and is oblong in shape, fringed in gold and bearing in the top corner nearest the pike a gold sun surrounded by sixteen golden stars; in the centre of the flag is the silver star and crescent and across the base of the flag is the regimental designation in gold. The pike is wood, covered in red leather and the tip is the gold star and crescent. This flag is held in great regard and handled with the utmost care. It is awarded medals just like a serving soldier and has a soldier's record sheet. If damaged in action the flag is awarded the Turkish equivalent of the American Purple Heart, and an entry is made on to the record book. The medals are kept on a velvet cushion together with the flag in the regimental commander's office.

The second or regimental colour is the same size and has the same pike as the first colour but is in cloth of the regimental facing colour and bears in the centre a device in gold relating to the regiment (infantry – crossed rifles, artillery – crossed cannon barrels behind a rocket, air corps regiments – the winged star and crescent). Across the top in gold the divisional designation; across the bottom the regimental designation. At battalion level only one triangular flag is carried; this is in the regimental facing colour and bears the regimental device as shown above. Each company has a smaller, triangular flag in the facing colour and with the regimental device.

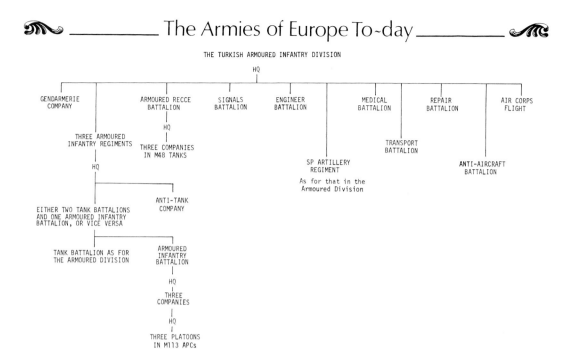

THE TURKISH ARMOURED INFANTRY DIVISION

```
                                              HQ
    │          │            │          │          │          │          │
GENDARMERIE  ARMOURED RECCE  SIGNALS   ENGINEER   MEDICAL    REPAIR     AIR CORPS
COMPANY      BATTALION       BATTALION BATTALION  BATTALION  BATTALION  FLIGHT
                 │
                 HQ                                 TRANSPORT
THREE ARMOURED   │                                  BATTALION
INFANTRY REGIMENTS  THREE COMPANIES
                 IN M48 TANKS
    │                                    SP ARTILLERY          ANTI-AIRCRAFT
    HQ                                    REGIMENT              BATTALION
    │          │
    │         ANTI-TANK                  As for that in the
    │         COMPANY                    Armoured Division
EITHER TWO TANK BATTALIONS
AND ONE ARMOURED INFANTRY
BATTALION, OR VICE VERSA
    │          │
TANK BATTALION AS FOR   ARMOURED
THE ARMOURED DIVISION   INFANTRY
                        BATTALION
                            │
                            HQ
                            │
                          THREE
                        COMPANIES
                            │
                            HQ
                            │
                       THREE PLATOONS
                       IN M113 APCs
```

Below, a photograph taken some ten years ago showing a platoon of Turkish Army infantry. Note British-style helmets, generally British appearance of the battledress, and the elderly German Mauser K.98 rifles and leather pouches. Right, a bugler of today's Turkish Army wears the same basic dress but of a neater appearance, and with American accessories. Note helmet decal. (Camera Press)

Centre, the Turkish Army cap badge motif; left to right, collar patches of the Armoured, Signals, Imams (chaplains) and Medical branches.

Officers rank badges (gold, five pointed stars; aspirants, a gold bar)

Aspirant (Asteğmen)	– one gold bar.	
Second Lieutenant (Teğmen)	– one star.	
Lieutenant (Üsteğmen)	– two stars.	
Captain (Yüzbaşi)	– three stars.	
Major (Binbaşi)	– one star	worn above a gold oak wreath with a small crescent and star in its tips – the centre of the wreath bearing the facing colour.
Lieutenant-Colonel (Yarbay)	– two stars	
Colonel (Albay)	– three stars	
Brigadier (Tuğgeneral)	– one star	worn above a golden oak wreath, star and crescent as before but backed with crossed silver sabres and all on a red cloth ground.
Major-General (Tümgeneral)	– two stars	
Lieutenant-General (Korgeneral)	– three stars	
General (Orgeneral)	– four stars	
General of the Army (Maresal) (Field Marshal)	– a gold shoulder-strap, edged with gold oak leaves and bearing the generals wreath, star, crescent and sabres badge on a red ground.	

Facing Colours on Collar Tabs (also worn behind hat badges and in field officers' wreaths)

Tanks – black, yellow tank badge, guns pointing outwards.
Artillery – dark blue.
Engineers – dark blue.
Signals – light blue with two yellow lighting flashes.
Infantry – dark green.
Transport – light blue with yellow wheel.
Supply – black with yellow wheel.
Medical – crimson with:

        a. medical – two yellow snakes wound around a glass.
        b. apothecaries – two yellow snakes interwound.
        c. meat inspectors – one yellow snake wound around a glass.

Music – light crimson with a yellow "key" on five lines.
Generals – red, square topped with gold oak leaves.
Education service and priests – light green with a yellow flaming torch.
Army Air Corps – dark blue (wings worn on left breast).
Paratroops – dark green (wings worn on left breast).
Military Police – dark blue with a narrow red edging.
Legal Services – dark green with a yellow sword and scales badge.
"Domestic Services" (bakers etc) – pink.
Officers on the General Staff – crimson.

THE WARSAW PACT

As far as the public in the Iron Curtain countries is concerned the Warsaw Pact was a purely defensive measure, forced on the peaceful socialist community by the entry of the "revanchist" Federal Republic of Germany in NATO on 9 May 1955. Two days later the party chiefs of Albania*, Bulgaria, Hungary, Poland, Rumania, Czechoslovakia, the German Democratic Republic and the Soviet Union met in Warsaw at a "Conference of European Countries for the Realisation of Peace and Security in Europe". On 14 May they signed a "Treaty of Friendship, Co-operation and Mutual Support" – the Warsaw Pact.

Although introduced as a retaliatory measure against the Federal Republic of Germany's entry to NATO, the eastern bloc signatories of the Warsaw Pact had threatened to form the Warsaw Pact organisation as far back as November 1954.

The most important articles of the Pact read as follows:

"*Article 1*: The signatories declare that in accordance with the Charter of the United Nations they will refrain from the threat or the use of force in their international relations and, in the case of international disputes, will settle them by peaceful means so as not to endanger world peace and security.

Article 2: The signatories declare their readiness to partake in all international negotiations, whose aims are world peace and security, in the spirit of sincere co-operation and will support the realisation of these aims with their entire forces. The signatories will also strive, in union with other states, who may desire such co-operation, to put into action such measures as may lead to general disarmament and to the banning of atom and hydrogen bombs and other weapons of mass destruction.

Article 3: The signatories will consult about all important international questions which affect their common interests and will be guided by the considerations of the securing of world peace and security.

They will consult jointly in the interests of their common defence and the maintenance of peace and security immediately that it seems to one of the signatories that there is the danger of an armed attack on one or more of the Pact members.

Article 4: In the case of an armed attack in Europe on one or more of the Pact members by any state or group of states, each signatory, in realisation of the right of individual or collective self defence as laid down in Article 51 of the United Nations' Charter will render to that member or those members subject to such an attack, support, individually and in concert with the other signatories, with all the means which appear necessary including the use of military force. The members of the Pact will consult immediately concerning those common actions which are to be taken in order to achieve the re-establishment and maintenance of world peace and security.

In accordance with the United Nations Charter, the Security Council will be informed of those measures to be implemented under this article. These measures will cease to be applied as soon as the Security Council takes such action as is needed to restore and maintain world peace and security,

Article 5: The signatories agree to establish a united command to control those forces which it shall be

---

* Since 1961 Albania has taken no part in the proceedings of the Warsaw Pact.

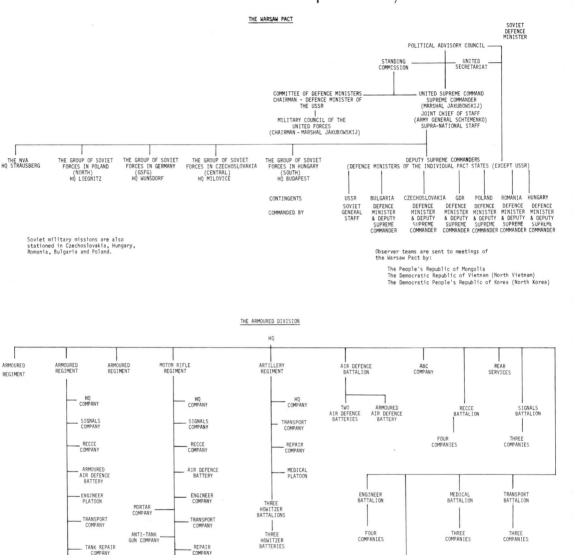

THE WARSAW PACT

```
                                                                                    SOVIET
                                                                                    DEFENCE
                                                                                    MINISTER

                                              POLITICAL ADVISORY COUNCIL _____|

                                     STANDING _____ UNITED
                                     COMMISSION                       SECRETARIAT

            COMMITTEE OF DEFENCE MINISTERS _____  UNITED SUPREME COMMAND
            CHAIRMAN - DEFENCE MINISTER OF                   SUPREME COMMANDER
                      THE USSR                               (MARSHAL JAKUBOWSKIJ)
                         |                                   JOINT CHIEF OF STAFF
            MILITARY COUNCIL OF THE                          (ARMY GENERAL SCHTEMENKO)
                 UNITED FORCES                               SUPRA-NATIONAL STAFF
            (CHAIRMAN - MARSHAL JAKUBOWSKIJ)
```

| THE NVA HQ STRAUSBERG | THE GROUP OF SOVIET FORCES IN POLAND (NORTH) HQ LIEGNITZ | THE GROUP OF SOVIET FORCES IN GERMANY (GSFG) HQ WUNSDORF | THE GROUP OF SOVIET FORCES IN CZECHOSLOVAKIA (CENTRAL) HQ MILOVICE | THE GROUP OF SOVIET FORCES IN HUNGARY (SOUTH) HQ BUDAPEST | DEPUTY SUPREME COMMANDERS (DEFENCE MINISTERS OF THE INDIVIDUAL PACT STATES (EXCEPT USSR) |

CONTINGENTS

COMMANDED BY

USSR	BULGARIA	CZECHOSLOVAKIA	GDR	POLAND	ROMANIA	HUNGARY
SOVIET GENERAL STAFF	DEFENCE MINISTER & DEPUTY SUPREME COMMANDER	DEFENCE MINISTER & DEPUTY SUPREME COMMANDER	DEFENCE MINISTER & DEPUTY SUPREME COMMANDER	DEFENCE MINISTER & DEPUTY SUPREME COMMANDER	DEFENCE MINISTER & DEPUTY SUPREME COMMANDER	DEFENCE MINISTER & DEPUTY SUPREME COMMANDER

Soviet military missions are also stationed in Czechoslovakia, Hungary, Romania, Bulgaria and Poland.

Observer teams are sent to meetings of the Warsaw Pact by:

The People's Republic of Mongolia
The Democratic Republic of Vietnam (North Vietnam)
The Democratic People's Republic of Korea (North Korea)

THE ARMOURED DIVISION

HQ

| ARMOURED REGIMENT | ARMOURED REGIMENT | ARMOURED REGIMENT | MOTOR RIFLE REGIMENT | ARTILLERY REGIMENT | AIR DEFENCE BATTALION | ABC COMPANY | REAR SERVICES |

ARMOURED REGIMENT
- HQ COMPANY
- SIGNALS COMPANY
- RECCE COMPANY
- ARMOURED AIR DEFENCE BATTERY
- ENGINEER PLATOON
- TRANSPORT COMPANY
- TANK REPAIR COMPANY
- ABC PLATOON
- THREE ARMOURED BATTALIONS
  - THREE ARMOURED COMPANIES

ARMOURED REGIMENT
- MORTAR COMPANY
- ANTI-TANK GUN COMPANY
- ANTI-TANK GUIDED WEAPONS BATTERY

MOTOR RIFLE REGIMENT
- HQ COMPANY
- SIGNALS COMPANY
- RECCE COMPANY
- AIR DEFENCE BATTERY
- ENGINEER COMPANY
- TRANSPORT COMPANY
- REPAIR COMPANY
- ABC PLATOON
- THREE MOTOR RIFLE BATTALIONS
  - THREE MOTOR RIFLE COMPANIES

ARTILLERY REGIMENT
- HQ COMPANY
- TRANSPORT COMPANY
- REPAIR COMPANY
- MEDICAL PLATOON
- THREE HOWITZER BATTALIONS
- THREE HOWITZER BATTERIES

ARMOURED BATTALION
- THREE TANK COMPANIES

AIR DEFENCE BATTALION
- TWO AIR DEFENCE BATTERIES
- ARMOURED AIR DEFENCE BATTERY

ABC COMPANY
- RECCE BATTALION
  - FOUR COMPANIES

REAR SERVICES
- SIGNALS BATTALION
  - THREE COMPANIES
- ENGINEER BATTALION
  - FOUR COMPANIES
- MEDICAL BATTALION
  - THREE COMPANIES
- TRANSPORT BATTALION
  - THREE COMPANIES
- ROCKET BATTALION
  - FOUR BATTERIES

decided, based on common agreement, to place at the disposal of such a command. They will also take other such agreed measures as seem necessary to strengthen their armed capacity in order to be able to protect the peaceful work of their peoples and the integrity of their borders and territories and the capability to resist possible aggression.

...   .

Article 7: The signatories bind themselves not to join any coalition or alliance nor to conclude any treaties whose aims contradict the aims of this Pact. They declare that their duties under existing international treaties are not in contradiction with the terms of this Pact.

Article 8: The signatories declare that they will act in regard to one another in the spirit of friendship for the further development and strengthening of economic and cultural ties with one another in accordance with the rules of mutual respect for their independence and sovereignty and non-interference in one another's internal affairs.

Article 9: Entry to this Pact is open to other states who, regardless of their social and political organisation, declare their readiness to work for the unification of the efforts of the peace loving nations for the purpose of the realisation of the peace and security of the nations. This entry will be effective with the agreement of the Pact members, after the deposition of an application of accession with the government of the Peoples Republic of Poland.

...   .

Article 11: This Pact will remain binding for twenty years. For Pact members who have not deposited a declaration of secession with the government of the Peoples Republic of Poland one year before the end of this period, the Pact remains binding for a further ten years.

Should a system for the collective security of Europe which would lead to the conclusion of a treaty whose aims coincide with those of this Pact come into being, this Pact becomes void on the day of ratification of such a treaty."

Apart from the already explained reason for the conclusion of the Warsaw Pact, other factors had led the Soviet Union to abandon the system of bilateral military pacts which she had used with her allies since the end of the Second World War in favour of this new, multilateral military pact complex.

Stalin had ruled the Iron Curtain countries with a rod of iron and had demanded utter obedience to his commands from the Communist parties of all Communist-controlled states of the world. Tito in Yugoslavia and Mao Tse-Tung in Red China had cracked open the apparent world-wide Communist monolith; and after Stalin's death Khruschev and his colleagues had sought for an integral strategy to maintain as much unity in the socialist camp as possible. The leading role of the Soviet Communist party was to be voluntarily acknowledged by the other Communist parties of the world. In the political sphere the conference of Communist party leaders was to be the tool of integration; economically, the Council for Mutual Economic Aid (COMECON) served its role; and militarily the Warsaw Pact was to play its part in keeping the vassal states true to Russia's party line.

Another factor was that since the evacuation of Austria by the victorious powers in 1955, Russia required a new military excuse for the continued stationing of her troops on Hungarian and Rumanian soil (the old excuse was the protection of her lines of communication with her occupation forces in Austria). It was thus no coincidence that the Warsaw Pact was signed one day before the conclusion of the international treaty on the state of Austria. Oberver nations at the conclusion of the Warsaw Pact were Red China, Mongolia, North Vietnam and North Korea; Red China soon withdrew from her "observer" capacity when she broke with Russia.

The following Pact organisations were called into being in order to carry out the decisions of the Pact members:

The Political Advisory Council to which each signatory state sent a government member or another representative. It meets twice a year and has its seat in Moscow, where a Standing Commission for the consideration of foreign affairs, co-ordination of plans, organisation, training and equipment policy, and the United Secretariat (made up of representatives from all signatories) are permanently active to implement Pact policy. The Political Advisory Council is responsible for all matters of the supra-national military organisation and for the strengthening of the armed potential of the member states. The general secretary of the

Council is at time of writing the Soviet deputy foreign minister Nikolai Pawlowitsch Firjubin. The post is always filled by a Russian.

The military organisation is headed by a *United Supreme Command* which commands those forces placed at its disposal by the Pact signatories. Deployment of Soviet forces within other Pact states is governed by a series of treaties drawn up between the Soviet Union and Poland, the GDR, Hungary and Czechoslovakia (between 1956 and 1958 Soviet troops were stationed in Rumania but were withdrawn during the latter year). The current supreme commander of the Warsaw Pact forces is Marshal of the Soviet Union Iwan Iwanowitsch Jakubowskij; his "Joint Chief of Staff" is Army General Sergej Schtemenko, also a Russian. The United Supreme Command has its seat in Moscow, and the Supreme Commander is always a Russian. Under the Joint Chief of Staff is a supra-national staff organisation made up of members of the staffs of the armies of the Warsaw Pact.

The Deputy Supreme Commanders of the War-

saw Pact are the defence ministers of the individual states or such army commanders as are nominated to command the national contingents. In theory the national contingents of the Warsaw Pact countries are commanded by their Deputy Supreme Commanders.

On 30 October 1956 the government of the USSR issued a statement to the effect that Soviet troops would in future only be stationed in foreign countries with the full agreement of the host state, this statement being prompted by the Hungarian uprising. The subsequent action in Czechoslovakia in 1968 speaks for itself: the conditions which must be satisfied before such "full agreement" is deemed to exist are not particularly rigorous.

Albania withdrew from the Warsaw Pact on 13 September 1968 in protest against the invasion of Czechoslovakia by the forces of the USSR, Poland, the GDR, Hungary and Bulgaria. The Warsaw Pact powers have refused to acknowledge this withdrawal even though Albania had not been invited to participate in any of the Pact's conferences or

THE MOTOR RIFLE DIVISION

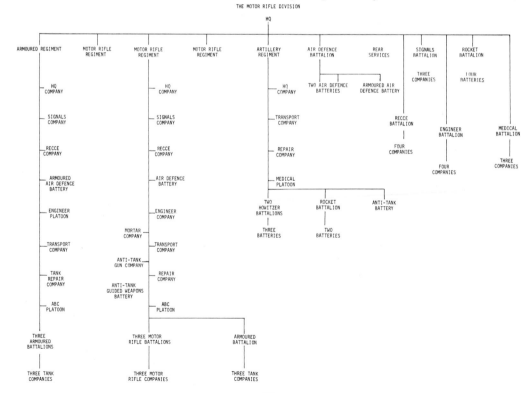

manoeuvres since 1962 due to Albania's adherence to China's brand of Communist doctrine.

During 1956 and 1957, the Soviet Union concluded treaties with Poland (17 December 1956), the GDR (12 March 1957), Rumania (15 April 1957) and Hungary (27 May 1957) regulating the stationing of Soviet troops in each of these countries. These treaties were of a very long term nature but in the case of Rumania Soviet troops moved out of that country in 1958. The common basis of these treaties is the threat posed to the socialist camp by the rearmament of West Germany and the presence of American forces in Europe. Although the phraseology of the individual treaties is not identical, the intent is the same. The most important articles of the Soviet-Polish treaty are as follows:

"Article 1: The temporary presence of Soviet troops in Poland can in no way affect the sovereignty of the Polish state and cannot lead to interference in the internal affairs of the People's Republic of Poland.

Article 2: a. The numerical strength of the Soviet forces temporarily stationed in Poland, and their deployment, will be regulated by special agreement between the governments of the USSR and the People's Republic of Poland. b. Movements of Soviet troops on Polish territory outside their places of deployment will, in each individual case, require the approval of the Polish government or of such Polish authorities as may be entrusted with this power by the Polish government."

In the years since the signing of the Warsaw Pact, the Iron Curtain countries have concluded a series of bilateral pacts of "friendship, co-operation and mutual support" among themselves. In each case the initial period of validity of these pacts is twenty years; unless positive action is taken to terminate them at this point, the treaties automatically extend themselves, usually for recurrent periods of five or ten years. The dates of the signing of these treaties are:

USSR – GDR	– 12 June 1964
USSR – Poland	– 8 April 1965
Poland – Czechoslovakia	– 1 March 1967
Poland – GDR	– 15 March 1967
Czechoslovakia – GDR	– 17 March 1967
Poland – Bulgaria	– 6 April 1967
USSR – Bulgaria	– 12 May 1967
Hungary – GDR	– 18 May 1967

Bulgaria – GDR	– 7 September 1967
USSR – Hungary	– 7 September 1967
Bulgaria – Czechoslovakia	– 26 April 1968
Poland – Hungary	– 16 May 1968
Hungary – Czechoslovakia	– 15 June 1968
Rumania – Czechoslovakia	– 17 August 1968
Hungary – Bulgaria	– 10 July 1969
USSR – Czechoslovakia	– 6 May 1970
USSR – Rumania	– 8 July 1970
Poland – Rumania	– 13 November 1970
Bulgaria – Rumania	– 19 November 1970

The reason for the appearance of this complex of treaties was a need by the USSR to reinforce its lead ideologically over its vassal states in the face of the Chinese heresy which threatened to split the socialist camp wide open. It is rumoured, for example, that in the spring of 1966 Rumania circulated proposals among the lesser Warsaw Pact members demanding that the post of Supreme Commander of the Pact's forces should rotate among the nations of the Pact and not be a Soviet monopoly. She also suggested that the costs incurred by the stationing of Soviet troops in a host country should be borne by that host country alone and not by the Pact as a whole, and that the use of nuclear weapons by the Pact must be agreed upon by all Pact members in advance. The Soviet Union and Poland (nervous of renewed German aggression) saw the break-up of the Pact ahead if things were allowed to slide and thus demanded that the Pact members bind themselves more closely together with the resultant series of bilateral treaties.

The Warsaw Pact in Action

Bearing in mind the text of the Pact document, one can scarcely suppress an ironic smile when one considers that the only two occasions to date on which the Pact powers have acted in earnest militarily have been in 1956 in Hungary and in 1968 in Czechoslovakia. In both cases, "comrades" have rushed to fasten their own "comrades" back into the Russian straight-jackets from which they were in danger of escaping!

On 24 October 1956 the then Hungarian government called for Soviet assistance, within the terms of the Warsaw Pact, to restore law and order in the land. On 31 October, Imré Nagy (Hungarian Premier) declared to the world that his government had now demanded that Russia withdraw her troops from Hungary immediately and also stated that it was his government's intention to leave the Warsaw

THE ARMOURED BATTALION

```
                              HQ
         ┌──────────┬──────────┴──────────┬──────────────┐
      TANK        TANK                  TANK            REAR
    COMPANY     COMPANY               COMPANY         SERVICES
                                                      PLATOON
                   │                              ┌──────┼──────┐
              THREE TANK    Each platoon       REPAIR  MEDICAL  SUPPLY
               PLATOONS    has three tanks     SECTION  SECTION SECTION
```

Pact in an attempt to become a neutral state. These points were delivered in writing to the Soviet government on 2 November 1956. In reply, Russia (also quoting the Warsaw Pact as the legal basis for her actions) put down the Hungarian revolution in a blood bath which cost 32,000 lives (7,000 of these Russian), using a call for help from Janos Kadar's rival Hungarian government (constituted on 4 November) as an additional sugar-lump to sweeten the bitter pill which Communists the world over have been trying to force down their throats ever since. No other Warsaw Pact troops participated in the suppression of the Hungarian revolution, but doubtless much active reflection took place.

The Czechoslovakian Crisis

The second occasion on which the Pact was actively engaged was in 1968 at the time of the Czechoslovak crisis. This time Russia, anxious to achieve a show of Pact solidarity to cloak her naked imperialism, raked together contingents from Poland, the GDR, Hungary and Bulgaria to march into Czechoslovakia with her own troops. Rumania, the Pact's problem child, was not even consulted about the operation and no Rumanian troops took part in the invasion.

The actual intervention, which took place on 20 August 1968, was preceded by a series of manoeuvres in the Warsaw Pact States, including one in Czechoslovakia itself ("Böhmerwald") which was ostensibly a staff exercise but which employed 42,000 men busily reconnoitering their future objectives – even if they did not at that moment realise it. As early as February 1968 the supreme commander of the Warsaw Pact forces, Marshal Jakubowskij, was in Czechoslovakia with a party of 35 very senior Pact officers. One of them, General Schadow, remarked to a Czech officer in a barracks in Leitmeritz, "Negative forces wish to remove socialism in Czechoslovakia. But the Soviet army also controls the armies of the allied lands and will help." Moscow had begun the spadework on the grave of emergent Czech liberalism.

During June, Jakubowskij set up his headquarters for the Warsaw Pact "staff" exercise "Böhmerwald" in Prague and a Russian army communications centre was installed on Ruzyne airport, just outside the city. This communications centre remained set up and manned after the end of "Böhmerwald" and played a key part in the landing of the Soviet airborne forces later used during the Czech operation. In early July 1968 units of the now-mighty Soviety fleet moved into the Atlantic from the Baltic thus placing themselves astride Europe's supply lines from America, in case NATO should contemplate resistance to Soviet action against Czechoslovakia later on. By mid-July 1968 Soviet, Polish and East German ships were in station in the Baltic, taking part in the exercise "Sever" (North) commanded by the Soviet Admiral of the Fleet S. Gorschkow. In late July extensive air exercises began in the area of the triangle, Baltic – Moscow – Black Sea. These were codenamed "Skyshield" and were controlled by Marshal of the Soviet Air Force Batizkij. From 23 July to 10 August 1968 there took place an extensive east-to-west logistics exercise, "Memel", involving the movement of thousands of reservists and vast quantities of warlike stores and vehicles from western Russia into her European satellites. The stage was being very carefully set for the public execution of the Warsaw Pact's most recent renegade.

After all the aforementioned operations were either under way or had been completed, from 11 August there began a new series of manoeuvres in southern Poland, in the GDR and in Hungary. These were the actual invasion preparations. The forces involved were divided into three army groups, A, B and C.

Army Group A, in south Poland, was commanded by Soviet Army General Pawlowskij with its headquarters in Liegnitz. It consisted of:

three Soviet tank divisions ⎫
one Soviet motor rifle division ⎬ the 20th Guards Army, normally garrisoned around Eberswalde
one Soviet airborne division* ⎭

one Polish motor rifle division
6th Polish airborne division
one Polish airforce division

7th GDR tank division

Total – 70,000 men and 1,800 tanks

Army Group B in the south of the GDR was commanded by Soviet Army General Iwan D. Velichko and had its headquarters in Leipzig. It consisted of: three Soviet tank divisions (the 1st Guards Tank Army)

11th GDR motor rifle division (less rockets and artillery)

Total – 35,000 men and 1,300 tanks

Army Group C concentrated in Hungary along the Czechoslovakian southern border with headquarters in Budapest. It consisted of:

1st Soviet tank division
2nd Soviet tank division

* This division included a Bulgarian regiment which was in the Soviet Union for training purposes.

Warsaw Pact solidarity, demonstrated by a posed group of (left to right) two Hungarians, a Polish tank soldier, a Soviet Guards artillery corporal, and a third Hungarian.

3rd Soviet tank division
one Hungarian motor rifle division
one Bulgarian motor rifle division**
one Bulgarian tank division**
four Bulgarian motor rifle companies**

Total – 40,000 men and 1,500 tanks

It is of interest that the GDR 7th Tank Division, although at that time in possession of T-55 tanks, actually used about one hundred T34/85's of World War Two vintage on the Czechoslovakian operation. While Polish units operated in their own sectors under their own formations during the invasion, the troops from the GDR, Hungary and Bulgaria were split up among Russian formations in regimental sized groups and General Ernst (commander of the 11th GDR Motor Rifle Division) found himself without a command and was "integrated" into the staff of a Soviet tank division.

Naturally the renewed presence of German troops on Czechoslovakian soil, even in a comradely capacity, was recognised by the Soviets as being an explosive situation and the GDR units were kept well hidden in the woods and finally sent home five days after the invasion.

The Hungarian contingent does not seem to have performed too well; to start with it was not a complete division which was used but a hotch-potch of units taken from various divisions of the Hungarian army. No logistic line of supply as such was set up from the Hungarian garrisons to the troops in the Czechoslovakian locations, and word has it that even the men's meals were cooked in Hungary and then transported daily over a hundred miles to the hungry recipients!

The operation of invasion itself went off well. At 11 pm Czechoslovak time on Tuesday, 20 August 1968, the gathered forces crossed the Czechoslovakian border at eighteen places and raced through the night at 60 kilometers per hour (36 mph) for their objectives. At 8.30 pm that same night an Aeroflot AN-24 machine on a special flight landed at Ruzyne airport with a cargo of 52 Soviet secret police heavily disguised as tourists and cultural officials. At 10 pm another AN-24 disgorged further tourists. The whole group now loitered innocently about the airport until midnight when, discarding their civilian clothes, they emerged in

** The Bulgars had been moved by sea into Hungary via the Soviet Union to avoid Rumanian territory.

their uniforms and took charge of the airport. The same thing happened at five other major Czechoslovakian airports and the way was thus clear for an unhindered landing of the airborne divisions – the Soviets at Ruzyne, the Poles at Pardubitz. Shortly before midnight NATO radar stations along the Iron Curtain were jammed and the movement of the hundreds of transport and fighter aircraft involved in the airlift of these divisions from their starting points in southern Poland into Czechoslovakia was controlled by the staff of the 24th Soviet Air Army, normally stationed at Wunsdorf near Berlin.

The movements of the ground troops during this invasion were apparently identical to those practised by the Warsaw Pact during the manoeuvre "Moldau" in 1966. In both cases, the main aim was to seal the Czech-West German border and this automatically involved the flooding of Czechoslovakia with Warsaw Pact troops, for the Soviets a happy accident of geography. A vital target for the invaders was the Czech railway system (Soviet logistics are heavily reliant on the railways) and by 11 pm on 20 August the important railway town of Kaschau in eastern Czechoslovakia had been captured by a Russo-Bulgarian task force from Army Group C. During the course of the night, Soviet ambassadors were busy informing various world governments of the extent and intent of the invasion.

At 1 am on 21 August Radio Prague announced the invasion to the world and stated that the Central Committee of the Czechoslovakian Communist Party regarded this as a breach of international law and that the Czech Army had been ordered to stay in its barracks and to offer no resistance.

This passive reaction undoubtedly saved thousands of lives; actual casualty figures reached about 72 Czechs killed and 702 wounded by gunfire in the period 20 August-3 September, and a further 26 killed and 104 injured in various road accidents with military vehicles belonging to the invaders. The impassioned pleas for justice and international aid which were broadcast from Czechoslovakia during the invasion produced no military reaction in the Western world, and might triumphed over right in the manner which has become only too familiar during our history.

On 16 October 1968 Czechoslovakia signed a treaty with Russia whereby the latter may station as many Soviet troops for as long as she sees fit in Czechoslovakia, and Soviet civilians may enter the country at will.

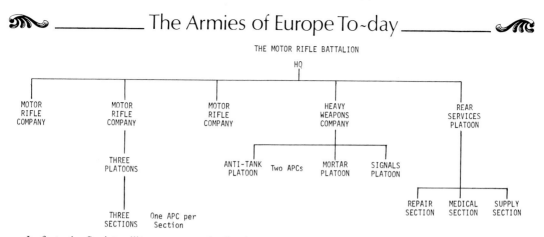

THE MOTOR RIFLE BATTALION

In fact, the Soviet military presence in Czechoslovakia today is about five divisions; the remaining Warsaw Pact invaders had all left the country by 12 November 1968.

The invasion of Czechoslovakia was an unpleasant shock for NATO in many ways. In the strictly military sense the Warsaw Pact had shown itself to be capable of launching a combined, large-scale operation in good security conditions, with a fair degree of efficiency and a high degree of speed and co-ordination. In particular, the quality and above all the apparent loyalty of the soldiers of the vassal states of the Pact proved to be higher than NATO had previously judged. The flexibility of the Warsaw Pact's logistic system, normally geared to an east-west flow and abruptly switched to a north-east-south-west axis for a period of months, must also be appreciated.

Above all, the undiminished ruthlessness of the rulers of the Soviet Union, which had lain dormant for over a decade, had been sharply brought to the forefront for those who had the eyes and the will to see it.

The Warsaw Pact in 1973

If the last decade has seen a loosening of the ties within NATO and a great degree of equalisation in the status of her members, almost the opposite can be said of the Warsaw Pact. Encouraged by her successful Czechoslovakian adventure and apparently unworried by economic pressures to reduce "defence" spending, the Soviet Union is now in firmer command of her East European empire than ever before. The expansion of the Soviet fleet has cost vast sums but the end result is that Russia must now be counted as a real world power as opposed to a continental power (which she was without an effective fleet).

During 1972 NATO invited the Soviet Union, the GDR, Poland, Czechoslovakia and Hungary to a series of talks aimed at Mutual Balanced Forces Reduction (MBFR). The now-familiar pattern of events to be expected at conferences involving Communist delegations is currently being played out in Vienna, with the Soviet Union delaying even the agreement as to who should take part in the talks and in what capacity, while she and her satellites continue to increase their conventional armed forces at a quite alarming rate.

These increases have been reported from behind the Iron Curtain for the last two or three years, and only recently was it heard that the GDR was supposed to have received deliveries of over 2,000 T62 medium tanks and that their tank troops have increased in size from three tanks to five. Similar drum-beats have been heard from other parts of the Pact jungle; new units being raised, establishments increased, new and improved equipment replacing the old.

The end effect of Communist strategy and delaying tactics in Vienna seems to be aimed at achieving agreement on reductions of forces in Europe so that, at the worst, the Warsaw Pact may have to disband their newly-raised forces (thus leaving them with armies at the same strength as they were in, say, 1971) while NATO will carry out genuine reductions thus tipping the balance fairly heavily in Moscow's direction. In fact, the Communists have only to drag out the Vienna MBFR talks for a little longer and NATO will be carrying out her own unilateral force reductions without any *quid pro quo* being demanded from the Warsaw Pact. (Economic pres-

SOVIET AIRBORNE DIVISION

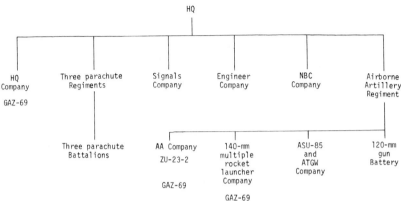

7,5000 men in all

sures have already forced Denmark, Belgium and Federal Germany either to reduce their forces or the length of their national service, to say nothing of America's obvious difficulties.)

A measure of the Soviet Union's dictatorial control of the lesser members of the Warsaw Pact is shown by the fact that at the MBFR talks in Vienna the Soviet delegation leader, Oleg Khlestov, demanded that Hungary (which currently has 40–50,000 Soviet troops stationed on its soil) should be excluded from the originally proposed list of direct participants at the talks; this demand came as a complete surprise even to the Hungarian delegate, Endre Ustor – although, being a well-trained party member, he would never admit it. This underlines the importance to the Soviet Union of the Warsaw Pact in recent years; it has become not only a convenient tool for the control of the Eastern European nations, it is now also a useful vehicle for East-West negotiations. The danger for the Soviets is that the carefully constructed myth of a treaty organisation drawn up among equals for their mutual benefit may become at least in part a reality, even though there is no sign yet of a weakening of Soviet domination. The principle of limited sovereignty seems to have become established among Russia's satellites, and the "Brezhnew Doctrine" is apparently widely accepted in Eastern Europe.

For the future it needs only to be said that any loosening of the ties within or outside the Warsaw Pact will be very gradual and carefully controlled by Moscow at each stage.

The Effects of the Warsaw Pact on the Armies of its Member States

It would be wrong to assume that Russian influence first began to be exercised over the other armies of the Warsaw Pact states only at the signing of the treaty in 1955. As soon as Russia entered (or was dragged into) the Second World War, she began to raise and train "foreign legions" from among the numerous refugees from Nazi tyranny in Eastern Europe. While Poland and Czechoslovakia both set up governments in exile in Britain after the occupation of their countries by the German armies, Communist party members of both these and other nations were hard at work in Russia preparing for the eventual march back into their homelands. This armed assistance on the one hand had not, of course, prevented Stalin's government from undertaking such exploits as the massacre of thousands of Polish army officers at Katyn Wood – a crime which was conveniently laid at the Nazis' door in 1945 but which subsequent disclosures have conclusively shown was carried out by Russia. Immediately following the end of the war, Russia moved her political system into all those territories within her sphere of power, "removed" undesirable elements and proceeded to produce minor mirror images of herself across the map of Europe. The Polish and Czechoslovak soldiers and airmen who had fought so well under British leadership on many fronts during the Second World War were subjected to a disgraceful ordeal when they returned "home" after the cessation of hostilities. The leading positions in the new armed forces of the liberated Eastern European nations went to politically reliable men, and nowhere was the Soviet model more diligently and slavishly copied than in the Soviet Occupied Zone of Germany, the present German Democratic Republic. Uniforms, equipment, weapons and doctrine were all straight off the Russian shelf for the present-day Warsaw Pact powers, and although several have now developed (or returned to) their own outer trappings such as uniforms, everything else is still very heavily under Russian influence.

The common armament policy has some exceptions mainly in the areas of small arms and radio equipment but even in the field of armoured fighting vehicles there are national deviations. The GDR produces the following vehicles for use in its "Nationale Volks Armee": the ES 250/2A motor cycle, the P-601/A Trabant, 4 × 4 quarter ton jeep, the Robur LO 1800A, 4 × 4 two ton truck, the W-50 LA/4, 4 × 4 three ton truck, the P2S, 4 × 4 amphibious half ton truck, the P3, 4 × 4 three

quarter ton command and signals vehicle and the Horch G5, 6 × 6 five ton truck.

Czechoslovakia, the most highly industrialised Warsaw Pact state, has a widely developed series of military vehicles including the 350 cc Jawa parachutists' motor cycle, the Tatra 805, 4 × 4 one and a half ton truck, the Praga – V3S, 6 × 6 three and a half ton truck, the Tatra-138, 6 × 6 eight ton truck, the Tatra-148, S3, 6 × 6 eight ton truck, the Tatra-813 Koloss, 8 × 8 ten ton tractor, the Tatra-814 6 × 6 six ton truck, the P-32 forty ton low loader tank transporter and its big brother the P-50 sixty-three ton trailer, the DOK (Dozer Kolovy) wheeled engineer vehicle and the Tatra-111C, 6 × 6 eight cubic meter fuel tanker. In the armoured fighting vehicle field, Czechoslovakia has produced the highly successful eight-wheeled amphibious armoured personnel carrier OT-64 which is also used by the Polish army and is there known as the SKOT. Czechoslovakia also produces a range of small arms, and even her own multiple rocket

Warsaw Pact equipment standardisation is extensive but certain non-Russian items are produced and exported within the system. Here Hungarian engineers wearing Polish-made helmets work with Soviet bridging equipment.

launcher. Hungary produces her own PSZH 4 × 4 armoured amphibious scout car. There is no doubt, however, that the centre of gravity of military strength within the Warsaw Pact lies firmly in Soviet hands; tanks and rockets, the backbone of offensive operations, are all supplied by the Soviet Union.

Military doctrine is also dispensed under monopoly conditions and the Soviet military academy churns out a regular stream of foreign disciples who return to their native Warsaw Pact countries sporting that important white, rhombic badge on their right breast pocket. Apart from educating and training officers of the Pact armies, Moscow ensures her command of the lesser armies by planting her own nationals in the armed forces of her allies. For example, the Polish army enjoyed the presence of thousands of Russian military advisers in the formative period after the war. In 1956 many of these, including Marshal of the Soviet Union Rokossowski, left Poland and returned home; but at the beginning of the 1960s Gomulka had a new flood of Russian officers forced down his throat, and care was taken to see that they occupied key positions within the Polish Army. It went so far that Russian officers and their families lived in Poland for years and "became" Poles (the "Deputy Polish Defence Minister and Chief of the Political Administration of the Polish Army", General J. Urbanowicz, is a Russian, as is the Quarter Master General of the Polish Army).

The Military Potential of the Warsaw Pact

In round figures the statistics show the following situations:

Population	352,195,000
Army (including Strategic Rocket troops)	3,142,000
Medium Tanks	78,900
Air force personnel	725,000
Planes	6,000
Naval personnel	525,500
Para-military forces	550,000
Militia	3,000,000

When it is considered that these forces are centrally controlled and motivated (at least to a degree) some idea of the military potential can perhaps be gained.

The Group of Soviet Forces in Germany (GSFG)

6th Guards Motor Rifle Division	– HQ Bernau.
6th Guards Armoured Division	– HQ Lutherstadt-Wittenberg.
7th Guards Armoured Division	– HQ Dessau-Rosslau.
9th Guards Armoured Division	– HQ Neustrelitz.
9th Armoured Division	– HQ Riesa.
10th Guards Armoured Division	– HQ Krampuitz near Potsdam (outside West Berlin).
11th Guards Armoured Division	– HQ Dresden-Klotzsche.
12th Guards Armoured Division	– HQ Neuruppin.
14th Guards Motor Rifle Division	– HQ Jüterbog.
19th Guards Motor Rifle Division	– HQ Döberitz near Potsdam.
20th Guards Motor Rifle Division	– HQ Grimma (near Leipzig).
20th Guards Armoured Division	– HQ Jena.
25th Armoured Division	– HQ Vogelsang (near Berlin).
27th Guards Motor Rifle Division	– HQ Halle.
32nd Motor Rifle Division	– HQ Perleberg/Prignitz.
39th Guards Motor Rifle Division	– HQ Ohrdruf in Thuringia.
47th Guards Armoured Division	– HA Hillersleben in the Altmark.
57th Guards Motor Rifle Division	– HQ Naumburg on the Saale.
94th Guards Motor Rifle Division	– HQ Schwerin.
207th Motor Rifle Division	– HQ Stendal in the Altmark.

THE UNION OF SOVIET SOCIALIST REPUBLICS

Population – 246,800,000.   **Capital** – Moscow.

Armed Forces:

Army – 2,000,000 men.

Strategic Rocket Forces (*offensive*) – 350,000 men with a total of about 1,530 ICBMs (Intercontinental ballistic missiles) including 210 SS-7s (Saddler) and SS-8 (Sasin), 290 SS-9 (Scarp), 970 SS-11s, 60 SS-13 (Savage); 600 Intermediate range ballistic missiles (IRBM) and medium range ballistic missiles (MRBM); 500 being SS-5 (Skean) IRBM and 100 SS-4 (Sandal) MRBM, the majority of which are sited near Russia's European borders; 560 submarine-launched ballistic missiles (SLBM) in 61 submarines – 29 Y Class nuclear-powered vessels each with 16 SS-N-6 missiles, 10 H-II Class nuclear-powered vessels with 3 SS-N-5 (Serb) missiles and 10 G-II Class diesel-powered submarines each with 3 Serbs; 12 diesel-powered GI Class submarines each with 3 SS-N-4 (Sark) missiles. Nuclear weapons can also be delivered by the following long range bombers: 100 TU-95 Bears and 40 Mya-4 Bison. Their basic range is extended by the use of 50 Mya-4 Bison tanker aircraft and mid-air refuelling technique. Medium range bombers include 500 TU-16 Badgers and 200 TU-22 Blinders.

Strategic Rocket Forces (*defensive*) also known as the PVO-STRANY – 500,000 soldiers and airmen and the following equipment: early warning and control radar systems, 3,000 combat aircraft including 1,060 MiG-17s, MiG-19s and Yak-25s, 800 Su-9s, 1,140 Yak-28P Firebars, TU-28P Fiddlers, SU-11 Flagon-As and MiG-23 Foxbat interceptors.

Ground (Henhouse) radar is complemented by sky-borne radar carried in 10 modified TU-114 Moss aircraft.

Anti-ballistic missiles (ABM) include four silo-based sites around Moscow holding 64 Galosh long range missiles in all. Galosh has a range of about 200 miles.

These fighter aircraft and ABMs are backed up by 10,000 SAMs distributed over 1,600 sites mainly based along Russia's European border, although about 25% of them are located in the Far East against China.

Missile types are: 5,000 SA-2s with Fan Song radar and HE warheads which can engage planes at altitudes from 1,000–80,000 feet (slant range 25 miles); SA-3 two-stage low altitude missiles (slant range 15 miles) HE warhead; SA-4s on tracked carriers. Air portable missiles: SA-5s, slant range 50 miles, and SA-6 SAM designed for use against low flying aircraft. Anti-aircraft artillery ranges from 14·5 mm and 23 mm to 57 mm guns, both towed and self propelled.

Navy – 386,000 sailors, 14,000 marines and 75,000 naval air arm. 34 nuclear-powered hunter submarines (C, N and V classes); 210 diesel-powered hunter submarines (B, F, Q, R, W and Z classes); 26 nuclear-powered long range cruising submarines (E class), and 25 diesel-powered long range cruising submarines (J and W classes) each with four to eight SS-N-3, 450 miles range missiles.

Surface ships include 2 anti-submarine helicopter-carrying cruisers each with 20 Ka-25 helicopters and 4 SAM; 1 Kara class cruiser with SAM and SSM, 4 Kresta I class and 2 Kresta II class cruisers with SAM and SSM, 4 Kynda class cruisers with SAM and SSM; 1 Sverdlov class cruiser with SAM; 10 without SAM or SSM and 4 older cruisers; 3 Krivak class destroyers with SAM and SSM; 5 Kanin class destroyers with SAM; 3 Krupny class destroyers with SSM; 4 Kildin class destroyers with SSM; 17 Kashin class destroyers with SAM; 6 modified Kotlin class destroyers with SAM, 17 Kotlin class destroyers; 40 Skory class destroyers.

112 ocean-going escorts.

250 coastal escorts and submarine chasers.

6 Nanuchka class escorts with SSM and SAM.

117 Osa class fast patrol boats with STYX SSM.

30 Komar class fast patrol boats with STYX SSM.

250 MTBs.

180 ocean-going minesweepers and 125 coastal minesweepers.

105 landing ships and many more landing craft.

The numerous Russian trawlers which haunt NATO naval manoeuvres bristling with radio and other electronic equipment are not taken into account here.

The main ports in the Soviet Union are protected by shore based SS-N-3 Shaddock missiles and batteries of guns.

The naval air arm is, as yet, shore based and includes the following bombers: 300 Tu-16 with either one Kipper or two Kelt ASMs; 60 Tu-22 Blinders, 40 Il-28 Beagle light bombers equipped with torpedoes, 50 Tu-95 Bear long range maritime reconnaissance planes and 150 Tu-16 Badgers in the reconnaissance or tanker roles.

Amphibious aircraft include 80 Be-12 Mail anti-submarine warfare (ASW) aircraft, and other ASW aircraft are 140 Il-18 Mays and 240 Mi-4 and Ka-25 helicopters.

The marines are organised into brigades and assigned to the various fleets. They are trained and equipped as for normal Soviet army infantry, and only their uniforms pick them out from their army colleagues. They use T54/55 medium tanks, PT-76 light tanks and the usual range of amphibious APCs.

Air Force

550,000 men and 9,000 combat aircraft, the long range component of which is shown in the offensive strategic rocket forces.

The tactical air force has about 4,300 aircraft being a mixture of MiG-17s, MiG-19s (older type fighters) and MiG-21J Fishbed Js and Yak 28P Firebars, representing the newer planes. The ground attack Su-7 Fitter and the Yak-28 Brewer light bomber are also modern, and the newest arrival is the variable geometry Flogger. Transport aircraft number about 17,000 and include 900 Il-14 and

An-24, 800 An-12 and Il-18 medium transports, and 10 An-22 heavy transports. In an emergency, the airliners of Aeroflot would also be pressed into service. Helicopters: apart from those 800 machines in use with army units, there are about 950 others used by the air force itself. Types include the Mi-6 and Mi-8 troop carriers and the Mi-10 and Mi-12 heavy load carriers.

Para-military forces – 175,000 border guards, 125,000 security troops, 1,500,000 militia.

Defence Spending – 17·9 billion roubles in 1972.

The breakdown of the member states of the Soviet Union:

State	Population	Capital	Population of Capital
Soviet Russia	131,394,000	Moscow	7,300,000
The Ukraine	47,910,000	Kiew	1,764,000
Bielorussia	9,152,000	Minsk	996,000
Usbekistan	12,500,000	Taschkent	1,461,000
Kazakstan	13,467,000	Alma-Ata	776,000
Georgia	4,785,000	Tbilissi	927,000
Azerbaijan	5,323,000	Baku	1,314,000
Lithuania	3,200,000	Wilna	400,000
Moldavia	3,669,000	Kischinjow	395,000
Latvia	2,412,000	Riga	755,000
Kirgizistan	3,080,000	Frunse	453,000
Tadschikistan	3,080,000	Duschanbe	400,000
Armenia	2,608,000	Jerewan	818,000
Turkmenistan	2,288,000	Aschchabad	266,000
Estonia	1,391,000	Tallin	387,000
TOTAL	226,259,000		

The Soviet Army and Military Doctrine

The Soviet Army of 1973 contains 106 Motor Rifle Divisions, 51 Tank Divisions, and six (some sources say seven) Airborne Divisions. Of these, 80 divisions are maintained at full peace strength in personnel and equipment; these are the "Category I" formations. Forty further divisions, "Category

II", have from 50-75% of the peace strength personnel and the full complement of equipment, although this will not be of the newest pattern. The missing personnel are reservists who could be recalled to their units on mobilisation within eight days.

The remainder of the army, "Category III", have less than 75% of their peacetime strength of personnel and equipment and this equipment is of older pattern. These formations would require some weeks to be brought up to full strength. All Soviet divisions deployed in the Warsaw Pact states of Eastern Europe are Category I units and it is common knowledge that extra forces, particularly armoured units, have been moved into these states from Soviet Russia in the last two years. It is thought that this escalation of the Soviet conventional forces (and of those of their Warsaw Pact vassals) is a well-thought-out gambit to precede the current SALT and MBFR negotiations in Europe.

The disposition of these Soviet divisions is as follows:

Western USSR	– 60
Volga basin and lake Baikal	– 8
Caucasus	– 21
Poland	– 2
GDR	– 20
Czechoslovakia	– 5
Hungary	– 4
Eastern USSR (Chinese border)	– 44

It can thus clearly be seen that even though China and Russia have their quarrels in the east, the military centre of gravity as far as the Soviets are concerned lies firmly in Europe; all the optimistic theorising that has recently been heard about massive transfers of Soviet divisions to the Chinese border areas is thus unfounded and misleading – the threat not only remains but has recently increased.

The Soviet Army is composed of professional officers and warrant officers and conscripted NCOs and men. Conscripts serve for two years in the army and the air force, three years in the navy.

In view of the importance which the Soviets attach to their Strategic Rocket Forces, these are considered not to be part of the army but have their own department in the Defence Ministry answering directly to the General Staff and on the same authoritative level as the High Command of the Ground Forces. Airborne formations (paratroops) are in a similar position although they do come under the High Command of the Ground Forces for administrative and technical control.

Political control of the Soviet army is ensured at every level of command down to company size units although military commanders now enjoy much greater independence from their political watchdogs than they did in former years.

The Communist Party machine is constantly in touch with conscripts during their military service and much of the Soviet soldier's free time is taken up supporting local party activities. The Young Communists' Party (Komsomol) is particularly heavily engaged with the political education of young soldiers. All ranks of the Soviet Army are fully aware that they belong to an invincible army (invincible largely due to its immense size) that is armed with the most modern weapons, commanded in the most advanced manner, and is the "Sir Galahad" of the contemporary· military scene because its principles, as formulated by Lenin, are unquestionably right. If there *were* a God, they feel, he would certainly be on Soviet Russia's side. Morale is high and trouble with conscientious objectors and other symptoms of capitalist decadence practically unknown. Unlike the situation in the armies of Sweden, Denmark, Holland and West Germany, soldiers' haircuts are severe and complaints against this fashion have not yet been heard.

The doctrine of the Soviet Army states that although Russia will not be the initiator of a nuclear conflict, it is inevitable that any future major war will degenerate to this level, and thus heavy emphasis is placed during basic training and exercises on practising troops in the use of their NBC defensive equipment. Based on the lessons of the Second World War, the Soviets also spend much time in training for night-fighting and in training in severe weather conditions. Survival in the field in the legendary Russian winter weather is extensively taught, and Soviet military equipments are all designed to operate in sub-zero conditions. This does not mean that the Soviet Army is not prepared to fight and operate in conditions of extreme heat; the Soviet Union includes plenty of areas in central Asia where desert conditions exist, and full advantage is taken of them for military training.

When it comes to evaluating modes of operations, the offensive is given clear pride of place in Soviet military doctrine. The defensive is accepted as being a phase which might have to be adopted for a limited period, but only in order to be able to concentrate forces at some other point along the front so that a decisive break through may be achieved after which all formations will at once resume the offensive. For the same long-term reasons a withdrawal will be countenanced.

The Soviets have scant regard for human life (as their casualty figures in both World Wars show) and leading formations will be fought ruthlessly to a standstill in order to achieve maximum combat value from them before following echelons pass through their exhausted comrades to take up the pursuit. Soviet armoured fighting vehicles are laid out with this strategic principle in mind; relatively little regard is given to crew comfort, the theory being that the crew will be either dead or relieved before they have time to become fatigued by their rough ride.

Projected rates of advance in war are high – in nuclear war 60-100 km per day is the target, although against a tough, well-organised defence 30–50 km per day would be acceptable. (It is the author's firm conviction that a well integrated, in-depth, anti-tank defence system would reduce these bombastic figures drastically.) This emphasis on speed *at all costs* has led to a spate of Soviet propaganda films in which the viewer is bombarded with the interminable spectacle of wave after wave of tanks and APCs roaring forwards with their crews firing with every available weapon over the side of their vehicles. Water obstacles are to be "forced" without serious reduction of speed, and heavy accent in training is laid on attacking "from the line of march". This phrase ignores the fact that the "line of march" is not a battle formation, and also that the enemy who are to be attacked may be resolute and well prepared. Nothing is easier than destroying one tank after the other if they appear in "line of march" in a well-chosen killing ground. Deployment into battle formation (line abreast) takes time which slows advance rates. Blundering on into the unknown regardless of resistance can be a very expensive tactic unless the enemy defence is thin.

Water obstacles in the Soviet Union (as far as can be judged from the Soviet military films which have been seen in the West) tend to be wide, shallow, clear, flat-bottomed and slow-moving. Thus one sees numbers of tanks "Schnorkeling" peacefully through crystal-clear water to fall upon the enemy on the hostile bank, while amphibious APCs surge invincibly across the surface of the same water-way.

Unfortunately for Soviet theorists, there are several major waterways in Europe which are deep, swift, murky and have precipitous banks. An APC or a tank may well be able to waddle or fall into such a watercourse; what he will achieve when trying to climb the hostile bank (equally steep, mined *and* covered with fire) is a different question. The sight of Soviet Motorised Rifle troops firing on the move (or through the ports of their BMP 76 APC) is equally unimpressive when examined in the cold light of day. Who has ever yet heard of a soldier who has *intentionally* hit his target from the unsure fire platform of a moving APC?

The West German "Marder" provides a quantifiable comparison: the rifleman sitting inside the vehicle "closed down" sees very little through his bull's-eye port and that which he can see can almost never be hit with a well-aimed shot when the APC is buffeting across country at some 30 km/h.

Soviet commanders below battalion level do very much as they are told, and little room is left for initiative in junior officers. Above this level the Soviet doctrine demands that the local commander should employ his individual judgement and initiative in executing his instructions. Penalties for failure incurred when following such individual quirks are not mentioned.

Soviet fighting units have a very limited "tail" compared to their Western counterparts. This has advantages (greater tactical mobility) but also disadvantages (reduced unit stamina).

In an advance, each formation is given:
a. an immediate objective.
b. a subsequent objective (the "immediate objective" of the next highest formation).
c. a direction of further advance (the "subsequent objective" of the next highest formation).
For various levels these read as follows:

	Battalion km	Regiment km	Division km	Army km
immediate objective	2–4	8–15	20–30	100–150
subsequent objective	8–15	20–30	50–70	200–280
direction of further advance	—	—	80–100	2504320

Armour is of vital importance to the Soviets and much emphasis is laid on concentrating available armoured strength at certain points. It is thus common for the combined armour of two neighbouring divisions to be concentrated at the junction of the divisions, which often leads to an unhealthy armour/infantry relationship at these points.

For operational purposes the Soviet forces are organised as follows:

Front – no fixed organisation; this depends upon its task, but it includes a number of Armies.

Army – this usually consists of about three motor rifle divisions and an armoured division and this would be a "Motor rifle Army". "Tank Armies" usually have three or four tank divisions but may also have a motor rifle division.

Division – the organisation of this formation is defined and may be seen in the relevant diagram.

Regiment – the regiment is also defined and may be seen in the relevant diagram.

Battalion – this is a "sub-unit" in Soviet parlance; its organisation is shown.

The Soviets favour the "pattern of threes" in their organisation; a regiment has *three* battalions each of *three* fighting companies each of *three* fighting platoons each of *three* vehicles.

A Soviet division in the advance breaks down into the following functional groups:
1. Motorised reconnaissance.
2. Forward detachment.
3. Advanced guard.
4. Main body.
5. Rear guard.
Flank protection is provided at all levels.

A division in the advance will occupy about 20 km of road and the frontages of attack allotted to the various formations are shown below:

	Nuclear	Non-Nuclear
Army	40–50 km	45–55 km
Division	10–15 km	11–16 km
Regiment	4–8 km	$4\frac{1}{2}$–9 km
Battalion	1–2 km	1–$2\frac{1}{4}$ km
Company	600–800 m	700–1,000 m

Soviet Guards officers march past the reviewing stand in Red Square during a military parade on 7th November 1973. (Novosti)

101

For defensive purposes the frontages are as follows:

	Nuclear	Non-Nuclear
Front	200–500 km	300–750 km
Army	100–200 km	140–280 km
Division	20–40 km	28–56 km
Regiment	8–10 km	11–14 km
Battalion	2–3 km	3–5½ km
Company	1 km	1·4 km

The Soviet High Command

Perhaps more in the Soviet Union than in any other country, the careers of military officers have been dependent upon the political climate of the day. Apart from the bloody Stalinist purges of the 1930s, there have been three major upheavals in the top-level Soviet military structure. The first, in 1946, swept away many wartime commanders so that Stalin could be sure of the loyalty of the Red Army in time of peace; the second, in 1957, consisted of a purge of those officers considered to have been in the following of Marshal Zhukow, who had just been ousted from the post of defence minister; the third major shake-up took place in 1972 when much dead wood was removed to make way for the younger technocrats of the Soviet Army who could understand a little more than the basic mechanics of a T34.

If the two former prunings were purely political in nature, this most recent one has been dictated by a recognition of the fact that modern warfare has become immensely complex and that in order to be able to use these highly technical forces to their best, commanders at Defence Ministry level must be capable of understanding the possibilities and limitations of the weapons under their command.

This meant that the majority of the classical "workers' sons" who had made it to the top of the military heirarchy were suddenly unsuitable, as at their time of life they were incapable of absorbing enough new facts to make up for the short-comings of their limited childhood education.

The hard bargaining to be met at the SALT tables was another, and sharp, spur demanding that men with modern technical know-how should be on hand to extract the maximum out of the wranglings. The arms race which has preceded these talks has also caused a heavy increase in the technical armoury of the Soviet forces and this accent on transistors and gadgetry is likely to increase rather than decrease in the future.

Another factor which speeded the shake-up at the top of the Soviet high command was that only two years ago the average age of fifteen of the most senior members of the defence ministry was 66. The deaths (from natural causes!) of three of these war-hardened warriors opened the gates to the new, younger, more educationally qualified generation of Soviet generals.

Among these "new boys" are the following:

Army General Viktor G. Kulikow, appointed Chief of the General Staff on 23 September 1971 to suceed Marshal Jakubowskij, who became C-in-C Warsaw Pact forces. Born in 1922, Kulikow was a tank commander in the Second World War; by 1950 he was commander of an armoured division and in 1967 he was appointed to command the Kiew Military District (a key post due to the heavy concentration of intermediate range ballistic missiles stationed there). In December 1969 Kulikow became commander GSFG, from where he moved to his present post.

Army General Vladimir Tolubko, appointed C-in-C Strategic Rocket Forces on 8 May 1972 to replace the deceased Marshal Krylow. Born in 1914, Tolubko can no longer be counted among the teenagers of the Soviet general staff in years; but in outlook and training he tends to fit their pattern rather than that of the older generation. Serving as a staff officer in the war, Tolubko commanded the Siberian Military District from 1968, later being transferred to command the Far Eastern Military District.

Colonel General Semyon Kurkotkin, appointed Deputy Defence Minister and Chief of Rear Services on 28 July 1972 in place of Army General Maryakhin, who died on 17 June 1972. Born in 1917, Kurkotkin entered the armoured corps and by the end of the war was a tank brigade commander. From 1966–1968 he was deputy commander GSFG and he then became commander of the Transcaucasian Military District.

Kurkotkin was succeeded as commander GSFG by *Army General Evgeny Iwanowsky*, 54 years old, who for the previous four years had commanded the Moscow Military District after being its deputy commander since 1966.

Colonel General Vladimir Goworow, born in 1924, replaced Iwanowsky as commander Moscow Military District in 1972. Goworow's father, Marshal Leonid Goworow, made his reputation as the defender of Leningrad in the Second World War. Vladimir Goworow is a past student of the Soviet

General Staff Academy and a close friend of Viktor Kulikow – now chief of the general staff. From 1971 until moving to Moscow, Goworow commanded the Baltic Military District; prior to that he had been Kulikow's second in command in the GSFG.

Colonel General Alexander Altunin, 51 years old, was appointed Chief of the Defence Ministry's Central Personnel Department (a very sensitive post) in early 1973. Altunin was one of those officers whose careers were greatly aided by Kruschew who promoted many younger officers during his term of office, presumably to gain their loyalty. Since 1960 he has served as deputy commander, and later commander, of the Kaliningrad garrison; in 1968 he assumed command of the North Caucasian Military District. Altunin is also a close ally of Kulikow.

While the main actors in the Soviet Defence Ministry's reorganisation drama were playing their roles in the centre of the stage the general staff "in the wings" were also undergoing quiet and bloodless turnovers as new faces, with technical or missile force backgrounds, replaced their older, less scientifically trained predecessors. These lower echelon figures include:

Colonel General Nikolai Ogarkow, new Deputy CGS, who is concerned with research and development and was a member of the Soviet delegation in the preparatory SALT negotiations.

Colonel General V. Druzhinin, a deputy defence minister, is a qualified engineer in the radar and radio fields and from 1961–1967 was Chief of the PVO Strany Radio Engineering Service. He also went to Egypt recently to advise on the problems the Egyptians were having with the newest Soviet radar equipments which had been supplied.

Apart from the officers mentioned above, about seventeen other high-ranking Soviet generals, considered by Kulikow to be ripe for less active pastures, have been posted or retired in the last eighteen months.

The Soviet Soldier

The Soviet soldier of today still comes mainly from a peasant background, although city-dwellers are forming an increasingly large proportion of the conscripts.

Like conscripted peasants the world over, such soldiers possess well-developed skills suitable for military applications such as fieldcraft, night fighting and living rough. In recent wars these soldiers have proved themselves to be brave, stubborn and undemanding, although their mood is liable to vary rapidly and extremely from intimate, garlic-laden cameraderie to brutal cruelty.

It is a fact that after the fall of Berlin in 1945, the Russian military at once set up organisations to feed and help the civil populace and individual Russian soldiers shared their rations with the Berliners.

Although over 60% of the Soviet army is made up of soldiers of Russian stock, the remaining 40% covers a spectrum of nations from Germans, Latvians and Finns to Kurds and Tartars. Such an army has to struggle with considerable linguistic problems (over sixty different languages are spoken) and although the Soviet government has directed that Russian must be the primary instructional language in all schools in the Union, there are many fringe areas where only the barest lip service is paid to this central directive.

With the rapid advances in the sophistication of modern weaponry, a major demand for qualified technicians has also been created in the Soviet Army. That these personnel could not be sufficiently trained in the numbers ideally required has doubtless been a major factor in Soviet equipment design and has resulted in a family of relatively simple and robust equipments requiring only uncomplicated maintenance. Great emphasis is placed on all equipments being as "soldier proof" as possible.

As far as morale is concerned the Russian soldier, being exposed since birth only to the party line on world affairs, is firmly convinced that the Russian nation invented and discovered everything, and his national pride is consequently very high.

It must be supposed that until this mental armour is cracked by "open" education the Soviet soldier will fight extremely well in any conflict against the fascist reactionary warmongers of the Western world.

The Czechoslovakian operation of 1968 showed us some very interesting examples of the breakdown of the inner convictions of the ordinary Soviet soldier when, instead of being welcomed by the Czechs as a socialist brother and saviour (as he had been told he would be by the Soviet party machine) he was exposed to insults and, more dangerous, logical and penetrating arguments which made it plain to him that he was somewhat less than welcome in the land he was supposed to be liberating! It must have cut the Soviets very deeply when the Czechs painted swastikas on the tanks of the

Above left, *Schellenbaum* of East German army band; above, reverse of Austrian infantry flag; left, colour party of Bulgarian army's Dimitroff Mausoleum Guard; below, British army rank and specialist arm badges: top to bottom, left to right, physical training instructor, sergeant, corporal, lance corporal; anti-tank specialist, Royal Tank Regt specialist, parachutist, Royal Artillery specialist, Royal Signals telegraphist, "B" Grade tradesman.

Warsaw Pact forces in the country.

The administrative needs of the Soviet soldier are relatively simple, and during his two years of military service the conscript is kept busy from 6 am to 10 pm. The day begins with physical training and ends with a twenty minute "Evening Walk" around the barrack square in full uniform by companies, each company singing a song of its commander's choice, which undoubtedly will be different from that sung by any other company! The Russian soldier receives three cooked meals a day: breakfast at 8 am, lunch at 3.30 pm and supper at 7.30 pm. The food is simple and nutritious and the choice non-existent, but complaints are few.

Conscripts serve for two years in the army and have no entitlement to leave during this time except as a reward for military and political excellence. A recent innovation has been the reintroduction of the rank of "Praporshchik" or ensign, a position which was abolished at the time of the Russian Revolution in 1918. Conscripts may apply for consideration as ensign candidates shortly before reaching the end of their service. If they are accepted, they progress up through the non-commissioned ranks and eventually reach their goal which is a post roughly equivalent to that of a warrant officer in the American army. Pay for conscripts is very low, approximately three roubles per month (DM 9, or $3.50, or £1·50 mid-1973 values).

As in many other armies today, courts martial in the Soviet Union still have the power to pass death sentences and lesser punishments include reduction in rank, detention and reprimands.

Apart from the stick the Soviets also use the carrot in their disciplinary system, awards for good conduct being leave, or a letter to the local Communist Party committee in the man's hometown including a citation or a photograph of the man in front of the unfurled unit flag. One of the highest honours to be awarded at unit level is an inscription in the unit "book of honour".

Political indoctrination within the armed forces is purely a continuation of the same thorough system to which the Soviet citizen has been subjected since the days of his Kindergarten. There is a daily ten-minute political session at 7.10 am (and that on an empty stomach) and further pep talks are injected into the training programme at regular intervals. The vast majority of Soviet recruits find this "Agitprop" intensely boring. Regular NCOs and even officers receive their political indoctrination and the latest changes to the party line from the unit political officer. The Party is very active within the army and members of the Young Communists (Komsomol) will be enlisted by the political officers to help spread the gospel. They will also be called upon to give extra instruction to fellow recruits who are either too slow to keep abreast of their fellows in the training programme or who have shown signs of reactionary tendencies and are in need of straightening out.

This system of the Party working within the armed forces has been adopted by all other Warsaw Pact states. The political officer of a unit, once absolute "king pin" and the bane of every commander's life in the early Stalin era, had his powers vastly reduced in 1942 and is now under his commanding officer's disciplinary power.

The Soviet officer of today is firmly entrenched in the ranks of his nation's élite and the military has a very high standing in Russia, as it does in all Warsaw Pact countries. There exist today Soviet families which can point with pride to sons following their fathers into a military career – almost a return to the old Tsarist days. The Soviet officer is selected from students who have completed the eighth grade of the Soviet education system, and successful candidates then receive further training at a "Suwarow" College (like Britain's Wellington College). Following this the officer cadet serves three or four years at a special-to-arm training college (equivalent of Britain's Sandhurst or America's West Point). These training colleges also accept officer candidates drawn from civilian life or from the non-commissioned ranks of the army. Entry to these colleges is by competitive examination except for those students of Suwarow Colleges who obtain automatic entry. This phase of career training is completed by the time the cadets are 21 years old.

Officers at the captain or major level receive further training at the Frunse Academy which gives a three-year command course (current commandant Army General Wladimir Iwanow), and this college also trains officers from other Warsaw Pact armies including that of the GDR. Officers who do not attend this course may be selected to attend a five-year technical course. Access to the higher ranks of the Soviet army is open only to those who have attended one of these courses.

Elite Formations

On 18 November 1941 four Soviet divisions engaged in the defence of Moscow were awarded the title "Guards" in recognition of their valiant conduct. The divisions concerned were the 100th, 127th, 153rd and 161st. This was the first use of such a title in the Red Army and was a distinct harking back to Tsarist days, although the Communist government of the day stressed that an ideological link was to be formed to the "armed workers of Krasnaja Presnja in the revolution and to the Red Guards of the Russian civil war". By the end of the Second World War the Guards title had been bestowed not only upon many regiments and divisions, but there were also "Guards Armies" to be seen. The majority of the eleven thousand Heroes of the Soviet Union were also Guards.

Nowadays the entire rocket artillery corps has been taken up into the ranks of the Guard, and the majority of the Group of Soviet Forces in Germany (GSFG) are Guards formations. Members of a Guards unit wear a red and gold badge on the left breast, and this same sign is painted on that unit's vehicles. Apart from these badges, a Guards unit will probably have been further distinguished by the award of the Order of Lenin, the Order of the Red Banner or the Order of Kutusow which means that suitable cravats will be attached to that unit's colours.

Parade units of Guards infantry have also been seen wearing a special hat badge on ceremonial parades; this badge is worn above the normal hat badge.

Although liberally spangled with badges and medals, the present day Guards units seem to set no extra high criteria regarding the quality of their members and conscripts may as easily be drafted to a Guards unit as to any other. To be really effective, an élite must be kept small in relation to the whole and must be called upon to achieve better results than other units. Neither of these rules apply to the modern Soviet Guards units and we may do well to seek the effective élite of the Soviet army today in the airborne forces. There are only (!) seven airborne divisions among the 160 of the Soviet army, and their training and dress certainly mark them out from their more conventional colleagues. The use the Soviets have made of their airborne forces in the past has not been convincing in building the case for their nomination as an élite formation, however, and although a Soviet airborne division was used in the Czechoslovakian operation in 1968, they made an unopposed entry and were not employed in the classical airborne manner.

Soviet Military Equipment

Since 1945 the Soviet Union has been the arsenal of the Warsaw Pact and has either sold equipment to these states, or permitted them to build Soviet pattern equipment under licence. In addition to being excellent for the Soviet economy, this policy has resulted in great standardisation of equipment and also means that the Warsaw Pact States are conveniently tied to Russia's apron strings for many years to come as the cost of re-equipping a modern army with a completely new range of weapons and fighting equipment would be enormous. A steady market for spare parts is also ensured for the Soviet arms industry.

Soviet military equipment is designed to be robust and simple to use and newer equipments make use, where possible, of proven sub-assemblies and spare parts already in use in the current equipment range. Thus the T62 tank bears an obvious resemblance to the T55 and the T54, and the PT76 amphibious tank chassis has been the basis for several vehicles since developed.

During annual training, it is usual for a Soviet/Warsaw Pact unit to use only about one-fifth of its tanks or APCs for training purposes; the rest of the vehicle stock remains in the garages and is used only once or twice a year during the large autumn exercises. The long term effects of this lack of usage may well be more damaging to the equipments than normal wear and tear. Certainly all rubber components will suffer, and vehicle batteries are also a problem, to say nothing of rust inside cylinder bores and other hidden crevices. Oils used for lubrication tend to degenerate after a long while and it is scarcely believable that the Soviets can afford to keep these huge numbers of tanks, APCs and wheeled vehicles, guns and radio and radar sets in dehumidified conditions. Perhaps it was fear of the consequences of a long period of disuse which caused the East German forces who took part in the invasion of Czechoslovakia in 1968 to use their old pattern T34 training tanks instead of the "mothballed" but much newer T62s which they also possessed. Major Soviet equipments will now be discussed by branch.

Photographed in the late 1960s, this group of Soviet infantry and T-54 tank crewmen display many typical features of dress and equipment. The infantry carry the AK47 assault rifle and (man immediately above tank spotlight) RPK light machine gun. Since 1970 the Gymnasterka *blouse has been progressively replaced as working and combat dress by a new jacket. (Camera Press)*

107

Armour

The great-great grandfather of the latest Soviet tank is the T34, which made its debut in the bitter fighting against the Germans in 1941. It was a complete surprise to the Germans that the Russians had such an advanced AFV, and although its crew comfort was very limited the T34 had a ballistically good hull and good cross-country performance and range. In post-war years the T34 was succeeded by improved progeny; the T54 with its turtle shaped turret, and the T55 which was a "corrected" version of the T54. The T62 started coming into service several years ago and is now to be seen in all Warsaw Pact countries, although in some their numbers may well still be small.

A novelty in the T62 was the use of a smooth bore gun, something which had fallen into general military disuse for field cannon since about 1880. Rifling had been introduced into gun barrels of all calibres to achieve stabilisation of the projectile fired from it, and thus greater accuracy. The disadvantage of rifling in high velocity guns such as those used on tanks is that the action of firing a round tears away part of the rifling, and after as little as 200 shots it may be necessary to change the barrel of a modern tank gun (if it has been firing shots at maximum charge). This is expensive in materials, in men and in time, and can cause the loss of battles due to inaccurate shooting. The problem of how to stabilise projectiles without using rifling has been solved by the Soviets by the use of fin-stabilised projectiles having a very high muzzle velocity. This development has been closely studied in the West and similar projects are under evaluation in several countries, West Germany and the United Kingdom being among them.

The most recent son of the T34 line (enjoying the designation "M1970" in the Western world) has been observed on troop trials in the central Soviet Union since 1972. Breaking with tradition, it has abandoned the famous Christy suspension system hitherto used and has six road wheels, front idler, rear driving sprocket, and three return rollers. The glacis plate of the hull is long and this angling gives greater effective armour thickness. The driver sits (lies?) in the centre of the front hull (as in the British "Chieftain"), and the smoothbore 115 mm cannon has a fume extractor half way along its length but no muzzle brake. The turret is very similar to that of the T62 and the vehicle may have a laser range finder. The gun is stabilised and the vehicle has the usual infra-red night firing and driving aids. Extra mileage can be given to the M1970 by fitting external fuel drums onto the rear of the hull.

Apart from these medium tanks, the T10 heavy tank is also in use but in limited numbers; they are mainly used grouped together in independent tank destroyer batalions.

All Soviet tanks can schnorkel through water obstacles and this is frequently practised on manoeuvres.

Although not actually tanks, the airborne assault guns used with the Soviet airborne forces fulfil the armoured role for these troops until tanks of the land forces arrive. There are two types, the ASU-57 and the ASU-85, the numbers giving the calibre in millimetres of the guns that they carry. Armour is very thin although a bit heavier in the front than elsewhere.

The ubiquitous PT-76 amphibious tank used in reconnaissance units has a fairly heavy gun (76 mm) but its armour plate is proof only against small arms fire and shell splinters.

Artillery

In the Soviet Army any gun worth the name is considered in the artillery fire plan and this includes the 82 mm, 120 mm and 160 mm mortars deployed in infantry units and the 82 mm recoilless anti-tank guns of the parachute battalions. Many field pieces currently in use with the Soviet Army date from the Second World War but while they can render good service they remain in use.

There are three types of towed 122 mm field piece; the M-30 howitzer (obsolescent but still to be seen), the D30 howitzer (which folds its barrel over the trails for transport purposes), and the D-74 field gun (a very old model with a shield; this gun is probably being withdrawn from service). The 122 mm Russian M63 gun howitzer has also been delivered to units of the NVA. The next largest calibre is the 130 mm M-46 towed field gun, which is employed at Front level, as is the 152 mm D-1 towed howitzer and the 152 mm D-20 gun howitzer. The 203 mm M55 gun howitzer can fire atomic ammunition as well as conventional.

Towed anti-tank guns include the 85 mm SD-44 with a small auxiliary motor to give it increased battlefield mobility; the old M-1955 100 mm gun; and its replacement the F12 100 mm gun, which fires fin-stabilised, discarding sabot rounds capable of penetrating over 40 cm of armour plate.

Multiple rocket launchers have fascinated the Soviets since before the Second World War and their armoury of these weapons is large and varied. Essentially an area weapon, a multiple rocket launcher is perhaps more impressive when one sees it actually in the act of firing a salvo than when one watches the salvo exploding on, or about, the target. For details of these weapons see the table provided.

Mortars

M-37 83 mm mortar. Weight – 56 kg; muzzle velocity – 211 m/sec; range – 0·1 to 3·04 km; Rate of fire – 25 rpm; ammunition type – HE and smoke (3·35 kg).

M-43 120 mm mortar. Weight – 275 kg at the firing point, 500 kg when being towed; range – 0·46 to 5·7 km; muzzle velocity – 272 m/sec; rate of fire – 15 rpm; amunition type – HE, smoke and incendiary (15·8 kg). This and the M-37 are used at battalion and regimental level.

M-53 160 mm mortar. Weight at firing point – 1,443 kg (1,670 when being towed); range – 0·75 to 8·1 km;

rate of fire – 2–3 rpm; ammunition type – HE (40·8 kg). This weapon is rear-loaded and exists at regimental and divisional level. VO – 340 m/sec.

240 mm M-53 Mortar. Although now no longer seen in Soviet units of the Category 'I' class, this weapon is still in use in Category 'II' and 'III' units and in the artillery of the other Warsaw Pact units. It is rear loading and is a divisional level weapon. Range – 9·7 km; rate of fire – 1 rpm; weight of round – 130 kg; weight of weapon – 4,150 kg; VO – 360 m/sec.

Anti-tank Weapons

RPG-7 (Reaktivnij Protivotankovyi Granatomet) or recoilless grenade launcher. Grenade calibre – 100 mm; weight – 2·5 kg; effective range – 300 m; armour penetration – 300 mm; rate of fire – 4 rpm. This is the section anti-tank weapon of the motor rifle battalion and fires a hollow charge projectile.

B-10 (Bezotkatnoje Orudie) Recoilless anti-tank gun. Calibre – 82 mm; weight of weapon in fire position – 91 kg; effective ranges; HE – 4,500 m;

Table of Soviet Multiple Ballistic Rocket Launchers

Name	Calibre (cm)	Number of barrels	Range (km)	Weight of Rocket (kg)	Vehicle on which mounted	Year into Service	Level Employed
BM14	14	8	9	41	GAS-63	1963*	Divisional
BM14	14	16	9	41	Towed (GAS-69A)	1964	Airborne battalions
BM14	14	17	9	41	Towed (GAS-69)	1959	
BM14	14	16	9	41	SIL-151	1954*	Divisional
BMD20	20	4	18	194	SIL-151	1954	Divisional
BM21	11·5	40	15	60	URAL-375	1964	Divisional
BM24	24	12	7	113	SIL-151	1953*	Divisional
BM24	24	12	7	113	AT-S	1957*	Divisional
BMD25	25	6	20	450	JAAS-214	1957	Army
BM28	28	6	30	455	KRAZ-214	1957	Army

* Obsolescent; being replaced by BM21.

hollow charge – 500 m; rate of fire – 6 rpm. This equipment has largely been replaced (except in airborne regiments) by anti-tank guided weapons (ATGW). It was deployed at a scale of 54 per motor rifle division (one platoon per motor rifle battalion).

107 mm Recoilless Gun Weight in firing position (complete with wheeled transport dolly) – 225 kg; range (hollow charge) – 1,000 m. There are six of these weapons in the anti-tank company of a motor rifle regiment.

SPG-9 Rocket Launcher Calibre of projectile – 76 mm; weight, range and rate of fire not known.

M-43, 57 mm Anti-tank gun (ATG) Weight of projectile (high explosive squash head HESH) – 3·14 kg; weight of kinetic energy projectile (KE) not known; range – 8·5 km; rate of fire – 25 rpm. Employment – one platoon (3 guns) in each motor rifle battalion.

M-55 57 mm Anti-tank gun Weight of HESH projectile – 3·14 kg; weight of KE projectile – ?; range – 8·5 km; rate of fire – 25 rpm. This weapon has a 20 hp auxiliary motor fitted to give it increased battlefield mobility; unlike the M-43, the M-55 has a muzzle brake. It is employed as for the M-43 and is replacing that weapon.

M-45 85 mm Anti-tank gun Weight of HESH projectile – 9·2 kg; weight of KE projectile – ?; range – 16 km; rate of fire – 20 rpm; weight of weapon with auxiliary power unit (22 hp, giving a speed on roads of 27 km/hr) – 2,300 kg; weight of weapon in firing position – 1,704 kg. This weapon is parachuted into action with airborne troops and is equipped with an infra-red searchlight. There are six such weapons in the anti-tank company of a motor rifle regiment and 18 in the artillery of a motor rifle division.

M-55 100 mm Anti-tank gun Weight of HESH projectile – 15·7 kg; weight of fin-stabilised KE projectile – ?; range – 21 km; rate of fire – 10 rpm; weight of weapon with auxiliary power unit – 3,455 kg; weight of weapon in firing position – 2,700 kg; employment as for M-45, 85 mm ATG.

ASU-57 (Aviadesantnaja Samochodnaja Ustanovka) Air portable, self-propelled ATG. Introduced into service in 1957, the chassis is a variant on the AT-P Artillery tractor theme. The gun is the M-55, 57 mm ATG. Vehicle weight – 5·5 tons; crew – 3; engine – 100 hp; speeds (roads) – 55 km/hr; range – 320 km; hull length – 3·72 m; height – 1·7 m; width – 2·1 m. There is no overhead cover for the crew; the armour is up to 12 mm thick.

ASU-85 This air portable, self-propelled ATG carries an 85 mm weapon with muzzle brake and fume extractor. The chassis is based on the PT-76 tank and there is overhead cover for the 4-man crew. It was introduced into service in 1962. Weight – 16 tons; hull length – 7 m; height – 2·3 m; width – 3·16 m; engine – 240 hp diesel; maximum road speed – 45 km/hr. This equipment is used in the tank-hunter battalions of the airborne divisions. Its armour is up to 40 mm thick in front and it is almost certainly not capable of being dropped by parachute.

Anti-Tank Guided Weapons (ATGW)

Schmel (Humming Bee) The NATO codename for this weapon is Snapper. It is mounted on the GAS-69A jeep or the BRDM scout car (three per vehicle) and can be fired either from the vehicle or from a remote position. It is widely used in other Warsaw Pact Armies. The warhead is 14 cm in diameter, hollow charge, the rocket weighs 22·3 kg, it is optically wire guided and the range extends from 500–2,000 m; speed – 100 m/sec.

Swatter The Russian name for this weapon is unknown. Calibre – 13 cm; weight – 27 kg; hollow charge warhead; radio guided; range – 400–2,500 m. This weapon is mounted on the BRDM scout car (four per vehicle); a Swatter "B" exists and has an increased range. Swatter may also be fired remote from its parent vehicle. Speed – 230 m/sec.

Sagger This is the NATO codeword for this Soviet ATGW. Calibre – 12 cm; weight – 13 kg; guidance – optical/infra-red and wire; range – 500–3,000 m; hollow charge warhead. Six such missiles are usually mounted on BRDM scout cars in the motor rifle regiment's ATGW battery or in the motor rifle division's AT battalion. Speed – 200 m/sec.

Sagger is man-portable and a team consists of vehicle, 3 crew and 4 missiles. The warhead is carried in a glass-fibre container with the motor as a one-man load but warhead and motor are only married up at the firing point when the warhead is clipped on to the motor unit.

Field Guns

M-63 122 mm gun howitzer This weapon folds its barrel over its trails for towing purposes and when in the firing position, the trails (three) are spread each at 120° to the other; the road wheels are raised and the gun then has 360° of traverse. In 1967 the Egyptian army was equipped with these guns. They are now the standard divisional towed artillery piece, the prime mover being either the URAL-375 or the JAAS-214 lorry. Weight of weapon at the firing point – 5,000 kg; range – 18 km; rate of fire – 6 rpm.

M-55 122 mm gun Modern piece; the gun's wheels can be driven from the prime-mover by means of a flexible drive cable. The prime-mover is either the AT-L tracked tractor or a lorry (JAAS-214). The recuperator mechanism is concentrically mounted around the barrel and there is a muzzle brake. Weight in firing position – 5,000 kg; weight of projectile – 25·5 kg; range – 21 km; rate of fire – 5 rpm; ammunition types – HE, smoke, incendiary and HESH.

M-55 152 mm gun howitzer This is the sister weapon to the M-55 122 mm gun and enjoys the same chassis and recuperator, the 152 mm barrel is shorter than that of the 122 mm gun. Weight in firing position – 5,900 kg; weight of projectile – 48 kg; range – 18 km; rate of fire – 4 rpm; ammunition natures – as for M-55 122 mm gun. Lateral traverse is limited to ±30°.

These weapons are very versatile and are capable of laying anti-tank minefields at threatened spots in a remarkably short time, using rockets which include dozens of bar-shaped anti-tank mines which are scattered over the target area and automatically armed as they land. They can also fire high explosive rockets, smoke and chemical rockets. Vehicle mounted versions include the BM-13 (BM = Bolewajamaschina) of 1941 vintage (mounted on the SIL-151 or GAS-63 trucks); the BM-14, 16-barrelled version on the SIL-151; the BM-20 (four rockets per salvo on a SIL-151 truck); the BM-21 (also known as the M64), 122 mm, 40- tube rocket launcher on SIL-151 truck; the twelve-barrelled 24 mm launcher on the AT-S tracked carrier; the towed, 16-barrelled, 140 mm M-1965; and the 8-barrelled WP-8Z towed weapon of the Polish airborne forces. The Czechs have come up with an improved version of the BM-21 mounted on their Praga 6 × 6 trucks whereby the launcher carries a second loading on the same vehicle so that the vehicle can fire two salvoes rapidly from the same launching site (before moving off to avoid the inevitable enemy counter bombardment) instead of only one salvo. The disadvantages of these weapons are that they use large quantities of ammunition within short periods and that they require a long

re-load time (15 minutes in the case of the "non-Czech" BM21).

Rocket artillery includes tactical rockets of the "Frog" (Free Flight Rocket Over Ground) range and operational-tactical missiles of the "Scud" (Surface to Surface Guided Missile) Group. At divisional level there are Frog 3 (range 40 km) on a tracked chassis based on the PT-76 model; the Frog 4 (range 50 km) on the same tracked chassis; Frog 5 (range 50 km) on PT-76 chassis; and the new Frog 7 (range 50 km) on the 8-wheeled, ZIL-135 carrier. These missiles are solid fuel rockets which makes for easier storage and quicker firing procedures than their big brothers, the liquid fuelled Scud missiles.

At army level the Scud-A (range 150 km) and Scud-B (range 165 km) are to be seen in their older versions on the adapted "Josef Stalin III" heavy tank chassis, while newer versions are carried on the 8-wheeled MAZ 543 vehicle.

Currently the largest in-service weapon in the rocket armoury of the Soviets is "Scaleboard" – although firm details of performance are very sparse. Like Scud, it is carred on the MAZ-543 launching vehicle.

Engineer Equipments

To support their doctrine of rapid advances against the enemy, the Soviets have developed a well-thought-out and very effective array of bridging and mine laying and clearance equipments.

Mine laying equipments (apart from the rifleman's bare hands) come in two versions, one towed by an APC and known as the PMR-60 and the other a tracked, armoured vehicle. These enable mines to be laid at speeds of up to 10 km per hour. Mine clearance devices range from hand-held magnetic mine detectors through vehicle mounted arrays of the same equipments, to rollers and ploughs mounted before AFVs (T54, T55 or T62) and helicopters. The Soviets are also in possession of rocket propelled explosive minefield clearance devices on the lines of the British "Giant Viper".

Bridges are designed to be built quickly and this has led to the development of the TPP (Tjasholyi Pontonnyi Park or heavy pontoon park) whereby the pontoons are brought to the water by the simple expedient of backing their SIL-157, six-wheeled carriers rapidly down to the water's edge and braking sharply, whereby the pontoons slide off into the water! Each division has one set of TPP which is sufficient to build a 150-meter long bridge of the MLC 50.

Similar launching action takes place with the TPP's larger counterpart, the PMP (Plitnyi Mostoroj Park or Platform Bridge Park). A set consists of sixteen central pontoons and two end sections which make up into a 120-meter MLC 50 bridge in only 36 minutes. It is held at army and front level and requires 22 six-wheeled JASSI214 vehicles to move it. When on the vehicles, the pontoons, in four hinged sections, are folded up like a letter "W". When launched into the river they unfold automatically into a flat platform. At divisional level sufficient PMP sections (four or five) are held to enable a ferry quickly to be built which will carry up to 110 tons. Motive power for this ferry is provided by motor-boats such as the BMK-130.

An MLC 60 bridge for vehicles, consisting of two tracks or runways can be built with the TMM (Tjasholyi Mekanizirovanny Mostowoj or heavy bridging equipment). This is carried folded scissor-like on the back of a JASS-214 lorry and is about 10 metres long. Sections can be joined together and to make a 40-meter bridge would take about 50 minutes. The TMM has been so successful that the Americans have developed a copy of it for their own army.

Similar to the TMM but only MLC 30 capacity is the obsolescent KMM (Koljeyno Mekanizirovnny Most or medium bridging equipment). Again providing just two tracks for the vehicle wheels, each section of KMM is about 7·5 meters long, and five sections can be joined together (as with the TMM) to bridge 35 meters in about 20 minutes. The KMM may be carried either on a SIL 151, SIL 157 or on the AT-L tractor.

Armoured bridgelayers appear in the form of the T54 and T55 MTU, both MLC 50, the former having a 10·5 meter span, the latter covering 17·8 meters. Launching time in each case is between 2 and 10 minutes.

Ferries

Apart from the PMP Ferry already mentioned above, the Soviets use the GSP (Gusenitschnyi Samochodnyi Parom) or tracked, self-propelled ferry at divisional level. Consisting of two halves, each mounted on a PT-76 chassis, this ferry has a capacity of 52 tons and it requires four minutes in the water to unfold and couple up the two vehicles.

Soviet Surface-to-Surface Nuclear Missiles

Weapon System	Frog 1	Frog 2	Frog 3	Frog 4	Frog 5	Frog 7	Scud A	Scud B	Scud B	Scaleboard
Fuel	Solid	Solid	Solid	Solid	Solid	Solid	Liquid	Liquid	Liquid	Liquid
Length (m)	10·2	9	10·4	10·2	9·1	9·1	10	11·35	11·35	11·6
Warhead diameter (m)	0·85	0·60	0·53	0·40	0·55	0·55	0·84	0·86	0·86	0·90
Lift-off weight (tons)	3·1	2·4	2·2	2·1	3·0	3·0	5·4	6·3	6·3	7
Range (km)	64	27	34/45	40/50	50/60	50/60	150/280	280	280	700/900
Launcher vehicle	JSIII	PT-76	PT-76	PT-76	PT-76	ZIL135	JSIII	JSIII	MAZ 543	MAZ 543
Vehicle length	6·65	7	7	7	7	10·7	6·65	6·65	12	12
Vehicle width	3·05	3·14	3·14	3·14	3·14	2·8	3·05	3·05	3·02	3·02
Vehicle height with rocket	3·30	2·95	2·95	2·95	2·95	3·6	3·30	3·30	3·08	3·08
Loaded vehicle weight	33	14·2	14·2	14·2	14·2	20	33	38	32	33
Engine hp	550	240	240	240	240	2 × 180	550	550	525	525
Max speed (km)	34	33	33	33	33	65	34	34	70	70
Road range (km)	190	240	240	240	240	500	190	190	500	500

Next in line of amphibious engineer vehicles is the PTS-M, a tracked vehicle capable of lifting 18 tons or 72 men. This is followed by the old K-61 tracked ferry with a lift of 9·5 tons or 35 men. Both these equipments may tow the PKP two-wheeled amphibious trailer in which field guns can be carried.

All Soviet engineer units still use the BAW (Bolschoj Plavajuschtschij Avtomobil) or Heavy Amphibious Vehicle which is a direct copy of the famous DUKW, the American Second World War vehicle. A four-wheeled amphibious jeep, the MAW (Malyi etc) or Light Amphibious Vehicle is used by reconnaissance units.

Soviet engineers employ frogmen to carry out reconnaissance of the beds of rivers it is proposed to force and these men will seek out the best available entry and exit points and explore the profile and nature of the river bottom.

Mechanical earth moving and digging equipments are also held by engineer units to speed up the process of digging-in in case of nuclear attack, to build roads and create river entry and exit points, or to make or clear obstacles.

Infantry
Personal Weapons – pistols
PM (Pistolet Makarow) 9 mm calibre with an 8-round magazine; 20 rpm; weight – 0·73 kg; range – 25 m; Muzzle velocity (Vo) – 315 m/sec.
APS (Automatitscheski Pistolet Stetschkin) 9 mm calibre, 20-round magazine, the wooden holster can be used as a butt, range up to 100 m. Rates of fire – single shot – 40 rpm; automatic – 90 rpm; weight – 1·78 kg; Vo – 340 m/sec.

Machine Pistols (sub-machine guns)
PPSH (Pistolet-Pulemet Schpagin) 7·62 mm calibre, 900 rpm, blow-back mechanism with either a 71-round drum or a 35-round bar magazine, range up to 100 m. This is a World War II vintage weapon and is produced in Hungary under the designation of the M48 machine pistol. Muzzle velocity – 335 m/sec.

Carbines
SKS (Samosarjadvij Karabin Simonowa) or self-loading carbine; 7·62 mm calibre, range up to 400 m; gas recoil mechanism with a 10-round magazine.

* Rpm = round per minute.

This weapon fires single shots or bursts; 40 or 95 rpm. Weight – 3·8 kg with empty magazine; Vo – 735 m/sec.
SKD (Samosarjadvij Karabin Dragunow or Snayperskaya Vintovka Dragunova) This is a sharpshooter's weapon and is equipped with telescopic sights. It has a 10-round magazine and a theoretical rate of fire of 30 rpm. Effective range up to 1,300 m. Weight – 4·3 kg; Vo – 830 m/sec.
AK-47 (Automat Kalaschnikowa) This is the main basis of the Soviet small arms family and has several variants within other Warsaw Pact states. The original Kalaschnikow appeared during World War II and was so admired by the Germans that they modelled their Sturmgewehr on it. Calibre – 7·62 mm; gas recoil mechanism, 600 rpm, 30-round magazine; range up to 400 m; weight – 3·8 kg. The bayonet of the AK-47 has a saw-toothed back and, together with its sheath, can be transformed into a wire cutting device of somewhat questionable efficiency. Vo – 710 m/sec.

Light Machine Guns
RPK (Roschnoi Pulemet Kalaschnikowa) Basically this is an elaboration of the AK-47 having a longer barrel with bipod legs and capable of taking either a 40-round bar magazine or a drum magazine with 75 rounds. The butt is also heavier than that of the AK-47. Rate of fire – 600 rpm; range up to 800 m; weight (empty) – 5·6 kg; Vo – 740 m/sec.
RPD (Roschnoi Pulemet Degtjarewa) 7·62 mm calibre; effective range up to 800 m; gas recoil action, 650 rpm with a 100-round belt/drum magazine. The barrel has bipod supports. Weight (empty) – 6·58 kg; Vo – 740 m/sec.
RP-46D (Degtjarew) An obsolescent weapon having the same characteristics as the RPD except range – 1,000 m, and belt/drum magazine capacity 250 rounds. It has been replaced at company level by the RPD.

Heavy Machine Guns
SGM (Stankovy Gorjunow Modernizovannyi) "M-49". Calibre – 7·62 mm; gas recoil action; range up to 1,200 m; 650 rpm, belt fed (250 rpb); tripod mounted with flash eliminator on the muzzle. The gun weighs 13·6 kg empty and the tripod 13·9 kg; Vo – 800 m/sec.
SG-43 This is a well known World War II weapon with an oval topped shield and two small wheels to facilitate its movement; it is now only rarely to be

seen. Calibre – 7·62 mm; effective range – 1,200 m; gas recoil action; 650 rpm, belt fed (250 rpb); weight of empty gun – 13·8 kg, weight of wheeled shield – 26·9 kg; Vo – 800 m/sec.

D Sh K (Degtjarew-Schpagin) This 12·7 mm weapon is the standard anti-aircraft machine gun mounted on Soviet AFVs. Weight – 52 kg; range – 1,500 m; gas recoil action; 125 rpm, belt fed (50 rpb); Vo – 860 m/sec.

KPV (Wladimirow) With a calibre of 14·5 mm, this is the heaviest Soviet machine gun. It is mounted on the T10 tank, the BTR 60PB APC and the BRDM-2 scout car. Weight – 52·5 kg; 150 rpm; belt fed, gas recoil action; range – 2,000 meters.

Anti-aircraft weapons

ZPU-2 (Zenito Pulemetnaja Ustanovka) Twin 14·5 mm MGs either mounted on a two- or four-wheeled trailer or on certain APCs (BTR 152). Weight of equipment – 400 kg; muzzle velocity – 1,000 m/sec; range – 1,200 m; rate of fire – 2 × 600 rpm. Optical control; 360° traverse.

ZPU-4 As for ZPU-2 but: weight – 2,100 kg; rate of fire – 4 × 600 rpm.

ZU-23-2 (anti-aircraft machine gun) Twin 23 mm MGs mounted on a towed, four-wheeled chassis; weight in firing position – 950 kg; muzzle velocity – 970 m/sec; range – 3,000 m; rate of fire – 2 × 1,000 rpm. This same AAMG is used in the ZSU-23-4 AA tank.

S-60 57 mm AAMG (also known as the M-50). Single-barrelled weapon on four-wheeled trailer (rather like the western Bofors 40 mm AAMG), 360° traverse; weight in firing position – 4,000 kg; muzzle velocity – 1,000 m/sec; range – 15 km (4 km against flying targets); rate of fire – 120 rpm; ammunition types – HE (with tracer)), HESH and KE. This weapon is radar controlled and uses the same barrel and ammunition as the M-43 and M-55 anti-tank guns, the SU-57 AA tank and the ASU-57 air portable SP gun. The prime mover is usually the SIL-157 truck.

ZSU-23-4 (Zenitnaja Samochodnaja Ustanovka) or self-propelled anti-aircraft MG. A cluster of four 23 mm MGs with target tracking radar mounted on a variation of the PT-76 chassis. Weight – 15 tons; engine – 240 hp, diesel; crew – 3; length – 6·5 m; height to top of turret (excluding radar antennae) – 2·2 m; width – 3·15 m. Employment – in the AA companies of armoured regiments and of GANNEF sites. This is a modern equipment which comple-

ments the old SU57 equipments of the AA regiments in armoured divisions.

SU-57 (Samochodnaja Ustanovka) or self-propelled vehicle. First introduced into service in 1957, this equipment has been seen in most Warsaw Pact countries as well as in Egypt. It (the gun) is optically controlled. Weight – 35 tons; engine – 520 hp diesel; crew – 6; length – 6·2 m; height – 2·75 m; width – 3·27 m; muzzle velocity – 1,000 m/sec; rate of fire – 15 rpm; range – 8·4 km; road speed – 50 km/hr; road range – 350 km.

M-44 85 mm AA Gun Mounted on a four-wheeled trailer, this heavy AA gun has radar control. Weight in firing position – 4,300 kg; weight of projectile – 9·75 kg; muzzle velocity – 792 m/sec; range (ground targets) – 15·5 km, AA – 9·4 km; rate of fire 20 rpm. Prime mover – SIL-157.

M-49 100 mm AA Gun As with the previous weapon, mounted on a four-wheeled trailer pulled by a SIL-157. It uses the same barrel and ammunition as AT guns, tank and tank hunter guns of this calibre. The gun is radar controlled. Weight in firing position – 11,000 kg; weight of projectile – 15·9 kg; muzzle velocity – 900 m/sec; range (ground targets) – 21 km, AA – 11 km; rate of fire – 20 rpm. An army level weapon.

M-55 122 mm AA Gun Four-wheeled trailer, SIL-157 prime mover, radar control, barrel and ammunition commonality with other weapons of similar calibre. Weight in firing position – 30,000 kg; weight of projectile – 25·5 kg; muzzle velocity – 800 m/sec; range (ground targets) – 20 km, AA – 15 km; rate of fire – 15 rpm. This weapon is employed in the defence of the Soviet homeland.

Recent additions:

SS7 Strela One-man AA projectile

Introduced into service in the Warsaw Pact states in 1967, the weapon resembles the American "Bazooka" but is longer and slimmer. The missile is an infra-red weapon like the American Redeye and homes in on heat sources. Calibre is about 100 mm; weight of the missile about 10 kg; length – 1·4 m; slant range – 3·7 km; max speed – 1·5 mach.

14·5 mm Vladimirov (KPVT) MG

This new heavy MG is replacing the 12·7 mm MGs until now mounted on the Soviet APCs. Ammunition types include AP and incendiary; range – 1,650 yards; rate of fire – 600 rpm.

Soviet Surface to Air Missiles

Title	Year of introduction	Range (km) Ground	AA	Length (meters)	Diameter (meters)	Weight (tons)	Fuel 1st Stage	Fuel 2nd Stage	Guidance System	Speed Mach	Towing Vehicle
Guild (SAM-1)*	1956	35	20	11·5	0·6	3	Liquid	NIL	Radio and self seeking (1R)	2·5	SIL-151 or 157
Guideline (SAM-2)*	1957	40	18	10·9	0·66	2·2	Solid	Liquid	Radio and self seeking (1R)	3·5	SIL-151 or 157
SAM-2 modified*	1960	40	24	10·5	0·5	2·5	Solid	Liquid	? and self seeking	3·5	SIL-151 or 157
Griffon (SAM-3)	1963	150	40	16	0·9	8	Solid	Liquid	Laser?	4	URAL-375D
Gannef (SAM-4)**	1964	80	24	8·5	0·9	2	Solid	Ramjet	Laser?	2·5	Modified PT-76
Goa (SAM-5)	1964	25	15	6·2	0·45	0·4	Solid	NIL	Radio and self seeking	2	SIL-157
Gainful (SAM-6)***	1967	30	16	5·8	0·33	0·68	Solid	NIL	Infra-red	2·5	Modified PT-76
Galosh (SAM-7)	1969	300	?	19	2·5	15+	?	?	Fully automatic	?	MAZ

A SAM-2 battery consists of six firing ramps, twelve SAM-2 missiles, command (including radar) vehicles and support vehicles including towed generators. Within 15 minutes all twelve missiles can be fired off.

  * Front and army level weapon.
 ** Army level weapon.
*** Divisional level weapon.

Strategic Soviet Rockets (Intermediate and Inter-continental)

Title	Year of introduction	Maximum Range (km)	Length (meters)	Diameter (meters)	Weight (tons)	Fuel	Guidance System	Carrier Vehicle	Remarks
Shaddock	1964	400	12	?	6·5	Solid	Inertial	4 × 4 wheeled	All these weapons belong to the Strategic Rocket Troops. Each Rocket Regiment consists of four-to-six batteries; a battery of two launcher vehicles and about twenty command, support and re-supply vehicles. All rockets have single-stage motors.
Shyster*	1961	1,000	21	1·7	23	Liquid	Inertial	4 wheeled trailer	
Sandal*	1962	2,000	27	1·6	21	Liquid	Inertial	4 wheeled trailer	
Skean	1964	3,500	24	2·4	30	Liquid	Inertial	2 wheeled trailer	
Scamp	1965	4,500	13	1·8	10	Solid	Inertial	JSIII tracked chassis	
Scrooge	1965	?	15	1·8	?	Solid	Inertial	JSIII tracked chassis	

* Only semi-mobile weapons.

UAS-469 4 × 4 ⅓-ton jeep

Produced by the Uljanowsker Autowerks, this new, 4-door vehicle has a soft top and is designed to carry either 7 men or 600 kg of equipment without major re-arrangement of the superstructure. This is achieved by a system of folding seats in the rear of the truck. Empty weight is 2,400 kg, length 4·02 m, width 1·81 m and height to top of canopy 2·01 m. Top road speed is 100 km/hr. The engine is the same as that used in the UAS-451 and UAS-452 trucks – a 72 hp, four stroke petrol engine and is equipped with a petrol pre-warming device for operation in Arctic conditions.

Uniforms of the Soviet Army

From the end of the Second World War until 1970 the Soviet Army's uniform remained practically unchanged, even to the extent that the men wore foot cloths in their jackboots instead of socks. By the end of 1971 it was intended that the entire army should be wearing the new uniforms but, inevitably when one considers the vast size of the army, old items of dress were still to be seen in 1973 as individuals continued to wear them out before being issued with the new pattern garments.

The main changes introduced by these new dress regulations may be summarised as follows:

1. The facing colour of the infantry (Motor Rifles) changed from magenta to red.
2. Branch badges, in the wearer's facing colour and bearing the badge of the wearer's parent regiment, were introduced to be worn on the upper left arm of the parade and walking out dress jackets, everyday dress jackets and on the greatcoat.
3. The collar patches on other ranks' jackets (in parade and walking out dress) received a gold coloured metallic edging as had previously been worn only by officers.
4. Officers' pattern cap badges were extended for issue to other ranks.
5. Armoured troops received a very modern tank badge to replace the stylised T34 (?) which had previously graced their collar dogs and shoulder-boards.
6. Engineers received a new badge, thus differentiating them from the great masses of engineering and constructional troops with whom they previously had shared a common badge.
7. The famous "Gymnasterka" blouse of the Russian soldier's combat and working dress was abolished.

8. Collars and ties were introduced for wear by NCOs and men.
9. Piping on officers' shoulder-boards and hats (which previously had varied in colour according to branch of service) were standardised at red.
10. Soldiers up to and including the rank of sergeant wear gold metal letters "CA" (Cyrillic = Cowjetskaja Armija: Soviet Army) on their parade and walking out shoulder-boards as well as on their greatcoat shoulder-boards.
11. Shoes were introduced for walking out and everyday wear.
12. Guards units in parade dress wear a special gold and red star-burst cap badge on their peaked caps above the normal cap badge, and gold metallic aiguillettes on the right shoulder, as well as a branch badge on their upper right arm to complement that on their left. Their shoulder-boards are edged in gold lace.
13. Airborne forces received a light blue beret and a blue and white striped shirt for wear on parades and walking out as well as everday dress.
14. New service badges (staged at one, two, three, four, five and ten years' service) were introduced to be worn on the lower left sleeve in parade and walking out dress.

We shall now consider the types of dress in detail:

Parade dress
1a. Officers and Ensigns (Praportschik), Summer

Dark green peaked cap with red headband and top piping, gold cord chin strap, gold buttons and gold and red badge, black peak. Dark green, single-breasted jacket with four gold buttons bearing a star enclosing the hammer and sickle; two horizontal, square pocket flaps at the sides of the skirts (no top pockets); white shirt, black tie; shoulder-boards according to rank, collar patches and arm badge according to regiment and branch of service, red piping across bottom of sleeve (about 10 cm above the end of the sleeve), white gloves, gold and black sash with oval gold buckle; dark green breeches with red side stripe, jackboots, medals and qualification badges. (Airborne forces parade dress is dark blue.)

1b. Winter

As above but with double-breasted grey greatcoat, with gold buttons and with the grey fur cap.

1c. Parade Dress NCOs and men, Summer

Khaki, single-breasted jacket of exactly the same cut as that in *a.* above except that the tips of the collar are angled down instead of up. The cap is khaki instead of dark green; the shirt and the breeches also khaki. All other details as in *a.* except that the waist sash may well be replaced by either a white leather belt with rectangular brass plate bearing a star and hammer and sickle or a brown leather belt with the same rectangular plate.

1d. NCOs and men, Winter

As in *b.* above; jackboots may be worn.

Walking Out Dress
2a. Officers and Ensigns, Summer

As in *1a.* above except that:
(1) Only medal ribbons are worn and not the medals.
(2) No white gloves.
(3) No waist sash.

(4) No jack boots.
(5) Dark green trousers and black shoes instead of breeches and jackboots.

2b. Officers and Ensigns, Winter

As in *1b.* Jackboots may be worn; brown leather gloves are worn.

2c. NCOs and men, Summer

As in *1c.* above except the changes listed in *2a.* apply and a brown leather belt may be worn.

2d. NCOs and men, Winter

As in *1d.* above, jackboots may be worn; brown leather gloves are worn.

Everyday Dress
3a. Officers and Ensigns, Summer

Khaki cap with red band and piping, small, oval gold, red and white badge, black chin strap and

A Soviet airborne unit on a winter exercise. (Novosti)

peak, gold buttons. Lime green linen blouse, khaki tie, gold pin. The sleeves are buttoned at the cuff with two small brown buttons; the two patch pockets on the chest are square with button-down pointed flaps having a point in the centre. The blouse is worn over the top of the trousers and over the pistol holster (if that is worn). Shoulder-boards are gold and red. Khaki trousers and black shoes or khaki breeches and jackboots may be worn.

When on duty requiring them to be armed, Soviet officers wear a belt and shoulder brace in brown leather with brass fittings very similar to the British Army's "Sam Browne" belt except that it is an unwritten law that a Soviet Officer's belt is never polished. The pistol, in its brown leather holster, is worn under the right elbow.

3b. NCOs and men, Summer

Kahki cap with red piping and headband; small, oval badge, black chin strap and peak, gold buttons. Khaki, single-breasted jacket of the same cut as that in *1a.* except that the collar is closed; the cuffs are buttoned with two small brass buttons and the sleeve is gathered at the cuff top with a slit about 15 cm long to the rear seam. The front of the jacket closes with five large brass buttons bearing, as usual, the five-pointed star and the hammer and sickle and the collar dogs have no gold edging. Collar dogs and shoulder-boards are in the branch facing colour and no "CA" initials are worn on the shoulder-boards. Qualification badges, guards' badge and Komsomol badge may be worn. Khaki breeches and jackboots will be worn and instead of the peaked cap, a khaki side cap with red star badge may be worn by conscripts and junior NCOs. For "tropical" service the headwear would be a "topee" shaped hat in khaki fabric, with a wide brim all the way round and a red star badge in front. Around the waist is a brown belt with yellow rectangular plate bearing the star, hammer and sickle.

3c. Officers and Ensigns, Winter

As in *3a.* but the hat may be replaced by the grey, fur cap with oval badge and the blouse by a jacket as described in *3b.* with "Sam Browne" and a greatcoat, double breasted and red-brown in colour may also be worn. Brown leather gloves, breeches and jackboots.

3d. NCOs and men, Winter

As in *3c.* above but the oval badge may be replaced by a red star badge for conscripts; no "Sam Browne"; grey gloves, single-breasted red-brown greatcoat, breeches and jackboots.

Combat Kit

General: This is roughly the same for all ranks except when accoutrements are considered, when the men inevitably tend to carry much more on their backs than the officers due to their different armament.

4a. European Summer Climate, Officers and Ensigns

Khaki cap with black chin strap and peak and khaki plastic oval badge and small buttons (this will, of course, be replaced by a khaki-painted steel helmet in combat). Khaki jacket of the cut described in *3b.* but with khaki collar patches, khaki buttons and khaki shoulder-boards with one or two red stripes and khaki plastic stars according to rank. A khaki plastic branch badge is also worn on the shoulder-board above the rank stars, and a small khaki plastic button. "Sam Browne" and pistol; khaki breeches and jackboots. A green and light brown mottled camouflage suit with hood may also be worn.

4b. NCOs and men

As in *4a.* but with the following differences; khaki side cap with red star badge (or helmet), shoulder-boards in khaki with red stripes according to rank and branch badges and plastic buttons. Brown leather equipment (waist-belt with rectangular brass buckle, two shoulder-straps at the front, one at the back centre, khaki webbing pouches and packs.

For tropical areas the hat is of the "topee" fashion and the uniform cloth is lighter in texture.

4c. Officers and Ensigns, Winter

As in *4a.* but a heavy, quilted khaki overjacket, reaching to mid-thigh and with a single row of concealed buttons may be worn. The collar patches are in the branch colour, the shoulder-boards khaki. The headwear may be the grey pile cap with oval badge. The red-brown, single-breasted great-coat may also be worn.

For combat in Arctic conditions a white camou-flage oversuit with hood and mittens would be worn.

4d. NCOs and men, Winter

As in *4c.* above.

Special Combat Clothing:
4e. Chemical

A chemical protective suit consisting of a grey plastic "boiler suit", grey plastic gloves and overboots and the regulation Soviet respirator with long corrugated rubber tube leading from the face piece to the filter unit may be donned over the normal combat clothing. Wearing this clothing is very uncomfortable as it causes excessive sweating and its protection against chemical and biological agents is limited to a few hours at the most.

4f. Airborne troops

Instead of the normal combat clothing, paratroops of the Airborne Forces wear a dark khaki jumping suit with dark brown close fitting leather helmet covering the ears and neck; goggles, jackboots, parachute and then the usual combat equipment.

4g. AFV crews

The crews of AFVs (but not their passengers, eg the riflemen carried in the backs of APCs) wear black battle uniforms (overalls) and padded leather helmets (either black or dark brown) which have earphones built into them. The crews of the motorcycle and sidecar reconnaissance teams also wear these helmets.

Branch facing colours

Motor Rifles ⎫
Military Bands ⎬ Bright Red

Armoured Troops
Artillery
Strategic Rocket Troops
Motor Transport troops
Road Construction Troops
Chemical Troops ⎬ Black
Engineers and Engineer Technical Troops
Pipelaying Troops
Railways and Military Communications
Signals and Radio Technical
Military Topography

Airborne Forces ⎫
Air Force ⎬ Light Blue

Medical Corps ⎫
Veterinary Corps ⎬ Magenta
Legal Services
Administration ⎭

Other formations outside the Soviet Army but who wear army pattern uniform are the MVD

(Ministry of Internal Affairs) and the KGB ("Komitjat Gossudarstrennaja Bezopasnost" or Committee of State Security) who are sub-divided into straight KGB and KGB Border Troops.

Their facing colours are as follows:

MVD	– Russet
KGB	– Royal blue
KGB Border Troops	– Mid-green

Examples of new Soviet branch badges worn on upper arm on patch of branch colour: Armour, Artillery, Motor Rifles, Airborne.

Soviet Army Rank Insignia, worn on shoulder-boards

Private	– no insignia except CA monogram.
Senior Private	– one yellow stripe across shoulder-board, CA monogram.
Corporal	– two yellow stripes across shoulder-board, CA monogram.
Sergeant	– three yellow stripes across shoulder-board, CA monogram.
Senior Sergeant	– one broad gold stripe across shoulder-board.
Sergeant Major	– one broad gold stripe along shoulder-board.
Officer Cadet	– shoulder-board edged with gold down both sides.
Ensign	– facing-colour shoulder-board, two gold stars spaced lengthways.

Officers

From Junior Lieutenant to Captain, all gold shoulder-board with red edging and one central red lengthways stripe. From Major to Colonel, all gold shoulder-board with red edging and two equidistant red lengthways stripes.

Junior Lieutenant	– one silver star on central stripe.
Lieutenant	– two silver stars, one each side of stripe.
Senior Lieutenant	– three silver stars, one on and one each side of stripe.
Captain	– two stars on stripe, plus one on each side of stripe.
Major	– one silver star between stripes.
Lieutenant-Colonel	– two silver stars, one on each stripe.
Colonel	– three silver stars, one on each stripe, plus one between stripes.

General Officers and Marshals

All gold shoulder-boards, patterned in the manner of Napoleonic period Austrian lace.

Major-General	– one large silver star.
Lieutenant-General	– two large silver stars spaced lengthways.
Colonel General	– three large silver stars spaced lengthways.
Army General	– four large silver stars spaced lengthways.
Marshal of Arm	– one large gold star edged red, below badge of arm.
Chief Marshal of Arm	– as above, but star enclosed in laurel wreath.
Marshal of Soviet Union	– very large gold star edged red, below enamelled badge of the Soviet Union.

THE PEOPLE'S REPUBLIC OF ALBANIA

Population – 2,250,000. **Capital** – Tirana.

Armed Forces:

Army – 28,000 men; 100 tanks, some SA-2 SAM.

Navy – 3,000 men; 4 submarines, 4 escorts, 40 MTBs.

Air Force – 4,000 men; 72 aircraft (MiG-15, MiG-17, MiG-19 and MiG-21).

Para-military forces – Internal security police – 12,000; frontier guards – 10,000.

Defence Spending – 1971 – 580 million leks ($1 = 5 leks).

The People's Republic of Albania turned Communist during the Second World War when Enver Hodscha came to power at the head of the Communist-inspired Army of Liberation. From 1944 to 1954 Hodscha was President of Albania; since then he has contented himself with the post of First Secretary of the Central Committee of the Communist Party (the Democratic Front) and thus still retains the reins of power in his hands.

Originally a member of the Warsaw Pact, Albania broke ideologically with Russia in 1961 and officially withdrew at the time of the Czechoslovakian crisis in 1968. She has since adhered closely to Red China's interpretation of the teachings of Marx and Lenin. This changing of sides has led to upheavals in all walks of Albanian life, including the army, where Russian equipment is being replaced by Chinese and all rank badges have been abolished as in the Chinese army. The titular head of state is Haxhi Lileshi as chairman of the fifteen-member Praesidium of the People's Assembly. The People's Assembly consists of 264 representatives, "elected" on 20 September 1970 in an election in which the Democratic Front achieved the usual 100% of the votes cast. The minister of defence is at time of writing Beqir Balluku who is also a member of the Politburo of the Albanian Communist Party. This means that under the usual Communist system, tight party control is exercised over the armed forces.

Military service liability is eighteen months in the army, and two years in the air force, navy and in special units. From a strength of 35,000 in 1970, the Albanian army has now (1973) been reduced to 28,000 (the navy has also been reduced from 4,000 in 1970 but the air force has increased from 2,500 men).

The army is organised into one tank brigade and six infantry brigades, but APCs are limited to the infantry in the tank brigade and most of the other infantry units are either lorry-mounted or (the major part) pure "foot-sloggers". Animal transport is used in the mountainous areas of the country and equipment is generally simple. Great difficulty is experienced obtaining sufficient qualified technicians to maintain the increasingly complex modern equipment. APCs are still mainly of Soviet manufacture. In 1972 armoured vehicles in the Albanian army included 70 T34s, fifteen T54s and T55s (in all, enough to equip three Soviet-style tank battalions) and one or two T62s. APCs included the BTR-152 (6 wheeled, open topped), and some BRDM scout cars (amphibious, 4 or 8 wheeled). There were also some SU 76 Chinese SP guns. Towed artillery pieces included 122 mm and 152 mm gun/howitzers. Anti-tank guns ranged in calibre from 45 mm through 57 and 76 to 85 mm weapons, and AA guns were 37 mm, 57 and 85 mm. ATGW were not held. Albania has some SA-2 missiles but apparently no more modern types. It is likely that Chinese medium tanks have now been introduced; these are the Chinese adaptation of the Soviet T54, generally known as the "T-59". It is thought that Chinese light tanks (T-62) have also been delivered. The logistical problems of this re-equipping programme can well be imagined and the difficulties of

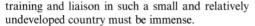

training and liaison in such a small and relatively undeveloped country must be immense.

In all, it may be deduced that the combat value of the technically equipped sections of the Albanian army (tanks and artillery) must have suffered some heavy blows in the last two years. How long it will take them to recover and whether the new "Chinese" standard will be above the old Soviet standard, remains to be seen.

By Warsaw Pact standards the Albanian army is primitive and the amount of its sophisticated equipment very limited. Logistic support is scarce, and discipline strict.

Organisation of the Albanian Army

The Albanian army is organised into one tank brigade of three tank battalions, and six infantry brigades. The tank brigade has a motor rifle component of about battalion strength; the infantry brigades are foot units with a certain lorry-lift capability. Animal pack transport is used in the more mountainous areas.

Albanian Army Equipment

Until recently, most weapons in the Albanian armoury were Soviet World War II pattern articles. Since the country has fallen under China's influence some of this has been replaced with more modern equipment such as the T-59 medium tank. Exact details of the nature and extent of this re-equipment programme are not known.

Small Arms include M-40 and M-41 7·62 mm machine pistols; G-44 rifles, Degtjarow 7·62 mm LMGs; Gorjunow 7·62 mm SMGs; DSCHK 12·7 mm MGs; 14·5 mm AT rifles; Czechoslovakian "T-21" 82 mm AT recoilless gun; 82 mm, 120 mm and 160 mm mortars.

Artillery 45 mm AT guns, 76·2 mm M-42 AT gun, 122 mm M-38 howitzers, 152 mm M-37 howitzers; 37 mm AA guns; SU-76 SP AT guns and SA-2 SAM.

Tanks Seventy T34/85 tanks; fifteen T54 and T-59 medium tanks; 20 APCs including BA-64s, BTR-40 4-wheeled and BTR-152 6-wheeled vehicles.

Albanian Army Uniforms

These used to be of Soviet pattern with rank and regiment shown on the shoulder-boards. It is likely that after the Chinese fashion, rank badges have been discontinued and "Mao" suits introduced. Prior to this, badges of rank were completely after the Soviet system.

Albanian Army Flags

The national flag fringed in gold; black flagstaff; gold, open spear point tip having in the centre the double-headed eagle.

* * *

T-59 Chinese Main Battle Tank

From 1950–1962 the Soviet Union supplied 3,000 T54 tanks to China. In 1963 China began producing a modified version of this vehicle which was entitled the T-59. In 1966 Pakistan received some T-59s after the rest of the world had refused to supply her with the necessary replacements for her losses in the 1965 war with India. Since 1968 Albania has also received them.

Compared to the Soviet T54 the T-59 is cramped, unreliable and poorly finished. Although very similar in appearance to the T54, the main differences lie in the lack of sophistication in the equipment. The gun has a fume extractor at the muzzle but is not stabilised, and the turret and gun are hand-traversed, which makes firing on the move impossible and engagement of second and subsequent targets very slow. There is no infra-red night driving or firing equipment. Dimensions are approximately as for the T54.

THE PEOPLE'S REPUBLIC OF BULGARIA

Population – 8,624,000.   **Capital** – Sofia.

Armed Forces:
    Army – 117,000 men; 2,300 tanks; 1,300 artillery pieces.
    Navy – 7,000 men; 1 destroyer, 2 frigates, 3 submarines and the Danube gunboat flotilla.
    Air Force – 26,000 men; 300 fighters and fighter bombers, one parachute regiment.
Para-military forces – Security Police and Border Guards – 25,000 men; People's Militia – 150,000 men.
      Reserves   – 750,000 men.
Defence Spending   – 324 million leva ($279 million) in 1970.

Until 1908 Bulgaria had spent a long period under Turkish rule after which she became a monarchy, the first king being Prince Alexander I of Battenburg (the English Mountbatten). Bulgarian rulers termed themselves "Tsars", and the last of the line (Simeon II) was removed from the throne by a referendum held on 8 September 1946.

During the Second World War Bulgaria joined the Axis powers when she signed the Three Power Agreement on 1 March 1941. On 25 November 1941 she also signed the Anti-Comintern Pact. Towards the end of the war (26 August 1944) Bulgaria requested America and Britain to agree to an armistice, and a few days later (5 September) Soviet Russia declared war on the unfortunate state, which was rapidly followed by an armistice on 28 October 1944. A peace treaty between all belligerents was signed on 10 February 1947.

A general election was held on 27 October 1946 and the "Fatherland Front" (Communists, socialists and independents) won 366 seats in the National Assembly (Narodno Săbranie) – 277 of which fell into the Communists' pockets. The inevitable happened; on 26 August 1947 the opposition party in the National Assembly (the Agrarian Union) was dissolved and its leader, Nikolai Petkow, was hanged. The Communists had arrived. In the "elections" of 27 June 1971, 99·9% of the votes cast went to the 400 Fatherland Front candidates – there were no other candidates.

The highest organ of state is the Council of State and the head of state is its Chairman (currently Todor Zhiwkow) who is also first secretary of the Bulgarian Communist Party and, of course, head of the Politburo. The defence minister, Army General Dobri Dzhurow, is not a member of the Politburo.

Bulgaria is a member of the Warsaw Pact and one of Moscow's most willing tools in her European colonialism. In May 1967 she signed a second twenty-year treaty of friendship with the Soviet Union. In time of war, the Bulgarian armed forces would come under command of the C-in-C of the Warsaw Pact forces (presently Marshal Jakubowskij of the Soviet Union).

The army has a strength of 117,000 men, with officers and most NCOs being professionals, the men conscripts serving for two years.

There are three geographical army commands: the Military Regions of Sofia, Plovdiv and Sliven. The field forces of the army comprise eight motor rifle divisions (of which three are manned only by cadres in peacetime and would be activated by reservist call-up in case of mobilisation) and five tank brigades. Military service liability extends to all citizens of the age of 19 years, and women would be called upon in time of emergency, although this is rarely the case nowadays. Terms of service are two years in the army and air force, three in the navy. Students at university can have their military service delayed until after they have completed their studies. Professional officers and NCOs are retired at the following ages: generals – 60; field officers – 50; junior officers – 40; NCOs – 55. Pre-military training is given in the "DKMS" organisation.

Bulgarian military training is recognised as being hard even by Russian standards and much time is spent in the field in winter conditions. There are no

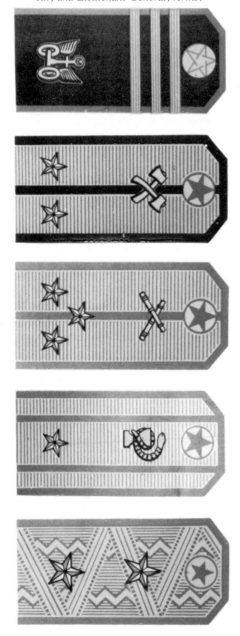

Soviet divisions stationed in Bulgaria at the moment. The army tradition goes back to 23 September 1923 when the Bulgarian Communist party organised a rebellion. Another Communist-inspired rebellion took place on 9 September 1944 against the then-Nazi-orientated Bulgarian army.

Bulgaria has no arms industry of her own and receives Soviet military equipment. Although she has some APCs (BRDM, BTR-50, BTR-60 and BTR-152) they are few in number and most of her motor rifle formations are either lorried or pure "foot-slogging" infantry. Medium tanks include T-34/85, T54, T55 and some T62s, and for reconnaissance purposes the ubiquitous PT-76 amphibious light tank is used. Anti-tank guns are the 57 mm, 85 mm and 100 mm towed guns; the SU 100 self propelled gun is operated. ATGW are the Snapper and Sagger mounted either on the BRDM scout car or the GAZ jeep. Artillery pieces range from calibre 85 mm through 122, 130 and 152 mm cannon, and rocket artillery is equipped with Frog and Scud SSMs.

Bulgarian units have been to Russia to undergo training (one of the Bulgarian regiments used in the 1968 invasion of Czechoslovakia was in fact in the Soviet Union and was sent into the operation from there) and individual officers attend the Soviet staff college. Military doctrine is thus as for the Soviet army.

The efforts of the government to industrialise and modernise Bulgaria have not yet caused that nation to cease to be mainly a peasant-based state. The armed forces occupy a position of prestige in the country and officers are counted among the élite. Conscientious objection to military service is extremely rare and not tolerated even if displayed.

Organisation of the Bulgarian Army

Of the eight motor rifle divisions, three exist only as cadres in peacetime and would be made up to strength by reservists in case of war. The five tank brigades are also only at about 70% full strength. The order of battle and organisation of the divisions, regiments, battalions and companies is on the Soviet model.

Bulgarian Army Equipment

Small Arms 9 mm Pistolet Makarow, 7·62 mm PPSH M-41 machine pistols, 7·62 mm Simonow SLRs, 7·62 mm AK-47 Kalaschnikow assault rifles; 7·62 mm RPK, RP-46 and RPD LMGs; Gorjunow,

7·62 mm M-49 SMGs. 82 mm and 120 mm mortars. *Artillery* 57 mm, 85 mm and 100 mm AT guns; 85 mm, 122 mm, 130 mm, and 152 mm guns, SU-100 SP guns, Sagger and Snapper ATGW; 37 mm and 57 mm AA guns. Frog and Scud SSM. *APCs* BTR-152, BTR-50, BTR-60 APCs and BRDM scout cars.

Tanks Some JSIII heavy tanks; about 1,900 medium tanks, mainly T54/55s with some T34/85s and a few T62s. PT76 light tanks.

Bulgarian Army Uniforms

The "Dimitroff Mausoleum Guard" in Sofia

Conscripts are selected for this ceremonial duty on a basis of height (minimum 1 m 76 cm) and good conduct. There are two ceremonial uniforms; a white dolman with red lace for summer and a red dolman with white lace for winter. Summer headwear is a white lambskin "colpack" with red top bearing a yellow cross; silver chin scales worn hooked up behind an oval white-within-green-within-red cockade, which is worn over the usual white-over-green-over-red cockade bearing the five-pointed red star. Behind the top oval cockade is a grey eagle's feather. The winter hat is the same but in grey lambskin.

The dolman has a closed collar about 4 cm high and edged in red (white for winter) lace; across the chest are seven rows of red (or white) lace, wider at the shoulders than at the waist. On the sleeves are red (or white) Hungarian knots and the back of the dolman is decorated with red (or white) lace along the seams.

Black riding breeches with white side stripes and black, straight-topped boots with white edging and buckle-on silver spurs are worn. Red (or white) barrel sashes and white gloves complete the outfit.

There is a colour party of three men who all wear red sashes (trimmed with gold and having two golden tassels at the lower end) from right shoulder to left hip.

Officers of this unit carry curved steel sabres and rank is indicated by gold and red shoulder-boards. The men carry breech-loading Simonow M1955 semi-automatic carbines with fixed bayonets, the escorts to the colour carry Kalaschnikow assault rifles slung across their chests, muzzles at the level of the left shoulder. Haircuts are extremely short.

Service Dress

Single-breasted, olive-brown, open-necked jacket,

four button front. Buttons are gold for officers, dark brown plastic for men and both bear a five-pointed star design. Khaki-green shirt and tie, olive-brown trousers, black shoes. Olive-brown peaked cap with red piping to crown and red head-band, black plastic peak and chin strap (for privates; gold cord for officers), oval national cockade in white, green and red bearing the red star. Regimental badges are worn on the collar, badges of rank on the shoulder-boards.

Fatigue and Barrack Dress

Khaki-green forage cap with small, red star badge in the front and triangular white-over-green-over-red patch on the left-hand side; khaki-green hip length, single-breasted jacket with six button front and two patch pockets with buttoned flaps on the chest; khaki-green open-necked shirt, khaki-green trousers, short black boots and puttees or black jackboots.

Summer Service Dress

Light khaki-green blouse with open neck, sleeves buttoned at the wrist, two patch pockets with buttoned flaps on the chest. This is worn outside the olive-brown trousers. Hat and shoes as for service dress.

Combat Dress

Helmet and equipment as for the Russian army, jacket and trousers khaki-green.

Specialist Dress

Tank suits and NBC Clothing as for the Russian Army.

Bulgarian Army Facing Colours

Worn on the collar patches in parade, walking out and service dress. The collar patch is trapeze-shaped; the first colour shown is the centre colour, the second colour is the piping around it. The regimental badge is worn on the collar patch.

Armour	– Black and red
Artillery	– Black and red
Engineers	– Black and dark blue
Signals	– Black and dark blue
Infantry	– Red and black
Medical	– Red and black
Motor Transport	– Black and red
Administration	– Brown and red
Intendance	– Purple and black

Internal Security Troops – Red and light blue
Frontier Troops – Dark yellow and red

Rank Badges

Worn on the shoulder-boards. For other ranks parade, walking out and service dress these boards are in the same colours as the collar patches; officers' shoulder-boards for these forms of dress are gold with red edging and five-pointed silver stars (silver with gold stars for medical). The regimental badge is worn at the base of the shoulder-board for other ranks and at the top of the shoulder-board for officers up through the rank of colonel. Internal

Security Troops and Frontier Troops wear no special badges.

Private	– no badge
Senior Private	– one thin lateral silver stripe
Corporal	– two thin lateral gold stripes
Sergeant	– three thin lateral gold stripes
Staff Sergeant	– one very wide lateral gold stripe
Sergeant Major	– one very wide lateral gold stripe and a wide gold stripe from the bottom of the shoulder-board to the lateral stripe.

(For medical personnel the stripes are in the reversed colour, ie for gold read silver and vice-versa.)

Second Lieutenant	– one small star
Lieutenant	– two small stars placed laterally
Senior Lieutenant	– three small stars placed in a pyramid
Captain	– four small stars (a pyramid and one above it)
Major	– one small star
Lieutenant-Colonel	– two small stars placed laterally
Colonel	– three small stars in pyramid
Major-General	– one large star.
Lieutenant-General	– two large stars one above the other.
Colonel-General	– three large stars one above the other.
Army General	– four large stars one above the other.

one red stripe along the centre of the shoulder-board.

two red stripes along the centre of the shoulder-board.

The shoulder-boards of major-generals and above are patterned as for those of Russian general officers. This pattern is the Austrian general officers' lace of the 1800 period and it is still worn today on Austrian general officers' collar patches. Field and fatigue shoulder-boards are in the uniform colour with red stripes and lace and green plastic stars and badges as in the Soviet Army.

Bulgarian Army Flags

The national flag, in the centre the rampant lion within a wreath of ears of corn all in gold. The flag is edged in gold fringes; the flagstaff is yellow and the tip an open gold spearpoint within which is the golden rampant lion. From below the tip depend gold cords and tassels.

THE CZECHOSLOVAKIAN SOCIALIST REPUBLIC

Population – 14,800,000. **Capital** – Prague.

Armed Forces:

    Army – 145,000 men; 3,500 tanks.

    Air Force – 40,000 men; 504 combat aircraft: 12 ground attack squadrons with SU-7s, MiG-15s, and MiG-17s; 18 interceptor squadrons with MiG-19s and MiG-21s; 6 reconnaissance squadrons with MiG-21s, Il-28s and L-29s. Transports – 50+ Li-2, Il-14 and Il-18. Helicopters – 90+ Mi-1, Mi-4 and Mi-8. Some SA-2 SAM.

Para-military forces – 35,000 Border guards (Pohranicki Straz); 150,000 Peoples' Militia (eventually to be 250,000).

Reserves   – 1,000,000.

Defence Spending   – $1,875 million in 1972 (5·8% of GNP).

Head of State – President Ludvik Svoboda, elected on 30 March 1968 for a five-year term. Parliament consists of the Federal Assembly, a two-chamber body with full executive and legislative powers. The lower house is the Peoples' Chamber with 200 members elected by the voters; the upper chamber is the Chamber of the Nations (President – Dalibor Hanes), with 150 members equally divided between the Czech area of the country and the Slovak area. No one may be member of both chambers simultaneously, and both chambers are elected for four-year terms.

Czechoslovakia is subdivided into the republics of Czechen (Bohemia, Moravia and Silesia) which have together 220 members in their "National Council" (President – Euzen Erban), and Slovakia which has 150 in her National Council (President – Ondrej Klococ).

External affairs, defence, etc are handled by the Federal Government consisting of the prime minister, his deputy, the ministers and those state secretaries of cabinet rank.

Prime minister is, at time of writing, Lubomir Strougal (a Czech) and defence minister is Colonel-General Martin Dzur (a Slovak). First secretary of the Czechoslovakian Communist Party (and thus the holder of real power) is Gustav Husak; born on 10 January 1913, he has been a member of the party since 1933. In April 1969 Husak replaced Alexandre Dubcek, who was removed on Russian insistence because of his liberal tendencies.

Czechoslovakia is a member of the Warsaw Pact and has general military service liability for all men between 20 and 50 years. Service in the army is two years, in the air force three. Subsequent to this service, all ex-conscripts are then transferred to the 1st Reserve until the age of 40, when they revert to the 2nd Reserve until 50.

The country is divided into two military districts, with headquarters at Prague and Pisek. Since the 1968 invasion the country has played host to five Soviet divisions (three motor rifle and two tank). Training is closely supervised by Russian advisers as is staff work at all levels. Due to their passive attitude during the invasion, the Czech army has not suffered a bloody purge like that which their Hungarian "comrades" went through after 1956.

In spite of the heavy-handed Communist commercial and industrial policy, Czechoslovakia has remained the most highly developed nation behind the Iron Curtain; she produces much of her own armaments and also exports to other Warsaw Pact countries such as Poland and Hungary. Her army is very well equipped, but it is of course almost impossible to arrive at a satisfactory assessment of the morale of the individual soldiers and officers, and thus no accurate forecast of combat value can be attempted. It is likely that the army would be utterly reliable if a Soviet offensive were successful; what would happen if the Soviets suffered a reverse is pure conjecture.

Military doctrine, strategy and tactics are

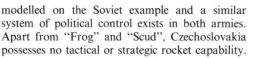

modelled on the Soviet example and a similar system of political control exists in both armies. Apart from "Frog" and "Scud", Czechoslovakia possesses no tactical or strategic rocket capability.

As a result of the First World War, the Austro-Hungarian Empire was dissolved and the previous domains became independent states. Czechoslovakia was created on 14 November 1918 and consisted of Bohemia, Moravia, parts of Silesia, Slovakia and Ruthenia. The notorious Munich agreement, signed by Britain, France, Germany and Italy on 29 September 1938, doomed this state and in March 1939 Slovakia proclaimed her independence (really an alliance with Germany) and Germany established a protectorate over Bohemia and Moravia. A Czech government in exile was set up in London in July 1940 and was headed by Dr Benes. Many Czechs made their way to England during the war and served in the armed forces. A particularly strong contingent became fighter pilots. By May 1945 American, Russian and Russian-sponsored Czech units had liberated the country and Czechoslovakia was reconstituted except for Ruthenia, which fell into Soviet Russia's eager hands. The post-war elections (May 1946) returned about 38% Communist representatives and a Communist (Klement Gottwald) became prime minister of a coalition government. Dr Benes was president and head of state. Infiltration of communists into powerful positions in the police began and this led to the resignation of twelve non-Communist ministers on 20 February 1948. This led to immediate elections and by May '48 the Communists had achieved an all-too-familiar 89%. President Benes resigned, and the usual form of Communist government followed until 1968.

Czechoslovakian Army Organisation
Five tank divisions, five motor rifle divisions, one airborne brigade, all organised on Soviet lines.

Equipment
Small arms All home-produced weapons shown in the national section.
Artillery Mostly home-produced weapons but also Soviet M-43 and M-55 57 mm AT guns and JSU-152 SP guns; Sagger, Snapper and Swatter ATGW; Frog and Scud SSM.
APCs Home-produced.
Tanks Some JSIII heavy tanks, about 3,400 medium tanks including T-34/85s, T-54/55s and T-62s.

Helicopters 200 Mi-1 and Mi-4 Soviet machines.

Czechoslovakian-produced equipment
M-50 Machine pistol
Calibre – 7·62 mm; loaded weight – 4 kg; effective range – 100 m; operation principle – blowback; rate of fire – 600 rpm; magazine – 32 rounds. Similar in appearance to the Sten gun; this weapon has a wooden butt.

M-24/26 Machine pistol
Calibre – 7·62 mm; loaded weight – 3·9 kg; effective range – 100 m; operation principle – blowback; rate of fire – 600 rpm; magazine – 32 rounds. A weapon which looks remarkably like the M-50.

M52/57 Self loading carbine
Calibre – 7·62 mm; loaded weight (with bayonet) – 4·35 kg; effective range – 400 m; operation principle – gas assisted; magazine – 10 rounds.

M58 Machine carbine
Details as for Russian AK-47 except: loaded weight – 4 kg; rate of fire – 700–800 rpm.

M1952/57 Light machine gun
Calibre – 7·62 mm; unloaded weight – 8 kg; effective range – 800 m; operation principle – gas assisted; rate of fire – 1,100 rpm; magazine – 25 rounds or belts of 100 rounds. This weapon is equipped with bipods or with a tripod chassis.

P-27 "Pancerovka" Light anti-tank rocket projector
Missile warhead calibre – 112 mm; warhead nature – hollow charge; weight of loaded projector – 10·15 kg; effective range – 150 m; armour piercing capability – 230 mm.

T-21 "Tarasnice" Recoilless anti-tank gun
Calibre – 82 mm; effective range – 450 m; loaded weight – 23·5 kg; warhead nature – hollow charge; armour piercing capability – 250 mm; muzzle velocity – 250 m/sec; rate of fire – 6 rpm. This equipment has two small wheels to increase its mobility.

M-59A Recoilless anti-tank gun
Calibre – 82 mm; effective range – 1,000 m; loaded weight – 392 kg; warhead nature – hollow charge; armour piercing capability – 250 mm; muzzle velocity – 745 m/sec; rate of fire – 4 rpm.

Left, Italian 6th Alpine Battalion cap badge, and collar patch of the *Artigliera a Cavallo*. Above, group of Italian army officer cadets in walking-out dress. Below, Italian infantrymen in camouflaged combat dress with adaptation of wartime German MG 42 machine gun, still widely used throughout Europe.

This is a towed weapon, developed by the Skoda firm as were the P27 and the T21.

M-52 85 mm anti-tank gun
Range – 16·2 km; muzzle velocity (HESH) – 820 m/sec, APDS – 1,070 m/sec; armour piercing capability – 123 mm at 1 km. This towed gun is employed as for the Russian M-45 85 mm anti-tank gun.

M-55 100 mm towed anti-tank gun
Details as for Russian M-55 100 mm anti-tank gun except – muzzle velocity – 900 m/sec; armour piercing capability – 110 mm at 1 km. The Czechs use the Tatra 138 6 × 6 lorry as prime mover.

Anti-Aircraft Weapons
12·7 mm DSchK
Quadruple heavy machine gun (Russian guns, Czech chassis). Muzzle velocity – 860 m/sec; weight in firing position (on three-legged platform) – 641 kg; range (AA) – 1 km; rate of fire – 4 × 600 rpm. This weapon is equipped with two wheels and is used in motor rifle regiments.

M-53 30 mm twin cannon
Range (AA) – 1·4 km; muzzle velocity – 1,000 m/sec; rate of fire – 2 × 500 rpm. As well as a four-wheeled, towed equipment, the Czechs also produce a self propelled version based on an armoured Praga, 6 × 6, "V3S" truck which is employed in the tank regiments.

57 mm AA MG
Details and ammunition as for the Russian M-50 57 mm AA MG.

Armoured Vehicles
Středni Kolový Obojživelný Transportér (SKOT) APC·
This eight wheeled, light armoured vehicle was a common Czech-Polish development which was introduced into service in those countries in 1964 and has also been delivered to Hungary. It is based on the Tatra lorry; the engine is in the centre of the vehicle, all wheels are driven and the tyre pressure can be varied from within the vehicle. It is the most common motor rifle APC in Czechoslovakia and is inherently amphibious. Weight – 12·5 tons; engine – 270 hp air-cooled diesel of a modified Tatra 803 V8 model; speed – 95 km/hr on roads, 9 km/hr in water; road range – 600 km; length – 7·4 m; width – 2·5 m; height – 2·3 m. Crew – driver, commander and 8 men; armament – one 12·7 mm MG (Skot-2A – Polish version – has a turret mounted 14·5 mm MG and a co-axial 7·62 mm MG). The vehicle has twenty forward and four reverse gears; water propulsion by two screws. Overhead cover gives ABC protection.

Transportér Obojživelný Pašový Středni ("Topas") APC
This tracked, amphibious APC is a Czech adaptation of the Soviet BTR-50P which was introduced into Russian service in 1958 and into other Warsaw Pact states in 1962. Also termed the OT-62, the Czech versions include an ambulance; and the OT-62 of 1964 vintage has a 57 mm recoilless anti-tank projector mounted alongside the right-hand turret. Weight – 14 tons; crew – commander, driver and seven men; height, length and width, water propulsion etc as for BTR-50PB. ABC protected.

OT-810 APC
A half-track vehicle, remarkably similar to the World War II German "Halbkettenfahrzeug". It has a Tatra diesel motor and is used in the Czech army instead of the BTR-152.

Vyproštovací Tank (VT)-34 Armoured Recovery Vehicle
This is the Czech version based on the T-34 tank.

Wheeled (soft skinned) Vehicles
Tatra T805 4 × 4, 1·5 tonner
Weight (empty) – 2,150 kg; length – 4·72 m; width – 2·04 m; height – 2·61 m; engine – 75 hp, eight cylinder, air-cooled, petrol; speed – 80 km/hr; road range – 400 km. Apart from load carrying vehicles, command, signals and ambulance versions are produced.

Praga V3S 6 × 6, 5 ton lorry
Weight (empty) 5,470 kg; length – 6·91 m; width – 2·32 m; height – 2·35 m; engine – 98 hp, 4 cylinder, air-cooled diesel; speed – 62 km/hr; road range – 450 km. This vehicle has many variants and functions; load carrier, tanker, artillery tractor, weapon platform for multiple rocket launcher and AA guns, command; signals-workshop bodies are also in use. The Bulgarian army also uses the vehicle.

Tatra T137, 4 × 4, 7 ton lorry

Weight (empty) – 5,700 kg; length – 7·32 m; width – 2·35 m; height – 2·44 m; engine – 160 hp, eight cylinder, air-cooled diesel; speed – 70 km/hr; road range – 480 km. An obsolete vehicle, fast going out of service. Used as artillery tractor and load carrier.

Tatra 111R, 6 × 6, 8 ton lorry

Weight (empty) – 9,100 kg; length – 8·3 m; width – 2·4 m; height – 2·55 m; engine – 180 hp, twelve cylinder, air-cooled diesel; speed 62 km/hr; road range – ? General purpose transport vehicle, also used by the Rumanian army.

Tatra 141, 6 × 6 tractor

Weight (empty) – 18,000 kg; length – 7·45 m; width – 2·58 m; height – 2·8 m; engine – 180 hp, twelve cylinder, air-cooled diesel; speed – 38 km/hr; road range – ? Equipped with crane and 8-ton winch; this vehicle is also used in the armies of Rumania and Hungary.

Tatra 138, 6 × 6, 12 ton lorry

Weight (empty) – 8,750 kg; length – 8·75 m; width – 2·45 m; height – 2·44 m; engine – 180 hp, eight cylinder, air-cooled diesel, speed – 70 km/hr; road range – 400 km. Introduced in 1965, this vehicle replaces the Tatra 111R.

Tatra 813 Kolos, 8 × 8, 10 ton lorry

Weight (empty) 13,500 kg; length – 8·67 m; width – 2·5 m; height – 2·7 m; engine – 270 hp,

Czechoslovakian artillery crew in winter combat clothing, 1971. (Keystone)

twelve cylinder, air-cooled diesel; speed – 80 km/hr; road range – 600 km. A very capable cross-country vehicle which is also the basis of the OT-64 APC. A derivative of this lorry is the Tatra 814, 6 × 6 vehicle.

Engineer Equipment
Střední Mostová Souprava (*SMS*) medium bridging equipment

This pontoon bridging equipment replaced the old Lehká Mostová Souprava (LMS)-20B light bridging device. Its big brother is the Těžká Mostová Souprava (TMS) or heavy bridging equipment. It is used as for the Russian PTT system and it can be used either as a bridge or to make ferries each of three pontoons.

*   *   *

In 1973 the Czech version of the Soviet BM21 multiple rocket launcher was introduced. It replaces the Czech 32-barrelled RM-130 rocket launcher which was mounted on the Praga 6 × 6 vehicle. The new Czech rocket launcher uses the Tatra-813 Kolos 8 × 8 truck as a prime mover and the vehicle has a lightly armoured driver's cab. The 40-barrelled launcher is mounted at the rear of the truck on a swivel pedestal, and between the launcher and the cab are 40 rockets in a storage cage. It is thought that by loading the launcher initially from the accompanying logistics vehicle, firing one salvo and then reversing the launcher and loading it for a second time with the "indigenous" rockets, a second salvo can be delivered onto the same target within only a few minutes of the first. This increases the "shock" effect of this area weapon immensely over the Soviet model (and those of Western states), which require a considerably longer reload period.

Czechoslovakian Army Uniforms
Ceremonial Parade Dress

Light olive-brown peaked cap with red headband and red piping to crown; black peak and chin straps; pentagonal badge with lion and star.

Light olive-brown, wrist length, single-breasted, open-necked jacket with four button front, two patch breast pockets with pointed button flaps, two slit skirt pockets with plain flaps, plain cuffs; shoulder-straps; single rear vent. Regimental badges in gold or silver on the collar. Officers and other ranks wear black and yellow striped waist sashes with gold buckle plates. Light khaki shirt, black tie, light olive-brown trousers, black boots and gaiters or black shoes (or light olive-brown riding breeches

and black jackboots), black gloves. Buttons: There are three types, gold for officers, silver for NCOs and green plastic for conscripts. The design on the button is crossed swords, hilts down.

Parade Dress

As above but officers wear brown leather Sam Browne belts, other ranks black leather waist-belts with rectangular steel buckle plates bearing a five-pointed star.

Walking Out Dress

As above but without the belts. Officers wear brown shoes and gloves.

Conscripts do not wear the peaked cap, they wear instead a fore-and-aft forage cap in light olive brown cloth with the pentagonal badge on the left hand side. For winter wear there is a Soviet pattern fur cap with pentagonal badge on the front flap and with the side and rear flaps also buttoned up.

Officers' Shirt Sleeve Order

Light grey blouse with open neck, sleeves buttoned at the wrist, two breast pockets with buttoned flaps and the waistband worn outside the light olive-brown trousers. Shoes or boots, peaked cap or forage cap.

Other-Ranks' Shirt Sleeve Order

Light grey shirt, open neck, cuffs buttoned at the wrist, no pockets; light olive-brown "denim" trousers, brown leather belt with square, open, steel buckle, black boots and black leather gaiters, forage cap.

Greatcoat

Light olive brown, double breasted with five pairs of buttons, mid-calf length, half belt in the rear.

Combat Dress

Peaked cap with ear and neck flaps buttoned over the small crown, hip length jacket and trousers all in light green material covered with brown camouflage stripes. The jacket has concealed buttons and two breast pockets. Black boots and black leather gaiters. Steel helmet and equipment are Soviet pattern.

Specialist Clothing

NBC protective equipment and tank crew suits are as for the Soviet Army. Paratroopers have close fitting, brown leather helmets with chin straps, jackets and trousers as for the normal troops but with a "blotty" mottled light green, dark green and brown pattern. Tank troops wear black berets, paratroopers red.

Miscellaneous

On the upper left arm of parade, walking out and service dress is worn a badge consisting of a tri-angular outline in yellow (point down) within which is the national roundel divided into three equal parts, white on top, blue to the left and red on the bottom. With the light grey, shirt sleeve order blouse a similar badge (but with less depth vertically) is worn on the upper left breast.

THE GERMAN DEMOCRATIC REPUBLIC

Population – 17,285,000.   **Capital** – East Berlin.
Armed Forces:
    Army – 130,000 men (including 40,000 Border Guards); 3,000 tanks.
    Navy – 16,000 men; 2 destroyers, 25 coastal escorts, 49 minesweepers, 12 Osa class patrol boats
        with Styx SSM, 65 MTBs, 18 landing ships and landing craft; 16 Mi-4 helicopters.
  Air Force – 25,000 men, 304 combat aircraft; 19 fighter squadrons (2 with MiG-17s, 17 with MiG-21s);
        30 transport planes (An-2s and Il-14s); 30 helicopters (Mi-1s, Mi-4s and Mi-8s); five air
        defence regiments equipped with 130 AA guns of 57 mm and 100 mm, and SA-2 SAM.
Para-military forces – 20,000 security troops and 350,000 workers' militia (Kampfgruppen); the latter form
        the national reserves.
Defence Spending – DM (East) 7,600,000,000 in 1972 – approximately £1,100,000,000 (approx. 5%
        GNP).

Tightly shackled into the fabric of the Warsaw Pact, the East Germans have fallen over backwards since the end of the Second World War to show their Soviet masters that they have become the most reliable of their allies. The SED (Sozialistische Einheitspartei Deutschland) – the only permitted political party in the GDR – takes its orders directly from the Soviet government and thus from the Central Committee of the Communist Party of the Soviet Union. The Ministry of Defence is a directly controlled organ of the SED administration; the defence minister of the GDR is at time of writing Armee General Heinz Hoffmann, who was trained in the Soviet Union in the Frunse Akademie and fought in the International Brigade in Spain. Hoffman has also been trained in the Soviet Military Academie since the end of the war.

The Defence Ministry is located at Strausberg near Berlin and is also the "Militärbezirk I" (Military District I). As well as receiving directives from the SED, the Defence Ministry of the GDR is also instructed from the following sources:
a. the Supreme Command of the Warsaw Pact in Moscow.
b. the Ministry for State Security (a GDR body under Colonel-General Mielke in East Berlin who, in turn, gets his orders from the KGB in Moscow).

Military Doctrine

All military doctrine, strategic and tactical teach-in the NVA (Peoples' Army) is a slavish copy of the Soviet military gospel. As in the Soviet army, there is an overwhelming accent on the political education of all ranks in the Nationale Volksarmee, and even down to company level there is a political officer (usually the second-in-command of the unit) whose

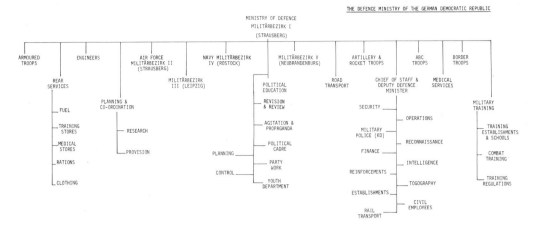

THE DEFENCE MINISTRY OF THE GERMAN DEMOCRATIC REPUBLIC

special duty it is to ensure that continuous and relentless political indoctrination takes place both on and off duty, in the camp and on manoeuvers, and that all ranks attend. Officers undergo eight hours political training each month; soldiers get four hours per week. New recruits to the NVA are not unused to such schooling, however; it begins in the Kindergarten, is intensified throughout later education and continues when the child enters the "voluntary" Freie Deutsche Jugend (FDJ or Free German Youth) and later the Gesellschaft für Sport und Technik (GST or Sport and Technical Society), both of which are also para-military organisations working closely with the SED and the NVA.

Army History

The NVA was formed on 3 July 1948 as the "Hauptabteilung Grenzpolizei-Bereitschaften" (Border and Riot Police) on instructions of the Soviet Military Administration in Germany (SMAD). Recruits came from the members of the "Nationalkomitee Freies Deutschland" (National Committee of Free Germany), a Communist-inspired organisation raised among Russian-held German prisoners of the Second World War. By October 1949 this organisation had assumed military form and in September 1952 the title was changed to the "Kasernierte Volkspolizei" (Barracked Peoples Police) which now boasted four "Army Groups". Uniforms, initially dark blue and with police rank badges and designations, were now changed for Russian pattern, khaki coloured clothing.

This was the situation until 1955, and volunteers (mostly straight out of Russian prison camps) were supposed to provide sufficient recruits. This was not the case, however, and on 26 September 1955, Article 112 of the GDR Constitution was suddenly altered to include the phrase that "the Republic is responsible for the protection of its homeland and the population". On 18 January 1956 the "Nationale Volksarmee" was proclaimed in being and conscription was the order of the day, conscientious objectors not being tolerated. Military service lasts for eighteen months (female "volunteers" serve for three years). By the end of 1957 total armed forces in the GDR were 115,000 men.

In 1956 the Russian-style uniforms were replaced by those still in use today: a mixture of the old Wehrmacht uniforms of World War II with certain modifications to include Russian commissioned ranks. The colour of the uniforms was described as "Stone Grey" to make a clear distinction from the Fascist clothing of Hitler's army, but many other minute details of the Wehrmacht uniforms were retained (such as the pattern on the silver lace edging to NCOs' rank badges).

Recently the paratroops of the NVA have been the vehicle for some uniform changes, which will be discussed later, but the sight of a marching NVA unit is enough to stir the heart of the most depressed National Socialist – until he remembers their current political leanings!

Organisation of the NVA

As in the Soviet Army, levels of military organisation range from "Front" through "Army", "Division", "Regiment", "Battalion", "Company", and "Platoon" to "Section". Corps and brigades are unknown, and the Soviet division is a weaker unit than the average NATO division. The NVA has currently six divisions; four Motor Rifle (mechanised infantry) and two Armoured. Apart from this there are the usual army troops and training establishments. The Border Troops are not included in this total although there are currently rumours that this body may soon be reorganised and placed under direct NVA control.

The Motor Rifle and Armoured divisions are organised completely according to the Russian models, and charts of their make-up are included in this chapter.

As is well known, the Soviet Army is designed almost exclusively for offensive purposes and is thus very heavy in armoured fighting vehicles but relatively weak in infantry.

The Motor Rifle Division

The 27 infantry companies of the division are all mounted in armoured personnel carriers (APCs) of the following types.

BTR 152 – an obsolescent vehicle with an open fighting compartment. It is now largely replaced by more modern equipments.

BTR 50P – this tracked APC is built on the chassis of the PT76 light reconnaissance tank and has now been modified so that the fighting compartment is closed, thus affording protection against ABC attack. It is still to be seen in quite large numbers in the NVA. It is amphibious.

BTR 60P – the replacement for the BTR 50P has eight wheels, a closed fighting compartment and is amphibious. It has a good cross-country performance and later versions are equipped with a turret-mounted machine gun.

BMP 76 – this newest Soviet APC has been issued in limited numbers to all armies of the Warsaw Pact but as yet has not made a general appearance in normal divisional units. It is thought that training units have them and that it will be some time before they are "on the ground" in any great numbers.

Reconnaisance units use either the PT76 amphibious tank or the BRDM series wheeled scout cars. In the divisional Reconnaisance Battalion motor cycle and side car combinations are also to be seen.

Each Motor Rifle Regiment has its own organic tank battalion and there is also the Armoured Regiment of the division with three more battalions thus making a total of eighteen tank companies to the 27 APC infantry companies – a rather heavy armour mix for all but attack purposes. These armoured troops mainly use the T54/55 tank,

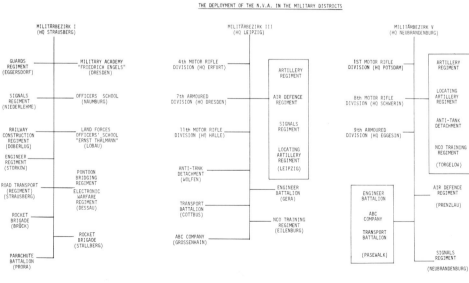

THE DEPLOYMENT OF THE N.V.A. IN THE MILITARY DISTRICTS

although these are increasingly being replaced by the superior T62. In 1968 those NVA units which took part in the invasion of Czechoslovakia used the T34s normally reserved for training purposes.

Equipment
Air Defence

At divisional level is an air defence battalion and each Motor Rifle or Armoured Regiment has its own organic air defence battery. Considerable effort is thus expended countering any possible low-level air attack threat from NATO. The 57 mm gun is used in both the armoured and towed batteries.

Artillery

Each Motor Rifle Regiment has a 120 mm mortar company and this usually fires from the dismounted position. The Artillery Regiment of the division has two howitzer battalions each with three batteries whose guns are a mixture of the 122 mm M1938 howitzer, the 122 mm D-30 howitzer and the 100 mm gun. Up to 5% of the total Warsaw Pact artillery ammunition is of a chemical or biological nature and delivery to the target can be achieved either by conventional guns or with rockets.

Anti-Tank Defence

As in NATO states, this is a mixture of rockets, anti-tank guns and tanks.

Anti-tank Grenade Launcher RPG 7

Carried at a scale of one per motor rifle section, this weapon works on the "Bazooka" principle and fires an 85 mm shaped charge grenade. It has an effective range of 550 metres and has been much used in the Vietnam War; it has also appeared in the hands of the terrorists of the "Irish Republican Army" in the British province of Northern Ireland.

The B-10 82 mm Recoilless Gun

This is found only in the parachute battalion; as well as shaped charge shells, it can fire normal high explosive projectiles and thus functions as artillery support for the parachutists in their very vulnerable phase directly after landing. Its effective range is 5,000 metres (high explosives) and 400 metres.

Rocket Launcher SPG-9

This is a 76 mm calibre weapon, two of which are held in each motor rifle battalion.

"Swatter" Anti-tank Guided Weapon (ATGW)

This weapon is mounted on the BRDM light reconnaisance vehicle and is held at motor rifle regiment level.

"Sagger" ATGW

This is the standard equipment of the motor rifle regiment's ATGW battery and of the motor rifle division's AT battalion. It is also possible to fire this weapon from a "remote" position, ie the firer can control the weapon from a position away from the carrying vehicle.

Atomic, Biological and Chemical Defence

As in the Soviet army, much training time is spent in practising defence against atomic, biological and chemical attack. Exercises frequently include the erection of major decontamination points in which personnel, weapons and even tanks are "decontaminated". Russian pattern equipment and doctrine are used and soldiers become accustomed to living and working in the highly restrictive and uncomfortable equipment.

Apart from certain wheeled vehicles and most of their signals and electronic equipment, the NVA is completely dependent on the Soviet Union for its fighting vehicles and weapons. The characteristics of these weapons can be seen in the relevant tables elsewhere in this book.

Small Arms

The Marakow pistol, the Dragunow and Simonow carbines, the Kalaschnikow assault rifle and the Kalaschnikow light (and heavy) machine guns.

Anti-tank Weapons

The RPG-7 anti-tank rocket launcher; the RPG-6 and RKG-3M anti-tank grenades.

Armoured Vehicles:
Scout cars BRDM and BRDM-2.
Armoured personnel carriers BTR-152, BTR-50P, BTR-60P, BTR-60PA, BTR-60PB, BMP-76.
Tanks Amphibious scout tank PT-76, battle tanks T-34/85, T-54A, T-54AM, T-55, T-62.

Anti-Aircraft Equipment

14·5 mm machine gun; ZSU-23-2 twin 23 mm cannon; ZSU-23-4 radar controlled, quad mounted 23 mm cannon on tracked, armoured chassis; S-60 57 mm cannon; ZSU-57-2 twin 57 mm cannon on tracked, armoured chassis; 100 mm cannon. Surface-to-air missile SA-2.

Artillery

120 mm Mortar M-43; 122 mm howitzer M-1938; 122 mm howitzer D-30; 152 mm howitzer D-1; 152 mm gun-howitzer D-20; 100 mm gun; 130 mm gun.

Rockets

122 mm BM-21 rocket launcher; 240 mm BM-24 rocket launcher; "Frog"; "Scud" and "Scud-B".

Engineer Equipment

Amphibious vehicles P2S; BAW; K-61 (GPT); PTS-M; GSP; PMP bridging train; TMM bridging train; MTU bridging tank; PT-54 mine clearing equipment; PMR-3 mine clearance equipment; BAT roadmaking equipment; BTM excavator; GP-60 trench digging equipment.

Light Wheeled Vehicles

ES-250-A motor cycle; P3 jeep; GAZ-69 jeep; Robur-LO 1800A four wheeled lorry; ZIL-157 lorry; G-5 lorry; Ural-375D 8 ton lorry; KR AZ-214 12 ton lorry; Tatra 813 10 ton lorry.

Recruitment and Recruit Training

With a conscription period of eighteen months, the NVA is geared to change over 33% of its conscripts at six-month intervals. The first four weeks of a conscript's military life are spent in the "Rekruteneinheit" (or basic training unit) where they learn drill, marching and basic combat training. During this four-week period the other conscripts, in their second and third half-year periods, undergo intensive individual training in their allotted skills. Recruits come from the basic training unit to take up the simpler positions in their units.

At the end of each half-year period, training is tested in division scale exercises. Heavy emphasis is placed on training at night, in adverse weather conditions and under "nuclear" conditions. Physical fitness is constantly maintained at a high level.

After the four weeks of basic training the conscripts are taken into their units and sworn in on the flag of that unit in a ceremony which is played up to the highest degree, with all members of the unit on parade in best dress, the band present and a few well-chosen words being spoken by a local party

* Produced in the GDR.

Soviet SA-2 "Guideline", in service throughout the Warsaw Pact.

dignitary. The oath is long and binds the conscript to loyalty to the government of the GDR and to alliance with the Soviet army. Coupled with this swearing in, the recruit receives his Kalaschnikow assault rifle presented to him by a veteran of the local Kampfgruppen or home guard, thus symbolising the idealogical link between the proletariat and "their" army.

Each regiment has a flag which is accorded a status almost as holy as that of Lenin himself. Regiments which are awarded honour title (usually names of obscure heroes of the class struggle) are presented with cravats to attach to their flags. The design of these flags is standard and consists of the GDR national flag with the cockade in the centre surrounded by the inscription: "FÜR DEN SCHUTZ DER ARBEITER UND BAUERN-MACHT" (for the protection of the workers' and peasants' power); a golden laurel wreath surrounds this inscription and the flag has a heavy golden fringe. Cravats are red with gold tassels on the ends and the honour title is also embroidered in gold. The flagstaff is brown, the tip chrome and bearing the GDR crest. The flag is carried by an NCO in a

Command version of the Soviet BTR-50P tracked APC.

brown leather belt, and he is flanked by two officers who usually carry sabres.

The NVA Women's Army Corps

Female volunteers, who usually serve for three years, are trained for employment in the fields of medical care, signalling and staff work. They undergo a basic training which is only slightly less rigorous than that which their male comrades undergo.

Discipline and Combat Value

Discipline in the NVA is strict and the all-pervading Communist informant system effectively contains any discontent which may be (and undoubtedly is) present. Although very few convinced Communists may be in the ranks of the NVA, the system is so well constructed that it may be safely assumed that "every man this day will do his duty" and that the NVA must be regarded as an efficient and well trained army; reliable, in the Communist sense.

The Uniforms of the NVA

In many details the uniforms of the Wehrmacht of the Second World War have been retained but sufficient changes have been introduced to emphasise the socialist character of the new army.

Headwear:

a. *"Schiffschen"* (*or little ship*) – *the forage cap.* It is in stone grey material, very simple in design (rather Russian) and has the GDR cockade in the front centre. It is normally only worn in barracks or on field duty.

b. *Service dress cap.* This peaked cap is of exactly the same design as that in World War II. The upper portion is stone grey, the headband black and the piping in the facing colour. The front badge is the GDR cockade within an oak leaf wreath (silver for officers and men, gold for generals) and the chin strap over the black, plastic peak is black for the men, silver for officers and gold for generals.

c. *Steel helmet.* Based on a German design of the Second World War era, this is a refreshing change from the ubiquitous Russian pattern helmet worn by the rest of the Warsaw Pact countries. It is of a good ballistic shape, somewhat wide (rather like the British Army helmet) and has a well-fitting chin strap. It is worn for parades and guard duties as well as active service.

d. *Tankmans helmet.* This padded helmet is an exact copy of the Russian article.

e. *Beret.* The parachute battalion wore a bright red beret up until mid-1971 but this has since been changed to a sky blue one just like that worn by their Russian counterparts. On both the red and the sky blue berets the badge was the GDR cockade.

The legendary jackboots are still to be seen, as are the breeches which go with them. The tunic has changed its colour from "Feldgrau" (Field grey) to "Steingrau" (Stone grey) which has less of a green shade in it than its predecessor; otherwise it is identical in style and cut to the war-time garment. The collar is black and the buttons matt, white metal (gold for generals). On everyday service dress (Dienstanzug) the cuffs are plain but on walking out dress (Ausgehanzug) and parade dress (Paradeanzug) they are decorated with two silver lace loops each with a central stripe in the facing colour. On the collar of all the above-mentioned forms of dress are the "Spiegel", double silver lace loops, also bearing the facing colours. Facing colours appear also on the edges of the shoulder-straps (and the collar edging of officers' jackets) and the top edge of the cuff. Facing colours are as follows:

Armour – pink
Artillery – dark red
Engineers – black
Signals – lemon yellow
Infantry – white
Technical troops – black
Rear services – dark green
Medical corps – dark blue

Officers of general rank wear bright red facings and special pattern gold lace embroidery to collars and cuffs.

Badges of rank are worn on the shoulder-straps (except for combat kit) and there are different patterns of collar and cuff embroidery for officers and non-commissioned ranks. The collars of NCOs jackets are edged in silver lace. Officers may also wear a double-breasted jacket when walking out and this is the only jacket which is worn without a leather waist-belt. It is worn with a collar and tie. The single-breasted jacket is worn closed to the neck in winter or open, and with an open-necked shirt, in summer. Recently the parachute battalion has been observed wearing a new style walking out dress jacket with a stone grey collar (designed to be worn open) and a shirt and tie. It is likely that this will spread to the rest of the NVA soon.

The everyday belt of NCOs and men is black leather and has a rectangular white metal buckle plate bearing the GDR crest. Apart from the decoration, this and the officer's brown leather belt and silver and black sash (Feldbinde) are exactly as the World War II pattern.

Officers on parade with armed troops carry sabres and officers attending such parades, but not par-

Tank crews in NBC suits go through decontamination drill on their T-54/55 series tanks.

taking, carry the small "Dolch" (ceremonial dagger) on silver slings on the left side of their Feldbinde. Officers on parade wear white gloves; jackboots are worn on parade by all ranks.

Tank crews wear the Russian pattern, dark blue "boiler suits".

The combat clothing is camouflaged and badges of rank appear as white stripes on the shoulder-straps. Equipment is of canvas webbing (until recently it was of black leather, World War II pattern).

The greatcoat is stone grey, double breasted with two rows each of five white metal buttons. The collar is black and shoulder-straps are worn as for the service dress jacket. The "Hauptfeldwebel" (equivalent of the British Army's Regimental Sergeant Major) wears a broad silver stripe around the top of his cuffs in addition to his normal shoulder rank badges and silver collar edging.

Service badges

Soldiers who volunteer to serve longer periods than the normal conscription (which is eighteen months) wear a white chevron, point down, on the lower left sleeve. Professional non-commissioned ranks wear two such chevrons.

Trade badges

Badges are awarded for proficiency in a particular trade and these are in the facing colour and worn on the lower left sleeve (above the service chevrons if these also are worn).

Classification badges

In addition to trade badges, soldiers reaching a certain standard of proficiency in a particular skill are awarded "medals" which are worn on the left breast. They are in three classes – bronze, silver and gold – and resemble a pilot's "wings" with a central motif reflecting the particular skill.

Various other achievement decorations are awarded including a silver lanyard for marksman-ship, a military sports badge, a general proficiency badge and the "Bestenabzeichen" (awarded to the best soldier in the unit).

Officers who have successfully completed a course at the Soviet Army Staff College wear the small white diamond-shaped badge of that estab-lishment on their left breast pocket. Those officers who qualify at the NVAs own "Militärakademie Friedrich Engels" wear a red triangular badge in the same position.

Elite Unit Badges

Parachute Battalion: In addition to their light blue beret, these troops have a special collar badge. Instead of the normal silver "Spiegel" they wear a red trapezoidal patch bearing a white parachute over small, white wings.

The Guards Regiment: Together with its white facings, this unit wears a cuffband on the left sleeve reading: "NVA WACHREGIMENT". The troops of the Ministry for State Security, although not part of the NVA as such, wear NVA uniform with dark crimson facings and a cuff band reading: "WACH REGT F DZIERZYNSKI" (the founder of the Russian secret police).

THE HUNGARIAN PEOPLE'S REPUBLIC

Population – 10,500,000.　　　　　　　　　　　　　　**Capital** – Budapest.

Armed Forces:

　　Army – 90,000 men; 1,580 tanks.

　　Navy – 500 men in the Danube Flottila of 20 gunboats equipped with PT-76 turretted guns, and 40 minesweepers.

Air Force – 12,500 men, 108 combat aircraft; 9 squadrons MiG-19 and MiG-21 interceptors. Transports – 25 AN-2, Il-14s and Li-2s. Helicopters – 15 Mi-1s, Mi-4s and Mi-8s. Air defence – 2 battalions SA-2 SAM.

Para-military forces – 27,000 border guards and security police; 250,000 workers militia.

Defence Spending – $558 million in 1972 (3·5% of GNP).

Head of State is President Pál Losonczi (elected 14 April 1967). Parliament is the National Assembly (NA) of 352 elected members, all of the Peoples' Patriotic Front (Communist party) serving a four-year term. There is no other political party. Above this body is the Presidential Council consisting of the president, two vice-presidents and seventeen members elected by the NA. The government is formed out of members of the NA. The prime minister is currently Jenö Fock (appointed 12 May 1971); defence minister is General Lajos Czinege. As in most Communist states, real power lies in the Central Committee of the Communist Party and in Hungary this is now headed by Janos Kadar, the first secretary, and includes Jenö Fock.

Hungary is a member of the Warsaw Pact; there is universal military service liability for all men from the age of eighteen. Service is normally for two years (special units three years).

According to the peace treaty of 1947, Hungary's army was to be limited to 65,000 men and her air force to 5,000. Communist memories are selectively short. Hungary is divided into four military districts with headquarters at Budapest, Debrecen, Kiskunfélegyháza and Pécs. There are four Soviet army divisions in Hungary (two motor rifle, two tank) and a Soviet air division. The Hungarian army is firmly under Soviet control.

Military equipment (except for some APCs, armoured cars, artillery weapons and small arms) is of Soviet origin as is military doctrine, strategy and tactics. Apart from "Frog" SSM, Hungary possesses no tactical or strategic rocket forces. It is said that the Soviets were not impressed by the Hungarian army's performance in the Czechoslovakian invasion of 1968. Whether this was due to genuine military incapability or a conscious "dragging of feet" will probably never be known. Hungarian army officers enjoy a high position in society and are regarded as part of the nation's élite. For the men discipline is strict and pay low. Morale is difficult to assess accurately.

The two tank divisions are stationed in western Hungary, near Steinamanger and Raab, the motor rifle divisions in central Hungary near Stuhlweissenburg and Kecskemet; the air force division is east of Budapest near Szolnok.

Hungarian Army Organisation

Two tank divisions and four motor rifle divisions organised on Soviet lines; one of the tank divisions and one motor rifle division exist only as cadres in peacetime.

Equipment

Small Arms

9 mm Makarow pistols; 7·62 mm **PPSH M-41** SMGs; Simonow 7·62 mm semi-automatic carbine, 7·62 **AK-M** Kalaschnikow assault rifles (home manufactured); 7·62 mm RPK, RPD and RP-46 LMGs; Gorjunow M-49, 7·62 mm HMGs; DSchK M-38 HMG, 82 mm and 120 mm mortars.

Artillery

76 mm, 85 mm and 122 mm and 152 mm guns; 57 mm AT guns, Sagger, Snapper and Swatter ATGW, Frog SSM, 57 mm twin AA guns.

APCs

Home produced FUG-M scout cars, OT-65 Czech Scout cars and OT-64 APCs; Soviet BTR-152 APCs.

Tanks

Some JSIII heavy tanks; about 1,500 medium tanks mainly T-54/55s with some T-34/85s and some T-62s; 50 PT-76 light tanks.

Hungarian-produced Equipments

Small Arms:

M-41 Pistolet-Pulemet Schpagin (PPSH) Sub-machine gun

This is a Hungarian copy of the World War II Russian weapon. Calibre – 7·62 mm; weight – 3·65 kg; effective range – 100 m; operation principle – blow-back; rate of fire – 900 rpm; magazines – 71 rounds (drum) or 35 rounds (straight).

Machine Carbine 7·62 mm

This copy of the Russian AK-47 assault rifle weighs only 4·85 kg with magazine – this weight being achieved by use of hollow plastic butt and pistol grips – and can float (without a magazine). Other details as for the AK-47.

Armoured Vehicles:

Felderítő Úszó Gépkocsi (FUG) 65 amphibious scout car

Based on the Russian BTR-40P concept, this Hungarian development is also used by the Czech army where it is known as the OT-65, and the Polish army. In contrast to the BTR-40P, the FUG-65 has its motor in the rear. Retractable, metal cross-country wheels, chain driven, can be lowered to improve mobility. Engine – 100 hp Csepel D-144·44, air-cooled diesel. Water propulsion by hydrojets. Other details as for the BTR-40P.

FUG-65 with turret

First observed during the "Moldau" exercises in 1966, similar vehicles were seen in Poland later that same year. Crew – 4; armament – 1 × 14·5 mm MG and 1 × 7·62 mm MG.

Hungarian FUG "M66" turreted scout cars.

Soft-skinned wheeled vehicles:
Csepel D-352, 4 × 2, 3¼ ton lorry

Weight (empty) – 3,500 kg; length – 5·5 m; width – 2·13 m; height – 2·2 m; engine – 85 hp, four cylinder, water-cooled diesel; speed – 75 km/hr; road range – 300 km. This cargo vehicle is in fact a Hungarian licence copy of the Austrian Steyr lorry. It appears also as a tanker, command, signals and ambulance version. From 1955 it has been increasingly replaced by the Csepel D-420.

Csepel D-420, 4 × 2, 4 ton lorry

Weight (empty) – 4,000 kg; length – 5·5 m; width – 2·13 m; height – 2·2 m; engine – 85 hp, four cylinder, water-cooled diesel; speed – 75 km/hr; road range – 320 km.

Csepel K-800 tracked artillery tractor. (This is a licence production of the Soviet M-2 vehicle): length – 4·89 m; width – 2·4 m; height – 2·2 m; 105 hp, water-cooled diesel engine; max road speed – 48 km/hr; road range – 320 km; empty weight – 8,000 kg. Five small road wheels, front drive sprocket, rear idler, three return rollers, high flat bonnet and enclosed cab, open cargo compartment to the rear.

Hungarian Army Uniforms
Parade Dress

Soviet pattern steel helmet; light olive brown, single-breasted (open necked for officers, closed for other ranks), wrist length jacket with single rear vent, three button front, four patch pockets with square, button flaps. Regimental colours, badges and other ranks' rank badges are shown on the pentagonal collar patches; officers' ranks are shown on gold shoulder-boards. Officers wear brown leather Sam Browne belts with curved steel sabres with gold wrist strap and tassel, light olive brown riding breeches, black jackboots and brown gloves. Other ranks wear brown leather waist-belts with open, square steel buckles, light olive-brown trousers, black boots and brown webbing gaiters.

Walking Out Dress (Gala – officers only)

White peaked cap with oval badge (red-over-white-over-green and bearing a five-pointed red star), black peak and chin strap. (Generals' white hats have red headbands and crown piping and gold cord chin strap, band and crown piping in the facing and in gold). White jacket of the same cut as above but with three buttons at the cuff; gold shoulder-

boards. Light olive-brown trousers, black shoes. (Generals' trousers have broad red side stripes.)

Normal Walking Out Dress

Light olive-brown cap with black peak and chin strap, band and crown piping in the facing colour. Jacket and trousers as for parade dress, boots or shoes.

Shirt Sleeve Order

Hat as for normal walking out; light grey blouse, sleeves buttoned at the wrist, two patch breast pockets with square, buttoned flaps. Black tie or open neck; officers wear either gold or field shoulder-boards, other ranks wear collar tabs and plain shoulder-straps. The blouse buttons over the light olive-brown trousers, or can be worn inside the trousers if the Sam Browne with pistol is worn. Boots or shoes.

Hungarian soldier in combat dress, with "M66" scout car in background.

Hungarian branch collar badges, worn in yellow metal on service and walking out dress, left to right, top: Infantry, Armour, Artillery, Air Corps; bottom: Air Defence Artillery, Signals, Motor Transport, Rail Transport.

Barrack Dress

Khaki denim jacket and trousers of the same cut as Walking Out Dress; soft-topped light olive-brown peaked cap with side and rear flaps turned up; normal cap badge, boots and gaiters. No coloured collar patches. In summer a light grey shirt with open neck and rolled-up sleeves is worn.

Winter Wear

Grey fur Soviet pattern cap with normal cap badge; light olive-brown, double-breasted greatcoat with five pairs of buttons; regimental collar patches (and shoulder-boards for officers). The coat is mid-calf length with a single rear vent.

Combat Dress

Either: Light olive-brown battle dress with field shoulder-boards and regimental collar patches, light grey shirt, black boots and webbing gaiters; regimental peaked cap or Barrack Dress cap or steel helmet; Soviet pattern equipment: or a mottled green and brown camouflage suit with the above mentioned accoutrements.

Specialist Clothing

NBC protective clothing and tank crew clothing is of Soviet pattern.

Miscellaneous

The Guards Battalion wear infantry collar badges on red collar patches. Buttons are gold and bear crossed rifles.

On the upper left arm of all uniforms except barrack and combat dress, all ranks wear a shield in the uniform colour bearing the letters "MN". The letters and the edging of the shield are silver.

*   *   *

Hungarian Army Facing Colours

Worn on the cap crown piping and headband, the collar patches and officers shoulder-boards:

Generals	– red
Armour	– black
Field and Air Defence Artillery	– red
Engineers	– green
Signals	– green
Infantry	– green
Medical	– green
Technical Troops	– green
Motor Transport	– green
Quartermaster and Administration	– green
Legal Services	– green

THE POLISH PEOPLE'S REPUBLIC

Population – 33,600,000.   **Capital** – Warsaw.

Armed Forces:

Army – 200,000 men; 3,800 tanks.

Navy – 18,000 sailors, 1,000 marine infantry; 5 submarines, 4 destroyers, 30 submarine hunters, 55 minesweepers, 15 Osa class patrol boats with Styx SSM, 20 MTBs, 22 landing craft. Naval air force: 55 planes – mostly MiG-17s with some Il-28 light bombers and some helicopters.

Air Force – 55,000 men, 696 combat aircraft; four squadrons Il-28 light bombers; twelve squadrons MiG-17 and SU-7 fighter bombers; thirty-six squadrons MiG-17, MiG-19 and MiG-21 interceptors; six squadrons MiG-21 and Il-28 reconnaissance planes. 45 transport planes (An-2, An-12, Li-2, Il-12, Il-14 and Il-18s). 40 helicopters (Mi-1, Mi-4 and Mi-8). SA-2 SAM.

Para-military forces – 73,000 men in the Security Police, Border Guards and Territorial Defence Force.

Reserves – 300,000.

Defence Spending – $2,350 million in 1971 (5·2% of GNP).

Head of State is currently President Henryk Jablonski, and the Head of the Communist Party is Edward Gierek, who took over after the bloody revolts in 1970 when the populace protested against food prices under Gomulka's regime. Born in Porabka in the Bedzin district to a miners' family on 6 January 1913, Gierek has been a Communist Party member since 1931. In 1934 he was expelled from France as an undesirable alien and in 1939 he was in the Belgian mining area organising party work. During the war he was active in the Belgian resistance and returned to Poland in 1948 after having founded the Polish Workers' Party in Belgium. In 1954 he qualified as an engineer at Krakau mining academy and from 1956 he has been one of the secretaries of the Communist Party. Since 1959 a member of the Politburo, Gierek was a critical supporter of Gomulka.

Supreme governing body in Poland is the State Council (Rada Panstwa) which is elected by the parliament (Sejm). The State Council has seventeen members and the state president (Henryk Jablonski) is the chairman. The Sejm has 460 members, all Communists of the National Front Party serving a four-year term. Prime Minister is Piotr Jaroszewicz, and minister of defence Wojciech Jaruzelski. Ultimate executive power is vested in the Council of Ministers.

Poland employs universal conscription on the Soviet model.

Terms of service: army – two years; navy, air force and specialist units – three years; security troops – two years three months.

All males between eighteen and 50 are liable. As in the Soviet Union, military training begins in the Young Pioneers at ten years of age, and in all professional schools and universities the study of military affairs is compulsory. Diplomas are normally only granted to students at higher education centres after they have successfully completed NCO or officer training schools during their conscription.

Poland has about fifteen officer cadet schools and five military academies, and propaganda states that at least 25% of Polish officers have a diploma or degree. Membership of the Communist Party is 100% for staff-trained officers, while over 72% of other officers are party members.

Poland has a thriving arms industry, building T54s under licence from Russia and manufacturing her own infantry small arms, ammunition, lorries (Star-66) and APCs (SKOT). MiG-21s, Jak-18s and Il-18s are also produced under licence.

Polish military advisers are currently employed in North Vietnam, Cuba and the Arab countries.

Poland is divided into three Military Districts: I (Warsaw), II (Pommerania, HQ Bydgoszcz) and

Polish-built tracked amphibious APCs ("OT-62 TOPAS-ZAP", based on Soviet BTR-50PK) on a Baltic exercise; the high ventilators at the rear of the vehicle are discarded on landing. (Sobieszczuk)

III (Silesia, HQ Wroclaw) and seventeen civil administrative areas (Wojewodschaften): Bialystok, Bydgoszcz, Gdansk (Danzig), Katowice, Kielce, Koszalin (Koslin), Krakow, Lublin, Lodz, Olsztyn (Allenstein), Opole (Oppeln), Poznan (Posen), Rzeszow, Szeczecin (Stettin), Warszawa, Wroclaw (Breslau) and Zielona Gora, and five cities of equal status – Warszawa, Lodz, Krakow, Poznan and Wroclaw.

Many key positions in the higher echelons of the Polish army are occupied by Russians either openly or covertly, and the Poles are rigidly integrated into the Warsaw Pact military system. There are currently two Soviet tank divisions in the country. Much of the equipment of the Polish army is of Soviet origin and its characteristics can be seen in the Soviet equipment tables. Details of Polish-produced weapons are shown below.

As in most East European countries, the Poles are well used to discipline imposed from without and the army is as obedient as any other behind the Iron Curtain. Military doctrine, strategy and tactics are completely Soviet; the morale of the army is difficult to assess but those units involved in the 1968 Czechoslovakian operation performed well.

Polish Army Organisation

Five tank and eight motor rifle divisions, one airborne and one amphibious division all organised on Soviet lines. Most of these formations are at 70%

full strength, except in the Warsaw Military District where they are at 30% strength. One motor rifle division includes mountain troops in the Carpathians.

Equipment

Small Arms

M-63, 9 mm machine pistol (home produced); 7·62 Simonow semi-automatic carbine; 7·62 mm AK-47 and AK-M Kalaschnikow assault rifles; RPK, RPD and RP-46 LMGs, Gorjunow M-49 HMG; PKS 7·62 mm HMG, 82 mm and 120 mm mortars.

Artillery

57 mm, 85 mm and 100 mm AT guns; Sagger, Snapper and Swatter ATGW; 122 mm and 152 mm howitzers, ASU-57 and ASU-85 SP guns, Frog and Scud SSM; 23 mm and 57 mm AA guns.

APCs

FUG-M and BRDM scout cars, OT-62 and OT-64 home produced APCs and Soviet BTR-152 APCs.

Tanks

Some JSIII and T-10 heavy tanks; 3,400 medium tanks, mostly T54/55s with some T34/85s and some T62s. 250 PT-76 light tanks.

Polish-Produced Wheeled and Tracked Vehicles

Star 20 4 × 2, 3 ton truck: length – 5·86 m; width –
2·2 m; height – 2·8 m; engine – 85 hp, water-cooled,
petrol; max road speed – 72 km/hr; road range –
563 km; empty weight – 3,719 kg. (Replaced since
1961 by the Star-66).

Star-21 4 × 2, 4 ton truck: length – 5·86 m; width –
2·2 m; height – 2·8 m; engine – 88 hp, water-
cooled, petrol; max road speed – 64 km/hr; road
range – 560 km. (Replaced since 1961 by the
Star-66).

Star-66 6 × 6, 4 ton truck: length – 6·3 m; width –
2·4 m; height – 2·93 m; engine – 115 hp, 6 cylinder,
water-cooled, petrol; max road speed – 74 km/hr;
empty weight – 5,700 kg. As a troop carrier it takes
14 men, it is also used as an artillery tractor and a
workshop version ('Star-66-574') has been produced.

Mazur-D350 tracked artillery tractor. Production of
this vehicle ceased in 1964; it is also used in the
Czech army. It has a 300 hp tank engine, five road
wheels, front drive sprocket, rear idler, four return
rollers; long, high bonnet, enclosed cab and a
canopied rear compartment.

Polish Army Uniforms

Parade Dress

Light khaki, single-breasted, wrist length, four
button front jacket with open neck and four patch
pockets with square buttoned flaps. Buttons are
silver and bear the Polish eagle. Light khaki shirts
and ties, light khaki trousers, black shoes or light
khaki riding breeches and black jackboots. Black
gloves, black leather waist-belt. Regimental badges
(in silver) are worn on the collars; badges of rank
are worn on the shoulder-straps and on the cap band.
Certain arms have facing colours which are worn on
the cap band: military police – white; frontier
guards – green; internal security troops – dark blue.

The cap badge is a silver Polish eagle of the same
design as that worn in 1812 by the army of the
Duchy of Warsaw but minus the crown. The cap has
a black plastic peak and chin strap.

Walking Out Dress

As above but with shoes instead of boots and
without the waist-belt.

Service Dress

As for Walking Out dress.

Barrack Dress

Light khaki fore-and-aft cap with silver Polish

Polish T-55 tank on schnorkeling trials. (*Iwan*)

*Above, Polish soldier in grey and black camouflaged combat dress. (*Novosti*) Right, colour party of the Polish Guards Battalion in parade dress. The flag is red and white with silver eagle, silver and gold wreath and gold fringe. (*Syndoman*)*

eagle badge at the front and rank badges on the left-hand side; jacket, trousers and boots as before, no collar badges.

Shirt Sleeve Order

Light grey blouse, open neck, sleeves buttoned at the wrist, two breast pockets with square, buttoned flaps. This blouse can be worn over or inside the light khaki trousers. Peaked cap or fore-and-aft cap.

Combat Dress

Square-topped traditional Polish "Czapka", with peak, in light khaki cloth and having the Polish eagle in white embroidery on the front. (This is replaced by Polish pattern steel helmet when required.) Field grey, single-breasted combat jacket, hip length and with black camouflage dashes all over, trousers in the same cloth, black lace-up boots and black leather gaiters. Black leather Soviet pattern equipment.

Winter Wear

Grey fur Soviet pattern cap with silver Polish eagle badge. light khaki mid-calf length, double-breasted overcoat with four pairs of buttons; black gloves.

Specialist Clothing

NBC protective clothing and tank suits are Soviet pattern, but the Poles have introduced their own tank helmet which has a black plastic crown and brown leather ear and neck piece.

Airborne forces wear a bright red beret, tankmen a black beret and marines a dark blue one, each with the silver Polish eagle badge.

Mountain troops have their own uniform: khaki hat with brim turned down all around; silver Polish eagle badge in front; white eagle's feather on the left side and pointing to the rear; khaki jacket, of normal parade wear cut, voluminous brown cloth cape slung over the left shoulder, khaki trousers, brown webbing gaiters, black boots.

Miscellaneous

Generals' hat bands are covered in silver lace of the same pattern as worn by Polish generals in 1812.

THE RUMANIAN SOCIALIST REPUBLIC

Population – 20,600,000.   **Capital** – Bucharest.

Armed Forces:

    Army – 150,000 men; 1,800 tanks.

    Navy – 8,000 men; 6 coastal escorts, 30 minesweepers, 5 Osa class patrol boats with Styx SSM, 12 MTBs; 4 Mi-4 helicopters.

    Air Force – 21,000 men; 252 combat aircraft in twenty interceptor squadrons with MiG-17, MiG-19 MiG-21; one reconnaissance squadron with Il-28s. Transport – one squadron with Il-14 and Li-2 planes and 10 Mi-4 helicopters. SA-2 SAM.

Para-military forces – 40,000 men in internal security and border troops, and a militia of 500,000.

Defence Spending   – $725,000,000 in 1972 (3·5% of GNP).

Head of State   – President Nicolae Ceausescu.

Head of the Communist Party – Nicolae Ceausescu.

Rumania as a nation has a long and complex history, having changed masters continuously for almost two thousand years. In the XVIth century the Turks overran the country, and in 1775 Austria became the governing power. In 1866 Karl of Hohenzollern-Sigmaringen, a south German family connected to the Prussian ruling house, became King Carol I of Rumania. During the First World War Rumania remained neutral until 27 August 1916, when she entered the lists on the Allied side. As reward she was allowed to annexe Bessarabia in April 1918, and in December of that year the "Great Assembly of Alba Julia" (100,000 people) voted for the inclusion of Transylvania in the Rumanian state. In 1921 the Rumanian Communist Party was founded, and in 1924 it was banned. In 1938 King Carol II proclaimed a dictatorship, and on 26 June 1940 Rumania ceded Bessarabia and North Bukowina to the USSR. This was followed on 30 August 1940 by the surrender of North Transylvania to Hungary, and on 6 September King Carol II abdicated.

Ion Antonescu became dictator, and on 22 June 1941 Rumania entered the war on the Axis side. This position was reversed in 1944 when the Red Army invaded the country. Antonescu was "removed" and on 25 August 1944 Rumania declared war on Germany and Hungary. Following the end of

hostilities the monarchy was reinstated, but on 30 December 1947 King Michael was forced to abdicate under Communist pressure and parliament proclaimed the "Peoples' Republic", nationalising all major industries. In 1949 Rumania joined COMECON, and on 14 May 1955 the Warsaw Pact. Soviet troops left Rumania in June 1958. On 21 August 1965 the present constitution was adopted and Rumania became a "Socialist" rather than a "Peoples'" state. The usual Communist form of government prevails, with the seat of real power lying in the Central Committee of the Communist Party. "Elected" bodies are the Grand National Assembly of 465 members serving five-year terms. It meets twice a year and in between times delegates all power to the State Council, consisting of the head of state, four vice-presidents, one secretary and twenty-two members. In the last (1969) elections 99·6% of the authorised electorate (universal suffrage over 18 years of age) voted; of these 99·75% voted for the candidates of the only permitted party, the Socialist Unity Front.

Apart from being president, Ceausescu is General Secretary of the Permanent Presidium of the Rumanian Communist Party and Chairman of the Supreme Council of Economic and Social Development. He was born of peasant stock in 1918; a leading member of the Young Communist Movement, he was often imprisoned under the Antonescu regime. In 1945 he became secretary of the Communist party in Bucharest, and a member of the Central Committee. From 1950 to 1954 he was deputy defence minister; in 1965 he succeeded Gheorghiu-Dej as head of the party, and since 1967 he has been head of state as well. He has always followed a strongly nationalistic policy and has often criticised Moscow for her conduct in relation to her European satellites. Hungary and Czechoslovakia provoked Rumania's scorn, as did the so-called "Breschnew doctrine".

Prime Minister of Rumania is Jon Gheorghe Maurer, born in Siebenburgen on 23 September 1902 and Communist party member since 1936. From 1958 to 1961 he was Rumania's president, and also followed a strongly independent nationalistic

line. The defence minister is Col.-Gen. Jon Joniță; defence policy is formulated by the Defence Council, headed by President Ceausescu and subordinate to the Council of State.

Rumania has a 16-month universal military service liability. The country is divided into three military regions: Moldavia, Wallachia and Transilvania. The army is divided into three corps each containing three divisions and the usual divisional troops, all organised after the Soviet Model. There are two mountain regiments located around Tîrgu Mures and Sinaia, and two tank divisions at Bucharest and Lipova. Rumania also has an airborne regiment. The regional, and thus corps, headquarters are located at Bucharest, Timisoara (Temesvar) and Tîrgu Mures (Neumarkt), Rumanian army units are maintained at about 75%

Rumanian infantry in camouflaged combat dress leave a BTR-60P 8 × 8 APC. Weapons are the usual AK47 family.

strength in peacetime; upon mobilisation reservists
would provide the missing 25%.

Equipment

Small Arms Soviet pistols, SMGs, rifles, AK-47s,
LMGs and MMGs as well as 82 mm and 120 mm
mortars.
Artillery 57 mm, 85 mm and 100 mm AT guns,
Sagger, Snapper and Swatter ATGW; 76 mm, 122
mm and 152 mm guns, SU-100 SP guns, ASU-57
and ASU-85 airborne SP guns, Frog SSM.
APCs BTR-40, BTR-50P and BTR-152 APCs.
Tanks Some JSIII and T-10 heavy tanks; 1,700
medium tanks, mainly T54/55s with some T34/85s
and T62s.

Rumanian-produced wheeled vehicles

Carpati SR-132 4 × 4, 2 ton truck: length – 5·78 m;
width – 2·26 m; height – 2·97 m; 140 hp, 8 cylinder,
water-cooled petrol engine; max road speed – 95
km/hr; empty weight – 3,700 kg.

The degree of motorisation in Rumanian formations is not too high and many infantry units are
pure footsloggers. As Rumania still has a largely
peasant-based economy, her soldiers' logistic needs
are few and discipline strict and easy to enforce.

Rumanian Army Uniforms

Parade Dress

Soviet pattern steel helmet; light olive-brown,
single breasted, four button front, four pockets
with square, buttoned flaps, open neck, two buttons
at each cuff; light khaki shirt and tie, single vent
back. Regimental colours are worn on the collar
patches; regimental badges and rank badges on the
shoulder-straps. Officers wear light olive-brown
riding breeches and black boots (generals with
double red side stripes to the trousers and gold oak-
leaf clusters on the collar). Other ranks wear normal
light olive-brown trousers in black boots with short
black leather gaiters. Officers wear brown leather
Sam Browne belts and brown gloves. Buttons are
yellow and bear (for generals) the national crest, for
others a five-pointed star.

Walking Out Dress

Light olive-brown peaked cap with black plastic
peak and chin strap; headband and top piping in the
regimental facing colour, the officers' cap badge is
the national crest (an oil derrick, pines and moun-

*Rumanian branch badges, worn in white metal on
shoulder-boards, left to right, top: Armour, Artillery,
Air Defence Artillery, Signals; bottom: Infantry,
Reconnaissance, Cavalry and Mountain Troops.*

tains) within an oval. Other ranks wear the five-
pointed red star. Jacket, shirt and tie as above, light
olive-brown slacks, black shoes.

Service Dress

As for walking out dress for officers but the
peaked cap may be replaced by a fore-and-aft forage
cap in light olive brown and having a five-pointed
red star at the front.

For other ranks it consists of the forage cap, a
single-breasted jacket closed to the neck, regimental
collar patches, the front buttons are concealed as
are the pockets which have square-shaped buttoned
flaps. The jacket is wrist length and has buttoned
cuffs. Light olive-brown trousers, black boots and
black leather gaiters. A black leather waist-belt with
square steel buckle plate is worn.

Summer Dress

Hat as above; light grey, open-necked, hip length
blouse with two pockets on the chest, sleeves buttoned at the wrist. Trousers as above.

Combat Dress

Dark green Soviet pattern helmet, Soviet pattern
"Gymansterka" with standing collar or the single-
breasted, closed collar jacket with concealed front
buttons as described for other-ranks' service dress
wear. Soviet pattern equipment.

Specialist Clothing

NBC and tank crew clothing as for the Soviet
Army. Mountain troops wear large grey berets,
pulled down over the right ear and with the national
badge above the left eye.

Military police wear a white stripe around their
helmets and in the front centre a white-ringed, red
disc bearing the white letters "IC".

Large grey berets distinguish these Rumanian mountain troops.

Rumanian Army Flags

The national flag (three vertical stripes – dark blue nearest the pike – yellow and red with the national crest in the centre of the yellow stripe). The flag is fringed in gold, the pike tip is a gold spear point.

Rumanian Army facing colours

Cavalry	– crimson
Armour	– black
Artillery	– black
Engineers	– black
Signals	– black
Infantry	– red
Medical	– crimson
Technical troops	– black
Rear Services	– red
Security troops	– purple
Frontier troops	– light green
Motor transport	– black
Administration	– red

These colours are worn on the collar patches and shoulder-boards of parade and walking out dress. In service and combat dress no collar patches are worn but the gold rank bars on the shoulder are edged in the regimental colour. For officers, the shoulder-boards are gold (silver for those in technical troops) with edging and stripes in the regimental colour and a silver regimental badge above the rank stars.

Badges of rank

In the armour, artillery, engineers, signals and technical troops there is a special series of technicians' ranks indicated by gold chevrons on the shoulder-boards.

Badges of rank of other non-commissioned personnel are indicated by straight gold bars across the shoulder-boards as shown below:

Soldat (private)	nothing.
Soldar-fruntas (lance-corporal)	one wide stripe with regimental edging.
Caporal (Corporal)	two wide stripes with regimental edging.
Sergent (Sergeant)	one wide gold stripe.
Sergent-major (Staff sergeant)	one wide and one narrow stripe.
Plutonier (Company sergeant)	two wide stripes.
Plutonier-major (Sergeant-major)	two wide and one thin stripe.
Plutonier-adjutant (Regimental sergeant-major) ...	three wide stripes.
The technicians' ranks:	
Maistru militar clasa IVa	two gold chevrons, point down.
Maistru militar clasa IIIa	as above, under a short gold bar.
Maistru militar clasa IIa	the same under two short bars.
Maistru militar clasa Ia	the same under three short bars.
Maistru militar principal	three chevrons under three bars.

Officers ranks are exactly as for the Soviet army.

THE NEUTRAL AND NON-ALIGNED NATIONS

THE FEDERAL REPUBLIC OF AUSTRIA

Population ± 7,473,800.   **Capital** – Vienna.
Armed Forces:
    Army – 40,000 men; 320 tanks.
Army Air Corps – 3,000 men; 39 combat aircraft (SAAB 105 fighter bombers), 11 Magister, 5 Vampire and 26 Safir training aircraft. Light fixed wing aircraft – 19 Cessna L-19s; 2 Cessna 185s. Helicopters – 24 Agusta-Bell AB-204s, 12 Agusta-Bell AB-206s, 10 Agusta-Bell AB-47Gs; 15 Alouette IIs, 16 Alouette IIIs, 2 Sikorsky S-65s and 4 OH-13s.
Defence Spending – $200 million in 1972 (1% of GNP).

From her proud imperial past, Austria has nowadays been reduced to her historic heartland, the majority of her former domains now being members of the Warsaw Pact (Czechoslovakia, Hungary, Rumania, Bulgaria and parts of Yugoslavia).

On 12 March 1938 Nazi Germany absorbed Austria in the "Anschluss", and the Austrian army was completely integrated into the Wehrmacht for the duration of the Second World War. After the war, Austria was divided up into four zones of occupation (French, British, American and Russian) in the same way that Germany was. By the Four Power Agreement of 15 May 1955 Austria was given back her sovereignty and independence, and the occupation troops were withdrawn on the strict understanding that Austria would remain neutral.

The current head of the Austrian Federal Republic is Franz Jonas, who was first elected in 1965 and was re-elected in 1971. Political power lies in the hands of the Kanzler, currently Dr. Bruno Kreisky, who heads a socialist government based on an upper and a lower house (the 'Bundesrat" and the "Nationalrat") which together are called the National Assembly. The president is nominal head of the armed forces, and actual power is exercised by the Defence Minister – at time of writing Karl Lütgendorf.

Military service liability is currently six months in Austria, and experience shows that this is only long enough to allow the most basic military skills to be learned. Specialist corps like armour, artillery and the technical services have thus suffered badly, and a new plan is to be tried. A small force of well-paid professionals (15,000 men in 24 battalions) is to be recruited, entitled the "Ever Readies" (Bereitschaftstruppe). They will be trained to handle the more complex equipment. The remainder of the Austrian Army will be made up of conscripts on their six-months national service. Together with this innovation, the Austrian defence ministry is to reorganise the order of battle. At present the army is grouped as shown below:

Army Troops
Guard Battalion
Fortress Battalion (in Bruckneudorf)
Army Engineer Battalion
Army Signals Regiment
Electronic Warfare Battalion

Gruppenkommando I
Group Troops
Training Regiment No 2
Tank Battalion No 1
Artillery Regiment No 1
AA Regiment No 1
Engineer Battalion No 1
Signals Battalion No 1
Logistics Regiment No 1

1st Jäger Brigade
HQ Battalion No 1
Jäger Battalion No 1 (training)
Jäger Battalion No. 2
Jäger Battalion No 4

Artillery Detachment No 1

3rd Panzer Grenadier Brigade
HQ Battalion No 3
Panzergrenadier Battalion No 9
Tank Battalion No 10
Panzergrenadier Battalion No 11 (training)
SP Artillery Detachment No 3

9th Panzer Grenadier Brigade
HQ Battalion No 9
Tank Battalion No 33
Panzergrenadier Battalion No 34 (training)
Panzergrenadier Battalion No 35
SP Artillery Detachment No 9

Gruppenkommando II
Group Troops
Training Regiment No 10
Tank Battalion No 4
Artillery Regiment No 2
AA Regiment No 2
Engineer Battalion No 2
Signals Battalion No 2
Logistics Regiment No 2

5th Jäger Brigade
HQ Battalion No 5
Jäger Battalion No 17
Jäger Battalion No 18 (training)
Jäger Battalion No 19
Artillery Detachment No 5

7th Jäger Brigade
HQ Battalion No 7
Jäger Battalion No 25
Jäger Battalion No 26
Jäger Battalion No 27 (training)
Jäger Battalion No 28
Artillery Detachment No 7

Gruppenkommando III
Group Troops
Training Regiment No 8
Tank Battalion No 7
Artillery Regiment No 3
AA Regiment No 3
Engineer Battalion No 3
Signals Battalion No 3
Logistics Regiment No 3

4th Panzergrenadier Brigade
HQ Battalion No 4
Panzergrenadier Battalion No 13
Panzergrenadier Battalion No 15 (training)
Tank Battalion No 14
SP Artillery Detachment No 4

6th Jäger Brigade
HQ Battalion No 6
Jäger Battalion No 21
Jäger Battalion No 22 (training)
Jäger Battalion No 23
Artillery Detachment No 6
    Under the new organisation of the Austrian

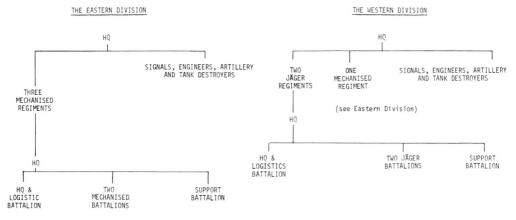

THE AUSTRIAN BEREITSCHAFTSTRUPPE
(15,000 men)

155

Above, Soviet GAZ jeep (note Guards insignia); crew wear 1970 transport corps ceremonial dress, passengers wear Guards infantry 1971 pattern dress. Below, *starshina* (Soviet sergeant-major) in transport corps parade dress – stripes indicate three years' service. Below right, colour party in pre-1970 Guards infantry parade dress.

Army (to be implemented in 1973 and 1974) Gruppenkommando I will become the Heereskommando and its Group Troops will join the current Army Troops as the new, enlarged Army Troops (Heerestruppenteile). The Brigades of the old Gruppenkommando I (1st Jäger, 3rd and 9th Panzergrenadier Brigades) will be distributed among the Gruppenkommandos II and III, which will each be reorganised into a division.

Austrian Small Arms

Walther P-38 9 mm pistol; weight – 0·87 kg; 8 round magazine; effective range – 50 m. A World War II German weapon.

Pistole-11 9 mm; 7 round magazine; weight – 1·1 kg; effective range – 50 m. A World War II American weapon.

Maschinenpistole 40 (_MP-40_) 9 mm; 3·7 kg SMG; blow-back action; 32 round straight magazine; rate of fire – 40 rpm; effective range – 200 m. A World War II German weapon with collapsible butt.

Maschinenpistole PPSH (M-41) Russian World War II weapon – for details see Soviet bloc equipment.

Karabiner M-1 7·62 mm; 2·37 kg; gas assisted, semi-automatic weapon; 0·9 m long; 15 round magazine; effective range – 150 m; 30 rpm.

Garand M-1 self-loading carbine 7·62 mm; 4·3 kg; gas assisted, semi-automatic weapon; 24 rpm; effective range – 300 m. An American World War II weapon.

Light Anti-Tank Projector M-72 (_PAR67_) Collapsible 66 mm rocket launcher; 2·14 kg in weight; effective range – 250 m. VO – 145 m/sec. American use-and-throw-away weapon; the rocket is transported in the collapsed firing unit.

Carl Gustav 84 mm heavy AT weapon (_PAR66_) Swedish weapon; for details see Sweden.

Tracked and Wheeled Vehicles

M-5 13 ton tracked artillery tractor American equipment used to tow the 155 mm M-1 medium howitzers.

M-4 18 ton tracked artillery tractor American World War II equipment; a larger version of the M-5.

M-24 light tank American World War II equipment; 18·4 tons weight, 5 man crew, two 110 hp petrol engines; top road speed – 160 km/hr; armament – 1 × 75 mm L/40 cannon (48 rounds carried); 2 × 0·5 inch MGs; 1 × 12·7 mm AAMG. Armour – 38 mm.

M-21 half track APC American World War II vehicle; 9 tons weight; 147 hp petrol engine; max road speed – 79 km/hr; road range – 345 km; 13 mm armour; crew – 1 + 12; armament – 1 × 12·7 mm AAMG and/or 1 × 7·92 mm MG; length – 6·33 m; width – 2·26 m; height – 2·53 m.

M-8 6 × 6 armoured car American World War II vehicle; 7·5 tons; 110 hp petrol engine; max road speed – 90 km/hr; road range – 645 km; crew – 4 men; armour – 20 mm; armament – 1 × 37 mm cannon; VO – 884 m/sec; length – 5 m; width – 2·54 m; height – 1·92 mm.

Alvis Stalwart High Mobility Load Carrier (for details see Great Britain). This vehicle is used by the engineer units.

Dodge ¾ ton 4 × 4 truck Length – 4·24 m; width – 2·09 m; height – 2·17 m; empty weight – 2,561 kg; 76 hp, 6 cylinder, water-cooled petrol engine; max road speed – 87 km/hr; road range – 385 km.

Corbitt 6 × 6, 6 ton truck Length – 7·27 m; width – 2·47 m; height – 3·05 m; empty weight – 10,020 kg; 202 hp, 6 cylinder, water-cooled petrol engine; max road speed – 60 km/hr; road range – 250 km. This American truck is used as an artillery tractor for the 155 mm howitzer.

Graf & Stift ZA-200/1 6 × 6 8 ton truck Length – 8·55 m; width – 2·4 m; height – 2·74 mm; empty weight – 9·72 kg; 200 hp, 6 cylinder, water-cooled, diesel engine; max road speed – 70 km/hr; road range – 670 km. Austrian vehicle, used in engineer units.

Graf & Stift ZA-210/3 6 × 6 10 ton truck Length, width and height as above; empty weight – 10,630 kg; 210 hp, 6 cylinder, water-cooled diesel engine; performance as above. Also used in engineer units.

Engineer equipments

Light aluminium bridge (MLC-50) with glass fibre, foam plastic filled pontoons permit bridges or ferries to be made. Heavier bridges are made from Bailey type sections produced by the firms Krupp and M.A.N.

Saurer APC In 1956 the Saurerwerke AG began development of this tracked vehicle known to the Austrian army as the "Schutzenpanzer (SPz)4K". Prototypes followed two years later and the SPz 4K-3F and 4FA were taken into army service in 1962.

The vehicle has an extremely low profile and well-angled hull, and the armour plate is very thin by British standards (front – 20 mm, other parts –

Austrian communications troops parade in Steyr-Puch "Halflinger" 4 × 4¼-ton jeeps. (Courtesy Austrian Army)

8 mm). The APC engine is front mounted and is a Saurer 4FA, 250 hp diesel engine giving a power/weight ratio of 18·5 hp/ton. Maximum road speed 70 km/hr, road range – 340 km; height (without armament) – 1·65 m; width – 2·5 m; length – 5·4 m. Access is by two rear doors and there is also a large crew-hatch and a commander's hatch in the roof. Armament – 1 × 12·7 mm Browning M-2 HB MG or 1 × 20 mm Oerlikon 204 GK automatic cannon in a turret (this is the Saurer 4H 4FA-G version). There are no gun ports; the crew is driver, commander and 8 men and the vehicle is not amphibious. The vehicle is NBC proof. The Saurer 4K 4FA is also produced as a command, 81 mm mortar carrier and ambulance versions. 450 in all have been built. In 1965 a variant of this basic vehicle was projected and is now coming into service; it is the:

Steyr-Daimler-Puch Saurer "Panzer Jäger Kanone" (Gun tank hunter)

This vehicle uses the same basic Saurer APC chassis but is rear engined and has been fitted with the French AMX-13 oscillating FL-12 turret carrying a 105 mm/44 cannon and a co-axially mounted 7·62 mm MG. Since 1954 the Austrians have employed the French AMX-13 in the SP anti-tank

role and are obviously pleased with the results.

The Panzerjäger K has a 6 cylinder 6FA, 300 hp diesel engine giving a top road speed of 65 km/hr; overall length is 7·78 m; width – 2·5 m; height – 2·35 m; weight – 16·8 tons. The 105 mm gun fires the same spin-stabilised, hollow charge ammunition as that used in the AMX-30 tank. VO – 800 m/sec; combat range – 2,700 m. Crew – commander, driver, gunner. Combat ammunition – 26 rounds with an automatic loading system using two magazines each of 6 rounds permitting a very high initial rate of fire. About 100 of these vehicles are planned to come into service to replace the current 70 AMX-13's with 75 mm guns.

Tanks

Apart from small numbers of M-24 Chaffee tanks – mentioned above – Austria has some 150 American M-47 and 120 American M-60 medium tanks, and 40 American M-41 Walker Bulldog light tanks.

Artillery

American 105 mm howitzers; 15 M-109 155 mm SP howitzers; 15 towed 155 mm howitzers; 21 Czech RM 130 mm 32-barrelled multiple rocket launchers mounted on Praga VS3 6 × 6 trucks. *Anti-aircraft artillery* 35 mm Oerlikon Super Bat guns.

Animal Transport

Mountain transport is by teams of Austrian "Halflinger" ponies – these animals carry less weight than the traditional mules used for this type of task by other countries, but are employed for reasons of national prestige.

Austrian Army Uniforms

Up until 1973 the Austrian Army has worn uniforms of a style, cut and quality which has changed but little since the 1930s. With the introduction of a new volunteer defence force the planners have seen fit to give the men a much smarter uniform of more modern texture and design. Badges of rank will remain as they now are, as will the facing colours and cap badges. Combat uniform will not change its present camouflage pattern.

Current Austrian Army Uniforms (up to September 1973):
Parade Dress

Steel helmet (US NATO pattern) with rank

badges on the front in yellow for officers, white for NCOs. Single-breasted, open-necked, four button front jacket with two pleated top pockets with trident-shaped buttoned flaps and two trident-shaped flaps with buttons on the internal skirt pockets. Plain cuffs, single rear vent. On the left shoulder is a Schulterspange or double shoulder cord, gold for generals, and officers, silver for NCOs; white for other ranks. Badges of rank and regimental distinctions are shown on the five-sided collar patches (see relevant sections). White shirt, black tie, grey gloves. Officers' parade leg wear is grey riding breeches and black jackboots. A silver and black Feldbinde or waist sash is worn by officers; it has a square silver buckle bearing the Austrian eagle. Other ranks wear a black leather belt with white metal square shaped buckle. Generals have twin red stripes on their trousers. Buttons are gold for officers, silver for NCOs and bronze for the men and bear the Austrian eagle.

Walking Out Dress

Jacket, tie, shirt and gloves as above; grey trousers, black shoes, grey peaked cap with black headband. Hat badge – the Austrian eagle within a wreath; gold for officers, silver for NCOs, bronze for privates. Gold or silver lace chin cords and decoration to black headband for officers and NCOs, black chin strap for men. The cap badge is surmounted by a red-within-white-within-red cockade on a gold base.

Working Dress

Same cut as above but of rougher material with plain buttons in gold, silver or bronze, grey shirt, black tie. Head-gear is a soft grey forage cap with small crown and grey cloth peak. The side pieces are buttoned together at the front by two small buttons and above these is the Austrian red-white-red cockade within a chevron of gold or silver lace according to rank. The trousers may be worn tucked into grey webbing gaiters if boots are worn.

Mountain troops wear either ski trousers and boots or knee breeches, grey socks and climbing boots.

Shirt Sleeve Order

Soft grey cloth cap with peak, buttons and cockade, grey shirt, open-necked but with an internal "fly" piece across the neck, long sleeved, buttoned at the wrist; two breast pockets with buttoned flaps, mid-grey trousers with narrow side stripe in the facing colour; narrow buff webbing waist-belt with oblong black buckle plate bearing the Austrian eagle. Badges of rank are worn on slides on the shoulder-straps.

Raincoat

Grey plastic, single breasted, with shoulder-straps and brown corduroy collar bearing (at each end) a patch in the facing colour and a button according to rank.

Greatcoat

Grey cloth, double breasted with half-belt at the rear.

Combat Dress

NATO pattern helmet, camouflaged smock and trousers, gaiters and boots. Black leather equipment of German World War II pattern (this is being replaced by grey webbing of the same design). Badges of rank are worn on slides on the shoulder-straps as in shirt-sleeve order.

Miscellaneous

Army pilots wear the Austrian red and white roundel in a silver wreath on grey, silver or gold wings on a black backing on the left chest above the pocket.

Those who have passed the "Schlangenfresser" (Snake-eater's) course at the Close Combat (Ranger) school in Hainburg near Wiener Neustadt wear a white parachute and wings with a vertical golden sword on a red-white-red centre piece all on a black backing, on the upper left chest. They also wear dark green berets with the same sign as a badge, worn over the left eye.

Members of the following military schools wear a red-white-red shield with a suitable device on the upper left arm of their jackets: National Defence College, Theresianische Military Academy, Army NCOs Academy, Jäger School, Tank School, Artillery School, Engineer School, Anti-Aircraft Defence School, Signals School, Air Defence School, Medical School, Technical School, Driving School, Flying School, Logistics School.

Army troops and Group troops also have red and white quartered shields with devices in black or in gold portraying their function and the formation to which they belong but these badges are not worn on the uniform, only on notice-boards and on

out and service dress and on the shoulder-straps in fatigues, shirt sleeve orders and combat dress.

New Pattern Uniform

The new uniforms have a distinctly American, "lean and hungry cowboy" look with a beret (black for armoured troops, green for Rangers, khaki for others) and calf length black boots. The cloth is olive brown and modern in texture, and the Austrian eagle is embroidered in black on the upper left breast.

Austrian Army Flags and Standards

Infantry and other dismounted units carry flags which are white and edged in white and red triangles. In the centre of the face side is the Austrian eagle, on the reverse side is the crest of the province in which the unit is stationed plus the designation of the regiment whose tradition the unit is maintaining. The flagstaff is polished black wood, the tip is a brass spear point bearing on one side the Austrian eagle and on the other the unit designation.

Cavalry (armoured) units carry standards which are similar in design to infantry flags but smaller in size.

vehicles. Each of the seven brigades has its own badge (worn on vehicles and on notice-boards but not on the uniform) as do the three training regiments, Nos 2, 8 and 10.

Badges of Rank

Worn on the collar patches in parade, walking

Austrian Army Facing Colours

Worn on the collar patches in parade, walking out and service dress.

Reconnaissance troops	– dark yellow.
Armoured troops (tanks and armoured infantry)	– black.
Field and AA Artillery	– bright red.
Anti-tank Artillery	– pink.
Engineers	– steel green.
Signals	– rust red.
Infantry and fortress troops	– grass green.
Guard Battalion	– bright red and white*.
Medical (doctors)	– black and dark blue*.
Veterinary surgeons	– black and light brown*.
Apothecary personnel	– black and purple*.
Ranger School	– light green.
Air Corps	– cherry red.
Medical orderlies	– light blue.
Quartermaster troops (supplies)	– dark blue.
Equipment provision troops	– dark blue.
Technical troops (repair)	– brown.
Administrative service	– crimson and dark blue*
Economy service (finance)	– sky blue.
Military padres	– violet and black*.
Military Academy in Wiener Neustadt	– bright red.
Generals	– bright red.
Officers on the general staff	– black and bright red*.

* Where two colours are shown, the second colour appears as a narrow chevron on the upper end of the collar patch, the main body of which is in the first colour shown.

Page 161:
* The collar patch is edged in silver cord.
** The hatband decoration is also worn as a chevron behind the cockade on the soft grey cap.

Rank		Collar Badges	Hat band decoration
Privates	Private (Wehrmann)	No badges	NIL.
	Senior private (Gefreiter)	One six-pointed white plastic star	One narrow silver stripe.
NCOs	Corporal (Korporal)	Two stars	Two narrow silver stripes.
	Junior sergeant (Zugsfuhrer)	Three stars in triangular shape	Three narrow silver stripes.
	Sergeant (Wachtmeister)	*One six-pointed silver star above a wide silver lace	**One narrow silver stripe.
	Staff sergeant (Oberwachtmeister)	*Two stars over a wide silver lace	**Two narrow silver stripes.
	Company sergeant-major (Stabswachtmeister)	*One silver star above one narrow and one wide silver lace	**One wide silver stripe.
	Regimental sergeant-major (Oberstabswachtmeister)	*Two silver stars over one narrow and one wide silver lace	**One narrow silver lace over a wide silver lace.
	Officers' Deputy (Offiziersstellvertreter)	*Three silver stars over one narrow and one wide silver lace	**Two narrow silver laces over one wide lace.
	Vice lieutenant (Vizeleutnant)	One silver star above a wide gold lace; the collar patch is edged in gold and silver lace	**One wide silver lace with a gold zig-zag along it.

The NCO who acts as RSM in the British sense has two silver chevrons (point up) on his cuffs.

Officer Cadets	a silver star over one or two wide gold laces; the collar patch is silver edged	one narrow silver band or two narrow silver bands.

Officers (collar patches are edged in gold)

Ensign (Fähnrich)	one silver star over one narrow and one wide gold lace	one narrow silver band over a wide silver band with a gold zig-zag along it.
Second Lieutenant (Leutnant)	one gold star	one narrow gold band.
Lieutenant (Oberleutnant)	two gold stars	two narrow gold bands.
Captain (Hauptmann)	three gold stars	three narrow gold bands.
Major (Major)	one silver star on a five-sided gold patch	one narrow and one wide gold band.
Lieutenant-Colonel (Oberstleutnant)	two silver stars on a gold patch	two narrow and one wide gold band.
Colonel (Oberst)	three silver stars on a gold patch	three narrow and one wide gold band.
Brigadier (Brigadier)	a silver star within a silver oak wreath on a large gold patch leaving only a narrow red piping showing	one narrow and one very wide gold band.
Major-General (General)	three silver stars and a wreath on a gold ground	three narrow and one very wide gold band.

161

THE FINNISH REPUBLIC

Population – 4·68 million.   **Capital** – Helsinki.

Armed Forces:

  Army – 34,000 men.

  Navy – 2,500 men; 3 frigates, 2 gunboats, 1 MTB with ship-to-ship GW, 15 smaller MTBs, 2 minelayers, 5 minesweepers.

  Air Force – 3,000 men; 47 combat aircraft including three fighter squadrons of MiG-21F and Gnat Mk. 1. The Gnats will be replaced by 12 Saab J-35BS Draken.

Para-military forces – 4,000 frontier guards.

Reserves   – 650,000 men.

Defence Spending $182 million in 1972 (1·4% GNP).

Head of state is Dr Urho Kekkonen (born 3 September 1900) who entered the Finnish parliament as a member of the "Bauernpartei" or peasants' party in 1936. In 1968 he was elected to a second six-year term as president and on 17 January 1973 the Finnish parliament extended this term of office by a further four years so that the good relations with the Soviet Union should not be disturbed. The parliament (Riksdag) is a demo-cratically elected, single chamber body of 200 members, elected for a four-year term, composed as follows: Social Democrats – 55; Agrarian Union (a centre party) – 35; Vennamo (Finnish National Party) – 18; Peoples' Democrats (Communists) – 37; Swedish Peoples' Party – 10; National Collective Party (Conservatives) – 34; Liberal Peoples' Party – 7; Christian Union – 4.

Since 1939 Finland has walked the political tight rope in Russia's mighty shadow and recently it seems the strain has begun to tell (five cabinet reshuffles since 1970). Prime minister (since 4 September 1972) is Kalevi Sorsa, a Social Demo-crat, and his government is a coalition of his own party with the Agrarian Union, the Communists and the Vennamo and Swedish Peoples' Party. Head of the armed forces is President Kekkonen who is advised by the Defence Council consisting of the prime minister, the minister of foreign affairs and three other ministers and the heads of the three armed services (there is no specific defence minister). The defence ministry comes directly under the president.

By virtue of her peace treaty with Russia of 10 February 1947 and the Mutual Assistance Pact (also with Russia) of 6 April 1948, Finnish defence policy is strictly limited to the defence of her neutrality, and her total armed forces are limited by these treaties to 41,900 men.

Organisation of the Finnish Army

The Second World War proved that, for Finland, the division was too clumsy an army formation and in 1951 a series of army reforms were undertaken which culminated with the present organisation which came into being in 1970. Under this new system, the country is split up into the following military regions each containing the forces shown below:

South Finland (Etela-Suomen Sotilaslaani)

Army Command HQ – Helsinki

Armoured Brigade HQ Parola

Rifle Battalion "Hämee"	Hämee
Armoured Car Battalion	Parola
Anti-tank Battalion	Parola
Field Artillery Battalion	Hämee
Armoured School	Parola

Uudenmaa Brigade HQ Dragsvik

Hämee Mounted Rifle Battalion	Lahti
Uudenmaa Rifle Battalion	Helsinki-Santahamina
Marine (coastal) Battalion	Porkkala-Upinniemi
Guards Battalion	Helsinki
Suomenlinna Coastal Artillery Regiment	Helsinki-Suomenlinna
Hanko Coastal Artillery Battalion	Hanko
Helsinki Air Defence Regiment	Hyrylä

Signals Regiment   Ruhimäki

North Finland (Pohjois-Suomen Sotilaslääni)
Army Sub-Command HQ – Oulu
East Bothnian Brigade   Oulu
Kainuu Brigade   Kainu
Lapland Rifle Battalion   Sodankylä
East Bothnian Artillery
Regiment   Oulu
East Bothnian Air Defence
Battalion   Rovaniemi

South East Finland (Kaakkois-Suomen
Sotilaslääni)
Army Sub-Command HQ – Kouvola
Karelian Brigade   Valkeala
Savo Brigade   Mikkeli
Kyme Rifle Battalion   Hamina
Uudenmaa Dragoon
Battalion   Lapeenranta
Parachutist School   Utti
Karelian Artillery Regiment Lapeenranta
Kotka Coastal Artillery
Battalion   Kyminlinna
Salpausselkä Air Defence
Battalion   Kuovola
Kyme Engineer Battalion   Koria

South West Finland (Lounais-Suomen
Sotilaslääni)
Army Sub-Command HQ – Turku
Pori Brigade   Pori
Satakunta Artillery
Regiment   Nünisalo
Turku Coast Artillery
Regiment   Turku
Turku Air Defence
Battalion   Turku

Karelia (Savo-Karjalan Sotilaslääni)
Army Sub-Command HQ – Kuopio
Karelia Rifle Battalion   Kontioranta
North Karelian Artillery
Battalion   Liperi-Ylämylly

Inner Finland (Sisa-Suomen Sotilaslääni)
Army Sub-Command HQ – Tikkakoski
Tampere Air Defence
Battalion   Tampere
Central Finland Engineer
Battalion   Keuruu

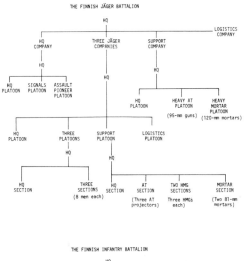

THE FINNISH JÄGER BATTALION

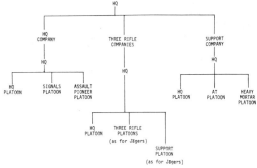

THE FINNISH INFANTRY BATTALION

East Bothnia (Pohjanmaan Sotilaslääna)
Army Sub-Command HQ – Vaasa
Vaasa Coastal Artillery
Battalion   Vaasa

Finnish Army Equipment
    Living as she does on the knife edge between the Soviet Union and the free world, Finland equips her armed forces with a mixture of Eastern and Western vehicles, equipments and weapons. She also manufactures indigenous weapons of certain categories, and some foreign weapons under licence.

Small Arms
9 mm Lathi M/35 pistol Weight – 1·02 kg; length – 25 cm; 9 round magazine; effective range – 50 m.
Also:
7·65 mm M/32 Parabellum pistol.

9 mm Makarow pistol (Soviet).

9 mm Suomi M/31 machine pistol (SMG) Weight – 4·6 kg; length – 0·87 m; blow-back action; rate of fire – 780 rpm; effective range – 100 m; either 36 round bar or 70 round drum magazine.

9 mm Peltikp M/44 SMG Weight – 2·9 kg; length – 62 cm (with extended butt 83 cm); blow-back action; rate of fire – 650 rpm; 36 round bar or 70 round drum magazine; effective range – 100 m.

9 mm Sten Mk III SMG British Second World War weapon, very simple construction. Weight – 3·18 kg; length – 76 cm; rate of fire – 550 rpm; blow-back action; effective range – 100 m; 32 round bar magazine to the left of the breech. Also:
7·62 mm PPSH SMG (see Soviet section).

7·62 mm M/39 Rifle Single action weapon with five round magazine taking old type rimmed M-08 or M-30 cartridges – a modified copy of the M-1891 Russian Mosin-Nagant.

7·62 mm Sturmgewehr M/62 Assault Rifle Weight – 3·5 kg; length – 86 cm; rate of fire – 650 rpm; gas-assisted action; 30 round curved magazine under breech. Finnish copy of the Soviet AK-47 Kala-schnikow, which is also used in Finland, as is the: 7·62 mm Simonova SKS.

7·62 mm M/62 LMG Weight – 7·6 kg; rate of fire – 1,000 rpm; gas-assisted action; effective range – 600 m; 100 round drum/belt magazine to right of breech. Can be used with bipod or, in heavy role, with tripod. Also:
7·62 mm Degtjarew M/27 LMG (see Soviet section).
7·62 mm Degtjarew RPD LMG (see Soviet section).

The Soviet 7·62 mm PK and PKS light machine guns are also used, and a few elderly 1909 Maxim heavy machine guns with water-cooled barrels are still held.

Support Weapons

81 mm M-38 Mortar (Latt Granatkastare) Weight in firing position – 60 kg; range – 3 km; rate of fire – 20 rpm.

120 mm M-40 Mortar (Tung Granatkastare) Details as for equivalent Swedish 120 mm M-41.

160 mm Tampella Heavy Mortar Weight in firing position – 1,700 kg; length of barrel – 2·85 m; weight of bomb – 40 kg; normal range – 9·5 km; range with supercharge – 13·8 km; rate of fire – 4 rpm. Also:
Soviet 82 mm M-37 and 120 mm M-38 or M-43 mortars.

55 mm M-55 light AT rocket projector (Latt Sinko) Weight of projector – 6·5 kg; weight of hollow charge rocket – 2·3 kg; range – 200 m; rate of fire – 5 rpm. Can pierce 30 cm of armour.

95 mm M-58 recoilless AT rifle (Tung Sinko) Weight on two-wheel trailer – 140 kg; weight of hollow-charge rocket – 10·1 kg; VO – 615 m/sec; effective range – 700 m; rate of fire – 8 rpm. Can pierce 30 cm of armour. Also:
American 106 mm recoilless AT rifle.
Soviet 85 mm PAK M-45 AT gun.
Soviet RPG-7 AT rocket launcher.
French SS-11 ATGW (see French section).
British Vigilant ATGW (see British section).

Artillery

150 mm M-40 medium field gun Weight – 5,530 kg; weight of shell – 43·5 kg; VO – 520 m/sec; range – 13·3 km; rate of fire – 4 rpm. This is an old German equipment and is being withdrawn from service.

122 mm Tampella M-60 Heavy Field Gun Weight in firing position – 9,500 kg; weight of shell – 25 kg.

105 mm M-61 Light Field Gun Weight – 1,800 kg; weight of shell – 14·9 kg; VO – 600 m/sec; range – 14 km; rate of fire – 7 rpm.

122 mm M-38 Medium Field Gun Weight – 2,450 kg; weight of shell – 21·76 kg; VO – 515 m/sec; range – 11·8 km; rate of fire – 5 rpm. This is an old Soviet weapon and is being withdrawn from service.

152 mm M-38 Medium Field Gun Weight – 4,150 kg; VO – 504 m/sec; range – 12 km; rate of fire – 4 rpm.

Also in use are the Soviet M-37, M-55 and M-63 120 mm gun howitzers; Soviet SBZ 130 mm gun howitzers; and Soviet 105 mm guns. Older pieces such as the 76 mm M-02 and M-36, 105 mm M-41, and 152 mm M-34 and M-37 were captured in quantity during Finland's campaigns against Russia, and are still held, although largely relegated to coastal defence emplacements.

Anti-Aircraft Weapons

35 mm M-63 Oerlikon twin-barrelled radar con-trolled AAMG (see Swiss section).
40 mm Bofors AA gun with radar control.
Soviet M-50 single-barrelled towed 57 mm and twin-towed 57 mm guns, and Soviet ZSU-57 SP twin AA guns.

Wheeled Vehicles

SISU-KB-45 4 × 4 3 ton truck; empty weight – 5,200 kg; length – 5·7 m; width – 2·3 m; height; 2·44 m; crew – 2 + 18; engine – 135 hp, 6 cylinder, water-cooled, diesel; max road speed – 88 km/hr; road range – 800 km. This is a Finnish-produced forward control vehicle which appears as a cargo and box-bodied vehicle in many roles.

Valmet Terra 865BM 4 × 4 articulated artillery tractor; empty weight – 6,250 kg; length – 7·06 m; width – 2·37 m; height – 2·55 m; crew – 2 + 6; engine – 90 hp, 4 cylinder, water-cooled, diesel; max road speed – 30 km/hr; road range – 550 km.

SISU-KB-46 6 × 6 4 ton artillery tractor; empty weight – 8,650 kg; crew – 3; engine – 165 hp; max speed – 70 km/hr. Like the KB-45, this vehicle has a hydraulic drive system to drive the axles of the towed guns and thus to increase mobility.

As in the Swedish army, guns are often towed by civilian agricultural tractors and a two-wheeled trailer limber carries the ammunition and the crew. The trailer wheels are driven via a flexible drive cable attached to the tractor's power take-off.

Other vehicles in use include the Soviet tracked AT-S artillery tractor; the Soviet GAZ-69M 4 × 4 half ton and ZIL-157 6 × 6 trucks; the West German Unimog 4 × 4 half ton tractor; and Sno-cat tracked vehicles. Engineering units have some Soviet K-61 amphibious tracked vehicles.

Armoured Vehicles
APCs Soviet BTR-50P tracked, closed vehicles.
Tanks Some British Charioteer vehicles of Second World War vintage; Soviet PT-76 light and T54 and T55 medium tanks.

Finnish Army Uniforms
Parade Dress
Grey-blue single-breasted, open-necked service dress jacket, 4 button front, four patch pockets with buttoned flaps (top pockets pleated), shoulder-straps, plain cuffs, single vent rear. White shirt, black tie. Officers wear Sam Browne style brown leather belts with pistol holsters on the front left-hand side; grey riding breeches, black jackboots, black leather gloves. All ranks wear light blue steel helmets of Finnish pattern which is rather like the French 1950–1970 style helmet. Other ranks wear white webbing and white, calf-length gaiters.

Service Dress and Walking Out Dress
Blue-grey, single-breasted blouse with hip-length skirt and two breast pockets (not pleated). The front buttons are concealed and the cuffs are closed with two buttons. The collar is closed and turned down.

Trousers are either normal, long or in riding breeches style and worn with jackboots or with black boots and gaiters or shoes. Headwear is a grey-blue peaked cap with two buttons and a blue-white-blue cockade.

Working Dress
A grey-blue denim suit of the same cut as Service Dress, same hat, boots and gaiters.

Combat Dress
Brown, light green and dark green camouflaged

Finnish collar patches, from top: Kenraalimajuri, Majuri, Luutnantti, Sotilasmestari.

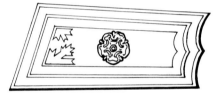

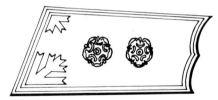

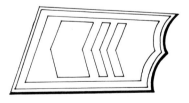

hip-length jacket and trousers with grey-blue peaked caps or German World War II helmet in camouflaged cover; jackboots; grey webbing equipment.

Special Clothing

Winter Combat Clothing: White camouflage suit, Russian pattern fur caps or steel helmets in white covers. Skis.

NBC Defence Clothing: Respirator with corrugated tube to filter unit on the hip, black rubber gloves, smock, trousers and boots, steel helmet.

Officer Cadets wear a very dark blue ceremonial uniform similar to British Army No 1 Dress with standing collar (edged in white), eight silver buttons, no pockets; red shoulder-straps edged white and bearing the cadet crest and one, two or three horizontal white bars beneath it to indicate rank: "Swedish" cuffs (with two buttons) edged in white; very dark blue trousers with broad white side stripes, black shoes, white gloves; peaked caps with very dark blue headbands and white tops and the cadet badge; white waist-belt.

Miscellaneous

There is a volunteer women's auxiliary corps who perform signals and nursing duties. A great variety of trade and skill-at-arms badges are worn on the upper left sleeve; and the paratroopers wear a silver winged parachute over crossed swords worn on the right breast above the pocket. Other skill badges are worn on the left breast pocket.

Finnish Army Flags

The Finnish Army has a great number of flags of very varied designs; each school has its own flag, each of the six brigades, the two cavalry regiments (dragoons and mounted rifles) and each of the six rifle battalions (Lapland, Uudenmaa, Kyme, Hämee, Karelia and the Marines), the tank and anti-tank battalions, each artillery, air defence and coastal artillery battalion as well as each signals and engineer company and the Guards Battalion. The dragoon, mounted rifle and rifle units have swallow-tailed flags, the rest are square and often bear the badge of the province in which the unit is located (Karelia: opposed arms holding swords; East Bothnia: six white mink). Flag tips are either a gilt spear shape with the gilt Finnish lion in the centre, silver spear points or "Prussian 1813 style" black and silver iron crosses within gold wreaths.

Finnish Army Facing Colours (worn on the collar patches in parade, walking out and service dress):

Armour	– Black with white edging.
Dragoon Battalion UUSEMAA	– Dark yellow with light blue edging.
Mounted Rifles Battalion HÄME	– Dark yellow with red edging.
Field Artillery	– Red with black edging.
Coastal Artillery	– Red with dark blue edging.
Air Defence Artillery	– Red with white edging.
Anti-tank Artillery	– Black with red edging.
Engineers	– Dark crimson with white edging.
Signals	– Dark crimson with yellow edging.
Guards Battalion	– Dark blue with white edging.
Infantry	– Dark green with white edging.
Technical Troops	– Dark blue with white edging.
Transport	– Light blue with white edging.
Veterinary	– Lemon yellow with light blue edging and gold snake badge.
Medical	– Grey with red edging and gold snake and staff badge.
Pharmacist	– Grey with red edging and two gold snakes intertwined.
Officer Cadet School	– Dark violet.
Military bands	– Dark blue, white edging and golden "key".
Military padres	– Black, crimson edging, golden cross within wreath.
NCOs Academy	– Dark green, red edging.
Border Guards	– Dark green with red edging.
Air Force	– Light blue with black edging.

Badges of rank parade and walking out dress (worn on the coloured collar patch):

General	– Three golden Finnish lions facing to the front, one thick and one thin gold edging to collar patch.
Lieutenant-General	– Two such lions and the same edging.
Major-General	– One such lion and the same edging.
Colonel	– Three large golden roses with two medium silver or gold lace edging.
Lieutenant-Colonel	– Two large golden roses with two medium silver or gold lace edging.
Major	– One large golden rose with two medium silver or gold lace edging.
Captain	– Three small golden roses, single edging in the regimental colour.
Lieutenant	– Two gold roses joined by a gold bar, regimental edging.
Second Lieutenant	– Two gold roses, regimental edging.
Ensign	– One gold rose, regimental edging.
Officer Cadet	– The Finnish lion on crossed swords within gold rays, gold edging.
Military official, technical provision branch	– Three six-pointed gold stars in triangular formation, behind them a sword through a cog wheel also gold.
Regimental Sergeant-Major	– One thick gold chevron followed by two thin ones.
Company Sergeant-Major	– One thick and one thin gold chevrons.
Staff Sergeant	– One thick gold chevron.
Senior Sergeant	– Four thin gold chevrons.
Sergeant	– Three thin gold chevrons.
Corporal	– Two thin gold chevrons.
Lance Corporal	– One thin gold chevron.
Senior Private	– A silver matt button and a piping in the regimental colour along the collar patch.

Badges of rank on combat dress (worn on six-sided grey patches on the lower sleeves):

General (Kenraali)	– One wide gold lace bar with oak leaf pattern under three narrow plain gold bars.
Lieutenant-General (Kenraaliluutnantti)	– One wide and two narrow bars.
Major-General (Kenraalimajuri)	– One wide and one narrow bar.
Colonel (Eversti)	– One medium plain gold bar over three narrow plain gold bars.
Lieutenant-Colonel (Everstiluutnantti)	– One medium over two narrow bars.
Major (Majuri)	– One medium over one narrow bar.
Captain (Kapteeni)	– Two narrow plain gold bars with a very narrow one in between them.
Lieutenant (Yliluutnantti)	– One narrow bar under two very narrow bars.
Second Lieutenant (Luutnantti)	– Two narrow bars.
Ensign (Vanrikki)	– One narrow bar.
Officer Cadet (Kadetti)	– Finnish lion on crossed swords within gold sun rays.
RSM (Sotilasmestari)	– Dark blue patch, one very wide gold chevron and two narrow gold chevrons, points to the top.
CSM (Ylivaapeli)	– One wide and one narrow gold chevron.
Ssgt (Vaapeli)	– One wide gold chevron.
Snr Sgt (Ylikersantti)	– Four narrow gold chevrons.
Sgt (Kersantti)	– Three narrow gold chevrons.
Cpl (Alikersantti)	– Two narrow gold chevrons.
LCpl (Korpraali)	– One narrow gold chevron.
Spte (Varvatty Mies) Pte (Sotamies)	– No badges.

THE FRENCH REPUBLIC

Population (including Corsica) – 52,000,000.   **Capital** – Paris.
Armed Forces:
   Army – 328,000 men; 600 AMX-30 tanks; 450 helicopters, 300 light fixed wing aircraft.
   Navy – 67,600 men; 2 aircraft carriers, 1 helicopter carrier, 19 submarines, 3 cruisers (1 command,
      1 SAM, 1 helicopter), 17 destroyers (3 command, 4 SAM, 4 aircraft direction and 6 anti-
      submarine); 29 frigates (2 with SAM); 91 minesweepers (various sizes); 23 MTBs; 23
      landing vessels. Naval air force: 150 combat aircraft – 2 squadrons Etendard IVM fighter
      bombers; 2 squadrons F-8F Crusader interceptors; 1 squadron Etendard IVP recon-
      naissance aircraft; 3 squadrons Alize anti-submarine aircraft; 1 squadron Super Frelon
      anti-submarine helicopters; 3 squadrons HSS 1 helicopters and 1 squadron Alouette
      helicopters, 3 squadrons Bréguet Atlantic and P-2 search and rescue and anti-submarine
      patrol aircraft.
   Air Force – 105,000 men; 500 combat aircraft split into two commands:
      Air Defence Command – 3 squadrons Mirage IIIC fighter bombers; 2 squadrons Mirage
      F-1 all weather fighters; 3 squadrons Super Mystere B-2 interceptors.
      Tactical Air Force – 13 fighter bomber squadrons (8 Mirage IIIE, 1 Mirage IIIB, 2
      Mystere IVA and 2 F-100D); 3 squadrons Mirage IIIR/RD recce planes.
      Air Transport Command has 1 heavy transport squadron (4 DC-6Bs and 4 Br-765
      Saharas), 7 tactical transport squadrons (4 with Noratlas and 3 with Transall C-160);
      2 mixed transport squadrons; 4 helicopter transport squadrons using Alouette IIIs and
      H-34s.
Para-military forces – 15,000 (Compagnies Républicaines de Sécurité).
Reserves   – 540,000 men.
Defence Spending – $6,241 million in 1972 (3·1% of GNP).

Head of State is the President – Valerie Giscard-d'Estaing, elected in May 1974 as successor to Pompidou after a hard-fought election. He remains in office until 1981. The national parliament is the Senate, with 283 elected members, and the National Assembly which is elected every five years. Current prime minister is Jacques Chirac, who belongs to the "Union des Democrates pour la République" (UDR), the Gaullist party. The government is a coalition of the UDR, the CDP (Centre Democratic and Progres) and some independent members.

Head of the armed forces is the president; he is assisted by the "Consiel Supérieur de la Défense Nationale" (CSDN), the "Comité de Défense" and the "Comité de Défense restreint". The president is chairman of the CSDN and the prime minister is his deputy. Other permanent members of the CSDN are the minister of defence, the marshals of France and the chiefs of staff of the armed services. Other members may be co-opted as required. The defence minister is assisted by the "Secretariat Generale de la Défense Nationale" (SGDN).

Although a member of NATO, France withdrew from military participation in that body in 1966 and caused NATO to remove her headquarters and all other military installations from her territory while simultaneously withdrawing many vital defensive forces from the NATO infrastructure. This left gaping holes in the Hawk anti-aircraft belt and severely weakened the Western alliance. French troops are still deployed in Germany however; there is a brigade in Berlin and a corps in Germany (Baden-Württemberg area). These troops are not under NATO command.

French troops are also stationed in East Africa (French Affars and Issas Coast) at the southern end of the Red Sea: army forces – two regiments (3,000 men); navy – 2 minesweepers and some landing craft; air force – 2 squadrons (550 men).

In Malagasy (formerly Madagascar) is a small

garrison of the Foreign Legion 3rd Infantry. In French Somaliland is the 13th Demi-Brigade of the Foreign Legion, a squadron of the French air force and a light naval squadron. France's atomic testing ground is in the Pacific ocean on the Mururoa atoll of the Tuamotu islands group and the main headquarters of this organisation (Centre d'Expérimentations du Pacifique or CEP) is on Tahiti. Units of the Foreign Legion 5th Regiment are deployed in the area for security purposes. In the French Caribbean territories one battalion is stationed.

The French army of today is divided into two main parts: the Territorial Army (Organisation Territoriale), and the Standing Army (Forces Permanentes).

The Territorial Army is responsible for the call-up and training of conscripts, mobilisation plans and internal security. It is organised in seven military regions (Régions Militaires) including 21 military divisions (Divisions Militaires), the city of Paris and the "military sector" of the island of Corsica. The geographical breakdown is as follows:

Military Region and headquarters	Military Divisions and their headquarters
I Paris	12th – Paris
	13th – Tours
II Lille	21st – Lille
	22nd – Amiens
	23rd – Rouen
III Rennes	31st – Rennes
	32nd – Caen
	33rd – Nantes
IV Bordeaux	41st – Bordeaux
	42nd – Poitiers
	43rd – Limoges
	44th – Toulouse
V Lyon	51st – Lyon
	52nd – Clermont-Ferrand
VI Metz	61st – Nancy
	62nd – Strassbourg
	63rd – Chalons
	64th – Duon
	65th – Besançon
VII Marseille	71st – Marseille
	72nd – Montpellier

The Standing Army is further subdivided into the "Forces de Manoeuvre" (FM), the "Forces à vocation de Défense Operationnelle du Territoire" (DOT) and the "Force d'Intervention".

The "FM" is deployed both in Europe and in French overseas territories and consists of the following troops:

The 1st Army (58,000 men in five mechanised divisions).

Berlin – one brigade with infantry, armour, engineer, logistic and Gendarmerie elements.

Germany (in the Baden-Württemberg area) – The 2nd Corps with two divisions: Corps HQ – Baden-

THE FRENCH "TYPE '67" MECHANISED BRIGADE

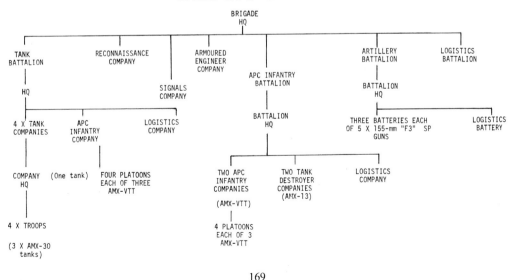

169

THE FIVE FRENCH ARMOURED RECCE REGIMENTS

THE FRENCH COMMANDO INFANTRY REGIMENT

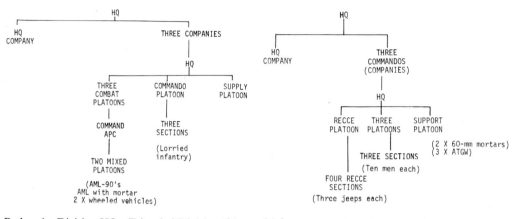

Baden, 1st Division HQ – Trier, 3rd Division HQ – Freiburg.

Since 1967 the French standing army has re-organised its forces so that a standard divisional establishment has been achieved. Each of the five "Type 1967" Divisions consists of three mechanised brigades organised as shown on the appropriate chart, and totals 16,100 men. Divisional troops include:

a security battalion (only raised in time of war).

an AA regiment (nine 30 mm AMX-30 AA Tanks, 12 Roland AAGW).

an engineer battalion with 48 Gillois amphibious bridging vehicles and 4 AMX armoured bridge layers.

an aviation squadron (Groupe d'aviation légère divisionnaire or GALDIV) of 38 PUMA SA-330 helicopters.

a transport battalion.

a supply battalion.

a signals battalion.

a Pluton nuclear rocket regiment of two batteries each of two launchers.

At corps level is a further regiment of Pluton of four batteries, making a total of 36 Pluton launchers in the 1st Army.

France – the 1st Corps with the 4th, 7th and 8th mechanised divisions. Corps HQ – Strasbourg, 4th Division HQ – Verdun, 7th Division HQ – Mulhouse, 8th Division HQ – Compiègne.

French North East African (Affars and Issas) – two battalions.

Elsewhere in Africa – 4,000 men.

Malagasy – two battalions.

Pacific Nuclear Test Ground Area – two battalions.

Caribbean – one battalion.

DOT (56,000 men) – two alpine brigades (the 17th and 27th); three armoured regiments; one artillery regiment; 25 infantry battalions which, on mobilisation, would increase to 80.

The Force d'Intervention consists of the 11th Parachute Division, the 9th Brigade and units of the French Foreign Legion specialising in parachute and commando type operations. The 11th Division is stationed in south west France and has an organisation which differs from that of all other French divisions due to its airborne role. It consists of two brigades each with their own light armour, artillery and engineer support all para-droppable or air portable. The 9th Brigade is stationed in western France and consists of marines, infantry, light armour and artillery and is designed to be used overseas. It is air portable and can also undertake amphibious operations.

Individual Arms of the French Army

Infantry

There are four different types of infantry in France today, differentiated from one another by their role and equipment.

Les Régiments Mécanisés Employed in mechanised brigades and equipped with AMX-VTT amphibious APCs. They are designed to operate closely with armoured formations.

Les Régiments Motorisés Mounted in wheeled vehicles for rapid mobility, these units are stronger in manpower than their APC counterparts and are designed to be used in difficult country where armour is not likely to be a great threat. They can be equated to the "Jäger-Brigaden" of the West German Army.

Les Régiments d'Infanterie Dismounted local defence units.

Les Unités Spécialisées Alpine battalions and parachutist units.

Cavalry (L'arme Blindée et Cavalerie)

This arm is the marriage of the traditional cavalry regiments and the younger tank battalions. As with the infantry various types of armoured units exist today:

Les Régiments de Chars de Bataille Equipped with AMX-30 medium tanks and designed for shock action and rapid thrusts.

Les Régiments Mécanisés Having light tanks (AMX-13), these units operate in the mechanised brigades.

Les Régiments de Reconnaissance The true followers of the light cavalry of old, these armoured car units are charged with the vital task of gathering intelligence of the enemy and screening the movements of their own troops.

Les Unités de Parachutistes Very lightly equipped with armoured cars and ATGW, these units form part of the Force d'Intervention.

The Artillery (L'Artillerie)

France has a long and proud tradition of an artillery arm always in the forefront of tactics, development and research, and their armament has recently been augmented by the French-developed tactical nuclear weapon system Pluton mounted on the AMX-30 chassis. Anti-aircraft artillery includes Hawk SAM, and the twin-barrelled, radar controlled 30 mm SP AA gun on the AMX-30 chassis. This same chassis is used for the 105 mm and 155 mm F-3 SP guns. Target data for nuclear strikes is gathered by surveillance using the R-20 unmanned photo-reconnaissance drone.

The Engineers (Le Génie)

As in other armies, the engineers have the task of aiding their own army to move, fight and live in the field and of hindering the movements of the enemy. Among their equipments is the Gillois amphibious bridging equipment.

Logistic Services (Le Train)

First organised on a military basis by the Emperor Napoleon I in 1807, the "Train" is responsible for route allocation, transport by land, rail, river and coasted waters and air, of rations, ammunition, petrol and spare parts, evacuation of sick and

The AMX-13 light tank, here photographed with an FL-11 turret and 75 mm gun. Widely exported and still in use at home and abroad, this design, progressively up-gunned, serves on as a tank-destroyer in the French armoured infantry battalions. (RAC Tank Museum)

wounded and the recovery of damaged vehicles and equipment.

Administrative and Repair Service (Le Service de l'Intendance Militaire)

The functions of provision and storage of material, equipments and spare parts is part of the task of this service as well as administration and other things such as baking bread.

Le Troupes de Marine

The old French colonial troops were reshuffled into "Les Troupes de Marine" on 1 January 1968, and consists of: l'Infanterie de Marine, l'Artillerie de Marine, and le Cadre des Télégraphistes des Troupes de Marine.

It is this corps which provides training teams to the armies of France's former colonies.

La Légion Etrangère

Still embodying much of the mystique of an earlier age, the French Foreign Legion has been retained and still accepts men from other lands without question (except when serious crime is suspected, when the applicant will be handed over to the police for further investigation). As in past days, many of the men of the Legion are of German origin. Some of the officers of the Legion are drawn from its own ranks but the majority are up-and-coming officers seconded to the Legion for two or three years at a time.

When France withdrew from North Africa in the 1960's, the Legion lost its traditional home at Sidi-Bel-Abbes and moved lock, stock, barrel and monuments to a new depot at Aubagne, where the 1st Foreign Regiment is now housed. The 2nd Infantry and 2nd Parachute Regiments are based in Corsica, while the 3rd Infantry Regiment is in Madagascar. The 1st Cavalry Regiment is at Orange (equipped with AML armoured cars and AMX-13 tanks); the 13th DBLE is in East Africa and the 5th Regiment is in the Pacific.

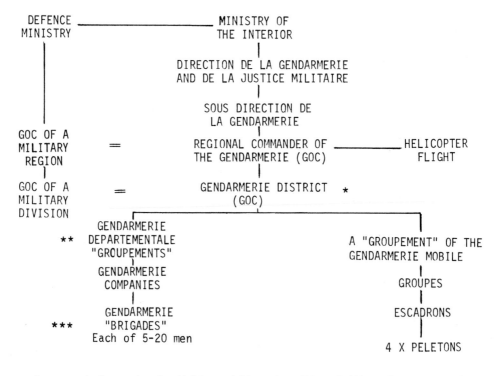

*= named after province in which located. ** = about 100 in all. *** = about 3,800 in all.

Army Aviation (L'Aviation Légère de l'Armee de Terre)

Each division in the Force de Manoeuvre has a "Groupe" of 40 helicopters, and each of the two corps has 50. In each military region is a flight of light helicopters, and the schools of infantry, cavalry, artillery and train also have flights attached. Apart from reconnaissance and liaison duties, helicopters are used in the anti-tank role with four SS-11 ATGW mounted on an Alouette III. Transport helicopters are of the SA-330 type.

The Gendarmerie Nationale Française

All members of this arm of the French army are professional soldiers. The Gendarmerie Départementale are distributed over the country in groups of two or three and function much as civil police. The Gendarmerie Mobile, however, are concentrated into barracks. Apart from traffic control and criminal police operations, the peacetime role of the Gendarmerie includes the protection of France's borders and the maintenance of public order. Their support of the French army lies in providing military police personnel and assistance in the mechanics of mobilisation and the call-up of conscripts. In time of peace they generally receive orders from the Ministry of the Interior and the legal department, and have increasingly been used to relieve catastrophe areas and for "civil defence" purposes. In time of war they continue to perform these functions and in addition form combat units which are integrated into the French order of battle; for this purpose they are then also subordinate to the Defence Ministry. At present the entire Gendarmerie has a strength of 65,000 men. Its command structure is integrated into that of the Territorial Army at every level and is shown in the attached chart.

Special Gendarmerie Départementale Brigades include – "Brigades de Recherche" – criminal police

The French AMX-30 main battle tank. (RAC Tank Museum)

task forces; "Brigades Motorisés" – traffic police; "Brigades de Montagne" – mountain rescue and security specialists employed in the Alps, the Pyrenees and the Auvergne; "Brigades Fluviales" – river police; and the mounted squadron of the "Garde Républicaine de Paris".

Each Escadron of the Gendarmerie Mobile is about 130 men strong and there are currently about 100 Escadrons. Where six or more Escadrons exist within one Groupe, they may be collected into two Detachements. Some Escadrons are armoured (Escadrons Portés) and mounted in APCs or there are also Escadrons with APCs and a Peleton of AML armoured cars (Escadrons Mixtes).

There is also the "1er Groupement Blindé" in Versailles consisting of two Escadrons with AMX-13 tanks, three APC – mounted Escadrons Portes, and a reconnaissance Escadron equipped with AML armoured cars.

Although all Gendarmes wear very dark blue uniforms, those of the Départementale have silver buttons and white facings, the Mobile gold buttons and red facings.

French-Manufactured Equipments

AM-50 120 mm Mortar

Apart from being capable of being fired from its two-wheeled chassis, this heavy weapon can be fired with a bipod or can also be broken up into mule or man loads for use in mountainous country. This weapon is used in the Yugoslavian Army and is there known as the "sGrW UBM-52".

Weight (on wheels – 402 kg, (with bipod) – 242 kg; length of barrel – 1·75 m; range – 500 m–7,000 m; ammunition type – HE, smoke and flare.

M-51 120 mm Mortar

Similar to the AM-50 except that this weapon can only be fired from its travelling carriage.

Weight – 530 kg; barrel length – 1·737 m; range – 500 m–6,650 m; muzzle velocity – 290 m/sec; ammunition type – HE, smoke and flare.

120 mm (B) Mortar

A heavier version of the AM-50; can be fired either from wheels or bipod. It breaks down into seven loads for mountain use.

Weight – 484 kg (wheels), 260 kg (bipod); length of barrel – 1·75 m; range – 500 m–6,700 m; muzzle velocity – up to 285 m/sec depending upon ammunition type.

MO-120-60 120 mm Mortar

Designated "Léger", this weapon weighs only slightly more than the 81 mm mortar and is now in use in the French, Belgian and Italian armies. It is a bipod supported weapon.

Weight – 92 kg; length of barrel – 1·63 m.

MO-120M65 Mortar

While retaining the ballistic performance of the old AM-50, this weapon has been lightened by the employment of modern techniques so that only two men are needed to move it across country. It can also be split into three man loads or carried on a mule.

Weight – 144 kg; barrel length – 1·64 m.

MO-120-TR-61 Mortar

In contrast to the preceding weapons, this mortar has a rifled barrel which enables it ballistically to equate to a light howitzer while being much lighter than such a piece. It can only be fired from its wheeled chassis and can fire at such low angles as 28°. At present it is in use in the Dutch Army. The ammunition has pre-cut driving bands.

Weight – 580 kg; length of barrel – 2·08 m; range – 1,200–12,850 m.

RAP-14 22 barrelled 140 mm rocket launcher

As in many other countries, a multiple rocket launcher has recently (1973) been developed in France. The existing equipment is towed on a two-wheeled trailer but it can also be mounted on wheeled and tracked vehicles. The rockets are single-stage, solid fuel, ballistic missiles with warheads having 5·5 kg of HE. Each rocket is 2 m long and weighs 54 kg. Maximum range is 20 km, covered target area 10,000 square metres, error tolerance 90 m. Rate of fire of salvo – 1 rocket per half second. The launcher is 5·05 m long, 2·57 m high, 2·5 m wide and weighs 3·6 tons empty, 4·8 tons with rockets. The crew is five men and the launcher can either be re-loaded by hand or the rocket "pod" can be unclipped and a new, full pod (weight *over* 1·2 tons!) placed on it.

AMX DCA twin armoured SP 30 mm AA guns

Used in the AA batteries of the mechanised brigades, this weapon system is mounted on the AMX-13 light tank chassis. The crew is 3 men, combat weight 17·2 tons; length – 5·4 m; width – 2·5 m; height to top of turret (without extended radar antennae) 2·7 m, with antennae – 3·8 m.

Radar range – 12 km; armament – 2 × 30 mm HSS-831A L/75 cannons; rate of fire – 2 × 650 rpm; muzzle velocity – 1,000 m/sec; combat ammunition – 600 rounds.

Roland I (*fair-weather*) and Roland II (*all-weather*) SP SAM

This is a joint Franco-German venture and is coming into service with both armies in 1973. Crew – 3; vehicle – Marder APC; both systems have twin launchers, Roland I has target acquisition radar with IFF, target tracking is optical and Roland II has both target acquisition and tracking radar. Both systems employ computer control translation equipment. The missiles (ten on each vehicle) are 2·6 m long and their maximum speed is Mach 1·5; combat range, 6,000 m.

Berliet VXB wheeled armoured vehicles

Based on the same basic 4 × 4 chassis, Berliet have developed a family of vehicles for use in the combat zone. The vehicle is a rear-engined, four-wheeled, inherently amphibious, enclosed, armoured truck whose dimensions are as follows: length – 5·99 m; width – 2·44 m; height (without turret) – 2·05 m; combat weight is 11,500 kg, empty weight – 8,900 kg. It can carry a 2,000 kg load or take 13 fully equipped men. Wading depth is 1·5 m and when swimming water propulsion is by wheel rotation giving a speed of 5 km/hr. Max road speed – 80 km/hr; road range – 750 km; fuel capacity – 200 litres. The engine is a Berliet V-8 168 hp power plant with a gearbox giving 12 forward and 2 reverse gears. A 4½ ton winch can be mounted at the front of the vehicle. The armour plate is proof against 7·62 mm rounds; access is by two side and one rear door or two roof hatches.

The versions already developed include:
Command Vehicle: Crew – 8; armament – 2 × 7·62 mm MGs (each with 4,000 rounds) (one on the

The Panhard EBR-75 armoured reconnaissance vehicle, with FL-10 turret mounting a 75 mm gun. This design has been progressively up-gunned to 90 mm. (RAC Tank Museum)

175

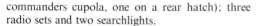

commanders cupola, one on a rear hatch); three radio sets and two searchlights.

Reconnaissance: Crew – 10; armament – 1 × 20 mm automatic cannon in T20-13 turret with 750 rounds; 1 co-axial 7·62 mm MG with 4,000 rounds and 1 dismountable 7·62 mm MG also with 4,000 rounds. Equipment includes 2 searchlights.

Fire support: Crew – 5 men; armament – 1 × 81 mm mortar with 100 rounds; 1 × 7·62 mm MG with 4,000 rounds mounted on the rear hatch. The mortar fires through a hatch in the roof and the vehicles chassis is specially strengthened.

A second mortar fire support version merely transports two 81 mm mortars and their crews (8 men), the mortars are fired externally from their normal baseplates.

Logistic version: Crew – 4 men; armament – 2 × 7·62 mm MGs each with 4,000 rounds; payload – 2,000 kg. Variants as recovery and workshop vehicles fitted with the aforementioned winch can also be seen.

APC: Crew – 13; armament either 1 × 7·62 mm MG on rotating armoured mount with 4,000 rounds or 1 × 12·7 mm HMG with 1,100 rounds.

Ambulance: Crew – 3 + 7 wounded (4 lying, 3 sitting).

Other versions of this versatile vehicle are under development and include a 120 mm Mortar carrier (range – 10 km; ammunition – 30 rounds); an AA version with twin or single 20 mm cannon and radar control equipment and an anti-tank vehicle with a variety of ATGW armament, either ENTAC, SS-11, SS12, Swingfire or Milan.

Pluton tactical nuclear SSM

This French produced missile is mounted on the AMX-30 medium tank chassis and is employed at divisional and corps level. The basic Pluton unit is the Detachment of two batteries each of two launchers. Each of the five divisions of the 1st French Army has one Detachment and each of the two corps a further two Detachments; this makes a total of 36 launchers. The launcher vehicle can travel short distances carrying one armed missile and it is accompanied by a 1 ton 4 × 4 truck carrying the "Iris 35-M" fire control computer and another housing the tracking and control radar. Each battery is supported by a reconnaissance and survey troop who seek out and survey prospective launching sites.

The missile normally travels in two loads and the warhead is married up with the rocket motor shortly before moving into the chosen firing position. The warhead has a yield of about 15 kilotons, a range of from 15–120 km and an error tolerance at the target of from 200–400 metres. From the time of moving into the pre-surveyed firing position to blast-off, at least 15 minutes are required for the count down.

The missile is 7·59 m long, 63 cm rocket diameter (1:415 m including fins) and the warhead weighs 1,200 kg while the whole missile weighs 2,350 kg. The motor is solid fuel which makes for easy storage and handling. Like other weapons of its type, it is a "shoot 'n' scoot" system; once the missile has been successfully directed onto its target the launcher group rush off to a new location in order to avoid the inevitable enemy counter stroke. Pluton is being introduced into service in 1973 and by 1975 will have replaced all the Honest John missiles which have been the French tactical nuclear field missile to date.

Crotale all-weather SAM

Although produced in France, this AA system is not in use with the French army, although it has been exported to the Union of South Africa where it is known as Cactus. Specifically designed to combat fast, low-flying aircraft, four missiles are mounted on each of the three launcher vehicles in a battery. These vehicles are equipped with target tracking radar while a fourth vehicle has the target acquisition radar, data being passed to the launcher vehicles by cables. All vehicles are of the same basic type, lightly armoured, 4 × 4 trucks, weight (with missiles) – 13 tons; length – 6·2 m; width – 2·6 m; height – approx 2·4 m with missiles; engine power – 230 hp diesel electric; road range – 600 km. The missile has a single stage, solid fuel rocket motor; it is 2·89 m long; 15 cm in diameter (54 cm fin-tip to fin-tip); weight 75 kg (of this, the warhead weighs 15 kg and contains 5 kg of HE with proximity and impact fuses). The missile range is from 500–8,000 m (max height 3,000 m) and its speed is Mach 2·5. The target acquisition radar has a range of 18·5 km, the tracking radar – 16 km.

155 mm armoured SP howitzer GCT

Built on an AMX-30 chassis, this weapon has a fully enclosed fighting compartment and the rear of the turret is a magazine housing 42 rounds. The howitzer can be operated in the automatic mode whereby a rate of fire of 8 rpm can be achieved.

Types of ammunition include HE, smoke and illuminating.

Maximum range – 23·5 km; crew – 4 (commander, driver, gun layer and loader); weight with 25 tons of ammunition – 41 tons. Road performance as for the AMX-30D. This weapon is still undergoing troop trials.

DCAN Bridge layer

This new 4 × 4 equipment is now undergoing troop trials. It consists of a four-wheeled bridge carrier similar in appearance to the West German M2 but carrying a scissor-folded MLC 40 bridge on its back. This bridge can be laid and used independent of the vehicle and will then cover a 20 m gap. By using itself as part of the finished bridge, a 38 m obstacle can be spanned and by coupling two such vehicles together with an extra ramp, this distance can be increased to 40 m. Weight of equipment – 33 tons; max road speed – 60 km/hr; max road range – 600 km; wades – 1·5 m.

AMX-10P tracked air-portable amphibious APC

Now coming into service with the French army, this vehicle is somewhat similar in external appearance to the Soviet BMP 76 infantry combat vehicle except that its armament is much lighter calibre. Crew – 2 + 9; armament – one turret-mounted 20 mm MK M621 cannon and a co-axially mounted 7·62 mm MG. Engine – 280 hp Hispano-Suiza, diesel; max road speed – 65 km/hr; max water speed – 7·2 km/hr using hydrojet and/or track propulsion. Night driving and fighting equipment is a passive, light intensifier system. Other versions of this vehicle include the AMX-10PC (Command) and the AMX-10TM which tows a 120 mm mortar. All these vehicles are ABC protected.

AMX-10RC 6 × 6 wheeled amphibious armoured car

A sister equipment of the tracked APC described above, this vehicle maintains the French belief in fast, mobile armoured cars with a heavy punch as stated by the AML 245-H90 and the EBR-90. This rear-engined vehicle is in the evaluation stage and is armed with the British 105 mm cannon. Fire control is by computer (COTAC) which is coupled to the laser rangefinder. Engine and gearbox are as for the AMX-10P; max road speed – 85 km/hr;

Right, the new French olive-green combat dress.
(Ét. Ciné-Armées)

max road range – 800 km; water propulsion by hydrojet.

M-8 Panhard 8 × 8 amphibious armoured car

Using the same turret and gun as the AMX-10RC, this rear-engined armoured car is still undergoing troop trials.

Berliet 680-T 4 × 4, 4 ton lorry

Now being developed for the French army, this forward control vehicle has a drop-sided load platform; 115 hp diesel engine; max road speed – 90 km/hr.

Saviem SM-8 4 × 4, 4 ton lorry

Similar in appearance to the '680-T', the engine is 115 hp; max road speed – 90 km/hr. This vehicle is now in issue to the French army.

French Army Uniforms

The following forms of dress are worn by officers:

"Bleu Armée" (Ceremonials)

Regimental kepi, midnight blue, single-breasted jacket with five button front, white shirt, black tie, white gloves, midnight blue trousers and black shoes, medals and lanyards as entitled. The jacket has no pockets on the breast; rank is shown on the epaulette and by silver/gold cuff bands. Collar badges and arm badges are not worn.

Tenue de Sortie Hiver No 1 (Winter Service Dress)

Khaki, single-breasted, four button jacket with patch pockets on breast and skirts, plain khaki, turned-up cuffs, regimental collar patches, and epaulettes, white shirt and gloves, black tie, regimental kepi. Khaki trousers with twin dark brown side stripes, black shoes.

Tenue de Sortie Été No 1 (Summer Service Dress)

Style as for winter service dress but of a much lighter weight, lighter coloured khaki material. The trousers have no side stripes. All other details as for winter service dress.

Tenue de Sortie Été No 2 (Shirt Sleeve Order)

Khaki shirt and trousers in the same material as for summer service dress, black tie, regimental epaulettes and kepi (a beret may also be worn), black shoes, narrow khaki web waist-belt with yellow buckle plate. Regimental collar patches are not worn, instead the regimental arm patch is worn.

Tenue de Travail d'Hiver No 3 (Winter Working Dress)

The kepi is replaced by the dark blue beret, regimental epaulettes by khaki shoulder-straps with gold/silver rank straps, no collar badges are worn, instead the arm badge; shirt and tie are khaki, gloves and shoes brown.

Tenue de Travail d'Été No 3 (Summer Working Dress)

Kepi replaced by beret, tie khaki, no regimental epaulettes but khaki shoulder-straps and brass/chrome rank stripes, regimental arm badge, brown gloves and shoes.

Tenue de Combat

The post-war French helmet of slightly Japanese-like shape, the light green combat clothing and the light brown leather equipment have now all given way to new pattern items. The helmet is shallower and broader (more like the British model), the combat jacket and trousers are now dark olive green, and the equipment is of a dark green plastic and webbing compound. Boots and puttees are black. Badges of rank are worn on shoulder-slides for officers or on the upper arm for men.

NCOs' Dress

Tenue de Ceremonie As for officers Tenue de Sortie Hiver No 1.

Tenue de Sortie Hiver As for Tenue de Ceremonie except light khaki shirt and tie, brown leather gloves.

Tenue de Sortie Été No 1 As for officers' Tenue de Sortie Été No 1 except light khaki tie and shirt, brown leather gloves.

Tenue de Sortie Été No 2 As for officers' Tenue de Sortie Été No 2 except light khaki tie.

Tenue de Travail d'Hiver No 3 As for officers.

Privates only wear berets and do not wear collar badges at all, regimental arm badges being their distinctions. In summer walking out dress, shirt sleeve order and working dress they have no gloves. Specialist clothing is worn by tank crews, Chasseurs Alpins, paratroopers, and the Foreign Legion – whose other ranks always wear white Kepis, a reminder of the white campaign covers of the old desert days.

Epaulettes are in the colour of the kepi base.

Regimental distinctions are worn on the following appointments: epaulettes, collar patches, arm patches, buttons, berets and Kepis.

The Epaulette This will bear the badges of rank (for officers) and will be in the colour of the kepi base. Marine troops wear a golden anchor, the Foreign Legion gold or silver seven-flamed grenades.

The Collar Patches These are worn only by officers and NCOs in parade, walking out and service dress. Rank and file wear no collar patches. The patch is pentagonal in shape with a central device and perhaps one, two or three chevrons above it. In working dress no collar patches are worn.

The Arm Patches The patch is always diamond shaped and worn on the upper left arm except in dark blue ceremonials and parade dress. The arm patch is of the same colour and bears the same device as the collar patch.

They are in various colours and generally have an edging all round and a central device. The edging and device are in the facing colour for rank and file. For officers and NCOs the edging is in the facing colour, the central device (or number) will be in gold or silver according to the regimental button colour. The arm patch is not worn by officers and NCOs in ceremonial or parade dress.

The Buttons The French Army has retained a multiplicity of button designs. Colours are gold or silver and in accord with the kepi lace. Designs include: marine troops – an anchor within a ring; infantry –
a flaming grenade within a ring; hussars – spherical, plain buttons.

Berets The somewhat large "Basque" beret is worn with the headpiece pulled down to the left-hand side, the tie ribbons of the headband hanging loose at the rear, and a badge of arm worn over the right ear.

Kepis The front badge is the regimental number, a grenade, or an anchor (Marine troops).

French Army Flags

The design is very reminiscent of the flags issued by Napoleon I in 1810. The cloth is square and in the national colours – three vertical stripes of blue (next to the pike staff), white and red – fringed in gold and has on the face side: "LA REPUBLIQUE FRAN-CAISE AU – ᴱᴹᴱ REGIMENT D'INFANTERIE" (or whatever regiment is concerned). In each corner is a gold laurel wreath enclosing the regimental number. On the reverse is: "HONNEUR ET PATRIE" and a list of the regiment's battle honours embroidered in gold; once again in each corner a gold wreath enclosing the regimental number. The pike staff tip is a four-sided spear point on a flat disc bearing the initials "RF".

According to the regiment's battle record it will have various cravats, medals and citations attached to the pike tip, and may also wear the lanyard ("Fourragere") of the Medaille Militaire or the Croix de Guerre.

Kepi colours

Arm	Base	Top	Lace	Badge
Marine troops				Golden anchor.
Artillery	Black	Black	Gold	Golden grenade.
Engineers				
Signals				
Infantry	Dark blue	Red	Gold	Golden/silver grenade or regimental number.
Cavalry	Light blue*	Red*	Silver	
Schools	Light blue*	Red*	Gold	
Technical Troops (Materiel)	Light blue*	Red*	Silver	Silver grenade.
Chasseurs, Alpins and Mechanisée	Black	Black	Silver	Silver grenade.
Train	Dark blue	Red	Silver	Silver grenade.
Foreign Legion (infantry)	Dark blue	Red	Gold	Golden/silver grenade of special design.
Foreign Legion (cavalry)	Dark blue	Red	Silver	
Gendarmerie Départementale	Black	Mid blue	Silver	Silver grenade.
Gendarmerie Mobile	Black	Mid blue	Gold	Gold grenade.

* Differing from other colours of the same apparent shade.

THE REPUBLIC OF IRELAND

Population – 2,971,000.　　　　　　　　　　　　　　　　　　　　**Capital** – Dublin.
Armed Forces:
>　**Army** – 9,000 men; at time of writing a recruiting drive was launched for some 4,000 extra personnel.
>　**Navy** – 500 men; 1 corvette, 3 minesweepers.
>　**Air Force** – 450 men; 2 Vampires, 6 BAC Provosts, 6 Chipmunks, 3 Alouette III helicopters, 3 DH Dove transport planes.

Reserves　　　　　– 17,500 men in the Territorial Army.
Defence Spending　– $53·3 million in 1972.

Head of state is Erskine Childers, elected by plebiscite in 1973 for a seven-year term. The parliament consists of two chambers, the Senate (Seanad Eireann) with 60 members (11 of which are nominated by the prime minister) and the lower chamber (Dail Eireann) with 144 members elected for a maximum of five years. The main political parties are the Fianna Fail (69 seats); Fine Gael (54); Labour (19) and Independent (2). The government (from 14 March 1973) is a coalition of Fine Gael/Labour and the Prime Minister, Liam Cosgrave, is a member of the latter party as is the defence minister, Patrick Donegan.

The terrorist activities of the illegal Irish Republican Army (IRA) in Northern Ireland and in the mainland of England, Scotland and Wales since 1969 caused severe strain to be placed on Cosgrave's predecessor, Jack Lynch, who sought to keep the Irish Republic in a peaceful state by a policy of non-interference with the IRA organisation in the country. The political voice of the IRA in Ireland is Sinn Fein, a party which received 1·1% of the cast votes in the 1973 election.

Since Cosgrave's assumption of office, more active measures have been taken against the IRA including the recent (September 1973) arrest of the leader of the Provisional IRA in Dublin, Seamus Twomey. Strong British pressure is suspected to have been exercised in this case as Twomey is thought to be the moving force behind the recent wave of letter bombs which have plagued London and Birmingham. Twomey later made a sensational escape by hijacked helicopter from a prison yard.

Due to the heavy losses incurred by the IRA in their terrorist campaign against the British (and the Protestant population) in Northern Ireland, a split occurred among the top leadership. Part of this group (known now as the Official IRA) wished to abandon terror and seek a political settlement in Northern Ireland; another part (known since the split as the Provisional IRA) were in favour of even more desperate attacks.

Even before the notorious subjugation of Ireland by Cromwell in the XVII Century, the British have been involved, more or less bloodily, in Irish affairs, nowadays much against their will. Since 1 July 1937 the southern part of Ireland has been an independent sovereign republic and was, in fact, neutral during the Second World War.

The Irish Army (Oglaigh na hEireann)

The Irish Army is essentially defensive in character and tailored to fit the tasks likely to confront it in a small island which has been officially at peace for almost fifty years. All its members are volunteers. Defence ministry organisation is shown on the appropriate chart; in explanation can be added:

Chief of Staff's branch	– operational planning, co-ordination of the three services.
Adjutant General's branch	– discipline, personnel matters, recruitment.
Quartermaster General's branch	– provision of equipment, arms, supplies and accommodation.

Ireland is divided into three military regions. *Eastern* – HQ Dublin – includes the counties of Louth, Monaghan, Meath, Dublin, Leix, Wicklow,

Carlow, Kilkenny, Wexford and Kildare and the eastern portions of Cavan, Offaly and Waterford. Command badge, worn on the tunic sleeve, is a yellow shield bearing a crimson spearhead. *Southern – HQ Cork –* includes the counties of Cork, Limerick, Kerry and Tipperary, the southern parts of the counties of Clare and Offaly and the western part of Waterford. Command badge is a blue crenellated wall bearing three crowns, in the orange "sky" a blue winged spear. *Western – HQ Athlone –* includes the counties of Donegal, Leitrim, Mayo, Sligo, Roscommon, Longford, Galway and Westmeath with the western portions of the counties of Offaly and Cavan and the northern party of County Clare. Command badge is a blue shield bearing an arm holding a sword in white.

The Curragh Camp forms an independent command and is a major training centre; its badge is a red shield bearing a sprig of yellow oak leaves and acorns.

Field Formations

The regular army consists of six brigades located as follows (brigade organisation is shown on the attached diagram):

1st Brigade – Southern Command
2nd Brigade – Eastern Command
3rd Brigade – Southern Command
4th Brigade – Western Command
5th Brigade – Western Command
6th Brigade – Eastern Command

Infantry

There are seven regular infantry battalions numbered 1, 2, 3, 4, 5, 6 and 12. The companies of a battalion are lettered A, B, C and D. The battalions are located as follows: 1st – Galway; 2nd – Dublin; 3rd – Curragh; 4th – Cork; 5th – Dublin; 6th – Athlone; 12th – Limerick and Clonmel. Apart from these 4,000 regulars, there are seventeen volunteer or reserve battalions in the "Forsa Cosanta Aitiuil" (FCA) numbered and located as shown below:

7th Battalion – 5 companies in Dublin and Meath.
8th Battalion – 5 companies in Louth, Monaghan and Cavan.
9th Battalion – 6 companies in Kilkenny, Callan, Castlecomer, Portlaoise, Abbeyleix.
10th Battalion – 5 companies in Wexford, New Ross, Carlow and Muine Bheag.
11th Battalion – 5 companies in Bandon, Bantry, Clonakilty, Macroom and Skibbereen.
13th Battalion – 5 companies in Fermoy, Cahir, Dungarvan, Kanturk and Mallow.
14th Battalion – 5 companies in Nenagh, Adare, East Limerick, Newcastle West and Tipperary.
15th Battalion – 6 companies in Tralee, Cahirsiveen, Dingle, Killarney, Killorglin and Listowel.
16th Battalion – 5 companies in Athlone, Ballinasloe, Tullamore, Loughrea and Athenry.
17th Battalion – 6 companies in Longford, Granard, Strokestown, West Cavan, Roscommon and Mohill.
18th Battalion – 4 companies in Westport, Tiveragh, Swinford and Ballina.
19th Battalion – 5 companies in Boyle, Carrick-on-Shannon, Ballymote, Manorhamilton and Castlerea.
20th Battalion – 5 companies in Dublin city; D Company is composed of students and E Company is completely Irish speaking.
21st Battalion – 3 companies in North Wicklow, South County Dublin and Wicklow.
22nd Battalion – 4 companies in Ennis, Ennistimon, Killaloe and Kilrush.
23rd Battalion – 3 companies in Cork and Middleton.
24th Battalion – 4 companies in Letterkenny, South Donegal, Inishowen and North Donegal.

In recent times, active service in the Irish army has been limited to UNO operations; in 1960 a volunteer battalion went to the Congo and by 1965 the "9th Brigade" consisting of the 32nd and 33rd Infantry Battalions and two independent armoured car units were representing the Irish peacekeeping force there. Twenty-six of these volunteers were killed and 57 wounded or injured. In March 1964 Ireland supplied another infantry battalion for UNO, to UNFICYP in Cyprus; there are currently moves afoot to recall them. Five men of the contingent have died in Cyprus, none in action.

Three Soviet
army generals in
parade dress,
1971.

The Artillery

There are six Field Regiments and one Anti-Aircraft Regiment, a number of Coastal Defence Forts, an Artillery School, a depot and a directorate. There are over 1,000 regular all ranks and over 3,000 reservists in the FCA. Location of units is as follows:

1st Field Regiment – Cork
2nd Field Regiment – Dublin
4th Field Regiment – Mullingar
1st Anti-Aircraft Regiment – Kildare

} HQ and 1 battery regular, the other batteries FCA. Equipment: British 25 pdr field guns and 120 mm mortars, now being replaced by 105 mm howitzers. AA weapons: 40 mm Bofors cannon.

3rd Field Regiment – Templemore
5th Field Regiment – Galway
6th Field Regiment – Kildare

} All batteries FCA.

The Cavalry

Not surprisingly, the Irish army has only a token force of tanks – British Comets of World War II vintage. The Cavalry is thus organised into the 1st Tank Squadron, the 1st Armoured Car Squadron and the 4th Motor Squadron, all in the Curragh camp; and the 1st Motor Squadron in Dublin and the 2nd Motor Squadron in Clonmel. All of these are regular units, while the remainder of the units (3rd Motor Squadron in Castlebar, 5th Motor Squadron Dublin and 11th Motor Squadron) are all FCA-manned. Apart from the tanks mentioned above, the Irish cavalry are equipped with four Panhard AML 90 French armoured cars with 90 mm guns, 30 Panhard APCs and 17 "Unimogs" (half-ton 4 × 4 German-built trucks). There are also some Swedish Landswerk armoured cars. Each squadron has nine officers and 127 ORs.

The Corps of Engineers

Six Field Companies (one per brigade), one survey and four maintenance companies located as follows:

1st Field and 3rd Maintenance Companies – Cork
2nd Field and 2nd Maintenance Companies and the 11th FCA Field Company } – Dublin
4th Field and 4th Maintenance Companies – Athlone
3rd FCA Field Company – Limerick
5th FCA Field Company – Galway
1st Maintenance Company – Curragh

There is also the Directorate of Engineering, and the Depot and School of Engineering at the Curragh.

The Signal Corps

This consists of the Directorate of Signals, a Depot, School and Base Workshops in the Curragh and six Field Signal Companies located as follows:
1st Field Signal Company – Cork
2nd Field Signal Company – Dublin
3rd Field Signal Company – Limerick
4th Field Signal Company – Athlone
5th Field Signal Company – Sligo
11th Field Signal Company – Dublin

The Air Signals Squadron provides communications for the Air Corps and Garrison Signal Sections link Army HQ to the Command HQs. Equipment is HF and VHF and ranges from man-pack to vehicle-borne stations; teleprinter multi-channel networks are maintained by the Garrison Signal Sections.

The Ordnance Corps

This corps is responsible for the provision, storage, maintenance, distribution, inspection and repair of clothing, weapons, ammunition, optical instruments, furniture and tentage. Establishment – 60 officers and 577 ORs.

The Supply and Transport Corps

The responsibilities of this body relate to "combat supplies" ie rations, water, petrol, oil and lubricants and ammunition (as was the case with the British RASC prior to 1965). The repair of non-armoured

H

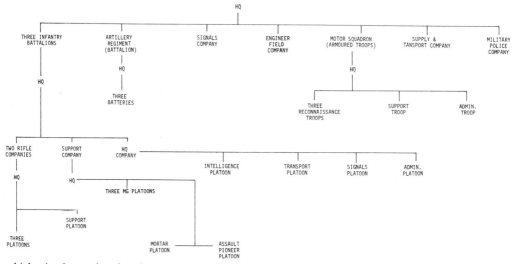

THE IRISH BRIGADE STRUCTURE

vehicles is also undertaken by the "S&T" Corps. The organisation is . a directorate, Depot and School at the Curragh, 3 Garrison Companies (one in each command), six Field Companies located as shown below, and a Base Workshops in Dublin.

1st Field Company and 3rd Garrison
Company   – Cork
2nd Field Company and 2nd Garrison
Company   – Dublin
3rd Field Company   – Limerick
4th Field Company   – Mullingar
5th Field Company   – Galway
11th Field Company (FCA)
4th Garrison Company   – Athlone

Regular establishment is 75 officers and 775 ORs.

The Military Police Corps

Established strength – 40 officers and 574 ORs. Organisation – Directorate; Depot and School in the Curragh, 3 Garrison Companies, 6 Field Companies (almost all FCA personnel). Locations:

1st Field Company   – Cork
2nd Field Company   – Dublin
3rd Field Company   – Limerick
4th Field Company   – Athlone
5th Field Company   – Galway
11th Field Company   – Dublin
2nd Garrison Company   – Dublin
3rd Garrison Company   – Cork
4th Garrison Company   – Athlone

Army Medical Corps

This is organised into a Headquarters, a Field Division and a Hospital Division.

The Air Corps

Strength – 101 officers, 724 ORs. Organisation – Headquarters, Flying Training Wing, Technical Wing and Administrative Wing (all at Aerodrom Mhic Easmuinn) and the Basic Flying Training School at Gormanstown. Aircraft include two DH Vampires, six BAC Provosts, six DH Chipmunks, three DH Doves, eight Reims-Cessna FR-172 trainers and three Alouette III helicopters.

Irish Army Equipment

Small Arms 9 mm Browning FN pistol (NATO pattern); 9 mm "Carl Gustav" SMG; 7·62 mm FN SLR (NATO pattern); 0·303 inch (7·7 mm) "Bren", British World War II LMG; Vickers 0·303 inch, water-cooled British World War II HMG; 2 inch (60 mm), 3 inch (81 mm) and 120 mm mortars; Swedish 84 mm "Carl Gustav" AT projector, and Swedish 90 mm, two-wheeled recoilless AT rifle.

Wheeled Vehicles

British Rover "8" and "9" $\frac{1}{4}$ ton and $\frac{3}{4}$ ton 4 × 4 trucks; Austin 1 ton 4 × 4 trucks; Bedford 1 ton 4 × 2, 3 ton 4 × 2 and 3 ton 4 × 4 trucks.

Irish Army Uniforms

Since 1962 the Irish Army has worn a light green mixture open-necked, single-breasted service dress jacket with four patch pockets remarkably similar in main detail to that worn by the British army. Officers (except cavalry officers) wear light green peaked caps, as do sergeant majors.

Cavalry officers wear a large-crowned caubeen-type beret with flowing black silk ribbons down to collar level, called a "Glengarry". Other ranks wear black berets with the badge situated over the left eye. Trousers are in the same colour as the jacket, boots and gloves black for men and officers.

Badges of rank take the form of horizontal red zig-zag bars on a yellow backing from acting corporal up through company sergeant (privates wear two or three five-pointed red stars with yellow edging according to grade). These badges are worn on the upper arms of the tunic and greatcoat and on the upper right arm in shirt sleeve order. Battalion quartermaster-sergeants (BQMS) and sergeant-majors (SM) wear a red embroidered badge (eight-pointed star of "Q" badge) on both cuffs and one

or two $\frac{1}{4}$ inch red silk bands across their shoulder-straps. Officers' badges of rank are worn on the shoulders, and major-generals and lieutenant-generals also wear scarlet gorget patches with gold loops and buttons.

Formation signs are worn on the upper left sleeve of the service dress tunics. Arm of service badges are worn in bronze on the collar, and other badges which may be seen are: Air Corps pilot – the silver, eight-pointed army star with the letters "FF" and a sun-burst in gold, with silver wings to either side all on green backing, worn above the left breast pocket. Air Corps air crew badge – as for pilots but only one wing to the left-hand side; worn in the same place as the pilot's badge. Champion Marksman's badge – a two inch diameter red circle edged in gold and bearing a blue diamond having a gold bow and arrow and red target on it. It is worn at the top of the right sleeve. Marksman's badge – a green cross in cloth bearing a yellow bow and arrow and a red target. Worn as for the Champion Marksman; the two badges may not be worn together.

Centre, Eire cap badge. Top to bottom, left, collar badges of Cavalry, Infantry, Air Corps. Top to bottom, right, collar badges of Engineers, Signals; and officer's rank star.

Forms of Dress

Officers (and Sergeant-Majors and BQMSs):
Full Dress (No 1)

Black peaked cap, gold wire badge, black tunic with no collar badges or top pockets, four button front, two buttons at each cuff, black cloth belt with open square yellow buckle, white shirt, black tie, white gloves, black trousers with single red side stripe, black shoes, gold aiguilette on left shoulder.

Service Dress (SD) No 1

Light green peaked cap with black headband and brown chin strap (cavalry officers the light green Glengarry); light green tunic with four patch pockets and bronze collar badges; brown leather Sam Browne belt; light green trousers, brown shoes and gloves. Light fawn shirt and grey-green tie.

SD No 2

Hat and tunic as above, additionally regimental pattern sword in brown leather sheath. Light tan riding breeches, brown leather lace-up gaiters and boots.

SD No 3

As SD No 2 but with web equipment and steel helmet.

SD No 4 (Shirt Sleeve Order)

Shirt with tie, sleeves worn buttoned at the cuff, web waist-belt, shoes.

Other Ranks:
SD No 1

Black beret with star badge, light green tunic with

Collar Badges

Cor Coisithe (Infantry)	– A target with crossed rifles superimposed, with a scroll below inscribed "COISITHE".
Cor Airtleire (Artillery)	– A figure representing "EIRE" seated on a Field Gun with a scroll below inscribed "AN COR AIRTLEIRE".
Cor Marcra (Cavalry)	– A breast plate, with crossed rifle and sabre beneath; the whole mounted on a wheel, with a laurel wreath and scroll surround; within the scroll the inscription "AN COR MARCRA".
Cor Innealltoiri (Engineers)	– A crescent inscribed "INNEALLTOIRI"; within the crescent a tripod and a theodolite.
Cor Comharthafochta (Signals)	– A figure representing the Angel Gabriel with scroll inscribed "AN COR COMHARTHAIOCHTA".
Cor Ordanais (Ordnance)	– A combination of axe, spear, sword and gun with a gunwheel, superimposed on a shield; a scroll inscribed "COR ORDANAIS AN AIRM".
Cor Solathair agus Iompair (Supply and Transport)	– Within a laurel wreath a castle, with a Celtic chariot in the foreground; a surround of wheat sheaves with scroll, inscribed "COR SOLATHAIR AGUS IOMPAIR".
Cor Liachta (Medical Corps)	– An upper scroll inscribed "OGLAIGH NA EIREANN", a lower scroll inscribed "COMRAIND LEGIS", the scrolls joined on each side by a staff around which a serpent is entwined; a silver hand in centre of badge.
Cor Poilini Airm (Military Police)	– An eight-rayed star, three tongues of flame between each ray; within the star a circle inscribed "AN COR POILII AIRM"; within the circle the letters "P.A."
Aer-Chor (Air Corps)	– A circle; within the circle an eagle; below, a scroll inscribed "FORFHAIRE AGUS TAIRISEACHT".
Scoil Cheoil Airm (School of Music)	– A lyre, with harp mounted on strings of lyre; harp of pattern known as Brian Boru Harp.

four pockets, four button front, bronze collar badges, black leather belt with open yellow buckle; very light green shirt and tie, light green trousers, black shoes or boots.

SD No 2 (*Parade Dress*)

As for SD No 1 but white web waist-belt (British '37 pattern); the trousers tucked into mid-calf length black boots, FN rifle with white web sling.

SD No 3

As for SD No 2 but with khaki coloured British

'58 pattern webbing and British pattern steel helmet. All buttons are gold and bear the gaelic harp.

On St Patrick's Day all ranks wear a sprig of shamrock behind their beret badge or on the left side of the peaked cap. (This custom is also observed by the Irish regiments of the British Army.)

Military police wear red-topped peaked caps and their helmets have a red stripe painted around the base.

A fawn raincoat or green greatcoat (double breasted) are also worn.

THE GRAND DUCHY OF LUXEMBURG

Population – 344,000.

Capital – Luxemburg.

Armed Forces – One battalion of infantry – 550 men.
Para-military forces – 350 Gendarmerie.
Defence Spending – $6,247,000 in 1972 (0·9% of GNP).

Head of State is Grand Duke Jean (born 5 January 1921) who came to the throne on 12 November 1964 after the abdication of his mother, the Grand Duchess Charlotte.

Parliament is the Chamber of Representatives, with 56 members elected for a five-year term (last election December 1968). The minister of state is Pierre Werner, a Christian Socialist.

The members of Luxemburg's army are volunteers serving a minimum of three years. The battalion is part of NATO's ACE mobile force.

Uniforms of the Luxemburg Battalion

In general, the style of these uniforms is similar to that of the Belgian army of today; that is, rather British in appearance.

Officers wear a khaki service dress with khaki cap having a brown leather chin strap and gold badge; the single-breasted jacket has an open neck, four button front, four pockets and pointed cuffs

with two buttons as for the British officer, brown leather Sam Browne belt and gloves, brown shoes. Light khaki shirt, khaki tie.

Alternative wear is a khaki battle dress (BD) of British style with '37 pattern web belt and gaiters and black boots, shirt and tie as above.

Badges of rank are worn on the shoulder-straps; the collar badges consist of the crowned cypher "J" on the upper collar point, crossed rifles on the lower collar point.

Shirt sleeve order consists of the shirt and tie, rank badges on the shoulder-straps, sleeves worn buttoned at the wrist, khaki trousers with narrow fawn web belt and yellow buckle plate, shoes or boots and gaiters. Combat dress is the olive green 1950s pattern British equipment with '37 pattern webbing. Berets are dark blue and are worn by other ranks in BD and combat dress and by officers in combat dress. Badges of rank for other ranks are worn on the lower sleeves.

Badges of rank: non commissioned men (chevrons, point uppermost)

Private 1st Class (Gefreiter)	– one red chevron.
Lance Corporal (Obergefreiter)	– one gold chevron.
Corporal (Unteroffizier)	– two red chevrons.
Sergeant (Feldwebel)	– two gold chevrons.
CSM (Hauptfeldwebel)	– three gold chevrons.
RSM (Stabsfeldwebel)	– three gold chevrons over a horizontal gold bar.

Officers (on the shoulder-straps)

Officer cadet (Fähnrich)	– a gold bar edged in red.
Second Lieutenant (Leutnant)	– one gold, eight-pointed star.
Lieutenant (Oberleutnant)	– two gold, eight-pointed stars.
Captain (Hauptmann)	– three gold, eight-pointed stars.
Major (Major)	– a gold and red crown.
Lieutenant-Colonel (Oberstleutnant)	– a crown over a star.
Colonel (Oberst)	– a crown over two stars.
Brigadier (Brigadegeneral)	– a crown over crossed gold sabres.

THE KINGDOM OF SPAIN

Population – 34,500,000.*

Capital – Madrid.

Armed Forces:

Army – 220,000 men.

Navy – 41,500 sailors, 6,000 marine infantry; 1 helicopter carrier, 4 submarines, 1 cruiser, 13 destroyers, 8 frigates, 2 corvettes, 1 anti-submarine PB, 3 MTBs, 17 minesweepers, 18 landing craft; 3 anti-submarine helicopters, 1 light helicopter squadron.

Air Force – 33,500 men, 215 combat aircraft: 36 F-4E and 30 Mirage IIIE fighter bombers; 70 F-5 and 55 HA-200 fighter bombers; 13 F-86F interceptors, 1 anti-submarine squadron of 11 UH-16B. 150 transport planes and helicopters including C-47s, C-54s, 21 Azor and 12 Caribou.

Para-military forces – 65,000 Guardia Civil.

Defence Spending – $879 million in 1972 (1·8% GNP).

Head of state is General Francisco Franco Bahamonde, born 4 December 1892 of a military family; he was trained in the infantry academy in the Alcazar at Toledo and later in Paris. In 1912 he was on colonial duty in Spanish Morocco and took part in the raising of the Spanish Foreign Legion which he commanded, as a general, in 1922. In 1927 he commanded the Saragossa military academy, in 1933 he was GOC-in-C in the Balearic Islands, in 1935 Chief of the General Staff, in 1936 GOC-in-C in the Canaries and at the outbreak of

the Spanish Civil War in that year he commanded the Moroccan troops. After his victory in 1939 he assumed the title "Caudillo" and found an authoritarian regime. On 23 July 1969 Juan Carlos, prince of Spain and a son of the old Bourbon royal family, was declared Franco's successor. Carlos is now being groomed to take over the reins of state when Franco retires or dies.

The head of state is advised by the "Council of the Kingdom" consisting of a chairman (President of the Cortes), Vice president of the Cortes, the senior member of the Cortes, the senior serving general-captain, the chief of the superior general staff, the president of the supreme court, the president of the state council, the president of the

* Includes Balearic and Canary Islands and West Sahara – 48,000.

THE SPANISH CAVALRY BRIGADE

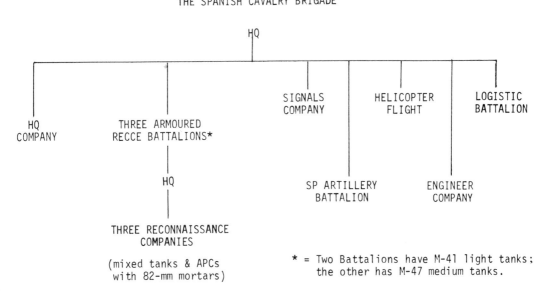

HQ

HQ COMPANY

THREE ARMOURED RECCE BATTALIONS*

HQ

THREE RECONNAISSANCE COMPANIES

(mixed tanks & APCs with 82-mm mortars)

SIGNALS COMPANY

HELICOPTER FLIGHT

LOGISTIC BATTALION

SP ARTILLERY BATTALION

ENGINEER COMPANY

* = Two Battalions have M-41 light tanks; the other has M-47 medium tanks.

Instituto Español and eight Cortes members. The parliament (Cortes) has 564 members drawn from various walks of society. Under the Spanish constitution, the head of state must be a male Catholic Spaniard, thus emphasising the important role which the church plays in Spanish life.

Voting rights can only be exercised by heads of families and by married women, and 104 Cortes members are elected by their votes. Head of the armed forces is Franco, who also appoints and dismisses officers, and he is advised in military matters by a special National Defence Council. There is no defence minister but a minister for each of the three services: Army – Lieutenant General Juan Castanon Mena; Navy – Admiral Adolfo Baturone; Air Force – Lieutenant General Julio Salvador. They are supported for executive purposes by their respective general staffs.

Spain has universal male conscription, terms of service being: army – 16 months; navy – 24 months; air force – 18 months.

Due to her geographical position and the world political situation, Spain is much sought after as an ally. There are currently 15,000 American servicemen in Spain at the air bases of Torrejon, Moron and Sanjurio-Valenzuela, and in the naval and air base at Rota (west of Gibraltar). The price America has to pay for these bases includes $125 million in

credit over the period 1971–76 and a free gift to Spain of $20 millions worth of arms, which will be used to speed up the current re-equipment programme of the Spanish army. Thus Spain, although not a NATO member, has a considerable finger in that pie, a fact which she undoubtedly uses as a lever in her current dispute with Great Britain over the sovereignty of Gibraltar.

Organisation of the Spanish Army

Field Army (*Fuerzas de Intervencion Inmediata – FII*)

One Tank Division, one Mechanised Infantry Division, one Motorised Infantry Division, one Cavalry Brigade, one Parachute Brigade and one Airborne Brigade.

Corps troops – a signals regiment, an artillery brigade (203 mm howitzers and Honest John SSM), an AA regiment (one battalion with Hawk SAM), an engineer regiment, army air corps units, medical, repair, transport and logistic battalions.

The Tank Division has its HQ in Madrid, and is composed of two tank brigades and one mechanised infantry brigade plus divisional troops.

The Mechanised Infantry Division is centred around Valencia, and has three mechanised infantry brigades plus divisional troops.

The Motorised Infantry Division is centred on Madrid, and has three motorised infantry brigades

189

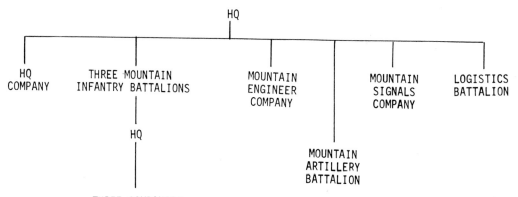

plus divisional troops.

Territorial Defence Forces (Fuerzas de Defensa Operativa del Territorio – FDOT)

Two Mountain Divisions (each of two brigades) in Barcelona and Burgos, and one High Mountain Brigade in Zaragosa; eleven Internal Security Brigades (one each for the nine military districts, two in Madrid); one Territorial Defence Brigade in Granada military region; a signals regiment, one coastal artillery brigade (around the Straits of Gibraltar), six coastal artillery regiments, four AA regiments, three engineer regiments, one medical regiment, one maintenance and one logistics regiment.

In addition to these formations are the 32,000 strong "Army of Africa" (the Spanish Foreign Legion and the Moorish Regulars or "Moros") who are stationed in the Sahara, in Ceuta and Melilla.

Independent formations (Army, Navy and Air Force) each 7,000 men strong are stationed in Mallorca, Minorca and Ibiza, Teneriffa and Gran Canarai.

Spanish Military Equipment

Small Arms (All Spanish-produced):

9 mm Superstar pistol Similar in appearance to the Browning; weight - 1 kg; 9 round magazine; effective range – 25 m.

9 mm Star Z-45 SMG This weapon has a collapsible butt and a magazine below the chamber and thus looks similar to the German World War II MP-40.

Blow-back weapon, 30 round magazine, 450 rpm; effective range – 100 m.

M-16 Carbine 7·62 mm calibre; weight – 3·8 kg; length – 1·04 m (without bayonet); 5 round magazine; hand action loading; effective range – 400 m. This is an old weapon used in reserve units and has been converted from its original 7 mm calibre.

M-58 SLR This is the Spanish version of the NATO weapon and is usually known as the CETME SLR (Centro de Estudios Tecnicos de Materials Especiales). It is identical to the West German G3 Gewehr and is used in many Nato and other armies. Calibre – 7·62 mm; blow-back action; weight – 5·13 kg; length – 1 m; 20 round magazine; rate of fire – 600 rpm; effective range – 600 m.

FAO LMG/HMG Calibre – 7·62 mm; weight with bipod – 9·1 kg; gas-assisted action; drum/belt magazine on left-hand side of breech with 50 rounds; rate of fire – 650 rpm; effective range – 1,000 m in the heavy role with 6·5 kg tripod mounting. This weapon is very similar in appearance to the World War II British Bren LMG.

FAO-M59 LMG A Spanish-licenced copy of the Czech MG ZB-26 with 7·92 mm calibre.

ALFA M-1944 HMG Calibre – 7·92 mm; length – 1·45 m; weight – 13 kg; weight of tripod – 27 kg; gas assisted action; 100 round cylindrical belt magazine to the left of the breech; rate of fire – 780 rpm; effective range – 1,000 m.

ALFA M-1955 HMG Almost identical to the M-1944 but with 7·62 calibre and a shorter barrel (1·1 m overall length).

89 mm Installaza recoilless AT rocket projector Length of weapon – 1·78 m; weight – 8·8 kg; weight of hollow charge projectile – 3·4 kg; VO – 185 m/sec; effective range – 250 m.

106 mm M40-A1 recoilless AT rifle This jeep-mounted weapon is an American product.

Mortars: 81 mm and 107 mm mortars (American weapons).

Artillery:

105 mm mountain howitzer – the Italian produced NATO weapon. The following American guns are also used: 105 mm M-2 light howitzer; 105 mm M-1 medium howitzer; 203 mm M-1 heavy howitzer; 155 mm M-2 medium cannon; 105 mm M-7B2 light SP gun on Sherman chassis; 105 mm M-37 light SP gun; 155 mm M-44 medium SP gun; 762 mm M-31 Honest John SSM. The Spaniards produced in 1966 a multiple rocket launcher mounted on a 2½ ton, 6 × 6 M-34 truck.

AA Artillery Spanish pattern Bofors 40 mm/L70 MG: Hawk SAM.

Armoured Vehicles:

American M-24 and M-41 light tanks; M-47, M-48 "Patton" medium tank; M-3A1, 4 × 4 APC; M-3 half-track APC; M-113 APCs, M-8, 6 × 6 armoured car, M-47 ARV.

Wheeled Vehicles:

American Willys, 4 × 4 jeeps, M-38 jeeps; M-274 "Mechanical Mule", 4 × 4, ½ tonner; ¾ ton Dodge, 4 × 4 trucks; 1½ ton Dodge, 6 × 6 trucks; 2½ ton, 6 × 6 M-34 and M-35 trucks; M-41, 5 ton, 6 × 6 trucks; M-543 and M-62, 5 ton, 6 × 6 crane vehicles, DUKW, 6 × 6 amphibious 2½ ton trucks; M-5 13 ton tracked artillery tractor; M-4 18 ton tracked artillery tractor.

British Rover ¼ ton, 4 × 4 jeeps ("Rover 8"); ¾ ton, 4 × 4, long wheel base "Rover 9" trucks; 1½ ton, 4 × 4 trucks; 1½ ton, 4 × 4 Rover Forward Control Vehicle. Many other British Vehicles (Austin, Bedford and Ford) dating back to World War II are also in use.

March-past by men of the Spanish Foreign Legion. (Keystone)

There are also Soviet "Ford" 4 × 2s, French and Spanish Citroen trucks, French Renault and Peugeot box-bodied vehicles. Modern Spanish vehicles include the licenced production of Rover ("Land-Rover-Santanda") and American "Kaiser CJ-3B" jeeps. Native vehicles include the 3 ton, 4 × 4 Barrieros TT.90.22 truck; length – 6·26 m; width – 2·4 m; height – 2·4 m; 6 cylinder diesel engine; max road speed – 85 km/hr. This is a forward control vehicle.

Spanish Army Uniforms

The Spanish Army has just introduced a new modern-style range of uniforms. Final details are not clear but a fairly accurate picture can be formed.

Parade Dress

Khaki peaked kepi with stiff crown, gold eagle badge, khaki chin strap, gold buttons. Khaki, single-breasted jacket; five button front, closed collar, knuckle length skirts, two pleated top pockets with buttoned flaps, slit bottom pockets with plain flaps; shoulder-straps; regimental badges are worn on metal rhombic badges worn on the collar points, rank badges are worn on the lower sleeves. The collar has a white insert which shows about 1 mm

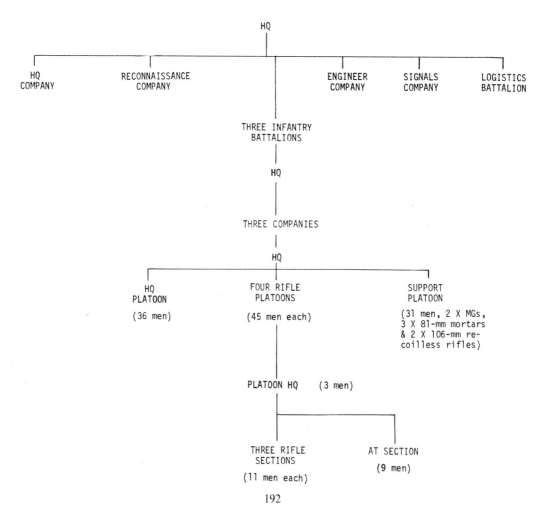

THE SPANISH INTERNAL SECURITY BRIGADE

HQ

HQ COMPANY — RECONNAISSANCE COMPANY — ENGINEER COMPANY — SIGNALS COMPANY — LOGISTICS BATTALION

THREE INFANTRY BATTALIONS

HQ

THREE COMPANIES

HQ

HQ PLATOON (36 men) — FOUR RIFLE PLATOONS (45 men each) — SUPPORT PLATOON (31 men, 2 X MGs, 3 X 81-mm mortars & 2 X 106-mm re-coilless rifles)

PLATOON HQ (3 men)

THREE RIFLE SECTIONS (11 men each) — AT SECTION (9 men)

above the khaki collar. Khaki trousers, mid-calf length black leather gaiters; black, lace-up boots. There is also a black leather waist-belt with upright, oblong brass belt plate bearing the eagle badge.

Walking Out Dress

Paratroopers have an olive green "battle dress" with open-necked blouse, white shirt, black tie, concealed front buttons, two pleated pockets with buttoned flaps and buttoned cuffs and shoulder-straps. The parachutist's badge (a gold, winged parachute) is worn on the upper right breast. Head-gear is a black beret pulled down over the left ear with the badge over the right ear. White gloves and black boots complete the outfit.

Other army units wear parade dress without boots and gaiters.

Summer Walking Out Dress

Parachutists – hat, shirt, tie, trousers and shoes as above. The shirt is worn with the sleeves buttoned at the wrist; parachute badge on the upper right breast, two pleated pockets with buttoned flaps, the metal rhombic regimental badge is worn on the right breast pocket; black leather waist-belt with

open brass buckle, black epaulettes without buttons.

Other units wear their own head-gear and khaki trousers, their own badges and epaulettes.

A mid-thigh length, double-breasted khaki mackintosh with regimental collar badges is worn.

Service Dress

Khaki denim jacket, trousers and open-necked shirt; the jacket has two pockets with square flaps on the chest and one pocket with a square flap on the upper left arm. The cuffs are buttoned, the skirts knuckle length. Brown laced boots to the lower calf; the trousers are tucked into the boots. A khaki, fore-and-aft forage cap with red piping is worn. The waist-belt is very similar to the British '37 pattern khaki webbing model. Badges of rank are worn on the shoulder-straps, regimental collar badges are not worn.

The Foreign Legion wears light green clothing, black webbing equipment with gold eagle buckle plate, rank badges worn on an oblong tablet on the upper left breast. The forage cap is khaki with red piping, red tassel hanging from the front peak, and a gold eagle badge on the front. Black boots and short black leather gaiters.

Top, left to right: rank insignia of Captain General; star motif used in rank insignia of Coronel (three), Teniente Coronel (two) and Comandante (one); cap and belt-plate badge; star motif used in rank insignia of Capitan (three), Teniente (two), and Alferez (one); and the rank insignia of a Teniente General. Bottom, left to right: branch of service badges worn on collar in gold for arms, silver for services, in a red diamond: Infantry, showing diamond backing; Cavalry, Construction Engineers, Logistics, Support Corps, and Cuerpo de Intervencion.

Combat Dress

American style NATO helmet, khaki jacket and trousers as for service dress; black webbing equipment or khaki webbing equipment (both British '37 pattern style) according to regiment; black boots and gaiters.

Paratroopers have a light green-dark green-white-brown-black mottled camouflage suit with knuckle length jacket skirts, olive green webbing equipment, black berets and black, mid-calf length boots. Marines wear a dark blue "battle dress" with black, calf-length boots, black beret with badge to the front centre and the crown pulled down over the right ear; khaki, open-necked shirt and white neckerchief. Foreign Legionnaires have light green, knuckle length jacket and trousers, black webbing equipment, black, mid-calf length boots and khaki forage cap with red tassel and gold badge.

Badges of Rank

Capitan General (General)	– four four-pointed stars around crossed sword and staff.
Teniente General (Lieutenant-General)	– as above but only the three bottom stars are worn.
General de Division (Major-General)	– as above but only the two stars at the sides are worn.
General de Brigada (Brigadier)	– one star on the crossed sword and staff.
Coronel (Colonel)	– three eight-pointed stars across the cuff.
Teniente Coronel (Lieutenant-Colonel)	– two stars.
Commandante (Major)	– one star.
Capitan (Captain)	– three six-pointed stars above the cuff.
Teniente (Lieutenant)	– two stars.
Alferez Alumno (Second Lieutenant)	– one star.
Alferez (Sergeant Major)	– one star.
Brigada (Staff Sergeant)	– a thick, vertical gold stripe on the bottom centre of the cuff.
Sergento (Sergeant)	– three gold stripes diagonally over the cuff.
Cabo Primero (Corporal)	– one such gold stripe.
Cabo Secundo (Lance Corporal)	– three diagonal red stripes above the cuff.
Soldado Especialista (Private first class)	– one red chevron, point up, on the upper sleeve.

THE KINGDOM OF SWEDEN

Population – 8,200,000.   **Capital** – Stockholm.

Armed Forces:

Army – 48,200 men (11,700 regulars, 36,500 conscripts).

Navy – 12,100 men (4,700 regulars, 7,400 conscripts); 22 submarines, 8 destroyers (2 with RB-08 SSM and 4 with Seacat SAM), 5 anti-submarine frigates, 33 MTBs, 2 minelayers, 37 mine-sweepers, 65 coastal artillery batteries with 75 mm, 105 mm, 120 mm, 152 mm and 210 mm guns and RB-08 and RB-52 (SS-11) SSM. 10 Vertol and 10 AB-206A helicopters.

Air Force – 12,200 men (5,800 regulars, 6,400 conscripts); 400 combat aircraft: 10 ground attack squadrons with Lansen A-32As using RB-04E ASMs and the newer Viggen AJ-37 (which will eventually replace the Lansen completely), 21 squadrons of J35 Draken all-weather fighters, 5 recce/fighter squadrons with S-32C and S-35E. Transport aircraft include 5 squadrons using C-130Es (2), C-47 Norseman (7), Beech Expediter, BAC Pembroke, DHC-2 Caribou and HS-104 Dove. 5 communications squadrons with SAAB 91, 130 SAAB 105 and 5 (eventually 98) Bulldogs. Helicopters are organised into ten Groups each of 3 or 4 craft of the following types: 10 Vertol 107, 6 Alouette II/III and 16 Agusta-Bell AB-204/206. Air defence is six SAM squadrons with Bloodhound-2. All air defence activity is co-ordinated and controlled by the computerised, fully automated "STRIL 60" air surveillance system.

Para-military forces – 500,000 Volunteer Home Guard.

Reserves	– Regular	Conscript
Army	– 13,700	100,000
Navy	2,600	14,000
Air Force	1,900	7,500

Defence Spending – $1,510 million in 1972 (3·7% GNP).

Head of state is King Carl XVI Gustav of the house of Bernadotte (founded by one of Napoleon's marshals). The Parliament (Reichstag) is a single chamber assembly having 350 elected members. Prime minister is Olof Joachim Palme, a Social Democrat, who has headed the government since 14 October 1969. Defence minister is Sven Andersson and Disarmament Minister (!) is Mrs Alva Myrdal. The government is responsible to Parliament for its policies although the King is theoretically responsible for his executive. The King is head of the armed forces and the GOC-in-C is directly answerable to the government. The GOC-in-C, supported by the defence staff, is responsible for executing government defence policy. The C-in-Cs of the three services, with their general staffs, are responsible for the training and operative efficiency of their formations.

All male Swedes between 18 and 47 years of age are liable for conscription. For the army and navy this consists of 9–15 months basic training with five subsequent refresher training periods of from 18–40 days; for the air force basic training is 9–14 months. Sweden is divided into six recruiting areas and the area commanders allot recruits as needed to the units of the three services within their areas.

In order to preserve the credibility of her political independence in peacetime and strict neutrality in war, Sweden has built up a strong and flexible defence system aimed at countering terrorism from within as well as invasion by a foreign power. Some 85% of Sweden's armament requirements are home-produced and Sweden is almost entirely self-sufficient as far as food supplies are concerned. Deep nuclear shelters have been constructed which could accommodate 3·5 million people if needed, and much of Sweden's industry is housed under-ground. The air force has atom-proof hangers and

Swedish ski-troopers being towed by snow-tractors, with reconnaissance helicopters in attendance. (Courtesy Swedish Army)

plenty of alternative airfields, and part of the fleet can also be placed in atom proof shelters in the naval base on the island of Musko.

Most of the Swedish army is concentrated either in the far north or in the south of the country at the Baltic approaches.

Swedish Army Organisation

The army is divided into the Field Army (Armén) and the Territorial Defence Force. In peacetime the Field Army consists only of fifty training units and twenty schools, and at time of mobilisation the combat formations (divisions and brigades) and the Territorial Defence units are activated.

For defence purposes, Sweden is divided into six military regions (Militärområden). All military formations come under command of the General Officer Commanding the military region in which they are located. Staff and headquarters personnel are drawn from all three services (navy, army and air force) and joint planning is thus ensured at all levels. The military regions are:

South	– HQ Kristianstad	– includes 4 military districts.
West	– HQ Skövde	– includes 3 military districts.
East	– HQ Strängnäs	– includes 6 military districts and the island Gotland.
Bergslagen	– HQ Karlstad	– includes 3 military districts.
Lower Norrland	– HQ Östersund	– includes 2 military districts.
Upper Norrland	– HQ Baden	– includes 4 military districts.

For peacetime administrative purposes the army is commanded by a "Chef för Armén" who is supported by an "Arméstab" and is responsible for organisation, equipment and personnel matters. The standing army consists of 12,000 professional officers and NCOs and 35,000 conscripts under training. There are also 12,000 officers and NCOs in the reserve.

The Territorial Defence Force is largely made up of volunteer organisations including the Home Guard (Hemwärnet) with over 100,000 men, the Swedish Red Cross (550,000) and the Swedish Women's Auxiliary Corps (Lotta-Korps) with about 100,000 members. Musketry practice takes place within the local shooting clubs.

The training units of the standing army are

196

located as follows: Military Region	Inf Regts	Jäger Batns	Recce Batns	Tank Regts	Tank Batns	Arty Regts	AA Regts	AA Batns	Engr Regts	Sig Regts
South	2	–	–	3	–	2	1	–	1	–
West	3	–	1	1	–	–	1	–	–	1
East	3	–	1	3	–	2	1	1	1	1
Bergslagen	3	–	–	–	–	1	–	–	–	–
Lower Norrland	2	–	–	–	–	1	1	–	–	–
Upper Norrland	2	1	1	–	1	1	1	–	1	1

There is also the "Leibgarde" in Stockholm, which is a horse-mounted unit.

The Field Army in time of mobilisation would be 500,000 men strong and would be formed into twelve divisions including six tank brigades, twenty-one infantry and three "Norrland" brigades (for organisations see the relevant charts). Apart from this Gotland would have its own "combat group". Each division would consist of a headquarters, two or three brigades and the usual divisional troops (signals, artillery, reconnaissance, AA, engineer, maintenance, medical, logistic and transport battalions).

Swedish Military Equipment
Small Arms:
9 mm Sig P210 Swiss pistol.
9 mm Browning NATO pattern pistol.
9 mm Lahti M/40 pistol with 8 round magazine.
9 mm Carl Gustav machine pistol with collapsible butt and 36 round magazine.
6·5 mm Ljungman AG-42B SLR. Weight – 4·7 kg; length – 1·26 m without bayonet; gas pressure operation; 10 round magazine; effective range – 300 m. An old Swedish weapon now replaced by the NATO pattern CETME SLR.
7·62 mm Automatkarbin 4 This is the Spanish CETME SLR and is the same weapon as used in the West German Army.
7·62 mm M-58 FN NATO pattern MG 1·2 m long; weight – 10·85 kg with bipod (tripod for heavy MG role weighs 10·5 kg); gas assisted action; 600–1,000 rpm (can be adjusted as required); effective range – 1,200 m; belt fed ammunition.
81 mm M/29 Mortar Swedish licenced production of the French Stokes-Brandt weapon. Weight in firing position – 60 kg; weight of bomb – 3·4 kg; VO – 190 m/sec; range – 2·6 km; rate of fire – 18 rpm.
120 mm M/41 Mortar Swedish licenced production of the Finnish Tampella weapon. Weight in firing position – 285 kg; weight of bomb – 13·3 kg; VO – 317 m/sec; range – 6·4 kg; rate of fire – 15 rpm.
74 mm Miniman light AT rocket projector

Length of weapon – 90 cm; weight – 2·6 kg; rocket weight – 0·88 kg (hollow charge); VO – 160 m/sec; effective range – 250 m. This is a use-and-throw-away weapon; the storage container is also

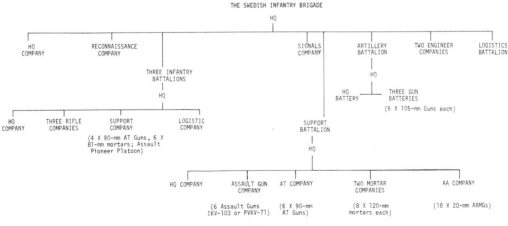

THE SWEDISH INFANTRY BRIGADE

the projector. All-up weight with two projectors in one case – 6·9 kg.

84 mm Carl Gustav heavy AT rocket projector

Length of projector – 1·13 m; weight – 13·2 kg; weight of rocket (hollow charge) – 2·5 kg; VO – 310 m/sec; effective range – 400 m; rate of fire – 6 rpm. Other armies also use this weapon, which can pierce 320 mm of armour plate.

90 mm Recoilless AT Gun (Pansarvarnspjas 1110)

Length of barrel – 3·7 m (towing hook at breech end); weight in firing position on two-wheeled trailer – 260 kg; weight of projectile – 3·1 kg; VO – 715 m/sec; effective range – 900 m; rate of fire – 6 rpm. This weapon has a co-axial 7·62 mm ranging MG and fires hollow charge projectiles which can pierce 380 mm of armour plate.

Apart from being towed by a farm tractor behind an accompanying limber trailer in the infantry brigades, it is also mounted on the ¾ ton, 4 × 4 Laplander jeep in the tank brigades.

11 cm ATGW Bantam (Bofors Anti-Tank Missile) Wire-guided, optically controlled missile, hollow charge warhead; start weight 7·6 kg; 85 cm long,

fin diameter – 40 cm; speed – 85 m/sec; effective range – from 300–2,000 m, can pierce 50 cm of armour. This weapon is carried by one man and can be fired from its storage container. Six missiles and all control equipment can be moved on a two-wheeled barrow pulled by two men.

Artillery:

105 mm M/39 and M/40 Light Field Howitzers – old weapons being withdrawn from service.

105 mm 4140 Light Field Howitzer. Swedish weapon with towing trails which form a cross-shaped firing platform giving 360° traverse when the gun wheels are switched up. Weight in firing position – 2,600 kg; weight of shell – 15·2 kg; VO – 610 m/sec; range – 14·6 km; rate of fire – 8 rpm.

150 mm M/39 Medium Field Gun/Howitzer. This gun is only used in tank brigades and is an old equipment. Weight in firing position – 5,700 kg; weight of shell – 42 kg; VO – 580 m/sec; range – 13 km; rate of fire – 6 rpm.

155 mm Medium Field Gun/Howitzer Swedish licenced production of the French M-1950 field gun.

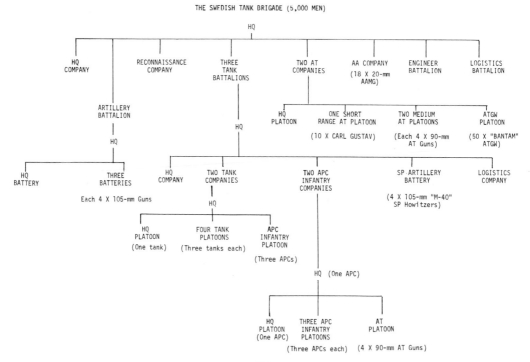

198

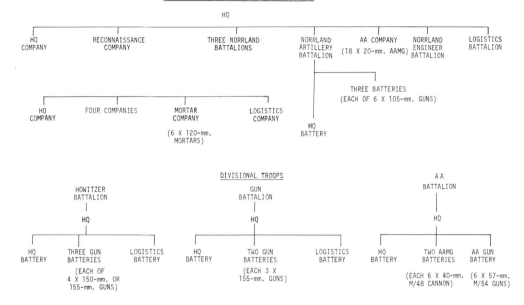

THE SWEDISH NORRLAND BRIGADE (5,500 MEN)

HQ

| HQ COMPANY | RECONNAISSANCE COMPANY | THREE NORRLAND BATTALIONS | NORRLAND ARTILLERY BATTALION | AA COMPANY (18 X 20-mm. AAMG) | NORRLAND ENGINEER BATTALION | LOGISTICS BATTALION |

HQ COMPANY — FOUR COMPANIES — MORTAR COMPANY (6 X 120-mm. MORTARS) — LOGISTICS COMPANY

THREE BATTERIES (EACH OF 6 X 105-mm. GUNS)

HQ BATTERY

DIVISIONAL TROOPS

HOWITZER BATTALION — HQ — HQ BATTERY — THREE GUN BATTERIES (EACH OF 4 X 150-mm. OR 155-mm. GUNS) — LOGISTICS BATTERY

GUN BATTALION — HQ — HQ BATTERY — TWO GUN BATTERIES (EACH 3 X 155-mm. GUNS) — LOGISTICS BATTERY

AA BATTALION — HQ — HQ BATTERY — TWO AAMG BATTERIES (EACH 6 X 40-mm. M/48 CANNON) — AA GUN BATTERY (6 X 57-mm. M/54 GUNS)

Weight in firing position – 8,000 kg; weight of shell – 43 kg; VO – 650 m/sec; range – 17·6 km; rate of fire – 6 rpm. This gun has a four-wheeled chassis and is used in both tank and infantry brigades.

155 mm SP Cannon VK 155 The chassis is an extended STRV-103-"S" medium tank chassis (two extra road wheels added) and the gun entered service in 1965. The fully enclosed turret has lateral rotation of 13°. The gun is automatically loaded and new magazines of 14 rounds can be placed in the turret from the accompanying limber by the crane on the gun in two minutes. VO – 860 m/sec; range – 25 km; rate of fire – 15 rpm; weight – 52 tons; length – 6·4 m (with gun barrel – 11 m); width – 3·4 m; height – 3·3 m; engine – 240 hp petrol engine and a 490 hp gas turbine; max road speed – 28 km/hr; armour – 20 mm. This is a divisional level artillery weapon.

LVKV 41 M/43 AA tank A World War II Swedish weapon having twin Bofors 40 mm/L60 MGs giving a rate of fire of 2 × 120 rpm. The turret is open, the chassis is that of the STRV-33 tank. Weight – 17 tons; crew – 4 men; length – 5·9 m; width – 2·45 m; height – 2·4 m; armour – 20 mm; engine – 290 hp petrol; max road speed – 55 km/hr. This weapon is still used in the tank brigades but is being withdrawn.

Bofors 20 mm Ivakan M/40 AA MG Mounted on a two-wheeled trailer, this weapon has a rate of fire of 360 rpm and an AA range of 1·6 km. A brigade weapon.

Bofors 40 mm L/60 M/36 AA gun Territorial defence weapon on a four-wheeled trailer, 120 rpm, 1·2 km AA range.

Bofors 40 mm L/70 M/48 AA gun This weapon is used by many other states and has already been described. It is radar controlled.

Bofors 57 mm M/54 AA Gun Similar in appearance to the above weapon, also radar controlled; weight in firing position – 8,100 kg; weight of shell – 2·6 kg; VO – 920 m/sec; AA range – 4 km; rate of fire – 120 rpm.

Armoured Vehicles:

STRV 74 Light Tank

Introduced into service in 1959; weight – 26 tons; length of hull – 6·08 m; width – 2·43 m; height – 3 m; armour – 40 mm max; engine 2 × 179 hp petrol engines; max road speed – 45 km/hr; crew – 4; armament – 1 × 75 mm gun (45 rounds carried), and 1 × AAMG. This is a development of the STRV 71 M/42 tank.

STRV 101 Centurion with 105 mm gun.

STRV 103 ("S")

The controversial Swedish "S" tank introduced into service in 1967. Having no turret, the gun is aimed by hydraulically altering the suspension posture of the whole tank. Weight – 37 tons; crew – 3; length with gun – 8·8 m (hull only – 6·9 m); width – 3·4 m; height – 2·14 m; front engined – 240 hp diesel and 490 hp gas turbine; max road speed – 50 km/hr; water speed – 6 km/hr.

IKV 91 Tank Destroyer (*Infanterikanonvagn*)

This light (15 ton) tank is designed to support infantry and is not itself a battle tank. With a crew of four (commander, driver, gunlayer and loader) it is inherently amphibious and is armed with a Bofors 90 mm cannon. It is constructed by the firm of **AB Hägglund** who have already developed several other light armoured vehicles for the Swedish army such as the PBV 302 (an amphibious APC introduced into service in 1966). The gun fires fin-stabilised projectiles with a muzzle velocity of 840 m/sec. Being a low pressure weapon, it is light in construction and requires less recoil mechanism than conventional rifled weapons of the same calibre. The ammunition is also less bulky than conventional ammunition. The gun is computer controlled (based on data fed in by the gunner's optical sight) and stabilised so that targets can be engaged while the IKV 91 is on the move. Auxiliary armament consists of one co-axially mounted 7·62 mm MG and another 7·62 mm MG on the loader's turret. Combat ammunition load is 68 rounds of 90 mm and 4,000 rounds of MG ammunition. The engine is a Volvo-Penta 330 hp four-stroke turbocharged diesel with a power/weight ratio of 22 hp/ton. Max road speed is 67 km/hr; road range – 600 km. Water speed is 8 km/hr and propulsion is by track movement.

The STRV 103 "S"; the 105 mm gun is automatically operated and can be handled, simultaneously with driving, by either of two of the three-man crew. (*Courtesy Swedish Army*)

IKV 103 (Infanterie Kanonvagn) Assault Gun

Based on the IKV 102 of 1952 vintage, this weapon came into service in 1956. Weight – 8·7 tons; crew – 4 men; length with gun – 5·85 m; width – 2·23 m; height – 1·84 m; armour – 18 mm max; engine – 145 hp petrol; max road speed – 55 km/hr; road range – 250 km; armament – 1 × 105 mm L/20 gun; VO – 475 m/sec; 24 rounds carried. Used in the infantry brigades.

PVKV 71 Tank Destroyer (Pansar Värnskanonvagn M/43)

A World War II weapon; weight – 23 tons; crew – 4; length of hull – 6·2 m; width – 2·4 m; height – 2·6 m; engine – 370 hp petrol; max road speed – 45 km/hr; armour – 40 mm max; armament – 1 × 75 mm gun (40 rounds carried); 1 × MG and 1 × AAMG. Used in the infantry brigades.

PBV 301 APC (Pansarbandvagn)

Introduced in 1962; weight – 11·5 tons; crew – 2 + 8 men; length – 4·66 m; width – 2·23 m; height – 2·64 m; armour – 20 mm; engine – 150 hp petrol; max road speed – 45 km/hr; road range – 300 km; armament – 1 × turret mounted 20 mm cannon (525 rounds carried); VO – 825 m/sec. This vehicle is used in the APC companies in the tank brigades and is a modification of the Czech "Pz 38" light tank.

PBV 302 APC

This is a modern, tracked APC, inherently amphibious. Weight – 13·5 tons; crew – 2 + 10 men; length – 5·45 m; width – 2·84 m; height – 2·41 m; armour – steel-plastic-steel sandwich; engine – 270 hp diesel; max road speed – 66 km/hr (water – 8 km/hr); road range – 300 km; armament – 1 × tur-

The IKV 91 is an inherently amphibious tank-destroyer of light construction. The 90 mm gun fires fin-stabilised projectiles, and is computer controlled. (Courtesy Swedish Army)

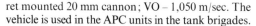

ret mounted 20 mm cannon; VO – 1,050 m/sec. The vehicle is used in the APC units in the tank brigades.

Ferret Mk 1 Scout Car British equipment.
SKPF M/42, 4 × 4 APC. Introduced in 1945, very "home-made" appearance; weight – 8·5 tons; crew – 2 + 13; length – 6·8 m; width – 2·3 m; height – 2·28 m; armour – 10 mm; engine – 115 hp petrol; max road speed – 70 km/hr.

Wheeled Vehicles:
Volvo "Laplander" – L3314, 4 × 4, ¾ ton jeep
   Empty weight – 1,510 kg; length – 3·99 m; width – 1·66 m; height – 2·05 m; crew – 2 + 6; motor 68 hp, 4 cylinder, water-cooled, petrol; max road speed – 97 km/hr. Also appears as radio vehicle.

Volvo P2104, 4 × 4, ¾ ton radio car
   Empty weight – 2,600 kg; length – 4·5 m; width – 1·9 m; height – 1·95 m; crew – 2 + 3; engine – 90 hp,

6 cylinder, water-cooled, petrol; max road speed – 105 km/hr.

Volvo L2204, 6 × 6, 1·5 ton truck
   Empty weight – 4,030 kg; length – 5·86 m; height – 2·56 m; engine – 115 hp, 6 cylinder, petrol.

Volvo L-3154, 6 × 6, 4 ton truck
   Length – 7·09 m; width – 2·13 m; height – 2·7 m; engine – 150 hp, 6 cylinder, water-cooled, diesel; max road speed – 80 km/hr.

Volvo L38545, 4 × 4, 4 ton truck
   Empty weight – 4,500 kg; length – 6·56 m; width – 2·32 m; engine – 115 hp, water-cooled, diesel; max road speed – 87 km/hr.

Bolinder Munktell BV202 over-snow tractor
   A tracked power unit with tracked trailer (tracks driven from the front power unit). Empty weight –

Swedish infantry armed with Carl Gustav SMGs deploy from a PBV 302 armoured personnel carrier. (Courtesy Swedish Army)

2,200 kg; length (both units) – 6·175 m; width – 1·76 m; height – 2·03 m; crew – 2 + 10; engine – 91 hp, 4 cylinder, water-cooled, petrol; top speed – 39 km/hr. This vehicle is amphibious and is used in the Norrland arctic regions.

Engineer Equipment

American Bailey and British MGB equipments are used together with pontoons to build ferries which are then propelled over Sweden's broad water areas by motorboats. Hovercraft with 8 ton capacity are also used.

Swedish Army Uniforms

Parade Dress

Medium grey peaked cap with black peak. Generals have gold chin cords and gold peak embroidery, field officers the same but thinner peak decoration, junior officers gold chin cords but no peak edging. In all the above cases the cap badge is a crowned light blue circle bearing the three gold Swedish crowns, all surrounded by gold oak leaves and imposed upon crossed swords. Senior NCOs have thinner gold chin cords and plain peak; the badge is generally as for officers but the central circle is white edged in blue and there are no oak leaves. Junior NCOs and privates have black silk chin cords and their badge is of the same shape as that of the NCOs but is in brass. The jacket is grey, open necked, single breasted with five gold buttons, four patch pockets with flaps (but without buttons). The jacket is wrist-length and has a single rear vent. Regimental badges, in brass, are worn on the collar. Light grey shirt, black tie, brown gloves, black shoes. Badges of rank are worn on the shoulder-straps.

Walking Out Dress

As for parade dress but the peaked cap may be replaced by a grey, fore-and-aft forage cap with gold edging for officers and having a gold button and loop over a light blue cockade bearing the three gold crowns. This cockade is silver for senior NCOs, brass for junior ranks.

Service Dress

Dark olive green peaked cap and battle dress with a very loosely cut blouse with two pockets and buttoned cuffs; all buttons concealed. Light green shirt, black tie, badges as before.

Barrack Dress

Dark olive green jacket (with four brass buttons) and trousers, the neck can be worn open or closed; two breast pockets, two pockets on the rear of the skirts, large pockets on the sides of the thighs, black leather belt with open, square brass buckle, brown boots and gaiters. Headwear is a forage cap in dark olive green with a peak, and having side and rear flaps which can be folded down. Rank and regimental badges are worn on the collar.

Combat Dress

Field-grey jacket and trousers of the same cut as barrack dress but having no breast pockets and with two slanted slit pockets on the front of the skirts. Field-grey caps as for barrack dress. Boots as for barrack dress.

The Women's Auxiliary Corps wear grey berets with badge and grey costume with five gold buttons, wrist length jacket with two slanted, slit pockets in the skirt (of the skirt); knee length grey skirt, black shoes and gloves, light grey blouse.

Swedish Regimental Badges

Armour – crossed swords.
Artillery – crossed cannon barrels.
Engineers – crossed axes over a wheel and a vertical sword.
Infantry – crossed rifles.

Swedish Badges of Rank

Generals Three gold oak leaves on the collar; gold shoulder-straps bearing at the base crossed golden batons and above this four emblems, a mixture of five-pointed gold stars and gold oak leaves above them as shown below:

	Stars	Oak leaves
General	3	1
General-löjtnant	2	2
General-major	1	3

Regimental Officers At the base of the shoulder-strap the regimental number in gold; above it one or more small five-pointed gold stars and above this a gold crown:

	Stars	
Överste (without regiment)	4	(no regimental number)

Överste	3
Överste-löjtnant	2
Major	1

Company Officers Stars as for regimental officers, above the regimental number:

	Stars
Kapten	3
Löjtnant	2
Fänrik	1

Senior NCOs The regimental number; above this round gold buttons bearing a five-pointed star:

	Buttons
Förvaltare	3
Fanjunkare	2
Sergeant	1

Junior NCOs Short, horizontal gold bars above the regimental number:

	Bars	
Rustmästare	4	(the top one thicker than the others).
Överfurir	4	(all thin)
Furir	3	
Korpral	2	
Vice-korporal	8	

Privates – the regimental number.

Officer cadets – one, two or three gold chevrons, point up, above the regimental number.

In barrack dress and combat dress, the regimental badge appears on the right hand collar patch and the rank badge on the left. Rank badges (in dull bronze) are also worn on the shoulder-straps but the regimental number is not.

The Carl Gustav 84 mm anti-tank rocket projector, a successful and widely-exported Swedish weapon.

THE SWISS CONFEDERATION

Population – 6,400,000.   **Capital** – Berne.

Armed Forces:

   Army – 2,500 regulars, 17,000 conscripts.

   Air Force – 3,000 regulars, 7,000 conscripts; 315 combat planes. 13 ground attack squadrons with Venom FB-50s, 2 interceptor squadrons with Mirage IIIS, 5 interceptor squadrons with Hunter F-85s equipped with Sidewinder AAM. 1 recce squadron with Mirage IIIRS. Transport planes include 3 Junkers JU-52/3 and 6 Dornier DO-27. Helicopters – 80 in all including 60 Alouette II/III.

Reserves   – Army 570,000; Air Force – 40,000.

Defence Spending – $561 million in 1972 (1·9% GNP).

Head of state is the president of the Bundesrat, who changes ever year; currently, Roger Bonvin. Parliament is the Bundesrat (upper chamber) elected by the lower chamber, the Bundesversammlung or Federal Assembly, which itself splits into the Standerat of 44 members and the Nationalrat of 200 elected members. Effective government lies with the Bundesrat, which has seven members – foreign affairs, finance, home affairs, justice and police, transport and energy, commerce and military affairs (Rudolph Gnagi); the deputy minister of military affairs is the president (Roger Bonvin) and Gnagi is deputy minister of justice and police affairs.

Switzerland consists of 22 independent Cantons – Zürich, Berne, Luzern, Uri, Schwyz, Unterwalden, Glavus, Zug, Freiburg, Solothurn, Basel, Schaffhausen, Appenzell, St Gallen, Graubunden, Aargau, Thurgau, Ticino, Vaud, Wallis, Neuenburg and Genf. Switzerland has no standing army as such, but a regular cadre and a peoples' militia. All male inhabitants of the cantons from 20–50 years undergo periodic military training with the emphasis lying on the years 20–32. Initial training takes place in military schools, later training with the units of the Heer or Army.

Promotion in rank is directly related to the time spent in training eg:

private	– 118 days
Sergeant	– 372 days
Lieutenant	– 499 days

Captain	– 664 days
Colonel	– 758 days

Men aged from 33–42 serve in the "Landwehr" and from 43–50 in the "Landsturm".

Head of the armed forces is the 7-man Bundesrat who command through the chief of the Military Department advised by the Commission for National

Camouflaged combat dress, now replacing grey in Swiss service; note metal-cleated boots and leather gaiters. (Courtesy Swiss Army)

Defence. Members of this commission include: the Chief of the Federal Military Department, the CGS, the Chief of Army Training, the Chief of Arma- ments, the four corps commanders and the commander of the air force.

The Swiss army is organised as follows:

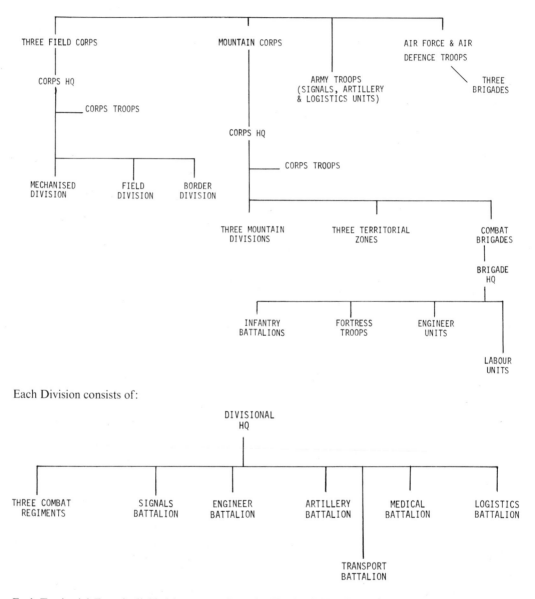

Each Division consists of:

Each Territorial Zone is divided into a number of Territorial Districts which may be grouped into Territorial Regions. Troops deployed are: infantry, air defence, medical and police units.

East German
army bandsmen.

Swiss Armoured Vehicles

"Panzer-58"

Combat weight – 35 tons; crew – 4; hull length – 6·55 m; width – 3·01 m; height to top of cupola – 2·63 m; armour thickness: front – 60 m; side – 40 mm; rear – 20 mm; armament – 1 × 90 mm L60 cannon, 1 × 20 mm Oerlikon co-axial cannon firing 820 rpm (VO – 1,100 m/sec); engine DB MB-837, V-8, 630 hp, water-cooled, diesel; max road speed – 50 km/hr; road range – 180 km; full capacity – 320 litres; wades – 1·1 m.

"Panzer-61"

As for Panzer-58 except as shown below: weight – 39 tons; hull length – 6·78 m; width – 3·06 m; height to top of cupola – 2·72 m; armament – 1 × Vickers L7A1 105 mm cannon (VO – 1,470 m/sec) (co-axial 20 mm cannon as before); fuel capacity – 760 litres; 105 mm ammunition capacity – 52 rounds; rate of fire – 10 rpm; 3,000 rounds of 7·5 mm for secondary machine gun MG 51.

"Panzer-68"

As for Panzer-61 except as shown below: weight – 38 tons; width – 3·14 m; height to top of cupola – 2·74 m; max road speed – 60 km/hr; engine – DB MB-837, V-8, 660 hp diesel; secondary armament – 1 × 7·5 mm MG-51 with a rate of fire of 1,000 rpm; VO – 750 m/sec; 4,600 rounds carried. The main armament is stabilised.

"Entpannungspanzer-65" (*Armoured Recovery Vehicle*)

Based on the Pz-68; length – 7·5 m; width (including dozer blade) – 3·15 m; height – 2·97 m; max road speed – 56 km/hr; crew – 3; armament – 1 × 7·5 mm MG-51.

"Bruckenpanzer-68" (*Bridge laying tank*)

Based on the Pz-68 chassis, it carries a 20 m bridge MLC 60. It is much slower and has a much lower range than the Pz-68.

"Panzerkanone-68" (*155 mm SP howitzer*)

Once again this weapon system uses the Pz-68 chassis and the 155 mm gun is also of Swiss production. The turret has a 360° traverse and is lightly armoured thus giving the crew NBC protection. The vehicle weighs 47 tons and the gun has a range of over 30 km.

Swiss Small Arms

Maschinenpistole 43/44 9 mm, blow-back weapon with wooden butt and 40 round magazine. This is a Finnish weapon of 1943 design; empty weight – 4·69 kg; rate of fire – 600 rpm; effective range – 100 m.
Sturmgewehr M-57 7·5 mm, blow-back weapon with curved, 24 round magazine; rate of fire – 500 rpm; effective range – 300 m; empty weight – 5·86 kg.
Light Machine Gun M-25 7·5 mm, blow-back weapon with 30 round curved magazine and bipod or on a tripod and belt-fed. Effective range – 800 m; rate of fire – 450 rpm. Empty weight (bipod) – 10·8 kg; weight of tripod – 10·7 kg.
Maschinengewehr M-51 7·5 mm, blow-back weapon which can be used with a 50 round drum magazine and bipod, or tripod and belt-fed. Rate of fire – 1,000 rpm; empty weight with bipod – 16 kg; weight of tripod – 24·2 kg.
The ubiquitous German MG42 is also used, designated *M2*.

Artillery

90 mm M-57 AT Gun Weight – 550 kg; VO – 600 m/sec; effective range – 1,000 m; rate of fire – 10 rpm; armour penetration (hollow charge) – 250 mm. Swedish weapon, used in the support companies of the infantry battalions.
105 mm Light Field Howitzer Swiss produced copy of the Swedish Bofors weapon, used at division level. Weight – 1,650 kg.

Vehicles

Steyr-Puch, 1 ton, 4 × 4 "Pinzgauer" truck

Length – 4·08 m; width – 1·68 m; height – 2·03 m; empty weight – 1,600 kg; 74 hp, 4 cylinder, air-cooled petrol engine; max road speed – 90 km/hr; road range – 400 km. Appears as load carrier and command vehicle.

Mowag 1 ton, 4 × 4 truck

Length – 4·64 m; width 2 m; height – 2·38 m; empty weight – 2,600 kg; 103 hp, 6 cylinder, water-cooled, petrol engine; max road speed – 88 km/hr; road range – 200 km. Crew 2 + 10.

Saurer M4, 4 × 4, 2¼ ton tractor

Length – 5·2 m; width – 2 m; height – 2·3 m; empty weight – 4,250 kg; 75 hp, 4 cylinder, water-cooled, diesel engine; max road speed – 58·5 km/hr; road range – 500 km; can carry 2 + 8 men.

Saurer M-6, 6 × 6, 2½ ton tractor
Length – 5·46 m; width – 2 m; height – 3·05 m; empty weight – 6,900 kg; 85 hp, 6 cylinder, water-cooled diesel engine; max road speed – 50 km/hr; road range – 500 km. Can carry 2 + 20 men.

Saurer-Berna, 4 × 4, 3½ ton truck
Length – 6·03 m; width – 2·25 m; height – 3·1 m; empty weight – 5,070 kg; 75 hp, 4 cylinder, water-cooled, diesel engine; max road speed – 54·6 km/hr; road range – 500 km. Can carry 2 + 25 men.

Saurer M-8, 8 × 8, 3·5 ton tractor
Length – 5·88 m; width – 2 m; height – 3·05 m; empty weight – 7,400 kg; 100 hp, 6 cylinder, water-cooled, diesel engine; max road speed – 50 km/hr; road range – 700 km. Can carry 2 + 20 men.

Saurer-Berna, 4 × 4, 4½ ton truck
Length – 7·37 m; width – 2·3 m; height – 3·2 m; empty weight – 7,100 kg; 135 hp, 6 cylinder, water-cooled diesel engine; max road speed – 75 km/hr; road range – 500 km. Can carry 3 men in the cab.

Saurer-Berna, 4 × 4, 5 ton truck
Length – 6·42 m; width – 2·2 m; height – 3·15 m; empty weight – 7,000 kg; 120 hp, 6 cylinder, water-cooled diesel engine; max road speed – 50 km/hr. Can carry 2 + 30 men.

Henschel, 6 × 6, 7 ton truck
A West German vehicle. Length – 8·15 m; width – 2·5 m; height – 3·14 m; empty weight – 9,700 kg; 192 hp, 6 cylinder, water-cooled, diesel engine; max road speed – 67 km/hr. Can carry 3 men in the cab.

Magirus-Deutz "Uranus", 6 × 6, 20 ton tractor
West German vehicle. Length – 7·65 m; width – 2·5 m; height – 3·22 m; empty weight – 18,500 kg; 250 hp, 12 cylinder, air-cooled, diesel engine; max road speed – 48·8 km/hr. Used to tow the AMX-13 tanks on low loaders.

"Super Atlantic", 6 × 4, 35 ton tractor
This British equipment is used with a 50-ton low loader trailer to transport the Centurion tanks. Length – 9·33 m; width – 3 m; height – 3·4 m; empty weight – 21,000 kg; 333 hp, 8 cylinder, water-cooled

diesel engine; max road speed – 64 km/hr. Can carry 3 men in the cab.

Engineer Equipment
M-61 Krupp-Man inflatable assault boat bridge as used by the West German army. MLC-16, 30 or 50 can also be used as a ferry.
M-35 Birago aluminium pontoon bridge MLC-3, 6, 9 or 12 (exceptionally up to MLC-16) difficult to transport; being withdrawn from service.
Bailey bridging equipment.
Krupp-Man-"D" bridging equipment.

Swiss Army Uniforms
The Swiss army is about to introduce new regimental and trade badges which are very modern in design and have been very controversially received. The following description applies only to the existing badges.

Parade Dress
The legendary Swiss steel helmet of huge dimensions (this is being replaced by a smaller one of more "NATO" appearance but retaining a distinctive Swiss signature).
Medium grey, open-necked, single-breasted jacket, four button front (the buttons gold and bearing the Swiss cross), four pockets with flaps but no buttons; the top pockets pleated; wrist length skirts; light grey shirt, black tie, medium grey trousers, black boots and gaiters (officers riding breeches and jackboots), black leather belt with steel buckle. Regimental badges are worn on the diamond-shaped collar patches and on coloured slides (bearing the unit number in yellow) on the shoulder-straps.

Walking Out Dress
Jacket, shirt, tie and trousers as above, black shoes; officers wear a stiff-topped grey kepi with black peak and chin strap and gold stripes according to rank around the crown. Other ranks wear a grey soft-topped peaked cap with national cockade on the left-hand side (a similar cap is worn by officers in barrack and field dress).

Service Dress As for walking out dress.

Barrack Dress
Grey denims without regimental badges; ranks in yellow on shoulder-slides.

Combat Dress

Steel helmet, field-grey jacket and trousers, jack-boots, black leather equipment as for the German Army in World War II.

Swiss Badges of Rank

Generals Black shoulder-straps edged in gold and bearing one or more, eight-pointed silver stars on a backing of gold laurel leaves:

	Stars
General (General)	4
Oberstkorpskommandant (Lieutenant-general)	3
Oberstdivisionar (Major-general)	2
Oberstbrigadier (Brigadier)	1

Oberst (Colonel)	– three wide stripes.
Oberstleutnant (Lieutenant-Colonel)	– two wide stripes.
Major (Major)	– one wide stripe.
Hauptmann (Captain)	– three narrow stripes.
Oberleutnant (Lieutenant)	– two narrow stripes.
Leutnant (Second Lieutenant)	– one narrow stripe.

Other Ranks' Badges of Rank These are worn on the upper arms in gold.

Gefreiter (Lance Corporal)	– one short horizontal gold bar.
Korporal (Corporal)	– one gold chevron, point up.
Wachtmeister (Sergeant)	– as for corporal but surmounted by the gold Swiss cross over gold laurel wreaths and under a thin gold chevron.
Fourier (Quartermaster Sergeant)	– two thick gold chevrons with the Swiss collage in between them.
Feldweibel (Sergeant Major)	– two thick gold chevrons together under the Swiss collage.
Adjutant Unterofficier (Adjutant NCO)	– as for the Feldweibel but the whole surmounted by another thick gold chevron.

Swiss Regimental Facing Colours

Armour*	– lemon yellow.
Artillery	– crimson.
Engineers	– black.
Signals	– light grey.
Infantry	– dark green.
Medical	– bright blue.
Air Corps AA Artillery	– dark blue.
Repair and maintenance	– dark violet.
Logistics troops	– medium green.
Territorial army	– orange.
Fortress troops	– red.

* Until mid '73 the Swiss army had a mounted Dragoon Regiment but this has now been disbanded; they also wore yellow facings.

Generals' stiff-crowned kepis have wide black headbands with gold laurel-leaf embroidery according to rank. On their soft-topped caps the star embroidery appears on the left side in miniature. Generals wear two broad black stripes flanking a narrow black piping on their trouser seams. Officers on the general staff have a single, wide black trouser stripe. Heads of arms and services have a single broad stripe in their facing colour on their trousers.

Officers Gold stripes, according to the system shown below, worn around the Crown of the stiff kepi, on the left side of the soft cap and across the base of the coloured shoulder-slide:

Legal services	– dark violet.
Military police	– brown.
Postal service	– dark grey.
General Staff	– black.

The collar patches of the uniforms bear an alarming variety of different badges and an edging embroidered in dark yellow.

The coloured shoulder-slides bear a large yellow number (the number of the wearer's unit) and for other ranks there is a strip along the bottom of the slide which shows the company to which the man belongs. These are: black – HQ; dark green – 1; brown – 2; yellow – 3; bright blue – 4; red – 5; mid-green – 6; dark blue – 7; dark green – 8; white – 9.

Specialist Qualification Badges

These are worn on the upper sleeves, above the rank badges, take the shape of shields in various colours bearing a number of badges in yellow thread.

Skill-At-Arms Badges

To complete the confusion, these badges, in gold metal, are worn on the upper left breast. Examples are:

Marksman	– crossed rifles.
Champion marksman	– crossed rifles in a wreath.
Pilot	– a vertical propellor between horizontal wings.
Observer	– a star between horizontal wings.
Mountaineer	– an Alpenstock and a crowbar crossed in a coil of rope.
Gun layer	– crossed cannon barrels.
Good driver	– a steering wheel, the shaft ending in laurel leaves.
Specialist Signaller	– a lightning flash.
Watermanship	– an anchor.
Ranger	– a winged parachute
Diver	– a frogman

The last parade by Switzerland's mounted Dragoon regiment in 1973. The decision to disband this unit caused national controversy, and not only for sentimental reasons. As several other nations have come to recognise, in certain types of terrain the horse-soldier still enjoys real advantages over opponents with more conventional modern transport and over enemy infiltrators. (Keystone)

THE FEDERAL SOCIALIST REPUBLIC OF YUGOSLAVIA

Population – 21,000,000.

Capital – Belgrade.

Armed Forces:

Army – 190,000 men; 1,200 tanks, SA-2 SAM.

Navy – 19,000 men; 1 destroyer, 5 submarines, 19 escorts, 30 minesweepers, 10 Osa class MTBs with Styx SSMs, 65 smaller MTBs, 30 landing craft, 25 coast artillery batteries; 1 brigade of marine infantry.

Air Force – 20,000 men; 342 combat planes; 12 ground attack squadrons with F-84, Jastreb and Kraguj; 8 fighter squadrons with 50 F-86D/E and 82 MiG-21. 2 reconnaissance squadrons with RT-33; 60 Galeb trainers; 13 Ilyushin-14 transports, 25 Beavers, C-47s and Li-2s; 60 helicopters (Alouette III, Whirlwind, Mi-4 and Mi-8). 8 air defence batteries with SAM-2.

Para-military forces – 19,000 Frontier Guards.

Reserves – 1·2 million People's Militia (final strength to be 3 million).

Defence Spending – $485 million in 1972 (4·7% GNP).

Head of state is President Marshal Josip Broz-Tito, born 25 May 1892 in Croatia. During the First World War Tito, as a member of the Austro-Hungarian army, was captured by the Russians and later joined the Red Army. In 1920 he returned to Yugoslavia and began to build up a Communist Party organisation there. In 1922 the Communist Party was banned and from 1928–1934 Tito was imprisoned. During the Second World War he led the Communist-dominated "Liberation Front" partisan organisation which later destroyed the Western-aligned partisans under Mihailovic. In 1945 Tito became prime minister and head of state of Yugoslavia, in 1963 President, and since 1971 also Chairman of the State Presidium. Although a staunch Communist and a Soviet protagonist in the current Sino-Soviet ideological struggle, Tito rejects the "Breschnew Doctrine" outright and has managed to maintain Yugoslavia's integrity as an independent state for some years.

Yugoslavia was for years under Turkish and then Austrian domination, and consists of the old states of Serbia, Croatia, Slowenia, Macedonia, Montenegro and Bosnia-Hercegowina. The population is 43·5% Serbian; 23·2% Croatian; 8% Slovene; 5·5% Macedonian; 2·8% Montenegran; 4·9% Albanian and 2·6% Hungarian and others. There are four written languages and six spoken; the rich northern Slovenian minority very much resent the fact that they have to support the poorer masses in the barren southern federal states. Yugoslavia has many internal problems and it is an open question as to whether Tito's death will lead to a bloody break-up of this uneasy alliance.

Tito is chairman of the Peoples' Defence Council and the State Security Council. The federal assembly (Savezna Narodna Skupstina) consists of five "chambers" or "councils".

The Socio-political Council (120 members).

The Economic Council (120 members).

The Council for Education and Culture (120 members).

The Council for Health and Social Services (120 members).

The Council of the Nations (140 members).

Above the Federal Assembly is the Federal Council, consisting of 100 members drawn from the Federal Assembly. The executive body is the

YUGOSLAV TANK BRIGADE

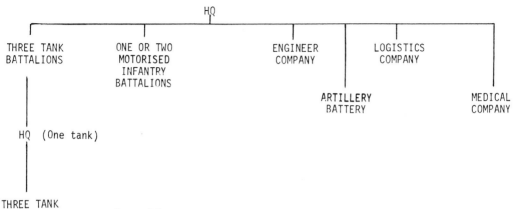

Federal Executive Council, currently presided over by Djemal Bijedic. Defence minister is Nikola Ljubicic.

Since the invasion of Czechoslovakia in 1968, Yugoslavia has modified her military organisation so that apart from the conscript army a Peoples' Militia has been raised for territorial defence. While the federal government is responsible for the standing (conscript) army, each member state raises, organises, trains and equips its own People's Militia units. Service in either the standing army or in the People's Militia is a liability for all males between seventeen and 50 years and all women between nineteen and 40 years. Men of sixteen years of age are also called up for public works service and up to the age of 65 years men are required to serve in the civil defence organisation.

The three Yugoslavian tank divisions are stationed at Sisak, Kragujevac and Skopje and consist of two tank brigades and a motorised infantry brigade as well as the usual divisional troops (artillery, engineers, signals, repair, logistics, transport and medical battalions). Brigade organisation is shown on the relevant chart. The infantry divisions consist of three or four infantry regiments each of four battalions (the 4th Battalion being the heavy weapons battalion), a tank battalion, anti-tank battalion, AA battalion and the usual divisional troops. Army level troops include one light and one heavy artillery regiment; one or two tank battalions, an AA battalion, signals, engineer, transport, repair, logistics and medical battalions.

Vehicle transport is limited and most infantry units march if required to move. Animal and pack transport is used in the mountain brigades.

Yugoslavian Army Equipment

7·62 mm pistol Tokarew Russian World War II weapon; empty weight – 0·85 kg; 8 round magazine.
7·62 Machine Pistol M-49 Yugoslav development of the World War II Soviet PPSH-M41; it weighs 4·3 kg, has a 32 round, curved magazine below the breech; blow-back action; rate of fire – 700 rpm; effective range – 100 m; wooden butt.
7·62 mm Machine Pistol M-56 Yugoslav development, based on the German World War II MP-40 and very similar in appearance; it has a tubular steel collapsible butt and can be used with a bayonet; weight – 3·06 kg; blow-back operation– 600 rpm; 32 round, curved magazine below the breech.
7·92 mm Sarac LMG Yugoslav copy of the German World War II MG-42; rate of fire – 1,050 rpm; weight with bipod – 12·5 kg, weight of tripod (for heavy role) – 22 kg.

120 mm UBM-52 mortar
Yugoslav-produced weapon. Weight in firing position – 400 kg; rate of fire – 15 rpm; range – 6 km. It is fitted with a towing hook on the muzzle and has a two-wheeled chassis and oblong base plate. Yugoslavia also produces her own 82 mm mortar which fires Soviet ammunition.

M-57 AT Grenade projector

Yugoslav-developed, light AT weapon firing an over-sized, hollow charge grenade; effective range – 200 m; rate of fire – 4 rpm; crew – 1; VO – 146 m/sec; weight – 8 kg; length – 1 m.

M-20, 75 mm recoilless AT rifle

American weapon mounted on the Zastava AR51 jeep.

M-60, 82 mm recoilless AT rifle (BO-82)

Yugoslav-produced, towed AT gun with two-wheeled chassis (tripod firing base), towing hook on the muzzle. 360° traverse; effective range – 500 m; rate of fire – 5 rpm. Towed behind Zastava jeep.

76 mm M-48 B-1 mountain howitzer

Yugoslav-developed weapon which can be towed by motor vehicles or horse team or broken down into pack-mule loads. Weight – 705 kg; VO – 398 m/sec; range – 11 km; rate of fire – 7 rpm.

105 mm M-56 light field howitzer

Yugoslav copy of the American M-2 105 mm howitzer with a different shield, muzzle brake and

towing facilities. Weight – 2,100 kg; VO – 570 m/sec; range – 13 km; rate of fire – 7 rpm.

130 mm M-54 field gun

Soviet equipment, used for coastal defence and AT combat. Weight – 7,500 kg; VO – 930 m/sec; range – 27 km; rate of fire – 6 rpm.

105 mm 18-M light field howitzer

A World War II German equipment: weight – 2·04 tons; range – 12·3 km; 6 rpm.

105 mm M-2 American light howitzer

World War II equipment: weight – 2·03 tons; range – 11·2 km; 8 rpm.

155 mm M-1 American howitzer

World War II gun: weight – 5·76 tons; range – 14·9 km; 4 rpm.

Soviet 122 mm M-38 and 152 mm M-37 weapons are also used.

M-63 128 mm Multiple Rocket Launcher

Yugoslav equipment, 32 barrels mounted on a 2-wheeled trailer which is also the firing platform and weighs 2·5 tons. The rockets can be fired as full, half, quarter or eight salvoes and are 80 cm long

Yugoslavian T-54/55 tank on manoeuvres, followed by a Yugoslav-built M-590 armoured personnel carrier. This 9½-ton tracked APC, which entered service in 1964, carries twelve men and has an externally-mounted 12·7 mm anti-aircraft machine gun.

A Yugoslavian Army mountain regiment parades with its flag; note details of rank insignia worn by colour-party in foreground. Below, a dramatically-posed mountain trooper with a Simonow self-loading rifle with permanently attached folding bayonet.

and weigh 23 kg. It takes 30 seconds to fire a full salvo. Range – 9 km; warhead – HE and smoke; crew – 8 men.

Triple 20 mm M-57 AAMG

Yugoslav-licenced production of the HS-804 MG on the two-wheeled HS-603 trailer. Weight in firing position – 1,170 kg; VO – 850 m/sec; AA range – 1·5 km; rate of fire – 3 × 800 rpm.

Soviet M-39, towed 37 mm and M-50 towed 57 mm AA guns, as well as German World War II 88 mm Flak-36 and Soviet SA-2 SAM are also used.

Armoured vehicles include American M-4 Sherman with 76·2 mm gun; M-18 Hellcat tank destroyer with 76·2 mm gun; M-36 Jackson tank destroyer with 90 mm gun; M-47 Patton medium tank with 90 mm gun; M-3 half-track APCs, M-8 6 × 6 armoured cars, and M-7B2 105 mm SP guns (based on the Sherman chassis).

Soviet armoured vehicles in use are represented by ASU-57 air droppable SP guns; SU-100 SP guns, SU-57 AA tanks, T34/85, T-54/55 medium and PT-76 light tanks.

The Yugoslavs also produce their own tracked APC (the M-590) which came into service in 1964.

It has five road wheels, weighs – 9·5 tons; length – 4·45 m; width – 2·7 m; height – 2·05 m; carries 12 men; armament – 1 × 12·7 mm AAMG; in each side are three peep-holes for the infantrymen.

Engineer Equipment

Soviet TMM MLC 60, 10-m bridge sections (a 40-m bridge can be built in 50 minutes) with JAAS-214 vehicles.

Soviet PMP pontoon bridge, MLC-50. One set of PMP consists of 16 main and 2 end pontoons, is carried on 22 JAAS-214 trucks and can make a 120-m bridge.

Soviet BTM tracked trench digger, mounted on the AT-T chassis.

Wheeled Vehicles

'ZASTAVA' AR-51' Yugoslav licenced copy of the Italian FIAT AR-51, 4 × 4 jeep. 63 hp petrol engine, top speed – 116 km/hr.

'TAM-4,500' Yugoslav licenced production of the German KLOCKNER-HUMBOLDT-DEUTZ 4 × 4 3-ton truck.

Yugoslavian Army Uniforms

Parade Dress

Steel helmet of a modernised German "coal-scuttle" style in grey. Light grey, single-breasted, open-necked jacket; wrist length, four front buttons; four pleated, patch pockets with square, buttoned flaps, pointed shoulder-straps, plain cuffs. Grey trousers, laced black boots, grey webbing gaiters, black leather equipment of German World War II pattern with steel fittings. Badges of rank are worn on the shoulder-straps, regimental badges on the collars. Light grey shirt, black tie. Buttons are brass and bear a five-pointed star. Officers wear a brown leather Sam Browne belt.

Walking Out Dress

As above but the helmet is replaced for officers by a grey peaked cap with black peak and for other ranks by a grey, fore-and-aft forage cap with red

Yugoslavian Collar Badges (in brass)

Generals	– oblong red patches, edges in gold and bearing crossed swords resting on oak leaves all in gold. (Tito, as marshal, wears gold laurel leaves on his collar patches and on both cuffs a five-pointed gold star at the top of a wreath of gold laurel leaves edged in red.)
Armour	– frontal view of a tank.
Artillery	– crossed cannon barrels.
Engineers	– an anchor on a ring with a bridge and a tyre across the centre.
Signals	– two interlocking, spear-headed lightning zig-zags.
Infantry	– crossed rifles on a wreath.
Medical	– a snake on a staff.
Veterinary	– as above but with a "V" on the snake.
Ordnance	– a cog wheel bearing a tank, a cannon barrel and a key.
Quartermaster (logistics)	– crossed swords over a chimney on a bridge all in a wreath of corn and laurel leaves.
Chemical	– crossed retorts behind a hexagon.
Legal services	– a sword on a torch with scales.
Military bands	– a lyre.
Frontier Guards	– a sword on a wreath.

Cap Badges

Generals	– a five-pointed, gold-edged red star on silver rays within a gold wreath.
Officers	– the star and rays.
NCOs	– the star in smaller size and silver edged.
Privates	– a smaller star with silver edging.

Tito Guard and Proletarian Units – as for others but with a hammer and sickle badge in the star (gold for officers, silver for other ranks).

star badge in the front centre; black shoes.

Barrack Dress

Grey denim suit without regimental badges.

Summer Dress

Light grey, hip length blouse; open neck, sleeves buttoned at the wrist, two pockets on the chest. Trousers, shoes, hat as before.

Summer Full Dress for Officers

A white jacket of the same cut as the usual grey jacket; the rest of the uniform as before.

Combat Dress

Steel helmet, rough grey jacket and trousers, boots, gaiters and equipment as for parade dress.

Specialist Clothing

NBC and tank clothing as for the Soviet Army; mountain troops wear a special soft-topped peaked cap, knee breeches, grey socks and mountaineering boots.

Yugoslavian Army Flags

The national flag – three horizontal stripes, blue over white over red with a gold edged, five-pointed red star in the centre. The flag is gold fringed with slogans embroidered in gold above and below the star. The pike has a spear point in gold and the pike is of polished wood. To the pike tip is attached a red cravat with gold fringed ends bearing the unit designation.

Yugoslavian light anti-aircraft artillery battery with 20 mm M-57 three-barrel weapons. The crews' personal armament appears to be the old German Mauser K.98 of Second World War vintage.

Badges of Rank

General Officers Shoulder-strap trimmed in gold; at the base crossed swords on a laurel wreath, above this one or more five-pointed gold stars.

Army General (Generalarmije)	– three stars in a pyramid and one above them.
Colonel General (General pukovnik)	– three stars one above the other.
Lieutenant-General (General potpukovnik)	– two stars one above the other.
Major-General (Generalmajor)	– one star.

Field Officers (gold edged shoulder-straps and gold stars).

Colonel (Pukovnik)	– three stars one above the other.
Lieutenant-Colonel (Potpukovnik)	– two stars one above the other.
Major (Major)	– one star.

Junior Officers (gold stars).

Captain 1st Class (Kapetan 1 Klasse)	– four stars one above the other.
Captain (Kapetan)	– three stars one above the other.
Lieutenant (Poručnik)	– two stars one above the other.
2nd Lieutenant (Potporučnik)	– one star.

Non-commissioned ranks (gold chevrons, point up, on the shoulder-strap).

Regimental Sergeant Major (Zastavnik)	– one broad chevron under one thin one.
Company Sergeant Major (Stariji vodnik 1 Klasse)	– four thin chevrons.
Staff Sergeant (Stariji vodnik)	– three thin chevrons.
Sergeant (Vodnik 1 klasse)	– two thin chevrons.
Corporal (Vodnik)	– one thin chevron.

Privates (red chevrons on the shoulder-strap).

Lance Corporal (Desetar)	– two chevrons.
Senior Private (Razvodnik)	– one chevron.
Private	– no chevrons.

APPENDIX I

Armoured Vehicle Characteristics

The following are some of the major armoured vehicles of various categories currently in use with European armies; data on other indigenous designs will be found under the national headings. The conventions followed in the short "specifications" are:

A = Number in crew.
B = Combat weight.
C = Hull length; hull width; height to top of turret – all in metres.
D = Main armament; types of ammunition; quantity carried.
E = Auxiliary armament.
F = Engine – petrol unless otherwise specified.
G = Power/weight ratio.
H = Armour thickness (at thickest point, usually hull front, unless specified otherwise).
I = Maximum road speed.
J = Maximum road range.
K = Fuel capacity.
L = Wading characteristics (normal; deep regime; schnorkel) in metres.
M = Night fighting equipment.

Not all these headings may apply, or may be available, for all vehicles. The data is followed by brief remarks, concluding with a summary of European users of the equipment, thus:

A   = Austria.
B   = Belgium.
CH   = Switzerland.
DK   = Denmark.
E   = Spain.
F   = France.
FRG   = Federal Republic of Germany.
GR   = Greece.
I   = Italy.
N   = Norway.
NL   = Netherlands.
P   = Portugal.
SW   = Sweden.
T   = Turkey.
UK   = United Kingdom.
AL   = Albania.
BG   = Bulgaria.
CZ   = Czechoslovakia.
DDR   = German Democratic Republic.
FN   = Finland.
H   = Hungary.
PL   = Poland.
RU   = Rumania.
USSR = Soviet Union.
YU   = Yugoslavia.

M41 "Walker Bulldog" light tank (USA)

A 4. **B** 25 tons. **C** 5·6; 3·26; 2·85. **D** 76·2 mm cannon; HE, AP, HESH. **E** 1 × 12·7 mm co-axial MG, 1 × 12·7 mm AAMG. **F** 500 hp. **G** 20 hp/ton. **H** 30 mm. **I** 65 km/hr (39 mph). **J** 260 km (160 miles). An obsolescent vehicle, this tank is being replaced in the US Army by the Sheridan M551. It was designed to replace the M24 Chaffee light tank in 1950 and came into service with the Bundeswehr in 1956. It has a limited road range and a badly shaped turret with many projectile traps. *A, B, DK, E, GR, P, T*

M42 anti-aircraft tank (USA)

A 5. **B** 22·5 tons. **C** 5·21; 3·26; 2·86. **D** twin 40 mm L60 cannon; AP; 480 rounds. **E** 1 × 7·62 mm hull MG. **F** 500 hp. **G** 23 hp/ton. **H** hull as M41, turret unarmoured. **I** 70 km/hr (42 mph). **J** 160 km (96 miles). **K** 530 ltr. **L** 1·2. This ageing vehicle represents almost the only anti-aircraft tank among the

219

European powers. It was introduced into US service in 1952; it is currently being replaced in Germany by the new Fla-Panzer I. The chassis of the M42 is that of the M41 light tank. *FRG, I*

M47 medium tank (USA)

A 5. **B** 44 tons. **C** 7·1; 3·5; 3·26. **D** 90 mm M36 cannon; HE, AP, HEAT; 71 rounds. **E** 1 × 12·7 mm co-axial MG, 1 × 7·62 mm AAMG. **F** 810 hp Continental AV-1790-5B. **G** 18·4 hp/ton. **H** 100 mm. **I** 50 km/hr (30 mph). **J** 125 km (75 miles). **K** 880 ltr. **L** 1·2. The Patton formed the basis of the armoured equipment of many NATO states in the immediate post-war period. Now mainly replaced by more modern equipments, it is still to be seen in Greece, Turkey and in the Federal German Territorial Army. *A, B, E, F, GR, I, P, T, YU*

M48A2C medium tank (USA)

A 4. **B** 48 tons. **C** 6·9; 3·63; 3·09. **D** 90 mm cannon; HE, AP, HESH; 60 rounds. **E** 1 × 7·62 mm co-axial MG, 1 × 12·7 mm AAMG. **F** 810 hp. **G** 16·8 hp/ton. **H** 110 mm. **I** 50 km/hr (30 mph). **J** 250 km (150 miles). **K** 1,230 ltr. **L** 1·2. **M** Infra red. The ageing M48, also known as "Patton II", is still rendering excellent service in many countries. Developed from the M47 in 1953, it began to be replaced by the M60 in European armies in 1963. *E, FRG, GR, N, T*

M48A2C Bridgelayer (USA)

A 2. **B** 44 tons, 58 with bridge. **C** 7·92 (11 with bridge); 3·65 (4); 2·3 (3·8). **F** 810 hp. **G** 18·4 hp/ton (14 hp/ton with bridge). **I** 48 km/hr (29 mph). **J** 250 km (150 miles). **K** 1,231 ltr. **L** 1·2. The bridge has a capacity up to military load classification 60, and is 19·2 metres long. It came into service in 1958. *FRG*

M60A1 battle tank (USA)

A 4. **B** 46·3 tons. **C** 6·95; 3·63; 3·26. **D** British 105 mm cannon; HE, AP, HEAT; 63 rounds. **E** 1 × 12·7 mm AAMG, 1 × 7·62 mm turret MG. **F** 750 hp diesel. **G** 16·2 hp/ton. **H** 110 mm. **I** 48 km/hr (29 mph). **J** 500 km (300 miles). **K** 1,120 ltr. **L** 1·2; –; yes, with extra equipment. **M** Infra red. This is a medium tank, with lower armour protection and higher mobility than such heavier designs as the British Chieftain. It was developed from the M48A2, and entered service in 1958. Some European countries are currently replacing it with the Leopard. *A, I*

The ubiquitous M113 armoured personnel carrier; this variant in Bundeswehr service mounts the British "Green Archer" artillery locating radar.

The Hotchkiss-Brandt SPZ Kurz ("short") light armoured personnel carrier.

M60A1E1 battle tank (USA)

A 4. B 48 tons. C 6·95; 3·63; 3·35. D 152 mm gun-launcher combination; HE, AP, or Shillelagh wire-guided anti-tank missile; 40 rounds, 6 missiles. E 1 × 12·7 mm AAMG, 1 × 7·62 mm co-axial MG. F 750 hp diesel. G 15·4 hp/ton. H 110 mm. M Infra red searchlight, headlights and aiming equipment. The first step towards the Sheridan M551 light tank, which also uses the gun-launcher combination, the M60A1E1 has a low turret profile.

M88 recovery tank (USA)

A 4. B 50·8 tons. C 8·26; 3·42; 3·12. E 1 × 7·62 mm AAMG. F 1,014 hp. G 20 hp/ton. H 110 mm. I 50 km/hr (30 mph). J 360 km (216 miles). K 1,710 ltr. L 1·6. This recovery tank was introduced in the US Army in 1959. The crane has a weight limit of 22 tons, and the dozer blade is a standard fitting. *A, B, DK, FRG, GR, NL, T*

M113 armoured personnel carrier (USA)

A 13. B 10·4 tons. C 4·86; 2·96; 2·5. D various 20 mm weapons; AP. E various. F 218 hp. G 20·9 hp/ton. I 64 km/hr (37 mph). J 320 km (192 miles).

K 305 ltr. L Inherently amphibious, propelled by track rotation. M Various, according to role. This is the most numerous armoured vehicle outside the Soviet bloc. Although introduced as long ago as 1958 it has proved itself in all parts of the world. It exists in many variants including ambulance, bridgelayer, command vehicle, mortar carrier, repair vehicle, etc. *B, CH, DK, E, FRG, GR, I, N, NL, T*

HS 30 (Long) armoured personnel carrier (Federal German Republic)

A 8. B 14·6 tons. C 5·56; 2·54; 1·85. D 20 mm cannon; AP; 1,075 rounds. F 229 hp. G 15·6 hp/ton. I 75 km/hr (45 mph). J 320 km (192 miles). K 325 ltr. L 0·7. Introduced in 1958, this Hispano-Suiza vehicle is now being replaced by the new "Marder". It is also used as a mortar carrier and command vehicle. *FRG*

Hotchkiss-Brandt armoured personnel carrier (Federal German Republic)

A 4 or 5. B 8·4 tons. C 4·47; 2·34; 2·0. D 20 mm cannon; AP; 575 rounds. F 164 hp. G 19 hp/ton.

The German Leopard medium tank, widely used in NATO armies.

I 58 km/hr (35 mph). **J** 380 km (228 miles). **K** 330 ltr. **L** 0·7. **M** Infra red or radar according to role. This vehicle is now being withdrawn from service; envisaged as a light scout tank, it has proved to be somewhat unreliable. Brought into service in 1958, it also exists in the conventional range of specialised variants. *FRG*

"Marder" armoured infantry fighting vehicle (Federal German Republic)

A 10. **B** 28·2 tons. **C** 6·79; 3·2; 2·9. **D** 20 mm cannon; AP; 1,250 rounds. **E** 2 × 7·62 mm MG. **F** 600 hp diesel. **G** 21·3 hp/ton. **I** 75 km/hr (45 mph). **J** 500 km (300 miles). **L** 1·5; 2·0; yes, with extra equipment. **M** Infra red. Introduced into Bundeswehr service in 1971, this infantry "APC tank" combination follows the Soviet BMP-76 in a new trend in armoured vehicle development. The Marder is the counterpart of the Leopard battle tank; at each side of the rear hull are two apertures through which the crew can fire if required to fight from within the vehicle. *FRG*

Leopard Medium tank (Federal German Republic)

A 4. **B** 39·6 tons. **C** 6·83; 3·25; 2·83. **D** British 105 mm cannon; HE, AP, HEAT: 60 rounds. **E** 1 × 7·62 mm co-axial MG, 1 × 7·62 mm AAMG. **F** 830 hp multi-fuel. **G** 21 hp/ton. **I** 64 km/hr (57 mph). **J** 500 km (300 miles). **K** 965 ltr. **L** 1·2; 2·25; yes, with extra equipment. **M** Infra red searchlight. This German-built replacement for the American types used by the Bundeswehr since its formation in 1956 was first issued in 1967. In 1973 two of Germany's

three corps are completely equipped with Leopard, and conversion of the third corps is well under way. *B, FRG, I, N, NL*

Jagdpanzer Kanone (Federal German Republic)

A 4. **B** 25·7 tons. **C** 6·24; 2·98; 2·1. **D** 90 mm cannon; HE, AP, HEAT; 51 rounds. **E** 1 × 7·62 mm co-axial MG, 1 × 7·62 mm AAMG. **F** 500 hp diesel. **G** 19·5 hp/ton. **I** 70 km/hr (42 mph). **J** 500 km (300 miles). **K** 475 ltr. **L** 1·4; 2·0; yes, with extra equipment. **M** Infra red. Since before World War II Germany has had a specific tank hunter, of which this "Tank Hunter, Gun" is the newest version. Cheaper than a battle tank, it is a dangerous opponent for such vehicles if it can operate from a concealed position. Gun traverse is limited, and the hull must be moved to engage targets outside these limits. *FRG*

Jagdpanzer Rakete (Federal German Republic)

A 4. **B** 23 tons. **C** 6·24; 2·98; 2·1. **D** SS-11 B1 anti-tank guided missile; 16 missiles. **E** 2 × 7·62 mm MG. **F** 500 hp diesel. **G** 21·7 hp/ton. **I** 70 km/hr (42 mph). **J** 500 km (300 miles). **K** 475 ltr. **L** 1·4; 2·0; yes, with extra equipment. **M** Infra red. This is the counterpart of the "Tank Hunter, Gun". It can engage targets at longer effective ranges than the 90 mm cannon-equipped version. *FRG*

Recovery tank "Standard" (Federal German Republic)

A 4. **B** 39·1 tons. **C** 7·4; 3·25; 2·46. **E** 2 × 7·62 mm MG. **F** 830 hp multi-fuel. **G** 21·2 hp/ton. **H** as for

Leopard tank. **I** 62 km/hr (37 mph). **J** 800 km (480 miles). **L** as AEV "Standard". Another variation on the Leopard chassis; the crane has a limit of 20 tons. *FRG*

Armoured Engineer Vehicle "Standard"
(Federal German Republic)
  A 4. **B** 39·6 tons. **C** 7·98; 3·25; 2·66. **E** 2 × 7·62 mm MG. **F** 830 hp multi-fuel. **G** 21 hp/ton. **H** as for Leopard tank. **I** 62 km/hr (37 mph). **J** 800 km (480 miles). **L** 1·2; 2·1; yes, with extra equipment. A variation on the Leopard chassis. In addition to the dozer blade and crane, weight limit 20 tons, it has a fox-hole auger which can bore 30 holes each 1·8 m deep, in gravel and shale soil, in one hour. Its winch can move 35 tons. *FRG*

AML 245/AML 245H90/AML 245-ENTAC
armoured car 4 × 4 (France)
  A 3/3/3. **B** 4·5 tons/5·5 tons/5·2 tons. **C** 3·68; 1·93; 2·18/3·79; 1·97; 2·1/3·7; 1·93; 2·2. **D** 60 mm mortar/90 mm cannon/60 mm mortar + 4 ENTAC ATGW; HE, smoke; HE, AP. **E** 1 × 7·5 AAMG, 1 × 7·5 turret MG common to all versions. **F** 90 hp. **G** 18·8 hp/ton/16·3 hp/ton/17 hp/ton. **I** 90 km/hr (54 mph). **J** 550 km (330 miles). **K** 115 ltr. **L** 1·1. **M** Infra red. A well-built and versatile scout vehicle, which in the H90 and ENTAC versions carries weapons capable of destroying tanks. Ammunition capacity is 53 rounds, 12 rounds and 30 rounds + 4 missiles, respectively. *F*

EBR-90 armoured car 8 × 8 (France)
  A 4. **B** 15 tons. **C** 5·56; 2·43; 2·24. **D** 90 mm cannon; HE, AP; 44 rounds. **E** 3 × 7·5 mm MG. **F** 200 hp. **G** 13·3 hp/ton. **I** 100 km/hr (60 mph). **J** 600 km (360 miles). **L** 1·2. **M** Infra red. Like the smaller Soviet BRDM, the EBR-90 (Engin Blindé de Reconnaissance) has two retractable pairs of central wheels, lowered when moving across country. There is a driver at each end of the vehicle, which is equally fast and manoeuvrable in either direction. An up-gunned version of the EBR-75, it is a dangerous adversary even for tanks, and forms the standard equipment of French reconnaissance units. *F*

AMX-30 medium tank (France)
  A 4. **B** 35·4 tons. **C** 6·63; 3·1; 2·85. **D** 105 mm cannon; HE, AP, HEAT; 50 rounds. **E** 1 × 12·7 mm MG, 1 × 7·5 mm AAMG. **F** 720 hp multi-fuel. **G** 20·4 hp/ton. **I** 65 km/hr (43 mph). **J** 500 km (300

miles). **K** 850 ltr. **L** 2·2; yes, with extra equipment. **M** Infra red searchlight. This well-formed tank replaced the M47 in French armoured regiments; fast and with a great range, it has a long "battlefield day". *F, GR*

Saladin armoured car 6 × 6 (United Kingdom)
  A 3. **B** 11·6 tons. **C** 4·9; 2·51; 2·39. **D** 76 mm cannon; HE, HESH; 43 rounds. **E** 1 × 7·62 mm MG. **F** 160 hp. **G** 14 hp/ton. **I** 72 km/hr (43 mph). **J** 400 km (240 miles). **L** 1·1; 2·1. **M** Infra red. Saladin belongs to the group of British six-wheeled armoured vehicles which includes the Saracen APC and the Stalwart cross-country amphibious load carrier. It has proved itself in service in many parts of the globe, and has been exported to numerous African and Arabian states. It has run-flat tyres. Saladin is the standard equipment of British armoured car regiments. *FRG frontier police, UK*

Centurion battle tank (United Kingdom)
  A 4. **B** 51 tons. **C** 7·82; 3·4; 2·96. **D** British 105 mm cannon; AP, APDS, HESH; 64 rounds. **E** 1 × 7·62 mm AAMG, 1 × 12·7 mm co-axial MG. **F** 650 hp. **G** 12·8 hp/ton. **I** 35 km/hr (21 mph). **J** 241 km (145 miles). **K** 890 ltr. **L** 1·45; 2·95; can swim, with added rubber skirt. **M** Infra red. A reliable tank, with limited speed and range, which has been modified many times throughout its long life (1945–72) with the British Army. Widely exported, it gave an excellent account of itself against the T54/55 in the 1967 Middle East war; although it is too early to assess results of the 1973 war, Centurion even seems to have inflicted severe loss on forces equipped with the T62. *B, DK, NL, SW, UK*

Chieftain battle tank (United Kingdom)
  A 4. **B** 51·5 tons. **C** 7·46; 3·5; 2·51. **D** British 120 mm cannon; HE, HESH, APDS, Canister; 53 rounds. **E** 2 × 7·62 mm MG, 1 × 12·7 mm ranging MG. **F** 740 hp multi-fuel. **G** 14·3 hp/ton. **I** 40 km/hr (24 mph). **J** 400 km (240 miles). **K** 888 ltr. **L** 1·06; yes, with extra equipment. **M** Infra red searchlight and gun sights. The Chieftain replaced the Centurion as the British Army's main tank, and has been sold to non-European countries. Its very low silhouette is achieved by several measures including the provision of a prone position for the driver when closed down. In view of the increased armour of the T62, the Chieftain is probably the most dangerous enemy of the former. It is now appearing in

the usual variations as a bridgelayer, armoured engineer and recovery vehicle. *UK*

T34/85 battle tank (*Soviet Union*)

   A 4. **B** 32 tons. **C** 6·1; 3·0; 2·7. **D** 85 mm cannon; HE, AP, HEAT; 56 rounds. **E** 1 × 7·62 mm co-axial MG, 1 × 7·62 mm hull MG. **F** 500 hp diesel. **G** 15·6 hp/ton. **H** turret 150 mm, hull 45 mm. **I** 55 km/hr (33 mph). **J** 300 km (180 miles); or 500 km (300 miles) with supplementary tanks. **K** 550 ltr + 360 ltr in supplementary tanks. **L** 1·3. This equipment saw much service during World War II and is still to be met today in the Warsaw Pact countries, where it is used for training. Variants such as bridgelayers and recovery tanks are also in use. As recently as 1968 this tank was used operationally by armoured units of the German Democratic Republic taking part in the invasion of Czechoslovakia. *AL, BG, CZ, DDR, H, PL, RU, USSR, YU*

PT-76 amphibious tank (*Soviet Union*)

   A 3. **B** 15 tons. **C** 6·9; 3·1; 2·2. **D** 76 mm cannon; HE, AP, HEAT; 40 rounds. **E** 1 × 12·7 mm AAMG, 1 × 7·62 mm co-axial MG. **F** 240 hp diesel. **G** 16 hp/ton. **H** turret 16 mm, hull 14 mm. **I** 40 km/hr (25 mph). **J** 250 km (150 miles). **K** 250 ltr. **L** Inherently amphibious. **M** Infra red driving and gun sighting equipment. Introduced shortly after World War II, this light reconnaissance tank has appeared in all Warsaw Pact armies as well as in the Middle East and Far East; recently the North Vietnamese have been mounting the T55 turret and gun on the original PT-76 chassis. Water propulsion is achieved by hydrojet equipment through two apertures in the rear hull, giving a water speed of 10 km/hr (6 mph). *BG, CZ, DDR, FN, H, PL, RU, USSR, YU*

T54 battle tank (*Soviet Union*)

   A 4. **B** 36 tons. **C** 6·0; 3·25; 2·4. **D** 100 mm cannon; HE, AP, HEAT; 34 rounds. **E** 1 × 12·7 mm AAMG, 2 × 7·62 mm co-axial and hull MGs. **F** 520 hp diesel. **G** 14·4 hp/ton. **H** turret 300 mm, hull front 100 mm, hull side 45 mm. **I** 50 km/hr

(30 mph). **J** 600 km (360 miles), with supplementary tanks. **K** 800 ltr, 1,200 ltr with supplementary tanks. **L** 1·4; 2·4; 5·0 with extra equipment. **M**. Infra red driving and gun sighting equipment. This simple, robust tank has been converted to the T55 by means of minor modifications such as stabilisation of the main armament and a more powerful engine. Introduced into service not long after the close of World War II, it is a direct development of the famous T34; like this whole family of tanks, it uses the Christie suspension system. *AL, BG, CZ, DDR, FN, H, PL, RU, USSR, YU*

T55 battle tank (*Soviet Union*)

   A 4. **B** 36 tons. **C** 6·0; 3·28; 2·4. **D** 100 mm cannon; HE, AP, HEAT; 43 rounds. **E** 1 × 7·62 mm co-axial MG, 1 × 7·62 mm AAMG. **F** 580 hp diesel. **G** 16·1 hp/ton. **H** as for T54. **I** as for T54. **J** as for T54. **K** as for T54. **L** as for T54. **M** as for T54. The basic difference between T54 and T55 is the more powerful engine, and the fact that T55's main armament is stabilised horizontally and vertically. As with all Soviet equipments, crew comfort comes low on the list of priorities. T55 did not do well in the 1967 Arab-Israeli war when pitted against the British Centurion. *AL, BG, CZ, DDR, FN, H, PL, RU, USSR, YU*

T62 battle tank (*Soviet Union*)

   A 4. **B** 36½ tons. **C** 6·5; 3·25; 2·2. **D** 115 mm smooth-bore cannon; HE, APDS, HEAT; 40 rounds. **E** 2 × 7·62 mm co-axial and AA MGs. **F** 580 hp diesel. **G** 16·1 hp/ton. **H** as for T54. **I** 50 km/hr (30 mph). **J** as for T54. **K** as for T54. **L** as for T54. **M** as for T54. The latest Soviet tank in general use; although only seen in very limited numbers in non-Warsaw Pact countries, about 100 tanks were used by both Egypt and Syria in the 1973 war with Israel. Largely due to the shorter engagement range, the T62 does not seem to have distinguished itself against the elderly Israeli Centurion. *AL, BG, CZ, DDR, H, PL, RU, USSR, YU*

NATO transport; above, the Unimog 4 × 4 1½-ton truck, below, the LARC landing craft.

APPENDIX II

NATO Artillery Equipments of American Origin

Weapon	Date into German Army Service	Weight in firing position (kg)	Range (km)	Rate of fire (rpm)	Muzzle velocity (m/sec)	Combat ammunition load (rounds)	Crew	Length Width Height (meters)	Remarks
105 mm Howitzer "M2A1"	1956	2,260	11·3	15	438	64	7		Standard brigade artillery piece; now replaced by the 105 mm "L" Howitzer.
105 mm "L" Howitzer	1962	2,500	14·6	15	640	64	7		More powerful barrel and German sights; six guns per battery.
105 mm Mountain gun	1961	1,273	10·2	15	420	36	9		Italian weapon modified by addition of a muzzle brake. Employed in mountain and air portable brigades. Can be broken down into 12 loads of up to 132 kg each.
155 mm "M1A2" Howitzer	1956	5,760	14·8	4	564	24	9		Division and Corps level weapon, six guns per battery.
155 mm "M2" Cannon	1956	12,565	23·5	1	856	30	15		Corps artillery weapon, pulled by the 12 ton Faun tractor.
203 mm "M2" Howitzer	1956	13,600	17	1	594	14	15		Corps weapon; six guns per battery, Faun 12 ton tractor
105 mm "M7B2" armoured, self-propelled (SP) Howitzer	1956	22,600	11·1	15	473	36	7	6·3 2·84 2·65	America's first SP gun, this was mounted on the Sherman tank chassis; six guns per battery in each armoured brigade. Engine – 506 hp, water-cooled, eight cylinder V petrol engine; consumption – 340 litres/100 km; tank capacity – 635 litres; road range – 185 km; max speed – 42 km/hr; wading depth – 0·92 m.
105 mm "M52" armoured SP Howitzer	1957	24,500	11·2	15	463	102	6	5·75 3·15 3·40	Successor to the a/m weapon. Engine – 506 hp, six cylinder air-cooled "Boxer" petrol engine; consumption – 500 litres/100 km; road range – 130 km; max speed – 56 km/hr; tank capacity – 660 litres; wading depth – 1·22 m.

Below, the towed 105 mm field gun, in use throughout Europe; bottom, the M109G armoured self-propelled 155 mm howitzer.

Weapon	Date into German Army Service	Weight in firing position (kg)	Range (km)	Rate of fire (rpm)	Muzzle velocity (m/sec)	Combat ammunition load (rounds)	Crew	Length Width Height (meters)	Remarks
155 mm "M44" armoured SP Howitzer	1956	28,400	14·8	4	573	24	9	6·03 3·23 3·15	Medium artillery piece; open crew compartment. 506 hp. six cylinder, air-cooled "Boxer" engine; consumption – 500 litres/100 km; road range – 120 km; max speed – 56 km/hr; tank capacity – 605 litres; wading depth – 1·07 m. Now replaced by the "M109".
155 mm "M109G" armoured SP Howitzer								3·58 2·80	Eight cylinder V 71-T diesel engine, air cooled. Max road speed – 56 km/hr; road range – 354 km; tank capacity – 492 litres.
203 mm "M55" armoured SP Howitzer	1961	45,000	17	1	594	10	10	8·26 3·56 3·56	Divisional artillery weapon, six per battery. Twelve cylinder. air-cooled, 810 hp "Continental" engine; consumption – 545 litres/100 km; max road speed – 48 km/hr; road range – 250 km; tank capacity – 1,440 litres; wades – 1·22 m. Enclosed firing compartment.
175 mm "M107" SP Howitzer	1962	27,896	32·5	1	?	2	10	11·3 3·15 3·47	Divisional weapon, open firing compartment, tracked chassis. Eight cylinder, water-cooled diesel engine; max road speed – 55 km/hr; road range – 720 km; tank capacity – 1,135 litres.
203 mm "M110" SP Howitzer	?	26,535	16	1	594	2	10	7·47 3·15 2·94	Divisional weapon; similar chassis as above; eight cylinder. water-cooled diesel engine; max road speed – 55 km/hr; road range – 720 km; tank capacity – 1,135 litres; wades – 1·06 meters.
Honest John "M836" Rocket Launcher M31-A2 Missile	—	2,678	5,000-24,000					8·305	Warhead: HE, Nuclear or "Special".
XM-50 Missile	—	2,140	5,000-37,000					7·582	

Below, the M107 self-propelled 175 mm howitzer; bottom, the M110 self-propelled 203 mm howitzer.

Above, the Raketenwerfer 110 SF 36-barrel rocket launcher; below, the "Honest John" missile on its launcher vehicle.

APPENDIX III

Summary of Anti-Tank Projectors and Guided Weapons of the Western World

Country of origin and year into service	Weapon title	Guidance System	Calibre (mm)	System weight (kg)	Warhead type and weight in grammes	Anti-tank Combat Range (meters)	Speed (meters/ second)	Crew
Belgium and United Kingdom (still under development)	"ATLAS" (Anti-Tank Laser Assisted System)	Optical/Laser	?	?	Hollow charge	1,000	?	1
France	"ACL-APX 80"	None (Optical)	80	12·6	Hollow charge, HE, incendiary and smoke. 550	500–700 (1,500)	400–540	1
France	"ARPAC"**	None (Optical)	68	1·85	Hollow charge, HE, illuminating, smoke	75–120	75	1
France	"LRAC-F1"	None (Optical)	88·9	7·3	Hollow charge, HE, incendiary and illuminating	400	300	1
France	"SARPAC"**	None (Optical)	68	2·2	Hollow charge	200	150	1
France	"ACRA" (Anti Char Rapide Auto-propulse)	Optical/ Infra-red, Radio	142	Vehicle borne	Hollow charge and HE 2,800	25–3,300	550 (Max)	2
France/Federal Republic of Germany	HOT (Haut subsonique Optiquement teleguide d'un Tube)	Optical/ infra-red, wire	136	27 Vehicle borne	Hollow charge	75–4,000	280	
France/Federal Republic of Germany 1973	MILAN (Missile d'Infanterie Leger Antichar)	Optical/ infra-red, wire	103	26·4	Hollow charge	25–2,000	200	1
Federal Republic of Germany	"Armbrust 300"	None (Optical)	80	5·4	Hollow charge, HE and illuminating	300	200	1
Federal Republic of Germany	"Mamba"	Optical, wire	100	12·9	Hollow charge	300–2,000	60–140	
Sweden	"Carl Gustav" (FFV 550 Mk I)	None (Optical)	84	4·7	Hollow charge, HE	550		

Country of origin and year into service	Weapon title	Guidance System	Calibre (mm)	System weight (kg)	Warhead type and weight in grammes	Anti-Tank Combat Range (meters)	Speed (meters/ second)	Crew
Sweden	FFV 550 Mk II	None (Optical)	84	6·6	Hollow charge, HE, illuminating	700 (HE 1,000 ill. 2,000)	350	
Sweden	"Miniman"**	None (Optical)	74	2·6	Hollow charge	250	160	
United Kingdom 1970 (BAC)	"Swingfire"*	Optical, wire	170	35·4	Hollow charge	150–4,000 (300–4,000 in remote mode)	190	
United Kingdom 1970 (BAC)	"Vigilant"	Optical, wire	131	28	Hollow charge	200–1,300		
USA 1972	"Dragon" (XM-47)	Optical, infra-red, wire	123	13·5	Hollow charge	30–1,000	95	1
USA (Still (1973) under development)	"Hellfire"	Optical, laser beam	?	?	Hollow charge	?	?	?
USA 1970 (Hughes)	"TOW" (Tube launched, Optically tracked, Wire-guided missile)	Optical, infra-red, wire	127	76 (3 × one-man loads)	Hollow charge	65–3,000	203	3

* Can be fired from a "remote" position by the operator.   ** "Use-and-throw-away" weapon.